SPEECH OUT OF DOORS

Even in an age characterized by increasing virtual presence and communication, speakers still need physical places in which to exercise First Amendment liberties. This book examines the critical intersection of public speech and spatiality. Through a tour of various places on what the author calls the "expressive topography," the book considers a variety of public speech activities, including sidewalk counseling at abortion clinics, residential picketing, protesting near funerals, assembling and speaking on college campuses, and participating in public rallies and demonstrations at political conventions and other critical democratic events. This examination of public expressive liberties, or speech out of doors, shows that place can be as important to one's expressive experience as voice, sight, and auditory function. Speakers derive a host of benefits, such as proximity, immediacy, symbolic function, and solidarity, from message placement. Unfortunately, for several decades the ground beneath speakers' feet has been steadily eroding. The causes of this erosion are varied and complex; they include privatization and other loss of public space, legal restrictions on public assembly and expression, methods of policing public speech activity, and general public apathy. To counter these forces and reverse at least some of their effects will require a focused and sustained effort – by public officials, courts, and of course, the people themselves.

Timothy Zick is Professor of Law at the College of William & Mary Marshall-Wythe School of Law. He has published numerous articles on freedom of speech and other constitutional issues.

Speech Out of Doors

PRESERVING FIRST AMENDMENT LIBERTIES IN PUBLIC PLACES

Timothy Zick

Marshall-Wythe School of Law
William & Mary

CAMBRIDGE
UNIVERSITY PRESS

CAMBRIDGE UNIVERSITY PRESS
Cambridge, New York, Melbourne, Madrid, Cape Town, Singapore, São Paulo, Delhi

Cambridge University Press
32 Avenue of the Americas, New York, NY 10013-2473, USA

www.cambridge.org
Information on this title: www.cambridge.org/9780521731966

First published 2009

Printed in the United States of America

A catalog record for this publication is available from the British Library.

Library of Congress Cataloging in Publication Data
Zick, Timothy.
   Speech out of doors : preserving First Amendment liberties in public places / Timothy Zick.
     p.   cm.
   Includes bibliographical references and index.
   ISBN 978-0-521-51730-0 (hardback) – ISBN 978-0-521-73196-6 (pbk.)   1. Freedom of
   speech – United States.   2. Assembly, Right of – United States.   3. Law and geography –
   United States.   I. Title.
   KF4772.Z42 2008
   342.7308′54–dc22   2008033691

ISBN 978-0-521-51730-0 hardback
ISBN 978-0-521-73196-6 paperback

For Brian Tamanaha – scholar, mentor, friend.

When one allows a political association to place centers of action at certain important points of the country, its activity becomes greater and its influence more extended. There men see each other; means of execution are combined and opinions are deployed with the force and heat that written thought can never attain.

Alexis deTocqueville, *Democracy in America*

At the heart of our jurisprudence lies the principle that in a free nation citizens must have the right to gather and speak with other persons in public places.

International Society for Krishna Consciousness v. Lee,
505 U.S. 672, 696 (1992) (Kennedy, J., concurring)

CONTENTS

LIST OF FIGURES

PREFACE

This is a book about the exercise of expressive liberties – speech, assembly, petition, and press – in public places. This may seem an odd time for a book about traditional – some might say "old-fashioned" – public expression. The growth in online discourse has been nothing short of phenomenal. Do protesting and pamphleteering still matter? Haven't we evolved beyond such seemingly primitive forms of communication? Haven't speakers already migrated from "meatspaces" to more virtual forums? Who cares whether citizens can engage one another in "bricks and mortar" places when they can reach a potential audience of *millions* online?

The short answer to this last question, at least, is that we should all care about the preservation of traditional First Amendment liberties. In many ways, public places were the birthplaces of American democracy. Our First Amendment was shaped and molded on the ground – by people who gathered out of doors to protest, proselytize about their faiths, and engage fellow citizens and officials on matters of public concern. Further, this sort of public expressive activity – "speech out of doors" – is perhaps the most tangible evidence of popular sovereignty, the idea that under our Constitution it is *the people* who ultimately govern. Public places remain important sites of public politics, contention, and democracy. This is particularly so with respect to poorly financed groups and causes, which, even in an advanced technological era, have little real communicative power. In sum, we all have a stake in the preservation of public First Amendment liberties and the places that facilitate their exercise.

Although this is first and foremost a book about particular First Amendment liberties, the subject matter necessarily touches upon broader themes. Our expressive culture is rapidly evolving. Fundamental terms like "assemble," "speech," "petition," and "press" have taken on new forms and meanings in the digital age. There are many expressive benefits associated with this transformation. As has been widely observed, speakers can communicate with larger audiences more cheaply and efficiently than ever before. But we ought also to note that the manner in which communication among public citizens occurs is changing in fundamental respects. In general, expression is becoming more virtual (and hence less physical), more distant in both space and time, more private, and more narrowly channeled to audiences based on individualized preferences and interests. These changes signal a critical divide in our expressive culture, between more traditional physical and tangible forms of expression and new virtual forms. Although this book is primarily about more traditional types of expression, its findings and conclusions are connected in important ways to our ongoing expressive evolution.

In conjunction with that dynamic evolution, a consensus seemed to be forming that traditional public expression had ceased to be either prevalent or important to American expressive culture. Although geographers, political scientists, and other social scientists remained intensely interested in public places, with a few devoting special attention to public expression, First Amendment scholars seemed to abandon the field for trendier subjects and agendas. Like the general public, they seemed to have concluded that speech out of doors no longer mattered. To the contrary, I observed first one, then another, and then still another incident in which speakers sought to engage in public expression in the most traditional of places – on public streets and sidewalks, in public parks and squares, and in the personal spaces of public audiences. Many of these speakers were not poorly financed either; they too had access to keyboards and modems. Still, they chose to engage the public in more physical and tangible ways and venues.

Some of these speakers and assemblies were allowed to exercise First Amendment liberties with minimal interference. But in many cases, speakers were denied the opportunity to reach intended audiences or permitted to speak only under the most restrictive conditions. In particular, I noted the frequent physical displacement of speakers and speech. Some of that displacement was owing to public order laws, regulations, and policing practices. Just as often, however, displacement resulted from various architectural, social, and political forces. In any event, my examination indicated that speakers have not, as the conventional wisdom suggests, simply abandoned either traditional forums or traditional forms of public expression.

As I was writing this book, I frequently wondered whether it was to be an obituary for or triumphant celebration of speech out of doors in

America. The book I have written is ultimately neither of these things. As noted, and as the many examples in this book show, the people have not abandoned public places or traditional public liberties. For those who remain skeptical, I invite you to visit the trove of photographs and videos now available on the Web and execute a simple search for "protest" or "demonstration." At the same time, much has changed since colonial Americans first took to the streets and public squares to protest taxes and present other grievances against public officials. Most of these changes – architectural, social, political, and legal – have resulted in a vastly diminished "expressive topography." This book is not a simplistic or naïve call for Americans to "take to the streets" or to reclaim public spaces in some revolutionary sense. It is, however, at once a reminder of the enduring significance of public expressive liberties and a warning with regard to their steady and continuing erosion.

As will become apparent, no single scholarly paradigm can explain something as complex and dynamic as the exercise of First Amendment liberties in public places. This book draws upon research in a host of disciplines, including law, history, geography, sociology, political science, philosophy, anthropology, architecture, and urban studies. As disparate as these disciplines may seem, they all have something important in common – each has devoted systematic attention to place, public protest and contention, or both subjects. Social science scholars have examined the character of public places and the relationship between place and socialization, citizenship, community, and political activism. When they have engaged speech out of doors, legal scholars have focused primarily on narrower doctrinal and theoretical concerns relating to freedom of speech. Although this is primarily a book about First Amendment liberties, interdisciplinary concepts like "place," "public contention," and "repression" are critical to the analysis. In brief, the present scope of our public expressive liberties is not solely a function of the content of casebooks, court reporters, and legal treatises. Speech out of doors is a social and political phenomenon; one must draw upon knowledge and information in diverse fields of study to understand it.

Social scientists who study place and public contention will benefit from this book's insights regarding the manner in which law conceptualizes and shapes public places and public expression. At the same time, lawyers, judges, and legal scholars will better appreciate the many *nonlegal* forces that affect public expressive liberties. The book's multidisciplinary examination will challenge (or, it is hoped, at least lead to greater reflection concerning) deeply ingrained ideas regarding public expression, free speech theories, and popular sovereignty. Finally, this book will contribute to contemporary discussions regarding the delicate balance between security and civil liberties. As we shall see, public places and speech out of doors are deeply affected by the prospect of terrorist attacks and other threats to public order and safety.

As a result of this study, I am convinced that speech out of doors remains critical to public life, public discourse, and public politics. It is therefore essential that we preserve adequate "breathing space" for First Amendment liberties in public places. Others may or may not ultimately share my convictions. Regardless, I hope at least to challenge those who believe that public speakers and traditional public expression are relics of little or no relevance to contemporary social, political, or expressive cultures; that public assemblies and speakers are, at worst, dangerous mobs or, at best, unnecessary inconveniences; that speech out of doors must generally be repressed in the name of "security" and "public order"; and that expression prohibited in one place can be just as effectively conveyed someplace else. In addition to addressing these and other fundamental issues, the book offers various proposals for preserving First Amendment liberties in public places. As is entirely fitting in a popular democracy, much will depend upon the people themselves. We are all ultimately responsible for the preservation of the expressive topography and our public expressive liberties.

ACKNOWLEDGMENTS

I am deeply indebted to scholars in a wide variety of disciplines whose research and ideas influenced my examination of public expression. This book relies upon and incorporates ideas from a range of disciplines. Two groups of scholars were particularly influential: geographers, anthropologists, urbanists, and other social scientists who have elevated space and place to subjects of serious scholarly attention, and political scientists who have studied the various facets of public contention. I have also benefited, of course, from the work of many First Amendment scholars. I would like to specifically recognize the late Harry Kalven, Jr., whose examination of First Amendment liberties during the Civil Rights Era convinced me of the *contemporary* importance of speech out of doors.

The research for this book has occupied me for several years. Although the book was conceived and written as a separate text, some of the central ideas are discussed in previously published articles. These include "Speech and Spatial Tactics," 84 *Tex. L. Rev.* 581 (2006); "Space, Place, and Speech: The Expressive Topography," 74 *Geo. Wash. L. Rev.* 439 (2006); and "Clouds, Cameras, and Computers: The First Amendment and Networked Public Places," 59 *Fla. L. Rev.* 1 (2007).

I would like to thank several scholars who took the time either to read all or portions of this book, or to discuss its premises and claims with me at various stages: John Barrett, Chris Borgen, Paul Kirgis, Peter Marguiles, Richard McAdams, Mark Movsesian, Michael Simons, Ellen Sward, Brian Tamanaha, and Nelson Tebbe provided criticisms and/or insights that have improved the manuscript. I would also like to thank the participants at workshops and panel discussions at Washington University Law School in St. Louis, Hofstra University Law School, and the annual meeting of the Law and Society Association. These events were particularly timely and helpful as the book first began to take shape.

I would also like to extend my appreciation to the several photographers who granted permission to use many of the images in the book. Last but certainly not least, I thank my research assistants – Rosa Castello, Valerie Ferrier, Chrisanthy Koumbourlis, and Annie Power – for their diligent work and support.

SPEECH OUT OF DOORS

1 INTRODUCTION: THE GEOGRAPHY OF EXPRESSION

The 2004 Democratic National Convention in Boston was a critical democratic moment. Delegates were gathering at the Fleet Center to choose a presidential nominee. Opponents of the nominees and various party detractors also intended to assemble there, to demonstrate and protest. Quite naturally, these speakers wanted to be both seen and heard – by the delegates and others near the Fleet Center. They also wanted the media to notice their assemblies and report on their criticisms and causes. Federal and local officials constructed a place for this purpose. The "Demonstration Zone (DZ)", as it came to be known, was located within a "hard" security zone around the immediate perimeter of the Fleet Center. This "hard" zone was located within a larger "soft" security zone stretching beyond the Fleet Center.

The DZ was an oppressive architecture. Barricades and fences marked its perimeters. Two layers of thick mesh were added to this imposing and restrictive shell. To prevent anyone from climbing out of the "pen" or "cage," as many demonstrators referred to it, officials placed coiled razor wire at its apex. National Guardsmen were strategically positioned to observe any activity within the DZ, and presumably to respond to any threats to public safety and order. Once inside, speakers would have no meaningful access to the delegates. No leaflets or other materials could be passed. No signs of any appreciable size would be allowed into the zone. Given the access points to the Fleet Center to be used by delegates, demonstrators would not be seen, or perhaps even heard (Figure 1.1).

A federal judge described the DZ as "a space redolent of the sensibility conveyed in Piranesi's etchings published as *Fanciful Images of Prisons*."[1] This "internment camp," the judge continued, was "a symbolic affront to

---

[1] Coal. to Protest the Democratic Nat'l Convention v. City of Boston, 327 F. Supp. 2d 61, 67 (D. Mass. 2004), *aff'd sub nom.* Bl(a)ck Tea Soc'y v. City of Boston, 378 F.3d 8 (1st Cir. 2004).

Figure 1.1. The "Demonstration Zone".

the First Amendment."[2] According to the judge, it was not even clear that the DZ was a *safe* place for protesters to be. Nevertheless, citing "security" concerns and the lack of alternative places, both trial and appellate courts held that the DZ did not offend any First Amendment doctrine or principle. Not a single protester ultimately used the DZ.

PLACE AND PUBLIC EXPRESSION

The DZ illustrates many of the themes discussed in this book. The protesters and demonstrators wanted to assemble and speak near the Fleet Center, in a public place. The historian Gordon Wood has shown that the impulse of the people to assemble "out of doors" – outside ordinary political channels and institutions and, more literally, in outdoor places – extends as far back as the prerevolutionary period.[3] As discussed in the next chapter, colonial Americans assembled in public committees, conventions, and "mobs" to petition authorities, make grievances known, and realize political goals. Popular sovereignty originated in this fashion – out of doors, on the ground, and in public places. Public protest, dissent, and

---

[2] *Id.* at 74–75.
[3] Gordon S. Wood, *The Creation of the American Republic, 1776–1787*, 319–28 (1969).

contention are venerable American traditions. In many contexts, but especially at critical democratic moments like national party conventions, people still want to be seen and heard in person by audiences large and small.

As the Supreme Court has observed on many occasions, "First Amendment freedoms need breathing space to survive."[4] Both doctrinal and *physical* space are required for a robust expressive culture. Today, of course, speakers can find many outlets for "cheap" speech – particularly on the Web. As the Supreme Court has noted, a speaker can communicate from a "virtual soapbox" to a potentially worldwide audience.[5] Virtual spaces and places are indeed a critical part of the modern expressive culture. As the Boston protesters were aware, however, material public places – also known in today's parlance as "bricks and mortar" places or, somewhat more derisively, "meatspaces" – possess unique characteristics and benefits as channels of public expression.[6]

For centuries now, public places have been important stages for the exercise of First Amendment liberties and sites of popular democracy. They remain so. Fundamentally, the proximity and physicality of expression in material public places often make it difficult to ignore. This sets tactile expression apart from the daily avalanche of words conveyed online, which can be readily avoided, ignored, or quickly deleted. Public places also assist in amplifying speakers' messages. The place itself may have symbolic power and meaning. Further, as conventional media are more likely to cover physical contest and dissent, public places can assist speakers in conveying messages to broader audiences.[7] Providing adequate public space for speech and assembly is especially critical to what the Supreme Court has called "the poorly financed causes of

---

[4] NAACP v. Button, 371 U.S. 415, 433 (1963) (emphasis added).

[5] Reno v. ACLU, 521 U.S. 844 (1997).

[6] The concepts of "space" and "place" are theoretically complex. Although it does not ignore notions of abstract or linear space, this book focuses primarily upon *concrete* places – those that are used and experienced by people. *See* William H. Sewell, Jr., "Space in Contentious Politics," in Ronald Aminzade, Jack A. Goldstrone, Doug McAdam, Elizabeth J. Perry, William H. Sewell, Jr., Sidney Tarrow, & Charles Tilly, *Silence and Voice in the Study of Contentious Politics* 52–54 (2001). As of the 1980s, this sort of space was referred to by many geographers as "place." *See* Doreen Massey, *Space, Place, and Gender* (1994).

[7] As we shall see, however, speakers must be careful not to lose control of their own message during media amplification. *See* Jackie Smith, John D. McCarthy, Clark McPhail, & Boguslaw Augustyn, "From Protest to Agenda Building: Description Bias in Media Coverage of Protest Events in Washington, D.C.," 79 *Social Forces* No. 4 (June 2001), 1397–1423; Pamela E. Oliver & Gregory M. Maney, "Political Processes and Local Newspaper Coverage of Protest Events: From Selection Bias to Triadic Interactions," *The American Journal of Sociology*, 106(2) (Sept. 2000), 463–505.

little people."[8] These causes still exist today. Finally, there is something unique, in terms of emotive quality and solidarity, about the experience of assembling with others and speaking in material public places. These characteristics of proximity, symbolism, emotion, and solidarity are very difficult, if not impossible, to replicate in existing virtual places.

The DZ also demonstrates that the power of place works in more than one direction. Spatial restrictions can limit or extinguish the benefits often associated with material public places. Governments have historically used place to exert disciplinary and sometimes repressive power over persons and groups. Officials have imposed public order by restricting access to and use of certain public places. In more recent times, governments have claimed that spatial control is necessitated by a special kind of public order problem – "security." As we shall see, fear of terrorism has significantly affected public liberties; public places and public expression are now situated on the much-discussed fault line between security and liberty. Whatever the reasons or motives for its imposition, displacement can and often does immobilize protest, mute speakers, and distort messages. The architecture of the DZ did just these things; it prevented movement, facilitated surveillance, and prohibited certain forms of expression. Place, in short, can be a useful tool of repression.

Finally, the DZ demonstrates the *vocality* of place. The area around the Fleet Center was a hotly contested social and political space. Speakers desired access to convey and amplify complaints and objections relating to the proceedings inside and to larger matters of public concern. Officials sought to militarize the area, constructing "soft" and "hard" security zones and the DZ itself. In this instance, militarization prevailed. The DZ's tactical architectures and the strategic placement of guardsmen sent an unmistakable message that public contest and expression posed serious threats. Had it been used, the DZ might have branded the persons confined and their speech as unworthy of serious attention and perhaps even dangerous to society. Places can be highly vocal – symbolic, evocative, and even communicative.

This book examines the complex and dynamic intersection of speech and spatiality. To be sure, that dynamic does not always resemble the DZ episode. My claim is not that place is *always* expressive or generally repressive; indeed, sometimes it is neither. But far more often than we generally appreciate, the character of a place substantially affects the exercise of First Amendment liberties. The remainder of this introductory chapter describes a conceptual and theoretical framework for

---

[8] *Martin v. City of Struthers*, 319 U.S. 141, 146 (1943).

better appreciating this connection. It also presents a roadmap for the
rest of the book.

THE EXPRESSIVE TOPOGRAPHY

As numerous examples in this book will show, assembly, expression, and
contention in public places remain significant to our social, political, and
expressive cultures. People still regularly engage in speech, assembly,
press, and petition activities out of doors. Some, no doubt, view such
activities as ineffective, silly, antiquated, disruptive, or some combination
of these things. In some of the instances we shall consider, these may be
entirely fair descriptions or criticisms. As a general matter, however, the
public exercise of First Amendment liberties cannot be so readily dismissed. For both historical and contemporary reasons, we ought to take
this aspect of our expressive culture more seriously. If we are poised to
lose it, we ought to understand why. We ought also to appreciate what this
loss might portend in terms of the scope of First Amendment liberties
more generally.

As noted, the public exercise of First Amendment liberties requires
an adequate supply of material space. This raises one of the fundamental
concerns of this book. As scholars in political science, sociology,
urban geography, and other disciplines have noted, there has been a
steady erosion of public space over the past several decades. Development and privatization have been critical forces in this diminution.[9] The
general physical erosion, in combination with a variety of legal, political,
and social circumstances, has severely diminished our *expressive topography* – the public space in which First Amendment liberties may be
exercised.

Imagine a simple map of the public places in and around a single city
or town anywhere in the United States. On this map are traditional public
thoroughfares like streets, sidewalks, parks, and squares. There are also
public buildings of various sorts, public gardens, large and small developments, shopping malls, auditoriums, museums, and stadiums. If the
city or town is near water, there might be a public beach and a boardwalk.
A college or university might occupy several acres or city blocks. On the
outskirts of the town, there might be an airport, highway rest stops, and

---

[9] For an insightful discussion of the manner in which privatization has affected public democracy,
see Margaret Kohn, *Brave New Neighborhoods: The Privatization of Public Space* (2004).

other transit hubs. In all of these places, we may assume that the general public is invited to be and often is present.

Now imagine that this same map is divided into zones of three different colors. *Green* spaces on the map represent the spaces in which public liberties are afforded the most robust constitutional respect and protection. Among other things, this means that speakers have a constitutional right to be in such places, and can be denied access only for valid and compelling reasons. This is, of course, an over-simplification. As we shall see, even in the "green" zones, expressive liberties can be substantially limited in terms of the time, place, and manner of their exercise. Thus, many of these spaces might just as well be colored *yellow*, to signify a state of conditional expressive liberty. Finally, *red* zones represent areas in which speakers have either no or minimal speech protections. In red zones, governments (and in situations like shopping malls and gated communities, private owners) may deny access altogether or remove speakers and assemblies for minimally rational reasons or even no reasons at all.

Although it is obviously very rudimentary, this mapping of the expressive topography highlights a rather serious and complex problem. In fundamental terms, the public areas on the expressive topography that are located within red and yellow zones now far exceed the areas that can genuinely be colored green. What is even more alarming, the green spaces are rapidly shrinking, while the red and yellow zones continue to expand. This steady erosion of the expressive topography has affected all forms and modes of public expression, from face-to-face citizen interaction, to expressive events intimately connected to particular places, to mass protests at critical democratic moments like the Democratic National Convention in Boston.

There have, of course, always been limits on the exercise of public liberties. The First Amendment is not a license to create chaos or do public harm. Thus there have always been red (and yellow) zones on the expressive topography. No one has a First Amendment right to deliver a message in the place of her choice. Assemblies cannot meet in the middle of the street, or in the Mayor's office. A speaker does not have the right to assemble with others and shout "No More War!" in the middle of the Pentagon – although that right certainly may be protected in some other place. As the legal scholar Harry Kalven, Jr. observed long ago, having and enforcing Robert's Rules for public places is a legal and practical necessity.[10]

---

[10] Harry Kalven, Jr., "The Concept of the Public Forum: Cox v. Louisiana," 1965 *Sup. Ct. Rev.* 1, 12.

As the next chapter demonstrates, the expressive topography has been shaped by a variety of forces, many of which have little or nothing to do with common sense and largely uncontested rules of public order and decorum. These forces include massive population shifts to suburban and exurban areas; large-scale privatization and commercialization of public places; architectural trends; zoning laws; conditions of general economic prosperity; deep cultural schisms; societal and political centralization; repressive law enforcement methods; tactical and other errors by speakers; public attitudes regarding public liberties; heightened security concerns; and the development and proliferation of new technologies. In conjunction with these social and political forces, First Amendment doctrines relating to place – principally the "public forum" and "time, place, and manner" doctrines (discussed in the next chapter) – have helped create an ossified and anemic expressive topography. As we shall see, these doctrines have generally failed to reflect, and have proven incapable of flexibly responding to, social forces like urban and suburban planning, population migration, and privatization. The combination of these and other influences has diminished the expressive topography and, with it, the scope of public First Amendment liberties.

Both present-day management and future preservation of the expressive topography require a delicate balance of competing interests. Throughout American history, public places have been sites of remarkable democratic displays. But they have also been sites of disruption and violence. The geographer Don Mitchell has referred to this as "the dialectic of public space."[11] Mitchell observes: "The central contradiction at the heart of public space is that it demands a certain disorder and unpredictability to function *as* a democratic public space, and yet democratic theory posits that a certain order and rationality are vital to the success of democratic discourse."[12] This "dialectic" will be one of the recurring themes in the book.

First Amendment doctrine grants public officials broad discretion to calibrate this balance. Officials, who have a natural tendency to favor order over disruption of any kind, have often found that speakers' interests in access, proximity, and manner of expression are outweighed by other interests. These include the privacy of the "unwilling" listener, the repose of the suburban homeowner, private property rights, preferred commercial and recreational uses, public order, security, and even aesthetics. A civilized society cannot, of course, exist without many of

---

[11] Don Mitchell, *The Right to the City: Social Justice and the Fight for Public Space* 130 (2003).
[12] *Id.*

these things. But neither can public liberties survive on an expressive topography designed, constructed, and regulated such that expressive interests are routinely sacrificed or curtailed in favor of a long and expanding list of nonexpressive interests. Courts can, and as we shall see sometimes do, correct or moderate this imbalance. But for a variety of reasons explored in this book, we cannot and should not rely too heavily upon the courts to maintain a robust expressive topography.

Writing during the pitched contest over civil rights in the 1960s, Harry Kalven, Jr. observed that the extent to which we make space for the exercise of public liberties is an "index of freedom."[13] So it remains, even as speech is digitized and migrates to virtual spaces. For this reason, too, we must carefully attend to speech out of doors. The health and vibrancy of our expressive topography is a direct reflection of undamental First Amendment values, theories, and commitments.

EXPRESSIVE PLACE

Commenting on political science scholarship regarding public contention and social movements, William Sewell has noted that "the literature has treated space as an assumed and unproblematized background, not as a constituent aspect of contentious politics that must be conceptualized explicitly and probed systematically."[14] The same can generally be said of judges' and legal scholars' treatment of the relationship between speech and spatiality. In First Amendment doctrine and scholarship, place has generally been treated as a background principle, not a *fundamental* aspect of assembly, expression, and other public liberties.

Place entered constitutional discourse as property, thing, or *res*. First Amendment scholars have acknowledged, with displeasure in most cases, that the treatment of place as *res* or thing is "deeply entrenched."[15] From

---

[13] Kalven, *supra* note 10 at 12.
[14] Sewell, *supra* note 6 at 51.
[15] Calvin Massey, "Public Fora, Neutral Governments, and the Prism of Property," 50 *Hastings L.J.* 309, 310 (1999). *See also* Lillian BeVier, "Rehabilitating Public Forum Doctrine: In Defense of Categories," 1992 *Sup. Ct. Rev.* 79, 117. ("It is quite possible that the Court started off with a fundamental error – misconceiving the speech issues involved in the public forum problem as *property* issues.") When scholars have occasionally proposed alternative approaches or refinements to the public forum doctrine they have done so from within the established property paradigm. *See, e.g.*, Massey, 50 *Hastings L.J.* at 311 (proposing that access to public spaces be determined "by making an analogy to the common law of nuisance"); Steven G. Gey, "Reopening the Public Forum – From Sidewalks to Cyberspace," 58 *Ohio St. L. J.* 1535, 1577 (1998) (proposing a focused balancing or "strong interference analysis" in forum cases).

its first consideration of place as an element of freedom of expression, the Supreme Court has used a series of legal property metaphors and principles to define rights of access to public places.[16] The government was initially considered the *owner* of traditional venues like public parks and streets, and some time later a *trustee* of these and other public properties on behalf of the people as beneficiaries.[17] More recent cases suggest that governments exercise a form of *proprietorship* with regard to public places. Over time, the people gained certain access and use *"easements,"* at least with regard to some public places.[18] As to a great many public places, however, governmental *title* has proved a powerful exclusionary and regulatory tool.

Thus, as a form of legal property, place appears in First Amendment discussions as a secondary, inert, mostly fungible, and (like other public resources) neutrally distributed backdrop for expression. This book will show that quite often place is, in fact, none of these things. We shall see that place can be as critical to one's expressive experience as voice, sight, and auditory function.

Although it is comfortable and familiar to lawyers and judges, the conception of place-as-property is too blunt and narrow to recognize the *expressive* qualities of place.[19] Place is often symbolic, vocal, and communicative – both in its own right, and in combination with a variety of speakers and manners of expression. This is not a metaphysical argument regarding place. Places like public streets and government buildings are, of course, properties – in the sense that they are material things ultimately owned and operated by someone or something. As many social science scholars have explained, however, tangible places have far greater significance than this for the people, including speakers, who occupy and experience them. To better understand the expressiveness of place, we must look beyond law, to disciplines in which place has been found to have greater meaning.

In general terms, material places are critical to human existence. People live in and through such places; indeed they cannot actually escape them, even in virtual realms. Many experience what the geographer Yi-Fu Tuan has called "topophilia" – an affinity for or connection to place.[20]

---

[16] *See* Massey, *supra* note 15 at 117.

[17] Hague v. Comm. for Indus. Org., 307 U.S. 496 (1939).

[18] *See* Kalven, *supra* note 10 at 13.

[19] *See* Timothy Zick, "Speech and Spatial Tactics," 84 *Tex. L. Rev.* 581 (2006); Timothy Zick, "Space, Place, and Speech: The Expressive Topography," 74 *Geo. Wash. L. Rev.* 439 (2006); Timothy Zick, "Property, Place, and Public Discourse," 21 *Wash. U. J. of Law & Policy* 173 (2006).

[20] Yi-Fu Tuan, *Topophilia* (1974).

People not only experience but actively shape and construct the spaces and places they occupy.[21] These acts of production give rise to a distinct spatial culture. When connections to place are severed or restricted, people may experience the condition or state of "placelessness."[22] In sum, places ground and give meaning to lives, activities, and cultures. Properties, as such, do none of these things; rather, their primary function is to order legal relationships.

The fundamental connection to place exists in many First Amendment contexts. The chapters in this book focus on several of these, in the process demonstrating that place is far more than a physical backdrop for expression. Message *placement* is often inextricably intertwined with message content. Choice of place is often an intentional act, one that facilitates a particular type of expression or conveys unique expressive meaning. Certain places provide critical proximity to target audiences. A particular place on the expressive topography may symbolize an ongoing contest, dispute, or grievance. As noted earlier, such places often help to maximize media coverage of a message or agenda. Places like public streets, parks, and squares are richly inscribed with memories, events, and histories. Still other places, like the National Mall, the White House, and Ground Zero, are sacred repositories of national memories and cultural moments. The public grounds of university campuses at one time facilitated robust political and social activism. Under the right conditions, these places may again serve as invaluable training grounds for public citizenship.

As this book also shows, places may be communicative or expressive in other respects as well. A spatial culture conveys a breadth of information regarding social and political conditions. Shopping malls, airport terminals, and other places in which public expression is generally prohibited or substantially muted symbolize commercialization, privatization, placelessness, and the general decline of our public expressive culture. The "militarization" of public places, especially during critical democratic moments like presidential campaigns, national party conventions, and meetings of world leaders (Chapter 7), signifies a new collection of threats to security, public order, and public liberties. The ongoing project to "network" public places, in particular by establishing ubiquitous public surveillance systems and wireless Web access (Chapter 9), signifies the

---

[21] *See* Henri Lefebvre, *The Production of Space* 73 (Donald Nicholson-Smith trans., Blackwell Publishing 1991) (1974); David E. Sopher, "Place and Location: Notes on the Spatial Patterning of Culture," 53 *Soc. Sci. Q.* 321–37 (1972).

[22] Edward Relph, *Place and Placelessness* (1976).

transformative effects of super-modernity on portions of our expressive topography. These and other communicative aspects are visible only when one thinks of place rather than property.

As the foregoing examples show, places, unlike properties, are not static or inert. The expressive topography is a dynamic and highly variable *system* of places. Its contours change as a result of a variety of events and circumstances. Places become more or less important to, or facilitative of, public liberties depending on external (population shifts or changes in First Amendment doctrine) and internal (demolition or privatization) spatial conditions. This variability and dynamism suggests the need for substantial flexibility in fashioning rules of access and other expressive doctrines. Yet as discussed in greater detail in the next chapter, the Supreme Court has held that all of the space on the expressive topography can be formally categorized as one of only *three* types of properties or "forums."[23] Unlike my earlier conceptual mapping of red, yellow, and green zones, the Court's categorization is not merely illustrative of a problem. It is, in fact, a large *part* of the problem. Legal rights and obligations flow directly from its rigid property categorization, which generally fails to account for the expressiveness of place.

Further, contrary to one of the apparent assumptions of the First Amendment's property construct, public places are not fungible commodities. Because place is so often communicative, where one is permitted to speak can be of critical importance. Whether a place is an "adequate" alternative or provides "ample" opportunity to convey a message under the "time, place, and manner" doctrine often depends heavily on context and circumstance. Thus, for example, it is incorrect to assume that sidewalks, parks, and streets are all more or less adequate substitutes insofar as public speakers are concerned. An assembly on a nearby public sidewalk is hardly an adequate substitute for a parade down Main Street. In short, whereas properties may be fungible, places are generally unique and distinctive.

Finally, the conception of place-as-property tends to treat place as a neutrally distributed thing. This assumes that place is a resource (like water or electricity) distributed according to neutral bureaucratic criteria. Place, however, is not a product of brute fact. It is not given but *made*. Henri Lefebvre has demonstrated the complex manner by which places are socially produced or constructed.[24] Michel Foucault has highlighted

---

[23] *See* Perry Educ. Ass'n v. Perry Local Educators' Ass'n, 460 U.S. 37, 50–51 (1983).
[24] *See generally* Lefebvre, *supra* note 21.

the power inherent in place – in particular, its ability to segregate persons and activities, facilitate surveillance, and brand individuals as misfits or outcasts.[25] One need not wholeheartedly embrace the concepts or philosophies of these prominent critical thinkers to question the neutrality of place. As we shall see, the distribution and regulation of public space is not typically a mere bureaucratic rationing. It is often the product of social, political, and legal contests and duelling conceptions of the public sphere. In many cases, the places on the expressive topography speak to the decidedly non-neutral production of public space.

In sum, this book generally treats place as primary to expression, dynamic, highly variable, distinctive, and constructed. Place is, in short, nothing like the property concept upon which First Amendment doctrines of place rest. Viewing place as expressive does not mean that one discounts legitimate public interests like security and public order, or assumes that all spatial regulation is a matter of power politics. It does not mean the speaker is always allowed to choose the most effective expressive place. Nor will this book advocate radical changes to fundamental First Amendment doctrines of place (although it will offer several criticisms). To the consternation of many First Amendment scholars, it is likely too late in the day to simply jettison these doctrines. But various changes in judicial perspective, speakers' practices, laws, physical places, and official policies can help secure public space for speech activities even within existing rules. These and other changes are explored in the various chapters that follow. More generally, viewing place as expressive will inform the debate regarding whether the First Amendment ought to be concerned, as some suggest, solely with preventing governmental "distortion" of speakers' messages rather than affirmatively "enhancing" or facilitating (public) expression.[26] Finally, and more tangibly, thinking in terms of expressive place can help us understand the considerable damage we have done and continue to do to our expressive topography.

---

[25] *See, e.g.*, Michel Foucault, *Discipline and Punish* 236 (Alan Sheridan trans., Vintage Books 1979) (1977) (highlighting the prison as the exemplar of containing and controlling space). *See also* Don Mitchell, "Political Violence, Order, and the Legal Construction of Public Space: Power and the Public Forum Doctrine," *Urban Geography* 17, 158–178 (1996); Nicholas L. Blomley, *Law, Space, and the Geographies of Power* xiii (1994) (positing judges and lawmakers as overlooked framers of space); Edward Soja, *Postmodern Geographies: The Reassertion of Space in Social Critical Theory* (1989).

[26] For a discussion of the enhancement versus distortion approach as it relates to public forum doctrine, *see* Lillian BeVier, "Rehabilitating Public Forum Doctrine: In Defense of Categories," 1992 *Sup. Ct. Rev.* 79, 101.

THE DEMOCRATIC FUNCTIONS OF PUBLIC PLACES

Fixing the damage to our expressive topography will not be easy. But if public places are to continue to serve their principal democratic functions, it will be necessary. The leading justifications for the First Amendment – the marketplace of ideas, the search for truth, and self-governance – are rooted in *public* deliberation and participation. Public places have always been critical to the creation of a marketplace of ideas.[27] They have been, and remain, instrumental to the search for truth, and citizen self-governance.[28] Public places are also important venues for self-actualization.[29] A vibrant expressive topography has encouraged public citizenship by facilitating interaction among diverse groups of citizens, and among citizens and public officials. More specifically, public places continue to serve three critical democratic functions: They facilitate speakers' identity claims, create necessary breathing space for democratic participation and self-government, and lend critical transparency to democracy and governance.

Place, Presence, and Identity

Public life today bears scant resemblance to that in the Greek agora, the Roman forum, or even the early American Republic. A once vibrant and communal public arena has been substantially diminished by, among other things, a proliferation of private enclaves – suburbs and exurbs, gated communities, private developments, and homes designed for long-term comfort and convenience.[30]

This does not mean, however, that the people have lost the basic desire for communal life. Far more people live in urban areas in America than in suburban or rural ones. Further, although new technologies facilitate isolation, people still flock to public places and events. They treat coffee houses as mobile offices, when they could as readily work from home. They populate parks and squares. They attend campaign rallies and

---

[27] Kent Greenawalt, "Free Speech Justifications," 89 *Colum. L. Rev.* 119 (1989) (discussing "marketplace" and other free speech justifications).

[28] *See* Alexander Meiklejohn, *Free Speech and Its Relation to Self-Government* 15–16, 24–27 (1948) (advancing self-governance theory).

[29] C. Edwin Baker, "Unreasoned Reasonableness: Mandatory Parade Permits and Time, Place, and Manner Regulations," 78 *Nw. U. L. Rev.* 937 (1983).

[30] *See* Jurgen Habermas, *The Structural Transformation of the Public Sphere* (1989); Don Mitchell, "The End of Public Space? People's Park, Definitions of the Public, and Democracy," *Annals of the Association of American Geographers* 85, 108–133 (1995); Kohn, *supra* note at 115–119.

conventions when, one supposes, they could "assemble" and communicate with one another online or simply watch the events on television or YouTube.[31] Even in our hyper-modern society, some level of physical presence in public places remains important to most people.

Presence matters, especially, to full democratic citizenship. In public places people are at their most *visible* – to government officials and one another. Only there are others forced in some sense to count and reckon with them. Through their mere public presence, people can forge public identities.[32] Indeed, presence in a public place is often itself an expressive claim – to political identity and democratic acceptance. The geographer Don Mitchell refers to this expressive use of public place as "representation."[33] When they function effectively, public places encourage and facilitate identity claims and "representation" by a diverse collection of speakers and audiences.

In the 1930s and 1940s, for example, Jehovah's Witnesses challenged conventional public norms by confronting audiences on the public streets.[34] The Witnesses engaged in this activity as a matter of faith. But they also sought to establish that their religious beliefs and practices were entitled to public presence, respect, and "representation." As discussed in the next chapter, the Witnesses were among the earliest architects of the expressive topography. They carved some critical space for public liberties – their own and that of future speakers. In the 1960s, civil rights protesters also pressed public identity claims. They routinely took to the streets, occupied public buildings, and staged sit-ins at public accommodations.[35] Protesters' public presence conveyed the message that African-Americans merited full inclusion in the community and equal justice under law. Public presence signified full legal identity, human dignity, and constitutional personhood.

Following the iconic civil rights example, gays and lesbians, religious proselytizers, women, homeless advocates, nuclear pacifists, peace activists, and "Million" marchers have all made identity claims in similar fashion. This traditional means of making and pressing public identity claims continues to be relied upon by a diverse range of persons and groups. In 2006, for example, nationwide public protests by immigrants

---

[31] One of my favorite examples is the annual convention of bloggers, where online commentators meet in person. Apparently they, too, desire some degree of tangible interaction.

[32] *See* Anne Norton, "Writing Property and Power," in Marcel Henaff & Tracy B. Strong (eds.), *Public Space and Democracy* (2001).

[33] Mitchell, *supra* note 11 at 33–36.

[34] William Kaplan, *State and Salvation: The Jehovah's Witnesses and Their Fight For Civil Rights* (1989).

[35] Taylor Branch, *Pillar of Fire: America in the King Years 1963–1965* (1998).

Figure 1.2. Immigrants' March, Downtown Los Angeles, CA (May 2006).
Source: Photograph by Eric Ju.

presented a quintessential identity claim (Figure 1.2). By assembling in the streets and demonstrating, thousands of immigrants to the United States conveyed a clear message: "We are here, and we are not going anywhere." Congress – and the nation – heard and witnessed these claims. Cable news media, talk radio, and Web sites vigorously discussed the marches and debated the protesters' specific identity claims.[36]

More recently, thousands of African-Americans descended on the tiny (and predominantly white) town of Jena, Louisiana to press claims of racial and criminal justice. For many participants, this was their first civil rights protest. The Jena demonstrations were hailed by some as a revival of the 1960s street protests. Whether or not this turns out to be the case, these and countless other recent protests remind us that public places remain critical to identity and "representation."

Place and Participation

Alexander Meiklejohn once wrote: "Our young women and men who enter into citizenship must learn what it means to be a member of a

---

[36] Congress ultimately considered comprehensive immigration reform legislation. Although the reform proposals failed, the demonstrations, school walk-outs, and other public activities sparked a national conversation about the country's immigration policies.

self-governing society. Our older citizens, if they have won that under-standing, must be saved from losing it."[37] A diverse and vibrant expres-sive topography can facilitate civic republicanism and self-governance.[38] An eroded and anemic public sphere, by contrast, signifies a rather weak foundation for self-rule.

We are fortunate today to have an array of outlets for public partici-pation in democratic affairs. Virtually every form of democratic participation takes both real and virtual forms. There are real and virtual signs and displays, petitions, campaign events, and even protests. Thus, if they choose, most citizens can at least offer their opinions on matters of public concern to some audience. Some might argue that the proliferation of "virtual" forums renders reliance on material public places as forums of self-governance entirely unnecessary. In fact, material places and cyber-places serve rather distinct participatory functions. A self-governing society needs both types of places.

As noted earlier, virtual places offer substantial efficiencies in terms of cost, time, and scale. But only in material places can speakers physically approach, interrupt, speak to, shock, and attempt to persuade a flesh-and-blood audience. The chances that an audience will be jarred or emo-tionally affected by an *online* display of contention are quite slim. Further, as the legal scholar Cass Sunstein has argued, democratic participation requires at least some exposure to speakers and messages that audiences do not wish to encounter or engage.[39] Modern audiences are adept at filtering speech and information that they do not wish to receive. Public places are the only remaining expressive venues in which dissent and contrary views cannot simply be avoided through the now-common practice of "narrowcasting." In sum, only in tangible places do the various advantages relating to physical proximity inure to the speaker. For these and other reasons, speakers continue to solicit petition signatures, picket, distribute pamphlets and leaflets, carry signs and placards, and participate in rallies and demonstrations in more traditional public places.

There is something romantic, yet ultimately naïve, in the notion that the people can self-govern from the comfort of their homes in front of keyboards and computer screens. To be sure, valuable forms of self-government, including the actions of an increasingly vigilant citizen-press, have already contributed to citizen governance and popular democracy. But democracy is and always has been something of a contact

---

[37] Alexander Meiklejohn, *Free Speech and Its Relation to Self-Government* 106 (1948).
[38] Michael J. Sandel, *Democracy's Discontent: America in Search of a Public Philosophy* (1996).
[39] Cass R. Sunstein, *Republic.com* (2001).

sport. The presidential campaign system is only one example of the physicality of self-governance. Candidates are still expected to "work the rope lines" and appear in front of live audiences. As inconvenient and disruptive as it can sometimes be, most of us cannot imagine popular democracy without some public displays of contention. Material public places allow for some rather unique forms of participatory contact, tangible contention, and physical display.

Finally, participation in more material spaces produces different democratic rewards than its virtual counterparts. Self-governance is not generally easy or convenient. As the civil rights era demonstrated, it can require a substantial investment of physical, emotional, and financial resources. Part of the payoff from demonstrations, assemblies, pickets, and other public displays of contention is the solidarity and self-actualization one experiences by participating with others in front of a public audience. This does not necessarily signify greater passion for a cause than, say, a blogger or online protester might possess. It may simply be a reflection of the desire of the speakers to engage with others in a collective public endeavor. Whether or not it ultimately changes minds or the course of events, however, expressive activity that occurs in public places likely leaves the participant feeling as if all that could be done on behalf of a cause has been done. One doubts that the virtual petitioner or blogger feels precisely the same way.

Obviously, the people cannot engage in effective political and social contention in the streets and public squares alone. Nor, however, can they self-govern from their keyboards. In light of their distinct strengths and weaknesses, the most effective path to self-governance would be to *combine* the participatory benefits of real and virtual places. Given their lower costs and broader reach or scale, cyber-places are ideal for organizing, broadcasting, shaping public opinion, and engendering certain kinds of social capital. With their visibility and physicality, material public places offer distinct advantages in terms of exerting pressure on fellow citizens and officials, counteracting the effects of citizen narrowcasting, and creating solidarity among activists.[40]

Place and Transparency

Political dialogue in this country is sometimes hampered by a lack of transparency. This includes an inability to ascertain the interests and

---

[40] *See* Susanne Lohmann, "A Signaling Model of Competitive Political Pressures," 7 *Econ. & Pol.* 181 (1995).

motivations behind a particular message. During extended election seasons, for example, shadowy sponsors and agendas tend to operate largely in the background. Lobbying and fundraising activities (both online and offline) also occur primarily in places removed from public scrutiny. Despite considerable efforts to shine light upon them, governmental deliberations are largely unknown or unknowable to the majority of the public. This general lack of transparency contributes to an unhealthy distrust of politics and political institutions. The proliferation of anonymous and pseudonymous expression in virtual spaces may add to this problem.

Public places lend invaluable transparency to the democratic process.[41] As the discussion of identity and representation indicated, a public place is "theatrical" in the sense that "it is a place in which one is seen and shows oneself to others."[42] In these common public places, audiences can witness first-hand speakers' identity claims, messages, and democratic participation. They may judge for themselves whether the speaker or assembly is motivated by genuine anger, frustration, or concern. They may ask questions of a petition gatherer in real time, debate the merits of a referendum with its proponents, and witness and react to speakers' public displays.

Public displays also challenge governmental authority in a manner that is direct and visible. In material public places, government officials can receive petitions and other communications *directly* from the public they serve. At its healthiest and most robust, the expressive topography allows speakers to see and perhaps (accounting for reasonable security concerns) even speak directly to candidates and public officials. It allows others to witness this activity – either in person or through media reports.

Through ceremony, force, and other means, public places also render the exercise of sovereign power more transparent. Owing precisely to this transparency, however, public places can be more difficult to control and "script" than contrived "town hall" meetings and other official events. People can then bear witness to any official reaction to the exercise of public liberties in public places. They can measure the First Amendment "index of freedom" in real time and space.

When they function as open and transparent venues, public places can check government entrenchment and promote tolerance.[43] They can even provide a "safety valve" for disruptive and potentially dangerous

---

[41] Marcel Henaff & Tracy B. Strong (eds), *Public Space and Democracy* (2001).
[42] *Id.* at 5.
[43] John Hart Ely, *Democracy and Distrust* (1980); Thomas Emerson, *The System of Freedom of Expression* (1970); Lee Bollinger, *The Tolerant Society: Freedom of Speech and Extremist Speech in America* (1986).

speakers. In this regard, at least, public places can actually assist officials in maintaining public order – by bringing potential threats to that order out into the open. Thus, citizens and governments alike derive benefits from an open expressive topography.

In sum, public places are important not only for their variable and dynamic intersection with speakers' individual messages, but also for their more general connection to public politics and popular sovereignty. The places that comprise the expressive topography are critical components of our marketplace of ideas and our system of democratic self-government.

PRESERVING PUBLIC LIBERTIES

Some have suggested that the preservation of public liberties and public places more generally will result only if and when the people commandeer or "take" public spaces.[44] America's political and expressive histories strongly indicate, however, that no populist revolution or massive pouring into public places is forthcoming. Polling data suggests that the American people generally support First Amendment liberties.[45] They are not, however, generally inclined toward mass participation; they are even less likely to support or participate in offensive, contentious and disruptive public displays or forceful (if necessary) repossession of public space.[46] Marginalized voices, in particular, lack the organizational structure and resources to refashion the expressive topography in any substantial way. In any event, a commandeering of certain public places would not be sufficient to sustain public liberties over the long term. The expressive topography is far too complex, and in some respects far too entrenched, to be altered in this blunt fashion.[47]

It is incumbent upon those who support an open and robust expressive topography to advance realistic proposals toward achieving that end. The solutions proposed in the various chapters of this book are as diverse as the

---

[44] Mitchell, *supra* note 11 at 14.
[45] *See, e.g.*, Julie L. Adsager *et al.*, *Free Expression and Five Democratic Publics* (2004); Marvin Ammori, "Public Opinion and Freedom of Speech" (2006) (white paper for The Information Society Project at Yale Law School).
[46] Bert Klandermans, *The Social Psychology of Protest* (1997).
[47] This does not mean that some of the commandeering tactics of the civil rights movement – sit-ins, occupations, demonstrations, and other contentious acts of civil disobedience – are no longer relevant or useful today. Today's public citizen has much to learn from the history of civil rights contention. New repertoires and strategies are needed, however, to respond to the changes in public places and public liberties that have occurred in the United States, especially since the middle part of the twentieth century.

expressive topography itself. Some are directed to speakers; others to public citizens generally; others to local and national officials; and still others to courts.

Although there are some common prescriptive themes, the proposals vary depending upon which *type* of place is at issue. One of the lessons of this study is that there can be no one-size-fits-all, global solution to the erosion of our expressive topography and our public liberties. Different places on the expressive topography raise distinct expressive issues and call for unique spatial knowledge, tactics, and solutions. Further, preservation efforts are substantially complicated by the need to consider a range of private and public interests, including security, that now dynamically affect certain portions of the expressive topography.

Despite these difficulties, there are steps that can be taken to strengthen our expressive topography. Among other things, preservation of public First Amendment liberties will entail encouraging and expanding citizen participation and activism; increasing general public awareness of and support for public speech and contention; identifying new spaces in which to exercise First Amendment liberties out of doors; using effective counter-tactics of protest and dissent; educating officials regarding the health and significance of the expressive topography and the responsibilities of public stewardship; relying on state constitutions and common law principles to create additional expressive breathing space; heightening judicial skepticism and review with respect to speech that occurs on the expressive topography; and designing (in some cases redesigning) public and quasi-public places with an eye toward making additional room for expressive activity. In sum, new attitudes and behaviors must be encouraged, different landscapes and architectures must be envisioned and constructed, and legal doctrines must be revisited and in some cases revised to reflect the diminished state of the contemporary expressive topography.

The proposals in this book are not motivated by any utopian vision of the public sphere. There is no agenda or program to turn *all* public spaces into freewheeling expressive forums. Even if we were to build such an expressive topography, there is little evidence that the American people would generally occupy and use it. We can, however, do much better in terms of creating the necessary breathing space for those who wish to engage in speech out of doors. In addition to explaining how and why we have reached a critical point with respect to public expression and our expressive topogrpahy, this book offers some suggestions for where and how we might begin to expand opportunities for public encounters and participation. Unfortunately, if none of these things are done, we may indeed be witnessing the slow but inevitable destruction of our expressive topography.

THE PLAN OF THE BOOK

Reflecting the conception of expressive place, the book is primarily organized with reference to the types of places on the expressive topography. These spatial types are not intended to be determinative of expressive liberties. Rather, they are identified, described, and examined with reference to the manner in which speech and spatiality intersect in certain places.[48] The typology is not so rigid that each place can be one and only one spatial type. A particular place may intersect differently with speakers and speech depending on the circumstances. Further, the places I have identified are not necessarily the only types of places on the expressive topography, although they are the ones most commonly involved in speech contests. In general terms, the typology of places will do two things: It will facilitate an examination of the broadest possible "surface area" of public space and will allow coverage of the complete range of public expression – from face-to-face encounters to mass public demonstrations and displays.

Chapter 2 begins with a brief historical examination of the nascent expressive topography during the colonial and revolutionary periods. There the foundation of the present-day expressive topography was laid. Most of the chapter, however, consists of an overview of the many forces and events – historical, social, political, and legal – that have shaped our contemporary expressive topography. The specific effects of these influences on public expressive activity are examined in the remaining chapters.

Chapter 3 inititates the detailed study of the contemporary expressive topography. It examines speakers' access to the *embodied* places of listeners and viewers. This is the "personal space" occupied by the listener or viewer in places across the expressive topography. In embodied places, petitions are signed, leaflets are distributed, and personal interaction and persuasion are possible. Speakers like abortion clinic sidewalk counselors, petition gatherers, solicitors, and beggars seek the critical expressive benefits of proximity and immediacy that inhere in such places. Unwilling

---

[48] Many of the spatial labels have been adapted from anthropological treatments of space and place. In particular, *see* the discussion of social spaces in Setha M. Low & Denise Lawrence-Zuniga, eds, *The Anthropology of Space and Place: Locating Culture* 1–22 (2003).

listeners and viewers possess strong competing interests in privacy and repose with regard to their personal spaces.

Chapter 4 considers speakers' access to *contested* places. Contested places broadly symbolize the conflicts of a particular era. In the 1960s, these were places like segregated public libraries, lunch counters, and jails. In the 1970s, speakers gathered near the Pentagon and White House to protest the Vietnam conflict. More recent contests, such as those involving speakers' access to abortion clinics and the homes of abortion providers, President Bush's Summer White House in Crawford, Texas, Armed Forces Recruitment Centers, and cemeteries where military funerals are held, manifest more contemporary social and political conflicts. As these examples indicate, contested places are often intimately connected to speakers' messages. They may afford the most effective access to target audiences and the media. Speakers must, of course, respect basic rights of ingress and egress with respect to contested places. As we shall see, however, additional limitations can extinguish the critical expressive value of contested places.

Chapter 5 examines what are effectively defunct spaces on the expressive topography. First Amendment and other constitutional precedents, suburban and urban planning, and other influences have created a variety of *non-places* on the expressive topography. For example, despite the presence of the general public in places like major transit hubs, these places are deemed "non-public forums." In such places, expression may generally be prohibited. Owing to their recent vintage, a variety of what I shall refer to as public and quasi-public "places of modernity" also fail to qualify as First Amendment "public forums." Other significant places on the expressive topography, such as shopping centers and gated communities, are treated as non-places owing to legal and constitutional principles of privatization. These substantial spatial gaps on the expressive topography have had a profound effect on the exercise of public First Amendment liberties.

Chapter 6 examines places that have traditionally been among the most significant outdoor democratic venues on the expressive topography. *Inscribed* places like public streets, sidewalks, parks, and squares often serve as public repositories of history, symbolism, and emotion. They are quintessential venues of civic and democratic participation. As mentioned earlier, certain inscribed places like the National Mall in Washington, D.C. and Central Park in New York City have become "sacred" by virtue of their relation to public democratic displays. Legal and other formal restrictions on public liberties in such places increased dramatically beginning in the 1970s, with the adoption and implementation of what social scientists refer to as the "public order management system."[49] Increasingly burdensome permit and financing requirements, along with new methods of protest policing, have effectively institutionalized public protests and other displays in inscribed and sacred places. Such places have also been downsized and "demoted" as a result of privatization, development and beautification projects, and the demolition and reconstruction of what once were places open to the public.

Chapter 7 examines the repressive tactics that have been used at democratic events like national campaigns, presidential inaugurals, globalization summits, and national party conventions. At these critical democratic moments, public places have been effectively *militarized*. Through spatial militarization, public protests and displays are channeled, contained, and (as the DZ shows) sometimes suppressed. Spatial militarization involves both overt and covert tactics, such as advance selection of public meeting sites, pre-event and real-time surveillance of protest groups and lawful protest activity, police infiltration of activist groups, physical barriers, aggressive public policing, and mass arrests. Militarization poses substantial obstacles to mounting effective public displays of contention during critical democratic moments.

Chapter 8 examines the state of public expression on the campuses of the nation's public colleges and universities. *Places of higher learning* are critical venues on the expressive topography. This is where young citizens first learn about self-governance and the power of public expression. Despite their importance to public liberties, in terms of First Amendment principles places of higher learning are the least defined and understood of all the places on the expressive topography. Aside from historical interest in the campus unrest of the 1960s, little academic or judicial attention has been paid to the *public* areas of our nation's campuses. Meanwhile, these places – or, perhaps more accurately, these collections of places – have become mirror images of other places on the expressive topography. Many restrictions on public liberties imposed outside the campus gates are now present within. Places of higher learning have traditionally been incubators for social movements. Whether they will continue to serve this and other democratic functions will depend upon a variety of things, not least the spatio-legal regime applied to campus places.

Chapter 9 looks primarily to the future and considers what sort of expressive topography we shall have once vast spaces are transformed

---

[49] *See* Donatella della Porta & Herbert Reiter, eds., *Policing Protest: The Control of Mass Demonstrations in Western Democracies* (1998).

into fully *networked* public places. New technologies have already begun to alter the nature and character of material public places. Cities, regions, and perhaps soon entire states will be covered by wireless clouds that deliver always-available Web access. Closed-circuit television (CCTV) monitors will provide constant surveillance of most public places, including inscribed and sacred places. Public surveillance technologies, which will become ever more advanced, will create a vast storable record of public events and a diminished sense of public privacy and anonymity. This surveillance may have serious chilling effects on public displays and other forms of public expression. Digital environments and pervasive personal computing will also make possible new forms of virtual speech and assembly. How we speak and associate in networked public places will depend primarily on future applications of surveillance and communicative technologies, and the manner in which the people adapt to the newly networked environment.

2 THE EXPRESSIVE TOPOGRAPHY AND PUBLIC LIBERTIES

Today, Americans enjoy greater "parchment" liberties than perhaps at any time in history. As a nation, we espouse and occasionally aspire to "export" a brand of free speech liberalism that is grounded upon the broadest *conceptual* breathing space for expression. *Physical* breathing space for public liberties is another matter. The surface area of our expressive topography – the amount of public space that is available for and actually facilitates the exercise of First Amendment liberties – has been drastically shrinking for many decades.

Americans today are not nearly as prone to public displays of contentious politics as, for example, citizens of some European nations. They are not generally inclined to assemble *en masse* to protest against social and political conditions, demand relief from officials, or present their collective grievances. When they do occur, public demonstrations and protests in this country are generally peaceful and largely *institutionalized* events.[1] The contemporary American style of public democracy might be considered rather tame and anemic in comparison to, say, that of the French.

It has not always been so. Our expressive topography has been forged by a variety of forces and events from the Revolution to the present day. The American people did not simply and suddenly abandon public places, public life, or their public liberties. Public contention was not institutionalized overnight. The transformation of our expressive topography is a fascinating story, one that has not received nearly the attention it deserves. This chapter presents an overview of the primary influences – historical, social, political, architectural, and legal – that have shaped the expressive topography and affected the physical "breathing space" for public expressive liberties in the United States. These signal events and

[1] *See* Sidney Tarrow, *Power in Movement* 9 (2d ed. 1998).

influences will be elaborated upon as we traverse the expressive topography in the chapters that follow.

"TIME OUT OF MIND": EARLY PUBLIC LIFE AND THE NASCENT EXPRESSIVE TOPOGRAPHY

Remarkably, public places did not receive any constitutional recognition or status until 1939, when the Supreme Court first recognized a minimal but fundamental right of access to certain public places.[2] The streets, parks, and public commons, the Court then said, have "immemorially been held in trust for the use of the public and, time out of mind, have been used for purposes of assembly, communicating thoughts between citizens, and discussing public questions."[3] Before turning to more contemporary conditions and events, let us first consider public places and public expressive liberties "time out of mind." What was the early expressive topography actually like? What kind of expressive liberties did it facilitate? What was its relationship to popular democracy?

Mobs, Riots, and Revolutions

Since before the nation's founding, the people have gathered "out of doors" – again, in the dual sense of being physically outside and outside mainstream political channels.[4] In population centers, the early expressive topography hosted a vibrant public expressive culture. People tended to spend substantial portions of their days in public places. The architectures of the era were critical in shaping this culture. Colonial-era homes were not built to accommodate extended periods of lounging and recreation. There were no "gated" communities, and few if any "private" enclaves.

The people appeared in early public streets and squares as assemblies and "mobs," rioters, soapbox orators, pamphleteers, proselytizers, provocateurs, and press agents. As the Court indicated, they used public places to "communicate thoughts" and "discuss public questions." Public pamphleteering was a common form of political activity. Indeed, many

---

[2] Hague v. Comm. for Indus. Org., 307 U.S. 496 (1939).
[3] Id. at 515.
[4] Gordon S. Wood, *The Radicalism of the American Revolution* 231 (1991). *See also* Thomas I. Emerson, *The System of Freedom of Expression* 287–88 (1970) (noting importance of public assembly to political life in the United States).

citizens received news of the day from this early public "press" activity. Following the example of their radical English forebears, the people also regularly met in public places like taverns. In these public halls one could discuss the issues of the day. There one could also regularly find – and informally "petition" – local public officials. These and other forms of traditional public speech were matters of necessity; if one wished to communicate with those in the community, public places were the only forums in which this could regularly and effectively be accomplished.

Eighteenth-century Americans also regularly assembled and engaged in public "riots" – predecessors of what today we would call protests or demonstrations.[5] Many believed it was not just their right but their *duty* to assemble in the streets and demonstrate, particularly when other political recourse was unavailable. As one writer has observed, "politics indoors, the normal channel of government, was to be checked by politics out-of-doors, the people in the mob."[6] In her study of pre-Revolutionary radicals, Pauline Maier noted that "in certain circumstances, it was understood, the people would rise up almost as a natural force, much as night follows day, and this phenomenon often contributed to the public welfare."[7]

Public displays and outbursts, in cities and countryside alike, were thus "a common form of political protest and political action" in colonial America.[8] Early public demonstrations in response to the Stamp Act of 1765 and other Crown directives were an "acting out" by the people and an early form of political theatre.[9] In terms of what political sociologists would much later refer to as "repertoires of contention," the people in these early public uprisings marched, chanted, sang, and burned objects in effigy.[10] So long as they did not seriously threaten public order, these riots or mobs were not only tolerated but generally supported. This sentiment was nicely summarized by Thomas Jefferson, who in 1787 wrote to James Madison that "a little rebellion now and then is a good thing, and as necessary in the political world as storms in the physical."[11] Public places

---

[5] Paul A. Gilje, *The Road to Mobocracy: Popular Disorder in New York City, 1763–1834*, 5 (1987); *See also* George F. Rude, *The Crowd in History* (1964).
[6] Gilje, *supra* note 5 at 8.
[7] Pauline Maier, *From Resistance to Revolution: Colonial Radicals and the Development of American Opposition to Britain, 1765–1776*, 3 (1972).
[8] Gordon S. Wood, *The Creation of the American Public, 1776–1787*, 320 (1969).
[9] Gilje, *supra* note 5 at 44.
[10] Tarrow, *supra* note 1 at 20.
[11] Letter from Thomas Jefferson to James Madison, January 30, 1787, in Merrill D. Peterson, (ed.), *The Portable Thomas Jefferson* 414 (1975).

thus served critical political functions during the period leading up to the Revolution. By facilitating the making of identity or representational claims and the participation of the common man in politics and self-governance, these common spaces helped propel Americans into the Revolution.[12]

Although there were occasional exceptions, participants in the Stamp Act "riots" and other public contentious displays generally sought to preserve public order. Aware that indiscriminate mob violence invited public disapproval, assembly participants designated one or more of their own to maintain discipline and prevent violence. Pauline Maier described the typical Boston Stamp Act display:

> Each day began with the parading of effigies, which were destroyed early in the afternoon so that "the Town might be perfectly quiet before Night." "General" Mackintosh presided in a blue and gold uniform, wearing a gold-laced hat and carrying a rattan cane and a speaking trumpet to proclaim his orders. His officers, marked by their lace hats and "wands," allowed no allegedly disorder-prone Negroes to join the 2000 paraders, and none but the officers were allowed to carry any stick or offensive weapon. Mackintosh walked arm-in-arm with Colonel William Brattle, a councilor and leading merchant, who "complimented him on the order he kept, and told him his Post was one of the highest in the Government." Business was conducted, the *Boston Gazette* commented, in the "most regular Manner," and dis-order prevented "as could hardly be expected among a Concourse of several Thousand People."[13]

Early public displays of contention were thus both well-organized and well-disciplined, if not egalitarian, affairs. The historian Gordon Wood has noted the temperateness of many such early public displays: "The severely ritualized nature of much of the crowds' behavior often kept the mobs from running amok."[14] It is important to note that protesters often had the support of a substantial number of community citizens and, in many cases, local governmental bodies. These, then, were not "mobs" in the pejorative sense; the state generally felt no need to put them down. Far from being radical displays, many early public protests and riots generally reinforced social norms and the premodern authority structure.

---

[12] Gilje, *supra* note 5 at 68.
[13] *Id.* at 69–70 (citation omitted).
[14] Wood, *supra* note 4 at 91.

Figure 2.1. A British Customs Official Is Tarred and Feathered.

Although order generally prevailed during public demonstrations, mobs were sometimes less kind to individual officials and their personal properties. The people would sometimes single out individuals such as tax collectors or agents of impressment for public admonishment and disapproval. Mobs regularly engaged in acts of violence against officials doing the King's bidding. Assault, tarring and feathering, and binding were common forms of mob violence (Figure 2.1).[15] Property damage was mostly limited to private places, such as homes, closely associated with the object of protest.[16] These early riots were typically acts of last resort, undertaken when all legal recourse had failed. Despite the passion they generated, such popular uprisings produced relatively little bloodshed and few fatalities.

As the radicals' faith in Britain and in law itself faded, officials feared that they would be unable to impose order on the publicly assembled

---

[15] Maier, *supra* note 7 at 4–11.
[16] *Id.* at 13.

masses.[17] Still, although there were some incidents of violence, public protests leading up to the Revolution remained generally civil and orderly. The unity of the revolutionaries' cause, the reluctance toward violence, the influence of elites, and the need for political solidarity all ensured that revolution did not generally lead to public anarchy.[18]

It is worth noting that had there been widespread disorder in the streets, officials would have been mostly powerless to stop it. At the time there was no extensive bureaucratic apparatus – municipal ordinances, permit schemes, large police forces, and so forth – to regulate or suppress public contention.[19] Prior to the transformation of cities into organized grids, the enactment of zoning laws, and the assembly of large police forces, the people were indeed far more difficult to control in public places. Magistrates were generally powerless to control public assemblies and other forms of contention. Even the militia could not necessarily be depended upon to act against mobs, which they both feared and in some cases sympathized with; indeed, in one instance when New York City ordered the militia to suppress a mob, most refused to report for duty.[20] Maintenance of order typically depended on the participation of members of the community. Antiriot acts, modeled on those enacted in Great Britain, were enacted subsequent to some popular uprisings. By their terms, these laws purported to severely limit public assemblies. Unlike their British counterparts, however, the antiriot acts in colonial America were temporary in duration and not typically enforced to suppress public assemblies.

In sum, the early expressive topography, which consisted primarily of rudimentary streets and town squares, was critical to the revolutionary spirit and cause. Public participation and contention were also critical to the early causes of "little people." As Gordon Wood has noted, public mobbing "was a means by which ordinary people, usually those most dependent – women, servants, free blacks, sailors, and young men – made their power felt temporarily in a political system that was otherwise largely immune to their influence."[21] Aside from the early antiriot acts and the occasional use of the militia to put down the rare violent assembly, governments did not act as agents of control or repression. Early demonstrations were often spontaneous and quite creative in terms of repertoires of contention; but they were rarely disorderly. The early streets and squares were communal places, held in trust by society's elites rather than the state. Indeed,

---

[17] *Id.* at 272–73.
[18] *Id.* at 280–87.
[19] *Id.* at 16.
[20] Gilje, *supra* note 5 at 81.
[21] Wood, *supra* note 4 at 90.

eighteenth–century elites would regularly invite the lower classes into the streets, for public theatre and community events.[22] In this sense, early public places served as critical safety valves for defusing class tensions.

The Rise of the State and "Indoor" Politics

As state governments began to form in the period following the Revolutionary War, reliance on public displays, mobs, and riots decreased. As local election and political party machinery took shape, public contention and "mobbing" became somewhat less important to democratic politics. Regularized and institutionalized "indoor" politics began to displace politics out of doors and in the streets.[23]

This is not to suggest that public politics and contention ceased to exist. As one student of the period notes, "many remained convinced that an occasional mob was one of the best ways to maintain a free government."[24] But protesters' repertoires of contention were also changing. With the rise of the state, the targets of public demonstrations were no longer individuals but governments themselves.[25] Public contention increasingly took the form of organized street demonstrations rather than targeted events focused on public officials.

By the 1780s and 1790s, governments, replacing the old societal elites, began to assert greater control over public places and public contention. The methods of control were informal at first; efforts to suppress public assemblies and other expressive activity were relatively rare. Urban officials would often attempt *negotiating* with the assembly or mob rather than (or at least prior to) suppressing it. This generally served to maintain the peace. Armed conflict, at least, was rare. When substantial disorder did occur, the militia, now more likely to comply, was called out to quell any disturbance. Disorderly mobbing and rioting were tolerated less and less by public officials charged with maintaining public order.

Even with these changes, however, the expressive topography remained quite vibrant. Political parties and elites now began to mobilize public contention for express *political* gain. During the framing period, for example, Republicans turned out mass assemblies to support Alexander Hamilton's fiscal plan for the new nation and to protest the Jay Treaty.[26]

---

[22] Gilje, *supra* note 5 at 17–18.
[23] *Id.* at 100.
[24] *Id.* at 78.
[25] *See* Tarrow, *supra* note 1 at 63–64.
[26] Gilje, *supra* note 5 at 100–03.

Federalists similarly used public assemblies to serve their political ends. Public participation became more egalitarian. A diverse group of participants joined in these early public political displays; assemblies were often led by elite members of the community, who joined the lower classes in marches and rallies. Like their revolutionary forebears, these events were generally orderly, minimally disruptive of public life, and nonviolent.

Certain early-nineteenth-century events led urban officials to take further steps to contain and at times even suppress public displays of contention. Ethnic and race riots in urban areas like New York City produced public and official backlashes against all forms of public disorder.[27] Labor and religious riots during this same period also reinforced the need for public order. Elites had begun to abandon public assemblies. Without elite supervision, the "bottom" or lower elements of society appeared prone to more indiscriminate public violence. The militia had to be called out to quell many public riots and disturbances.

In time, political parties began to use antimob rhetoric. Those in power, in particular, emphasized the dangers of public "mobs" and protests. The earliest "public order" laws were enacted in response to nineteenth-century urban disruption and disorder. Under these laws, certain "unlawful" assemblies were banned.[28] For the first time, public permit schemes were enacted to control access to streets and other common public areas. These early permit laws were often enforced to prevent certain speakers from appearing, or certain groups from assembling, in public places. Grants, denials, and revocations of permits typically occurred at the sole discretion of municipal officials. Public vagrancy and loitering statutes were also enforced, often arbitrarily, to clear public areas of disorderly persons and behaviors. By the close of the nineteenth century, a new regime of laws governing public behavior banned or severely limited assembly, expression, press, and petition activities.[29]

The manner in which public places were policed also changed dramatically during the nineteenth century. As urban areas and populations expanded, so did municipal police forces. By 1845, New York City had a full-fledged police force whose primary mission was to defuse racial and class tensions in poor immigrant neighborhoods such as the Irish Five Points. Calls for "law and order" led to increasing numbers of arrests by police and militia, as well as official violence directed toward public speakers. Officials no longer negotiated with mobs; they brutally

---

[27] *See id.,* Chapters 5 & 6.
[28] Glenn Abernathy, *The Right of Assembly and Association* 27–35 (1961).
[29] *See id.* at 27–35 (discussing limits on public assembly).

Figure 2.2. Rendition of The Haymarket Riot (1886).

suppressed them.[30] Police officers relied on the threat of force and, more commonly, its application to control the masses and enforce public order. The fact that police officers were themselves often the targets of mob violence only served to increase tensions and escalate the use of force.

In the years leading up to and during the Civil War, public rioting was commonplace, particularly in large cities. During the Draft Riots of 1863, New York City experienced four full days of rioting. Later, scores were killed or injured in the Orange Riots of 1870–71. Police efforts to disperse labor strikers and other public assemblies were also often violent affairs. For example, the 1886 Haymarket Riot in Chicago resulted in the deaths of seven police officers (four anarchists were also put to death) (Figure 2.2). The riot was precipitated by an unknown person lobbing a bomb into the crowd of officers and labor activists. The image of the "bomb-throwing anarchist" was thus born. Violent interactions between police and other demonstrators were relatively common throughout the nineteenth and into the twentieth century.[31]

---

[30] Marilyn Johnson, *Street Justice: A History of Police Violence in New York City* (2003), Chapter 1.
[31] *See id.*, Chapters 3 (Progressive era) and 4 (prohibition). *See also* Henry David, *The History of the Haymarket Affair* (1936).

Figure 2.3. Water Celebration on Boston Common, Lithograph by P. Hyman and
David Bigelow (1848).
Source: National Archives and Records Administration.

By the dawn of the twentieth century, the principle of governmental
ownership of public places had begun to gain acceptance and support
among officials and courts. This principle of ownership was demonstrated most poignantly by the opinion of then–Massachusetts Supreme
Judicial Court judge Oliver Wendell Holmes in *Davis v. Commonwealth*
(1895).[32] In *Davis*, the Massachusetts court upheld the conviction of a
preacher for making a public address on Boston Common (Figure 2.3)
without first receiving the permission of the mayor. Holmes wrote: "For
the Legislature absolutely or conditionally to forbid public speaking in a
highway or public park is no more an infringement of the rights of a
member of the public than for the owner of a private house to forbid it in
his house."[33] Using similar reasoning, the Supreme Court affirmed: "The
right to absolutely exclude all right to use necessarily includes the
authority to determine under what circumstances such use may be availed
of, as the greater power contains the lesser."[34]

The people continued, as they always had, to gather out of doors to
assemble, speak, and demonstrate. By this time, however, the institutionalization of public contention had begun. Authorities permitted
groups, such as those advocating women's suffrage, to use public streets
and other places. But such access was no longer, as it had been in pre-
Revolutionary times, a matter of social or community custom; it had in

---

[32] Commonwealth v. Davis, 4 N.E. 577 (Mass. 1886) and 39 N.E. 113 (Mass. 1895), *aff'd sub
nom.* Davis v. Massachusetts, 167 U.S. 43 (1897).
[33] *Davis*, 39 N.E. at 113.
[34] *Davis*, 167 U.S. at 47.

Figure 2.4. Suffrage Parade, Washington, D.C. (1913).
Source: Library of Congress.

many respects become a matter of official discretion. The state, not the community, now decided what was appropriate in terms of public contests and demonstrations. Orderly parades and processions were welcome; disruption and "rioting" were not (Figure 2.4).

This very brief overview shows that the people have indeed "time out of mind" used public places to assemble, address matters of public concern, and petition government officials. Early Americans claimed a public space for activities like mobbing and rioting that politicized citizens and spurred the Revolution. As the First Amendment scholar Thomas Emerson noted, this history demonstrates that the First Amendment "was meant to protect a broad right of assembly and petition as a vital part of a system of freedom of expression."[35] Nevertheless, as this history also shows, the tension between public order and public expression had led governments to legalize and regulate access to public places. While at times such regulation was conciliatory and cooperative, it could on occasion be violent and extraordinarily repressive. However it was enforced, Holmes's decision in *Davis* is evidence that by the early twentieth century, official "ownership" of public places was an unmistakable fact of law and public life.

[35] Emerson, *supra* note 4 at 290.

THE CONTEMPORARY EXPRESSIVE TOPOGRAPHY

Although there are important lessons in this early history, my primary goal in this chapter and the remainder of this book is to examine the *contemporary* expressive topography. In particular, this book examines the manner in which the topography's present-day contours and conditions affect the public exercise of First Amendment liberties. By the beginning of the twentieth century, the nation had substantial experience (both positive and negative) with speech out of doors. There was a very rudimentary and still-developing legal framework for the expressive topography. In general, however, the die was not yet cast insofar as public places and public expression were concerned.

Several critical events and circumstances in the twentieth century combined to shape the contours of the contemporary expressive topography. As the discussion that follows emphasizes, some of the most important events relating to the development of the expressive topography were not legal or constitutional in nature. Extraordinary transformations in the nation's social and political cultures were as or even more important than official acts and judicial decisions. The discussion that follows provides an overview of the events and forces most responsible for the contours of the contemporary expressive topography. These causes are varied and complex. They include, among other things, demographic and social trends, urban and suburban planning policies, architectural choices, judicially crafted doctrines of place, changes in public policing methods, speakers' own tactics and behaviors, and public attitudes regarding the public exercise of expressive liberties. These influences and others are identified and briefly discussed here, with elaboration occurring in the chapters that follow.

Socio-Demographic-Architectural Forces

Places, including those that together comprise the expressive topography, are constructed in response to social patterns and activities. The early expressive topography took shape in response to a largely urban and sedentary people, many of whom were actively engaged in some form of public life. As the twentieth century progressed, people started to migrate away from urban areas. The physical landscape and the infrastructure of the expressive topography underwent monumental changes. Homes became personal sanctuaries. Technologies – radio, television, and eventually the Internet – would bring entertainment (and work) home, facilitating prolonged periods of indoor presence. Public squares and parks were in many cases abandoned or severely underutilized. These and other fundamental changes profoundly reshaped the basic contours of what would become our contemporary expressive topography.

Although the connection might not be immediately apparent, the invention and mass production of the automobile was one of the most important twentieth-century events in terms of shaping the contemporary expressive topography. For one thing, the automobile occupied a substantial amount of public space. Entire cities and suburban communities would eventually be constructed or reconstructed to accommodate its use. The automobile's introduction into everyday life displaced people from the public streets, led to new (and newly necessary) limits on events like assemblies, demonstrations, and parades, and required a new level of public control over public spaces and public activities. As importantly, the automobile also allowed people to bypass many communal public spaces.

The automobile also facilitated a mass population migration – from the cities to the suburbs and, ultimately, to distant "exurbs." A host of social critics, geographers, demographers, political sociologists, and urbanists have catalogued the various social and political costs associated with this substantial population shift, which began in the 1950s.[36] Commentators and scholars have lamented what they view as substantial losses in terms of culture, community, aesthetics, and social capital.

Far less noted have been the substantial *expressive* costs associated with these demographic and landscape changes. Changing patterns of migration and new architectures built to suit migrants affected not only culture and community, broadly speaking, but also the physical "breathing space" required for expressive liberties. Suburban places were planned, architecturally and as a matter of public policy, as enclaves of tranquility, repose, and comfort – things that are generally anathema to public expression and contention. New suburbanites wanted to retreat into their castles, at a safe distance from the dangers and dysfunctions of urbanity. Many urban perils were explicitly associated in the public mind with public places, which were considered to be sites of crime, poverty, drug use, and other social ills. Suburbanites wanted separation – from both those evils and, to some extent, their fellow citizens. They craved

---

[36] Gerald E. Frug, *City Making: Building Communities Without Building Walls* (1999); William Severini Kowinski, *The Malling of America: An Inside Look at The Great Consumer Paradise* (1985); Jane Jacobs, *The Death and Life of Great American Cities* (1961).

private, not public, space. They demanded – and were willing to pay for – strong protections for private property and privacy.

Architects, planners, and public officials obliged. Suburban communities were designed with a minimal "street presence" or public life in mind. Plans typically featured narrow sidewalks, minimal common spaces, and sprawling private residential enclaves far removed from any public places (Figure 2.5). People drove past one another on their way to other places. They strolled down sidewalks that led them around the block, rather than toward common gathering places. In suburbia, there were substantially fewer public squares or other places suitable for the exercise of expressive liberties than there were in most cities. As noted, parking lots and parking facilities, built to accommodate the insatiable appetite for automobiles, commanded substantial public spaces. In short, the topography of suburban America did not (and generally still does not) facilitate spontaneous exchange or interaction. Indeed, the basic design of such places has actively discouraged such things. This topography has only become more exclusionary, isolating, and private. Particularly since the 1980s, for example, exclusive "gated communities" and exclusionary community associations have proliferated in suburban and exurban areas.[37]

Some of the places erected in response to the suburban migration seemed to offer at least a shred of hope that a semblance of traditional public life might survive. The "inverted" space of the shopping center, which featured faux *indoor* "public" streets and squares, looked at first glance like an antidote to the otherwise placeless suburban topography. Shopping malls and centers, mainstays of the suburban landscape, have steadily increased in both number and size since the 1960s. As discussed further in Chapter 5, however, the Supreme Court officially excised these places from the expressive topography in the early 1970s. As James Kuntsler presciently observed in his provocative and entertaining book, *The Geography to Nowhere*:

In a nation as politically complacent as the United States in the 1970s and 1980s, this might seem trivial. But imagine if America got involved in another war as unpopular as Vietnam, and the political temperature rose. Or if our dependence on cheap oil started to cause

[37] *See* Setha Low, "How Private Interests Take Over Public Space: Zoning, Taxes, and Incorporation of Gated Communities," in Setha Low & Neil Smith, eds., *The Politics of Public Space* (2006); *see also* Margaret Kohn, *Brave New Neighborhoods: The Privatization of Public Space* (2004).

Figure 2.5. Aerial View of Levittown, PA (ca 1959).
Source: National Archives and Records Administration.

political problems. Acme Development might not be so tolerant about political rallies held around their philodendron beds, or protest marchers interfering with sales at the Pet-O-Rama shop. Where, then, are you going to have your public assembly? On the median strip of Interstate 87?[38]

As suburbanites rushed to escape cities in the 1960s, many of those cities ironically became increasingly *suburban* in terms of their own planning, architecture, and culture.[39] Here law and social conditions plainly intersected. Insofar as contemporary urban landscapes are concerned, the legitimization and proliferation of public zoning laws was surely one of the transformative events of the twentieth century. In 1926, the Supreme Court for the first time upheld detailed public zoning laws.[40] Urban officials gradually realized that they had wide discretion under such laws to shape and plan urban communities – and they used it.

---

[38] James Howard Kuntsler, *The Geography of Nowhere: The Rise and Decline of America's Man-Made Landscape* 120 (1993).
[39] *See* Kowinski, *supra* note 36 at Chapter 28.
[40] Village of Euclid v. Amber Realty Corp., 272 U.S. 365 (1926).

In *The Death and Life of Great American Cities*, the late urban critic and activist Jane Jacobs famously lambasted the results of urban planning in New York City.[41] Jacobs focused in particular on the manner in which single-use zoning and other regulations physically segregated both spatial uses and populations. She criticized city planners, most notably New York City Parks Commissioner Robert Moses, for constructing a modernist "Radiant City" that all but eliminated (in her view) public identity and community.[42] Jacobs argued in favor of such things as mixed-use developments, shorter city blocks, and dense concentrations of people. She extolled the virtues of local communities in urban settings and emphasized the special importance of public streets, sidewalks, parks, and other public places to community.

Jacobs' was, however, a distinctly minority voice. Most city planners did not share her view that city spaces should be organic, spontaneous, and somewhat untidy. In the 1960s, planners began to commercialize vast public areas in cities across the United States. They planned and constructed "super blocks" of high-rise towers, structures critics claimed destroyed the "diverse, pedestrian-centered feel of city streets."[43] Urban areas, most of which have been heavily developed in the past three to four decades, now feature the very sorts of architectures Jacobs so ardently criticized – high-rise business districts and large-scale shopping malls built into mega-structures and surrounded by parking lots. Thus began the transformation often referred to by critics as the "malling" or "Disneyification" of public space.[44]

In part to stem the tide of suburban migration, the so-called "post-1965 city" was sanitized in other respects as well.[45] Many urban areas were cleansed of unwanted *people* and behaviors. Some of the targeted behaviors involved the exercise of expressive liberties. For example, to deter begging and sometimes to prevent the physical presence of the homeless, the destitute were placed in skid rows, harassed, and routinely arrested for vagrancy and other "public order" crimes. In places they otherwise had a right to be, picketers and protesters were told by police to "move along." Private property rights were more vigorously enforced, often to purify quasi-public areas of any sign of disorder. This purification

---

[41] Jane Jacobs, *The Death and Life of Great American Cities* (1961).
[42] For a critique of urban architecture, *see* Vincent Scully, *American Architecture and Urbanism* (1988).
[43] Frug, *supra* note 43 at 150.
[44] *See* Kowinski, supra note 36 at 64–68.
[45] Daniel Solomon, *ReBuilding* 6 (1992).

was sometimes brutally accomplished, by police forces prone to view the slightest public disturbance as a threat to public order and security.

In one seemingly positive development insofar as the expressive topography is concerned, large parks projects preserved vast areas of common space. As Jacobs and others noted, however, many of these parks were not designed in a manner that integrated park spaces with the surrounding communities. Others were not properly maintained, leading to their decay and that of their surrounding communities. Thus, even the designation of large public parks often failed to resuscitate a public life that was being choked off by poor planning and the surrounding built environment. This, unfortunately, continues to be the case today in many urban areas.[46]

By the 1970s, something of an urban malaise had set in. Like their new suburban counterparts, urban places generally failed to facilitate chance encounters between diverse citizens. Architects like Peter Calthorpe blamed city and suburban planning and architecture for a host of social ills, including "serious environmental stress caused by intractable traffic congestion, a dearth of affordable housing, *loss of irreplaceable open spaces*, and lifestyles which burden working families and isolate the elderly."[47] In these communities, the people largely remained isolated strangers.[48] James Kuntsler poignantly summarized many of the criticisms concerning contemporary urban and suburban spatial conditions in *The Geography to Nowhere*:

Eighty percent of everything ever built in America has been built in the last fifty years, and most of it is depressing, brutal, ugly, unhealthy, and spiritually degrading – the jive-plastic commuter tract home wastelands, the Potemkin village shopping plazas with their vast parking lagoons, the Lego-block hotel complexes, the "gourmet mansardic" junk-food joints, the Orwellian office "parks" featuring buildings sheathed in the same reflective glass as the sunglasses worn by chain-gang guards, the particle-board garden apartments rising up in every meadow and cornfield, the freeway loops around every big and little city with their clusters of discount merchandise marts, the

---

[46] *See* Setha Low, Dana Taplin, & Suzanne Scheld, eds., *Rethinking Urban Parks: Public Space and Cultural Diversity* (2005).
[47] Peter Calthorpe, *The Next American Metropolis: Ecology, Community, and the American Dream* 18 (1993) (emphasis added).
[48] *See* Lyn Lofland, *A World of Strangers* (1973); Richard Sennett, *The Uses of Disorder: Personal Identity and City Life* (1970).

whole destructive, wasteful, toxic, agoraphobia-inducing spectacle that politicians proudly call "growth." . . .

The newspaper headlines may shout about global warming, extinctions of living species, the devastation of rain forests, and other world-wide catastrophes, but Americans evince a striking complacency when it comes to their everyday environment and the growing calamity that it represents.[49]

In the past few decades, a group of architects and urban planners known as "new urbanists" have made a variety of proposals for improving suburban and urban spaces. As summarized by the legal scholar Gerald Frug, the principal elements of new urbanism involve "creating multiuse environments, constructing grid systems for public streets, giving priority to the needs of pedestrians, facilitating reliance on public transportation, highlighting the importance of centrally located public space, and establishing focal points and boundaries for urban space."[50] To be sure, new urbanism has its committed critics.[51] Nevertheless, its proposals and philosophy – if not all of its applications – are worth considering and will be referred to in several contexts in this book. Some new urbanist proposals, in particular those intended to preserve open spaces and to bring people into more regular contact with one another, may facilitate the exercise of expressive liberties in public places. Thus far, however, new urbanism seems to have had little effect on the man-made landscape or, as we shall see, the expressive topography.

With the exception of zoning laws, note that no reference has yet been made to any legal doctrines or principles. The contemporary expressive topography is a dynamic system of places, one that has been constructed in response to major social and demographic circumstances like those discussed above. Fundamental social choices regarding location and architecture have substantially affected the contours and dimensions of the contemporary expressive topography.

Early Public Contention and Expressive Breathing Space

The built environment represents merely the skeleton or foundation of the contemporary expressive topography. Like any dynamic organism, the

---

[49] Kuntsler, *supra* note 38 at 10.
[50] Frug, *supra* note 43 at 150–51.
[51] *See, e.g.*, Kohn, *supra* note 37 at 126–33.

topography is influenced and shaped by a variety of internal and external forces and events. The scope of public expressive liberties depends not only on having access to places but, as importantly, on what the people can actually *do or say* in such places. As noted earlier, this is a function of both physical and conceptual "breathing space." This section examines several important twentieth-century political and legal events that substantially influenced the overall breathing space afforded to contemporary public speakers.

Agitators, Wars, and Witnesses

The original expressive topography was shaped without any discussion of freedom of expression or consideration of whether First Amendment liberties existed there. The reason is simple; at the time, it was not clear that the First Amendment – which expressly prohibited "Congress" from abridging freedom of speech and other liberties – applied to states and local governments. As noted, from the Revolutionary period to the early twentieth century, regulation and control of the nascent expressive topography was entrusted first to societal elites and, later, to the state as "owner" of public places or properties. The courts generally remained on the sidelines.

It is often assumed that courts, legal scholars, and speakers paid little or no attention to the First Amendment aspects of public expression prior to World War I. As David Rabban has observed, however, First Amendment contests regarding access to the expressive topography substantially predate this period. In his important work, *Free Speech in Its Forgotten Years*, Rabban demonstrated that labor agitators took to the public streets and sidewalks in cities across the United States in the period between 1906 and 1913.[52] Members of the Industrial Workers of the World (IWW), or "Wobblies," set up soap boxes on busy street corners and provoked what were referred to as "free speech fights" with municipal authorities (Figure 2.6). These speakers were the first to expressly claim a *First Amendment* right to assemble and speak in public places. Their claims preceded – by nearly four decades – the Supreme Court's initial recognition of any such right.

Coming as it did on the heels of the nation's experience with mobbing and rioting, the Wobblies' civil disobedience produced a mixed reaction from the public and from public officials. Although they gained some support from civil libertarians and labor groups, some groups were

---

[52] David M. Rabban, *Free Speech in Its Forgotten Years* (1997), Chapter 2.

Figure 2.6. Wobblies Arrested During a "Free Speech Fight" (1912).

harshly critical of the Wobblies' actions. Many cities responded by enacting restrictive public ordinances. These municipal laws expressly limited the places in which Wobblies could assemble and speak to certain designated "free speech zones." One such ordinance barred labor activists from speaking within a *49-block* zone in the heart of the city. A few courts upheld this early form of "expressive zoning," although they did so without addressing the substantive First Amendment issues involved. Municipal officials were not the only threat to the Wobblies' public liberties. They also faced serious threats from vigilantes and others offended by their message and their use of public places to convey it. Some Wobblies were beaten and seriously injured.

Although they did not result in explicit recognition of any First Amendment right to access the streets, the Wobbly "free speech fights" of the early twentieth century demonstrated the continued importance of public places to public liberties. Wobblies were some of the earliest speakers to use public places strategically – to garner attention and support for their labor causes and to challenge authorities. As Rabban has shown, the Wobblies were at least partly successful in achieving their goals. Perhaps most importantly, the Wobblies were the first to claim specific *First Amendment* rights to use public places.

Not until World War I, however, did courts expressly address First Amendment rights to public assembly and expression. There was little support for such rights at the time. During both world wars (and, later, the Communist "Red Scare" of the 1950s) socialists, communists, and other dissidents assembled and spoke before public audiences. They appeared in the public streets, squares, ports, and other places where large audiences could be found. Dissidents and protesters were jailed for engaging in acts we now consider quintessentially protected public liberties – distributing pamphlets and making political speeches on the public streets. They were prosecuted and punished under sedition and syndicalism laws for little more than engaging public audiences on matters of what were then pressing national concern – war, ideology, and government foreign policy.[53]

Place or location had no effect whatever on judicial review of these convictions. In none of the sedition cases did the fact that the speaker occupied a public place even weigh in the constitutional balance. The place of expression seemed to matter only insofar as the physical proximity of the speaker and the "incited" audience would present, it was then argued, a "clear and present danger" of illegal activity. As Geoffrey Stone and other legal scholars have demonstrated, expressive and other constitutional liberties that seem to threaten national security are subject to a greater degree of suppression during times of war or conflict.[54] As we shall see, this remains true today, although methods of suppression have changed. In any event, during the world wars and subsequent national scares regarding Communism and sedition, public expressive liberties were generally sacrificed in the name of national security and public order. Agitation and seditious ideology were not to be granted any First Amendment breathing space.

Meanwhile, in contexts far removed from wartime strife or claims of sedition, some public speakers began to secure critical breathing space for public speech and contention. During the 1930s and 1940s, for example, the Jehovah's Witnesses carved out critical conceptual and physical breathing space on the streets and in other public places for making what were in the eyes of many people disruptive and offensive identity claims. As a matter of faith, the Witnesses rely on personal interaction with the public to convey their message.[55] In *Cantwell v. Connecticut* (1940), Jesse Cantwell, a Jehovah's Witness, was convicted of breaching the peace for playing a record deemed offensive to many on the public streets and sidewalks. One year earlier, the Supreme Court had issued its decision in

---

[53] *See* Schenck v. United States, 249 U.S. 47 (1919); Abrams v. United States, 250 U.S. 616 (1919); Gitlow v. New York, 268 U.S. 652 (1925); Whitney v. California, 274 U.S. 357 (1927); Dennis v. United States, 341 U.S. 494 (1951).

[54] Geoffrey R. Stone, *Perilous Times: Free Speech in Wartime from the Sedition Act of 1798 to the War on Terrorism* (2004).

[55] Merlin Owen Newton, *Armed With the Constitution: Jehovah's Witnesses in Alabama and the U.S. Supreme Court, 1939–1946* (1995). The Witnesses follow the example of Paul, teaching "publicly, and from house to house." Acts 20:20. They take literally the mandate of the Scriptures, "Go ye into all the world, and preach the gospel to every creature." Mark 16:15. *See* Murdock v. Pennsylvania, 319 U.S. 105, 108 (1943).

Hague, which finally confirmed that public streets were held "in trust" for the people, for the purpose of ensuring rights of assembly and speech. Invalidating the conviction, the Court noted that Cantwell had spoken "upon a public street, *where he had a right to be*, and where he had a right peacefully to impart his views to others."[56] *Cantwell* and other First Amendment victories by Witnesses established the right to peacefully approach public citizens and deliver, face to face and even in more private spaces like front porches and lawns, controversial and offensive messages.

By insisting on and obtaining access to public places and even the personal spaces of public audiences, Jehovah's Witnesses opened the public streets, sidewalks, and parks to public expression as a matter of constitutional right. Like the Wobblies before them, the Witnesses often paid a substantial price; public beatings were a common reaction to their public expression. But they ultimately achieved what the Wobblies had sought decades earlier – legal recognition of a right to use public places as channels of communication.

During the 1930s and 1940s, the Jehovah's Witnesses and other public speakers secured still more critical space for the exercise of public liberties. In addition to guaranteeing an expressive easement to the public commons in *Hague* and rights to public discourse and interaction in *Cantwell*, the Supreme Court also held that public pamphleteering and leafleting could not be banned solely on the ground that these activities caused litter or tended to annoy the public. These traditional activities have been granted special First Amendment consideration ever since.[57]

Finally, although it upheld the authority of officials to require permits for public expression and to regulate the "time, place, and manner" of public displays, in the 1930s and 1940s the Court invalidated several local schemes that vested unbridled discretion in officials to control speakers' access to public places. As noted earlier, such discretion had been lodged in public officials at least since the enactment of early-nineteenth-century public order laws. In these and other decisions, the Supreme Court officially acknowledged the importance of public places to First Amendment liberties. As the Court declared in *Schneider v. State* (1939): "[One] is not

---

[56] Cantwell v. Connecticut, 310 U.S. 296 (1940) (emphasis added).
[57] *See* Lovell v. Griffin, 303 U.S. 444 (1938) (invalidating conviction of Witness under city ordinance prohibiting distribution of circulars, handbooks and other literature without first obtaining permission from City Manager); Schneider v. State, 308 U.S. 147 (1939) (invalidating ban on distribution of leaflets); Martin v. Struthers, 319 U.S. 141 (1943) (invalidating ordinance prohibiting distribution of handbills to residences).

to have the exercise of his liberty of expression in *appropriate* places abridged on the plea that it may be exercised in some other place."[58]

The Civil Rights Era and Its Aftermath

Which places are in fact "appropriate" venues or forums for public expression is of course a central question for public speakers. That question lay at the center of the struggle for civil rights in the 1960s. Building on the victories of the Witnesses and other early public speakers, civil right activists sought to extend the contours of the expressive topography. Frequent activity by the people out of doors was critical to the advancement of civil rights in America. The expressive contests of this era created invaluable "breathing space" for expressive liberties on the expressive topography. Indeed, the expressive topography was indelibly altered – in both positive and negative ways, as we shall see – during the monumental struggle for civil rights.

As noted, more than two decades before the civil rights struggle began in earnest the Supreme Court had rejected the idea that the government wielded power to exclude the public from all public property solely on the basis of its legal title. In *Hague v. CIO* (1939), the Court stated that "[w] herever the title of streets and parks may rest, they have immemorially been held in trust for the use of the public and, time out of mind, have been used for purposes of assembly, communicating thoughts between citizens, and discussing public questions."[59]

Civil rights activists would test the outer boundaries of the commitment of public space to civil discourse. The civil rights movement relied heavily upon public contention and displays in a variety of public places (Figures 2.7 and 2.8). It used new repertories of public contention, including "sit-ins at drug stores, restaurants, draft boards, offices of public officials, and many other places; pray-ins at churches; lie-ins in front of trucks, bulldozers, and troop trains; vigils of varying duration; blockages of traffic at various points; shop-ins, love-ins and be-ins."[60] These repertoires placed additional stress on the expressive topography. They required greater physical and conceptual First Amendment breathing space than even the Jehovah's Witnesses had been allowed.

During the 1960s, the Supreme Court upheld speakers' rights to access a variety of public places. These places served as invaluable public

---

[58] Schneider v. State, 308 U.S. 147, 163 (1939) (emphasis added).
[59] 307 U.S. 496 (1939).
[60] Emerson, *supra* note 4 at 287–88.

Figure 2.7. School Segregation Protest.
Source: National Archives and Records Administration.

platforms from which activists could press identity claims and agendas.
The Court held, for example, that peaceful and nondisruptive protesters
could occupy the common areas of a public library.[61] It supported
activists' efforts to access and occupy streets and other public areas near
governmental seats of power like state capitols.[62] The Court even sanctioned some inroads on *private* property rights, as when it invalidated the
convictions of sit-in protesters who occupied lunch counters and other
quasi-public places.[63] The Court eventually indicated that so long as a

---

[61] Brown v. Louisiana, 383 U.S. 131 (1966).
[62] *See* Edwards v. South Carolina, 372 U.S. 229 (1963); Cox v. Louisiana, 379 U.S. 536
    (1965).
[63] Lombard v. Louisiana, 373 U.S. 267 (1963); Bell v. Maryland, 378 U.S. 226 (1964).
    Although the Court's majority did not base these decisions expressly on First Amendment
    principles or doctrines, the result was to allow activists to be present in places where private
    owners did not want them to be.

Figure 2.8. Civil Rights March on Washington, D.C.
Source: National Archives and Records Administration.

speaker's expression was basically "compatible" with the nature of the place at issue, it ought to be permitted there.[64]

The legal scholar Harry Kalven, Jr. interpreted the Supreme Court's civil rights precedents as establishing a First Amendment "easement" in certain public places.[65] By virtue of the Court's decisions, he wrote, the public had a right to "commandeer" public places such as streets for expressive purposes. Looking back at the periods in which syndicalism laws had nakedly suppressed public expression, Kalven predicted that "we may come to see the Negro as winning back for us the freedoms the Communists seemed to have lost for us."[66]

The opening of physical spaces to public contention during the 1960s coincided with a period in which conceptual or doctrinal space for public expression also continued to expand. Indeed, the commitment to public expression may have reached its apex in the 1960s and early 1970s, during the civil rights and Vietnam eras. In 1964, the Supreme Court emphasized

[64] Grayned v. City of Rockford, 408 U.S. 104, 115 (1972).
[65] *See* Harry Kalven, Jr., "The Concept of the Public Forum: Cox v. Louisiana," 1965 *Sup. Ct. Rev.* 1, 13.
[66] Harry Kalven, Jr., *The Negro and the First Amendment* 6 (1964).

in the famous libel case *New York Times v. Sullivan* that "debate on public issues should be uninhibited, robust, and wide-open."[67] In keeping with that philosophy, in 1969 the Court refashioned the definition of illegal "incitement" such that speakers were permitted to publicly or privately advocate even the overthrow of the government itself, so long as lawless action was not "imminent" and the speech was not "likely" to produce such action.[68] Further, in a series of decisions concerning "hostile" audience reactions to public speakers, the Court appeared to impose an obligation on police officers to protect public speakers rather than seek to suppress public contention based upon the mere possibility that violence or public disorder would occur.[69] Finally, the Court narrowed the definition of illegal "threats" in a manner that allowed for charged and heated rhetoric at public rallies and other events.[70]

The extent of physical and conceptual breathing space for public expression produced during this period is evident in *Cohen v. California* (1971). In *Cohen*, the Supreme Court reversed a breach of peace conviction occasioned by Cohen's wearing a jacket emblazoned with the words "Fuck the Draft" in the corridor of a public courthouse.[71] The Court flatly refused to extend privacy protections available in the home to such *public* places, insisting instead that viewers could "effectively avoid further bombardment of their sensibilities simply by averting their eyes."[72] It emphasized at length that local authorities lacked the power "to maintain what they regard as a suitable level of discourse within the body politic."[73] Notably, in the course of defending Cohen's rather inartful public statement about the draft, the justices invoked the loftiest of First Amendment theories:

> The constitutional right of free expression is powerful medicine in a society as diverse and populous as ours. It is designed and intended to remove governmental restraints from the arena of public discussion, putting the decision as to what views shall be voiced largely into the hands of each of us, in the hope that use of such freedom will ultimately produce a more capable citizenry and more perfect polity and in the belief that no other approach would comport with

---

[67] New York Times v. Sullivan, 376 U.S. 254, 270 (1964).
[68] Brandenburg v. Ohio, 395 U.S. 444 (1969).
[69] *See* Edwards v. South Carolina, 372 U.S. 229 (1963); Cox v. Louisiana, 379 U.S. 536 (1965).
[70] Watts v. United States, 394 U.S. 705 (1969).
[71] 403 U.S. 15 (1971).
[72] *Id.* at 21.
[73] *Id.* at 23.

the premise of individual dignity and choice upon which our political system rests.[74]

The "verbal tumult, discord, and even offensive utterance" one often encounters in public places, the Court said, were "in truth necessary side effects of the broader enduring values which the process of open debate permits us to achieve."[75]

During the Civil Rights Era and its aftermath, the Supreme Court firmly embraced the view earlier expressed by Justice Douglas in *Termi-niello v. Chicago* (1949): "[A] function of free speech under our system of government is to invite dispute. It may indeed best serve its high purpose when it induces a condition of unrest, creates dissatisfaction with conditions as they are, or even stirs people to anger."[76] Speakers now appeared to enjoy unprecedented First Amendment rights – to communicate *wherever* doing so was "compatible" with the functions of a particular public place, to cause or seek to cause public unrest, to offend public audiences, and even to publicly advocate the overthrow of government (so long, again, as this outcome was not imminent and likely). This open space policy was so firmly embraced that even the Ku Klux Klan could not be denied the opportunity to march through Skokie, Illinois, home to many Jews who had survived the Nazi holocaust.[77]

The 1960s and early 1970s were a heady time for supporters of civil rights and public expressive liberties. But the "easements" civil rights protesters had secured in public streets and other places had hardly been peacefully bestowed. Although their own tactics were generally peaceful, civil rights protesters gained both physical and conceptual breathing space for public liberties only as a result of enduring police brutality and racist mob violence.[78] Protesters who "commandeered" public space paid dearly, some with their lives, in Selma, Birmingham, and other flash-places of the Civil Rights Era.

The public disruption of the Civil Rights Era was televised to the nation. Images of violent encounters between police and protesters stunned a complacent nation and served as important catalysts for legal and social changes, including landmark civil rights legislation (Figure 2.9). But as the nation's early experience with mobs and riots showed, there are limits to the public disorder and violence officials and members of the

---

[74] *Id.* at 24.
[75] *Id.* at 25.
[76] 337 U.S. 1 (1949).
[77] Collin v. Smith, 578 F.2d 1197 (7th Cir. 1978).
[78] *See* Jerome Skolnick, *The Politics of Protest* (1969).

Figure 2.9. Alabama Police Attack Selma to Montgomery Marchers (March 7, 1965). *Source*: Federal Bureau of Investigation Photograph.

public will tolerate. As the civil rights protest era gave way to the Vietnam protest era, tolerance for public disorder began to wane. In particular, riots and public disturbances at the 1968 Democratic National Convention in Chicago, in cities following the assassination of Dr. Martin Luther King, and on campuses across the nation during the Vietnam War generally failed to produce the public solidarity that followed the civil rights protests. Images of Bull Connor and abusive law enforcement officials were replaced by pictures and news accounts of "hippies," student activists, and members of the Weather Underground and other radical groups engaging in public violence, occupying university and other government buildings, and destroying public properties. This looked to many more like mobocracy than self-government.

The backlash was predictable. Legal and political pendulums began to swing sharply in the direction of maintaining public order and security. Officials believed that access to public places, in particular, had to be restricted in order to maintain public order. Thus, beginning in the 1970s, officials enacted and enforced more restrictive permit requirements, police forces adopted increasingly aggressive forms of public policing, and college and university administrators initiated stricter limits on campus contention. At the level of national politics, "law and order" became a rallying cry – and part of the official platform of the National Republican Party.

The story of the Civil Rights Era is generally one of triumph for public expression. But the substantial progress made in expanding the expressive topography in the 1960s and 1970s must be placed in perspective. As of the early 1970s, speakers were indeed armed with robust First Amendment "parchment" liberties. As noted earlier, however, by the 1960s physical landscapes and demographic patterns had already changed in ways that made finding suitable or "compatible" expressive places in cities and suburbs far more difficult. Those changes, which did not halt or stall during the tumult of the 1960s and early 1970s, had already begun to fashion a new expressive topography. Further, the same desire for peace, tranquility, and public order that had driven so many people from urban areas was starting now to influence official attitudes regarding public contention and expression. Ultimately, the turmoil of the 1960s and 1970s would produce new legal and physical restrictions on speech out of doors.

The Judicial Bureaucratization of Place

Supreme Court justices are no doubt influenced to some degree by social and political events and circumstances.[79] The justices of the Burger and Rehnquist Courts had witnessed both the triumphs of the civil rights movement and the public turmoil of the 1960s and early 1970s. By the end of the 1970s many – including, apparently, a majority of justices then serving on the Court – perceived a need to impose greater order in public places. Urban and suburban planning was imposing order of its own, in the form of an increasingly exclusionary, commercial, and privatized built environment. But a legal and constitutional system for ordering public places and public expression had not yet been clearly articulated.

In the late 1970s and early 1980s, the Supreme Court finally agreed upon and announced a set of formal rules regarding access to the expressive topography. Notably, the Court jettisoned the idea that expressive activity ought to be permitted so long as it was "compatible" with the place under consideration.[80] This, apparently, was too loose and unpredictable a standard to provide guidance and maintain the requisite order. In place of generalized compatibility, the Court announced a formal *categorization* of places now referred to as the "public forum doctrine." Pursuant to the categorical approach, *all* of the public space on the expressive topography was to be categorized as one of three (possibly four) types of "forums." The scope of a speaker's public liberties would henceforth vary according to the type or category of forum she occupied.[81]

[79] Lee Epstein & Jack Knight, *The Choices Justices Make* (1998).
[80] Robert C. Post, "Between Governance and Management: The History of the Public Forum," 34 *UCLA L. Rev.* 1713, 1735 (1987).
[81] *See* Perry Educ. Ass'n v. Perry Local Educators' Ass'n, 460 U.S. 37, 45–46 (1983).

Under forum categorization, the Court explained, liberties expressive were to be broadest in "quintessential" or "traditional" public forums. This category was comprised of public streets, public parks, and (most) public sidewalks. The list presumably followed from the Court's recognition, in *Hague*, of the "immemorial" use by the people of these public places. In traditional public forums, government regulations expressly based on the *content* of the speaker's expression were prohibited unless there was a compelling interest for them and the government could not possibly draw the regulation in a content-neutral fashion. So long as it avoided content discrimination and left open "ample" and "adequate" alternative channels of communication, however, the government could still broadly regulate the "time, place, and manner" of expression in these and other public forums.[82]

The doctrinal rules announced by the Court were essentially the same in what it referred to as "designated" public forums. These, the Court explained, are public places as to which the government has demonstrated a *clear* intent to permit expressive activity. Such intent may be demonstrated by evidence of past government practices, the nature of the property at issue, and the compatibility of the property with the proposed expressive activity.[83] The Court made clear that the government was under no constitutional *obligation* to keep designated forums open to the public. It also explained that governments could choose to limit access to designated forums to certain "classes" of speakers or limited subject matters. This arguably created another type of public forum, sometimes referred to as a "limited" public forum.

According to the Court's categorical approach, all remaining public places were to be treated as "non-public" forums. This does not mean that the public is not invited to such places, or that the property has no public or quasi-public characteristics. The category label is, once again, principally a matter of governmental *intent* to preclude expression in the place to which the speaker seeks access. Speakers essentially have no expressive rights in nonpublic forums. After all, the government is not obligated to permit any expression there. If it does so, however, any regulation imposed will be upheld so long as the government has a "reasonable" basis for it and the regulation does not discriminate based upon the *viewpoint* of the speaker. Regulations very rarely fail these minimal standards.

---

[82] Ward v. Rock Against Racism, 491 U.S. 781, 791 (1989).
[83] Cornelius v. NAACP Legal Def. & Educ. Fund, 473 U.S. 788, 802–03 (1985).

On the surface, the public forum categorization approach appeared to offer predictability and order. The devil, as always, was in the details. Ever since the Court announced it, First Amendment and other scholars have been merciless in their critiques of the public forum doctrine.[84] The doctrine has been characterized as essentially unprincipled and theoretically bankrupt. It is said to depend upon a "myopic focus on formalistic labels" – "public" versus "non-public" forums.[85] Public forum doctrine has also been criticized as "crude, historically ossified, and seemingly unconnected to any thematic view of the free expression guarantee."[86] First Amendment scholars have argued that categorizing properties distracts courts' attention "from the first amendment values at stake in a given case."[87] Finally, forum doctrine has been criticized as an overbroad "declaration of deference to forum administrators" with regard to public spaces.[88]

Although these are all valid criticisms, we shall see that historical "ossification", has turned out to be a particularly glaring weakness of the public forum doctrine. The doctrine, as applied, has failed to respond adequately to the various forces and events that shaped public places beginning in the 1950s. For example, despite massive demographic and social changes, including suburban migration and an increasingly mobile citizenry, the Court has flatly refused to recognize any new "quintessential" public places where expressive rights are to be broadly construed. After nearly seventy years, the public streets, parks, and

---

[84] Representative critiques of the public forum doctrine can be found in Calvin Massey, "Public Fora, Neutral Governments, and the Prism of Property," 50 *Hastings L. J.* 309, 310 (1999); Steven G. Gey, "Reopening the Public Forum – From Sidewalks to Cyberspace," 58 *Ohio St. L. J.* 1535, 1577 (1998); Laurence Tribe, *Constitutional Law* 993 (2d ed. 1988); Robert C. Post, "Between Governance and Management: The History and Theory of the Public Forum," 34 *U.C.L.A. L. Rev.* 1713, 1715–16 (1987); Geoffrey R. Stone, "Content-Neutral Restrictions," 54 *U. Chi. L. Rev.* 46, 93 (1987); Keith Werhan, "The Supreme Court's Public Forum Doctrine and the Return of Formalism," 7 *Cardozo L. Rev.* 335, 341 (1986); C. Thomas Dienes, "The Trashing of the Public Forum: Problems in First Amendment Analysis," 55 *Geo. Wash. L. Rev.* 109, 110 (1986); Daniel A. Farber & John E. Nowak, "The Misleading Nature of Public Forum Analysis: Content and Context in First Amendment Adjudication," 70 *Va. L. Rev.* 1219, 1234 (1984); Ronald A. Cass, "First Amendment Access to Government Facilities," 65 *Va. L. Rev.* 1287, 1308–09 (1979); David Goldberger, "Judicial Scrutiny in Public Forum Cases: Misplaced Trust in the Judgment of Public Officials," 32 *Buffalo L. Rev.* 175, 183 (1983); Kenneth Karst, "Public Enterprise and the Public Forum: A Comment on *Southeastern Promotions, Ltd. v. Conrad*," 37 *Ohio St. L. J.* 247 (1976).

[85] Stone, *supra* note 84 at 93.

[86] Massey, *supra* note 84 at 310.

[87] Farber & Nowak, *supra* note 84 at 1224.

[88] Massey, *supra* note 84 at 319.

(some) sidewalks[89] remain the *only* "quintessential" public forums the Court has ever recognized.

Among other things, this means that places of modernity – shopping malls, airports, transportation terminals and facilities, highway rest stops – cannot achieve "quintessential" forum status.[90] Simply put, these places have not been around long enough to warrant such exalted treatment. The Court has also made clear that insofar as title to any of these modern properties is held by private entities, they apparently have the right to exclude expressive activity there – even if the general public is expressly invited to come.[91] Thus, other than the public streets, sidewalks, and parks – areas now used less by the people and substantially restricted in any event by automobile use, permit requirements, privatization, and architectural characteristics – no additional breathing space has been allocated for public liberties under the public forum doctrine.

As of the early 1980s, this was the new First Amendment regime that confronted speakers as they sought to reach the people, many of whom now lived in tightly zoned and commercialized cities or distant and exclusionary suburbs. Application of the public forum doctrine would thus exacerbate the stark contrast between robust *conceptual* public liberties (the liberty to speak *as* or in the manner one desires) and the *physical* breathing space (the liberty to speak *where* one desires) that remained once social, demographic, and other events had altered the contours of the expressive topography.

Public forum doctrine was not the only doctrinal force that limited public breathing space for expression. The First Amendment's "time, place, and manner" doctrine, which generally allows officials to regulate expression across the expressive topography so long as the regulation is "content neutral," serves important government interests, and is minimally tailored to serve those interests, became increasingly deferential during the 1970s and 1980s.[92] Critical decisions in the 1980s held that

---

[89] *See* United States v. Kokinda, 497 U.S. 720 (1990) (holding sidewalk adjacent to post office was nonpublic forum).

[90] *See* Int'l Soc'y for Krishna Consciousness, Inc. v. Lee, 505 U.S. 672 (1992) (holding airport terminals are nonpublic forums).

[91] *See* Lloyd Corp. v. Tanner, 407 U.S. 551 (1972) (holding that protestors of the Vietnam War had no right to distribute handbills in shopping center); Hudgens v. NLRB, 424 U.S. 507 (1976) (holding that labor picketers had no right to demonstrate at shopping center).

[92] *See* Ward v. Rock Against Racism, 491 U.S. 781, 791 (1989) (holding that any regulation "that serves purposes unrelated to the content of expression is deemed neutral"; this is so "even if it has an incidental effect on some speakers or messages but not others"). *See also* Susan H. Williams, "Content Discrimination and the First Amendment," 139 *U. Pa. L. Rev.* 615, 644 (1991) (noting substantial deference to authorities under time, place, and manner doctrine).

even in "quintessential" public forums, governmental regulations serving
an ever-expanding list of public interests – public order, listener repose,
suburban tranquility, privacy, and even landscape *aesthetics* – were entitled to substantial judicial deference.[93] Town planners, municipal boards,
sheriffs, and other governmental authorities had been effectively granted
the legal authority to shield urban and suburban citizens from various
forms of visually and otherwise offensive public expression, from suburban protesters to the "blight" of political campaign posters.[94] The
deference granted authorities during this period was a far cry from
the original justification for time, place, and manner regulations – the
maintenance of a basic set of Robert's Rules governing expression in
public places.

As noted throughout this book, the broad deference granted officials to
displace expression was particularly problematic for speech out of doors.
Given the primacy and expressiveness of place, spatial restrictions tend to
have a more substantial effect on public expression than time or manner
regulations. Restrictions on place are often different in character from
those on time and manner. Time and manner regulations can delay the
communication of messages, reduce the volume at which speech is
delivered, or impact such things as the size of placards or the activity that
accompanies speech. These can of course be more than mere inconveniences to speakers. As we shall see, however, spatial regulations can be
so physically coercive as to chill speech altogether. Unlike those relating to
time or manner, regulations of place often operate *directly on the body*. The
time, place, and manner doctrine ostensibly requires that "adequate"
alternative places be available to the speaker should she be denied her
preferred location. But courts are not required to, and rarely do, inquire as
to the physical, social, or expressive "adequacy" of alternative places. As
we shall see, courts generally consider public places to be more or less
fungible insofar as speakers are concerned.

In a word, by the 1980s the Supreme Court had fully *bureaucratized*
public places. Architectural and social forces had combined with constitutional precedents to create a system of bureaucratic property management that substantially diminished the physical breathing space for
public expression. Public places had now been placed under a kind of

---

[93] *See* Frisby v. Schultz, 487 U.S. 474 (1988) (upholding ban on targeted residential picketing);
Clark v. Cmty. for Creative Non-Violence, 468 U.S. 288 (1984) (upholding ban on public
camping on National Mall).
[94] *See* Members of the City Council v. Taxpayers for Vincent, 466 U.S. 789, 817 (1984)
(upholding prohibition on posting of signs on utility poles).

bureaucratic receivership, the terms of which extended beyond rudimentary "Robert's Rules" for public displays and expression. In general, public places would now be categorized by courts and managed by government "trustees." The bureaucratic regime shifted the balance from one that generally favored speakers' access to public places, with an emphasis on "compatibility" and the preservation of public "easements," to one that placed substantial faith in bureaucratic control and management of public properties. At the same time, increased respect for private property rights limited public expression that arguably diminished an owner's title, or that touched upon audience "privacy" and "tranquility." Henceforth, so long as governments remained "neutral" with regard to message content, courts would not seriously question their distribution of the resource of public space. Nor would they require that governments create or designate new physical forums for expression, or even retain those previously open to public speakers.

As we shall see in the chapters that follow, the bureaucratization of public place affects every aspect of the expressive topography. In their capacity as trustees of public places, for example, local officials and planners sometimes *privatize* public places, effectively "demoting" even traditional public forums like streets and sidewalks to "non-public" forums (Chapter 6). Places that have existed and operated as public forums for many years have been demolished, only to be reconstructed as "private" facilities. Using their aesthetic discretion, officials "beautify" public properties, in many cases without regard for the effects such improvements will have on public liberties. They also grant exclusive permits to private and official applicants, thereby ousting the general public from public forums for substantial periods of time.

Perhaps no phenomenon better symbolizes this bureaucratization of public place than the proliferation of "institutional free speech policies." These detailed codes, which are modeled on even more detailed permit and other requirements relating to public expression (*see* Chapter 6), set forth a variety of rules regarding expressive activity in and near an expanding list of public places – for example, sports arenas, public parking lots, transit hubs, and auditoriums. Today virtually all public places on the expressive topography, including most of the campuses of the nation's public colleges and universities, are subject to such institutional codes.

The bureaucratization of public places follows naturally from the First Amendment conception of place as property. Public forum and time, place, and manner rules, which flow naturally from the property conception, have combined with forces external to constitutional doctrine to further reduce the physical breathing space for speech out of doors. For the people out of doors, who generally enjoy broad conceptual breathing space for expression, the expressive topography contains fewer and fewer speech-facilitative places.

The Policing of Public Protest

As the discussion of the early expressive topography indicates, speakers' access to public places on the expressive topography is substantially influenced by the manner in which public places are policed. This is the case whether the public event involves a lone speaker on a soapbox or a mass demonstration in the streets. A wide variety of police tactics – informal and discretionary acts of policing, violence, covert surveillance, infiltration, and discriminatory enforcement of public order laws – can substantially affect access to public places and the exercise of First Amendment liberties in public places. As this book shows, public policing is among the most important factors affecting the contemporary expressive topography.

As political sociologists have noted, until the 1970s public policing generally followed an approach known as "escalated force."[95] The approach has roots dating to the nineteenth century, when the first large police forces were formed. As noted earlier, at the time officers exhibited little concern for public expressive liberties (formally, of course, there actually were none). They frequently used overwhelming physical presence and brute force to intimidate and sometimes intentionally harm "mob" participants and "rioters." If orders to disperse were not immediately followed, police promptly initiated repressive and violent tactics. Escalated force policing methods openly suppressed public expression and discouraged participation in public displays of contention.[96] From the Haymarket riot to clashes in the 1930s and 1940s, police engaged in violent confrontation with strikers and labor activists. Escalated force methods remained on full display during the civil rights and Vietnam eras.

By the 1970s and 1980s, escalated force had been replaced by an approach commonly referred to as "negotiated management."[97] This

---

[95] John McCarthy & Clark McPhail, "The Institutionalization of Protest in the United States," in *The Social Movement Society*, D.S. Meyer & S. Tarrow (eds) (1998); Clark McPhail, David Schweingruber, & John D. McCarthy, "Protest Policing in the United States, 1960–1995," in D. della Porta & H. Reiter, eds. *Policing Protest: The Control of Mass Demonstrations in Western Democracies*, (1998).

[96] Johnson, *supra* note 30 at 259–66.

[97] McCarthy & McPhail, *supra* note 95 at 96–100.

approach also has roots in early American practices relating to public contention. Recall that local officials sometimes sought to negotiate with protesters before brute repression became a more common response. Under a "negotiated management" policing system, protesters and police discuss the details of public displays – including, often, the places where they are to occur, the number of participants, and even arrest logistics – well in advance of a public event. Negotiated management has generally – although as we shall see by no means completely – prevented violence and injury at demonstrations and other public events. It has provided police with advance notice of the location and size of expressive displays, allowing for both effective public safety planning and better tactical responses to protester activities. But negotiated management has also had a variety of detrimental effects on public contention and expression. For example, negotiating every detail regarding a public display eliminates or at least substantially diminishes things like spontaneity and mobility. It may also distort speakers' messages, particularly those intended to convey opposition to the *status quo*.

Negotiated management is part of a broader regime of public place management that political sociologists sometimes refer to as the "public order management system".[98] The public order management system is another product of the judicial bureaucratization of public places. A typical public management system requires compliance with detailed permit and licensing requirements prior to public expressive events. In addition to limiting the places where people may gather and speak and requiring advance notice of events, public order management laws and policies also typically require that speakers post bonds, provide proof of insurance coverage, and pay license and cleanup fees. Today many public places, including those most critical to public expressive liberties, are managed in this fashion.

As political sociologists have observed, as a result of negotiated management and the public order management system public protest has been not only bureaucratized but largely *institutionalized*.[99] As a result, public contention has become just another aspect of ordinary, mainstream, "indoor" politics. As the institutionalization of protest has become more common, media and general public interest in public displays has decreased. In sum, methods of public policing, while certainly more peaceful today, are limiting the impact and effectiveness of public contention.

---

[98] *Id.* at 91.
[99] *See generally* McCarthy & McPhail, *supra* note 95.

Expressive Zoning

Channeling and repression of public expression can take many forms, from permit schemes to various forms of protest policing.[100] The most recent method of channeling speech out of doors – expressive zoning – combines methods of spatial bureaucratization and public policing. In essence, expressive zoning is the designation of areas or "free speech zones" in which public expression is permitted. Some zones, like the DZ discussed at the beginning of Chapter 1, are uniquely repressive. Others diminish public expressive displays in various ways – by separating speakers and audiences, restricting movement, and eliminating the symbolic and other advantages that inhere in particular places.

As noted above, the earliest "free speech zones" were constructed and enforced at the beginning of the twentieth century, to control and ultimately suppress the "free speech fights" instigated by Wobblies. Some accounts of the 1968 Democratic National Convention in Chicago indicate that officials there also sought – unsuccessfully, as it would turn out – to restrict protesters to certain areas.

These were isolated historical instances of the use of place as a unique regulatory tactic. Particularly since the 1990s, expressive zoning has proliferated across the expressive topography.[101] Today, regardless of where they are located, public speakers are likely to be affected by expressive zoning. Zones have been used at political conventions, abortion clinics, funerals, public auditoriums, national parks, campaign events, inaugurals, and on college and university campuses across the country. In the past few decades, expressive zoning has even altered the lexicon of First Amendment in America. Today speakers must navigate a gauntlet of official "demonstration zones," "free speech zones," "speech free zones," "buffers," "bubbles" (of, as we shall see, both the "fixed" and "floating" variety), "cages," and "pens."

There are a variety of likely causes for the relatively recent proliferation of expressive zoning. Zoning itself is a traditional means of regulating public places. Its use in distinctly *expressive* contexts has been encouraged, if not sanctioned, by the Supreme Court's bureaucratization of public places. As noted, public forum and time, place, and manner standards now provide ample authority to impose expressive zones. Further, as

---

[100] *See* Jennifer Earl, "Tanks, Tear Gas, and Taxes: Toward a Theory of Movement Repression," *Sociological Theory*, 21(1) (March 2003).
[101] *See* Timothy Zick, "Speech and Spatial Tactics," 84 *Tex. L. Rev.* 581 (2006). *See also* James J. Knicely & John W. Whitehead, "The Caging of Free Speech in America," 14 *Temple Pol. & Civ. Rts. L. Rev.* 455 (2005).

always there are sharp cultural divisions in this country, including those involving abortion, war, immigration, and globalization. To supplement negotiated management and public order management techniques, officials have turned to more tangible and physical spatial restrictions like expressive zones to neutralize these sometimes charged public controversies. Finally, as noted below and throughout this book, after September 11, 2001, "security" became an overriding public concern.[102] Expressive zoning has often been imposed in the putative interest of security. Like surveillance cameras, "Jersey" barriers, and other security apparatuses, expressive zones have become part of our post-9/11 landscape.

We shall see that zoning has been used across the expressive topography. Whatever accounts for its proliferation, expressive zoning now merits serious study as a distinct method of channeling and suppressing public speech and assembly (Chapter 7).

Security and Liberty

As all of the foregoing influences show, the expressive topography is quite dynamic. It changes in response to historical, social, and political events and circumstances. That transformation continues up to the present moment. As a result of the horrendous events of September 11, 2001, "security" has reshaped the contours of the expressive topography in numerous ways. The effects range from the visible (barriers, zones, surveillance cameras, demonstrations of force) to the far less transparent (covert infiltration of activist groups and official, but nonpublic, policies of repression).

It is simply impossible to overstate the influence of security concerns on present-day exercises of public expression. As we shall see, security concerns affect everything from access to architecture. Some of the changes we have witnessed to the expressive topography in the past seven-plus years have been common-sense reactions to concerns about violence and public safety. Others seem to be over-reactions or, worse, politically expedient measures designed to repress protest and dissent. When scholars, pundits, and commentators debate the delicate balance between liberty and security, public expressive liberties are among the things they should be, but generally are not, discussing. We shall have many occasions

---

[102] On the influence of security concerns on public places *see generally* Neil Smith & Setha Low, "Introduction: The Imperative of Public Space," in Setha Low & Neil Smith, eds., *The Politics of Public Space* (2006).

to consider the effects of the war on terrorism on our expressive topography and speech out of doors.

Activism and Attitudes – The People Themselves

Socio-demographic, political, and legal changes account for many of the features of the contemporary expressive topography. But as Justice Brandeis once wrote, "the greatest menace to freedom is an inert people."[103] The depleted condition in which we find our expressive topography is in part the product of choices speakers themselves have made – to pursue or not pursue access to public venues and to adopt particular strategies or repertoires of contention.

As the Supreme Court has said, public places are held *in trust* by government for the benefit of the people. To the extent the people, as beneficiaries, fail to make demands for physical space they bear at least some responsibility for the present condition of the expressive topography. Preservation of the expressive topography requires a certain level of commitment to public speech, assembly, petition, and press activities. This does not mean that the people must regularly pour into the streets and "riot," as they did in the eighteenth and nineteenth centuries. It does mean, however, that the people risk waiving expressive "easements" by not regularly insisting that officials honor them.

This book shows that many concerned citizens continue to insist on physical breathing space for public expression, and to resist governmental efforts to channel and suppress speech out of doors. More activism of this sort is required to preserve the expressive topography. This is not simply a function of the people showing up. It requires as well that speakers make *intelligent* choices with regard to the expression they convey and the restrictions they challenge. This is complicated by, among other things, the lack of any coordinating mechanism among public speakers. Speakers tend to be driven by personal agendas. They rarely consider the systemic effects of their expression. As we shall see, this can create harmful precedents which are then applied to limit access by future speakers and audiences.

Public speakers bear the particular burden of choosing wisely from among a variety of what political scientists and sociologists call "repertoires of contention."[104] As noted, early Americans engaged in mostly peaceful, nondisruptive, and often targeted protests. These

---

[103] Whitney v. California, 274 U.S. 357, 375 (1927) (Brandeis, J., concurring).
[104] Sidney Tarrow, *Power in Movement: Social Movements and Contentious Politics* (2d ed 1998).

displays were effective in defusing societal tensions, engendering solidarity, and granting limited power to the marginalized and powerless. As a result of the civil rights experience, in particular, today's speaker may seek real and momentous political changes. To achieve this goal, research has shown that public protests require at least some degree of disruption.[105]

This creates a serious dilemma for those who support more robust and effective public expression. Disruptive repertoires attract media coverage. They can sometimes generate public attention and solidarity. Taken too far, however, disruption can adversely affect the expressive topography by causing resort to new forms of official channeling, producing adverse legal precedents, or undermining public support for the exercise of public expressive liberties. Violent episodes in particular, from campus demonstrations to public riots, have negatively affected public tolerance for public expression and contention.

Opinion polls suggest that American citizens have great respect for the principle of self-government through expression. They broadly support the right to express an opinion and to protest governmental policies. But the form of that expression matters. Americans generally prefer peaceful discourse; they have little tolerance for disruptive or chaotic displays. Compared to citizens in other Western democracies, Americans are far more likely to engage in petitioning or leafleting than protests or demonstrations.[106] Today, there is relatively broad public support for restrictions on the speech activities of disruptive speakers like abortion protesters.[107] Americans also tend to look favorably upon protections for the unwilling or "captive" audience. In other words, there is sometimes a serious gap between our support for conceptual breathing space – for offensive and disturbing expression – and our preference for forms of public expression that do not actually offend, disrupt, or disturb anyone. The upshot is that today's public speaker often must walk a very fine line.

Except for a relatively small but determined group of public activists, the people have generally allowed long-held expressive easements on the expressive topography to lapse or weaken. To be sure, Americans still gather in public places during momentous public events like war protests and marches on Washington. The challenge is not only to maintain that presence, but to encourage participation in other places on the expressive topography, and to encourage greater tolerance for speech out of doors.

---

[105] William A. Gamson, *The Strategy of Social Protest* (1990).
[106] Bert Klandermans, *The Social Psychology of Protest* (1997).
[107] *See* Marvin Ammori, "Public Opinion and Freedom of Speech" 18–19 (2006) (white paper for The Information Society Project at Yale Law School).

3   EMBODIED PLACES

We begin our examination of the expressive topography with *embodied* places. These are places that we actually take with us as we traverse the expressive topography. Social scientists generally refer to this type of place as one's "personal space." Embodied place is critical to some of the most traditional forms of public expression – begging, counseling, pros- elytizing, soliciting, petitioning, and polling. Embodied places are often sites of high tension and uncomfortable exchange. Erving Goffman has described this as "the space surrounding an individual where within which an entering other causes the individual to feel encroached upon, leading him to show displeasure and sometimes to withdraw."[1]

Sociologists and legal scholars have likened embodied place to an "invisible boundary surrounding the person's body," a "bubble," a "shell," and "breathing room."[2] Embodied places are somewhat unique in that we "own" them; we live and experience this sort of place intimately and can readily detect intrusions upon it. Given the discomfort that often accompanies intrusions upon embodied place, as well as the increasing regard for privacy and tranquility, it is not surprising that efforts to reg- ulate or prevent access have been relatively common. Consider the fol- lowing recent examples:

- The enactment of "bubble" restrictions prohibiting abortion clinic "sidewalk counselors" from approaching within a specified number of feet from clinic patrons for the purpose of counseling them or advocating life.
- The arrest of a Colorado man on harassment and assault charges subsequent to his approaching Vice President Dick Cheney and stating that the administration's policies in Iraq were "reprehensible."

[1] Erving Goffman, *Relations in Public* 30 (1971).
[2] R. Sommer, *Personal Space* 26 (1969); Irwin Altman, *The Environment and Social Behavior: Privacy, Personal Space, Territory, Crowding* 53 (1975).

- A proposal by the Minneapolis police chief that panhandlers obtain a license and wear photo identification.
- The arrest of "Reverend Billy" (a/k/a William Talen) in Manhattan's Union Square Park for speaking *the words of the First Amendment* through a megaphone in close proximity to several police officers on the scene.

In First Amendment terms, speakers' demands for access to embodied places raise a fundamental tension between the speaker's interest in conveying a message from close distance and the audience's countervailing interests in repose, tranquility, and "privacy" in public places. A growing variety of contemporary restrictions – architectural, social, and legal – tend to keep particular speakers at a "safe" distance from their intended audiences. Although the serious tensions created by embodied expression cannot be ignored, preserving access to embodied places is critically important to the First Amendment and to the democratic functions of public places discussed in Chapter 1. Preservation of public expressive liberties must begin here, in the intimate spaces occupied by listeners and viewers.

THE EXPRESSIVE VALUE OF EMBODIED EXPRESSION

The dynamics of expression in embodied places are somewhat complex. An examination of the sociology of exchange in personal spaces can help us better understand the unique expressive dynamic in these places. Behavioral studies show that human beings use personal space to control public interactions and set communicative boundaries. These studies suggest that legal and other restrictions on access to personal space can fundamentally alter the expressive dynamic in embodied places. Embodied expression is critically important to speakers like sidewalk counselors, solicitors, panhandlers, proselytizers, and pollsters, who rely upon the proximity and immediacy of embodied places to deliver their messages or collect needed information. Indeed in certain instances, the message the speaker wishes to convey can only be effectively presented from a close distance.

The Sociology of Proximate Communication

Although it has received less attention in recent years, academic study of personal space was at one point quite vigorous. In the 1960s and 1970s, at the height of behavioral sociology, social scientists showed a keen interest in embodied places and, in particular, the communicative dynamic in such places. In laboratories, simulations, and field studies social scientists examined people's use of space as a means of social interaction and identity-building.[3]

The findings of social scientists contain various insights that relate to the analysis of embodied expression. Erving Goffman, among others, observed that human beings (like other species) actively use and manipulate space in personal encounters.[4] Even in public settings, people desire a certain level of personal space or "privacy." They use a variety of repertoires to maintain a personally optimal level of separation from others. These include verbal and nonverbal cues, territorial marking and alteration, and even flight. Thus in tense or otherwise uncomfortable encounters, people will avert their eyes, retreat to corners, and put distance between themselves and strangers.[5]

Social scientists have identified various differences among cultures, genders, and personality types in the intentional use and manipulation of personal space. For example, in some studies men tended to react more negatively to invasions of personal space than did women. Some studies suggest that Americans tend to prefer more personal space than, say, those from Mediterranean or Latin American cultures. Researchers have also observed how boundary control mechanisms differed when people encountered various groups, such as friends, the mentally ill, and persons perceived to be angry.[6]

The anthropologist Edward T. Hall provided an early and influential framework for the systematic study of personal space.[7] Although his methodology was rather crude, Hall's theory of "proxemics" – the study of man's use of personal space – continues to influence the study of proximate interaction today. For contemporary anthropologists, for example, Hall's proxemics continues to serve as "a model for understanding the creation of place through spatial orientation, movement, and language."[8]

Hall conceived of personal space as a "mobile spatial field" – "a culturally defined, corporeal-sensual field stretching out from the body at a

---

[3] For a summary and review of these studies, *see generally* Altman, *supra* note 2 at 69–72.
[4] Erving Goffman, *The Presentation of Self in Everyday Life* (1959); Erving Goffman, *Behavior In Public Places* (1963); Erving Goffman, *Relations in Public* (1971).
[5] Research indicates that these spatial rules may even apply in cyberspaces. *See* Stephanie Rosenbloom, "In Certain Circles Two is a Crowd," *N.Y. Times*, Nov. 16, 2006, G1.
[6] Altman, *supra* note 2 at 69–72 (summarizing research).
[7] Edward T. Hall, *The Hidden Dimension* (1966).
[8] Setha M. Low & Denise Lawrence-Zuniga, "Locating Culture," in Setha M. Low & Denise Lawrence-Zuniga eds., *The Anthropology of Space and Place: Locating Culture* 5 (2003).

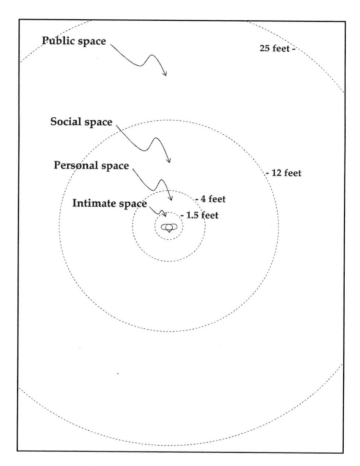

Figure 3.1. Hall's Proxemic Zones.
Source: Graphic by Libb Thims.

given locale or moving through locales."[9] Like others, he observed that people use personal space to maintain a degree of distance or separation between themselves and others. Hall was among the first social scientists to conceive of personal space as a "bubble" surrounding each individual. He noted that people associate different communicative activities and interpersonal relationships with different social distances or "zones."

Hall's interpersonal distance zones – which he labeled "intimate," "personal," "social," and "public" – were based upon observed vocal, visual, and behavioral shifts (Figure 3.1).[10] Each of Hall's interpersonal

---

[9] *Id.* at 108.
[10] Hall, *supra* note 7 at 108.

zones contains "close" and "far" phases. The primary emphasis in mapping these proxemic zones was on what sort of communication and interaction could occur from each of the identified distances. As we shall see, Hall's zones can therefore be useful in mapping the expressive dynamic in embodied places across the expressive topography.

Hall noted that the close phase of *intimate* distance is "the distance of love-making" and personal comforting. In this space there is essentially no distance between persons. The far phase of intimate distance, which Hall measured as six to eighteen inches, is characterized by low voice level and distorted visual perception. This is roughly the distance a person maintains on a crowded city subway.[11] In First Amendment terms, intimate distance, in both its close and far phases, is the distance perhaps most closely associated with the notion of audience "captivity." The audience within this zone finds it very difficult, perhaps impossible, to avoid the speaker's message.[12] Audiences can experience expression from this distance as not only uncomfortable but personally threatening.

According to Hall, *personal* distance is "the distance consistently separating the members of non-contact species."[13] This is the "small protective sphere or bubble that an organism maintains between itself and others."[14] In the close phase of personal distance ($1\frac{1}{2}$–$2\frac{1}{2}$ feet), one can reach out and physically grab another person. In its far phase ($2\frac{1}{2}$ – 4 feet), maintaining personal distance is essentially equivalent to keeping one "at arm's length."[15] Voice levels remain moderate at this distance, voice cues are rich, and "[s]ubjects of personal interest and involvement" can still be discussed.[16] Beggars, proselytizers, sidewalk counselors, and solicitors of various sorts typically seek to deliver their messages from personal distances, in either close or far phases.

Social distance is the normal distance at which business and general social contact occur. At this distance personal communication becomes more strained and difficult. In the close phase (4–7 feet), only impersonal interaction is possible.[17] This is the typical distance maintained, for instance, in most office settings between the person behind the desk and a visitor. Social distance-close phase has been observed in many public settings, including inside airports and on street corners. The far phase of

---

[11] *Id.* at 111–12.
[12] *See* Charles L. Black, Jr., "He Cannot Choose But Hear: The Plight of the Captive Auditor," 53 *Colum. L. Rev.* 960 (1953).
[13] Hall, *supra* note 7 at 112.
[14] *Id.*
[15] *Id.* at 113.
[16] *Id.*
[17] *Id.* at 114.

social distance (7–12 feet) is much more formal. Here one must maintain visual contact in order to communicate effectively. The voice becomes noticeably louder. As Hall observed: "A proxemic feature of social distance (far phase) is that it can be used to insulate or screen people from each other."[18] As we shall see, legal zones and other spatial regulations that codify such distances can have a substantial negative impact on embodied expression.

When one reaches *public* distance, Hall stated, she is "well outside the circle of involvement."[19] In the close phase (12–15 feet) one cannot see another person clearly; thus visual and other cues are not available. At public distances subjects can readily take evasive action. There may be a vestigial flight reaction.[20] In the far phase (25 or more feet) subtle shades of meaning are entirely lost, as are most of the details of facial expression. At this distance, people are and will remain strangers. Spatial zones and regulations that keep speakers at such distances from intended audiences effectively prohibit embodied expression.

The point of this discussion is not to suggest that Hall's proxemic framework ought to be adopted as a rigid constitutional baseline for access to embodied places. By Hall's own account, the zones are mere approximations.[21] The proxemic zones do, however, possess both intuitive appeal and some degree of scholarly support. As we all know, very close contact with strangers can often lead to substantial discomfort. This is particularly true in certain situations, as when the stranger approaching is perceived to be angry or to suffer some disability (mental, physical, or other). Research also shows, as we might expect, that viewers and listeners may discount messages delivered from social and public distances.[22] Distant speakers may be viewed as less trustworthy, less friendly, and not as well-meaning as those who communicate from closer distances. Studies have shown, for example, that counselors who communicate from personal distances were rated as more empathetic and understanding.[23]

As we shall see, there is considerable overlap between the sociological study of personal space and First Amendment concerns regarding access to embodied places. Understanding how people use personal space in communicative settings and how different proxemic zones affect

---

[18] *Id.* at 115–16.
[19] *Id.* at 116.
[20] *Id.*
[21] *Id.* at 109.
[22] Altman, *supra* note 2 at 83.
[23] *See,* e.g., F.D. Kelly, "Communicational Significance of Therapist Proxemic Cues," *Journal of Consulting and Clinical Psychology,* 39(2), 345, 1972.

embodied interaction can help us to appreciate how legal and other limits on access to embodied places affect First Amendment liberties.

Proximity, Immediacy, and Privacy

As noted in Chapter 1, on the early expressive topography interpersonal communication was a rather routine phenomenon. Avoidance of others was actually quite difficult, at least in densely populated areas. As people have gradually become more mobile and separated by greater distances, this form of public interaction has become less and less common. The explosion of communicative technologies has further reduced reliance on this and other traditional forms of public expression.

Despite these fundamental changes, however, certain speakers continue to try to connect intimately – face-to-face, if possible – with public audiences. A variety of counselors, proselytizers, beggars, petitioners, and pollsters still rely upon access to an embodied place or personal space to deliver their messages. For these and similarly situated speakers, the principal First Amendment values or benefits associated with embodied places are *proximity* and *immediacy*.

Proximity offers several advantages. In the most practical terms, speakers' displacement from embodied places can preclude traditional First Amendment activities such as the passing of literature, the solicitation of funds, the conducting of polls, or the conveyance of a personal grievance. Substantively, the content and nature of many messages delivered in embodied places may require intimate contact with a particular audience. To be even minimally effective, communicative activities like counseling, praying, begging, proselytizing, soliciting, and leafleting must occur from what Hall referred to as "personal" distances rather than from "social" or more "public" distances. From close distances, a dialogue can occur at an ordinary pace and volume. This is critical, as one does not typically hurriedly shout when she prays, or counsels, or empathizes, or begs for assistance. Sensitive matters of life, death, and morality require a degree of solemnity and intimacy that is simply not possible from far distances. Finally, as social science research suggests and intuition confirms, speakers who communicate from greater distances are sometimes viewed with greater wariness and skepticism by audiences. Whatever the message, the speaker who conveys it from social or public distances starts from a distinct sociological disadvantage.

Embodied places also provide the critical benefit of immediacy to speakers seeking to reach particular audiences. Obvious examples include the petition gatherer and political pollster, both of whom require immediate access to public audiences for purposes of gathering signatures or data. In a more message-oriented sense, abortion counselors and beggars require immediate access to their audiences. The sidewalk counselor may genuinely believe that the death of an innocent human being is imminent. As discussed below, the message of the beggar may be inseparable from the immediate matter of subsistence or survival. In seeking the clinic patron's attention or the public's assistance, the counselor and beggar must make an immediate human connection. They must overcome what Goffman referred to as a "relationship wedge"[24] that generally exists between strangers in public places. As the legal scholars Helen Hershkoff and Adam Cohen have observed: "The immediacy of [the beggar's] appeal breaks down the wall between speaker and listener and engages her interlocutor in a social interaction."[25] Like the sidewalk counselor and the beggar, the solicitor and proselytizer also seek to form immediate personal bonds with their public audiences. To do so, they too rely upon access to embodied places.

As critical as access to embodied place can be for these and other speakers, there are of course countervailing audience interests to consider. Audiences possess important interests in basic comforts like orderly movement, safety, and protection from fraudulent forms of public communication.[26] Overly aggressive forms of embodied expression, including those that interfere with movement or threaten the safety of public audiences, obviously cannot and should not be tolerated. Many public order laws prohibit physical obstructions and breaches of the peace. These laws can and should be enforced in appropriate circumstances.

More controversially, personal space is also related to both sociological and legal conceptions of *privacy*. Behavioral studies indicate that public audiences use place, among other "compensations," to defend against perceived invasions of privacy.[27] Most Americans, having perhaps internalized contemporary norms and customs associated with what now passes for public presence, do not appear to be receptive to public approaches by strangers. Access to, or "invasions" of, embodied places affect "privacy" interests in bodily integrity, mental and psychological repose, and avoidance of unwanted contact.[28]

---

[24] Goffman, *Behavior in Public Places, supra* note 4 at 105.
[25] Helen Hershkoff & Adam S. Cohen, "Begging to Differ: The First Amendment and the Right to Beg," 104 *Harv. L. Rev.* 896, 913 (1991).
[26] *See* Thomas I. Emerson, *The System of Freedom of Expression* 285 (1970).
[27] Altman, *supra* note 2 at 98–99.
[28] *Id.* at 17 (reviewing sociological definitions of privacy).

People can often create interpersonal boundaries by controlling access to personal space. Audiences can, for example, essentially "tune out" public interaction and expression they do not wish to experience. Allan Westin has referred to this notion of privacy as "reserve," which he has described as "the creation of a psychological barrier against unwanted intrusion."[29] But suppose the person cannot filter the message out socially, psychologically, or otherwise? The question then is whether, and if so to what extent, the *law* ought to protect the "unwilling" audience from intrusions upon embodied places.

In First Amendment terms, audiences have a strong privacy interest in private places like the home. But they have generally been granted a far weaker privacy interest in public places like the streets, parks, and sidewalks. No speaker has a First Amendment right – anywhere – to press a message on another in a harassing or physically threatening manner. Beyond that, however, the First Amendment has generally been interpreted to permit proximate and immediate expression – regardless of the offense or discomfort it causes an audience. As we shall see, however, recent practices and decisions have cast some doubt upon this longstanding principle.

The Democratic Functions of Embodied Places

As we consider the expressive significance of embodied places, we ought to keep firmly in mind the fundamental *political* functions these places serve. As noted in Chapter 1, all the places on the expressive topography serve, to a greater or lesser extent, one or more of three principal democratic functions associated with public places – identity, participation, and transparency. Embodied places are critical to *all three* of these functions.

Public places ought to facilitate a diversity of speech claims and forms. Many, although by no means all, of the speakers who typically rely upon embodied place lack any viable alternative channels of communication. Some of these intimate speakers may lack the money or other resources necessary to communicate with the general public. Further, for the reasons discussed earlier, some claims or messages must be heard in embodied places if they are to be heard at all. Finally, recall that a person can make an "identity" claim merely by *being present* in a public place.[30] Marginalized persons like beggars, however, are increasingly unwelcome

---

[29] Allan Westin, *Privacy and Freedom* 32 (1970).
[30] Don Mitchell, *The Right to the City: Social Justice and the Fight for Public Space* 33–36 (2003).

in public places. Insofar as geography, law, or both exclude these and other marginalized speakers, public places fail to serve critical identity functions.

Embodied places also support and facilitate the most fundamental and traditional forms of public political participation. Embodied speakers rely upon intensely participatory forms of speech like leafleting, polling, petitioning, oral persuasion, solicitation, and counseling. Limits on access to embodied places may restrict or even prevent the free flow of a range of personal, political, and commercial information. For example, as discussed below "buffer zones" at polling places may interfere with the press's efforts to collect and report information on electoral activity. Protective bubbles placed around political leaders may limit or prohibit public petitioning for redress of grievances. More generally, restrictions on access to embodied places prevent the sort of face-to-face communication that builds and sustains a public political community.

Finally, embodied places lend critical transparency to expression and governance. It is true that a substantial portion of our expressive culture has migrated to online and virtual spaces. Embodied expression is among the last remaining vestiges of a material and visible expressive culture. The expression that occurs there is physically and tangibly experienced in a manner that other forms of expression are not. As it interrupts and inconveniences, embodied expression forces audiences to take public notice. It makes tangibly manifest speakers' messages, functions, grievances, and intentions. Last, but certainly not least, embodied expression is a tangible and public manifestation of popular democracy.

EARLY INROADS – DISTURBING THE "COMPLACENT"

Embodied expression has a rich First Amendment tradition. Because it challenges social norms and interferes to some extent with public repose, this form of expression has always been somewhat controversial. Nevertheless, First Amendment values and jurisprudence have exhibited a healthy respect for embodied places and proximate expression. Before turning to recent limits on access to embodied place, let us first examine the origins of early breathing space for this critical form of public expression.

As noted in Chapter 2, the very early expressive topography was often tumultuous. "Mobbing" and "rioting" were relatively frequent occurrences. There is no indication, however, that public places were unpleasant in terms of the everyday interpersonal interaction that occurred there. During the colonial era, social norms and community controls rather than positive laws generally sufficed to regulate communication among strangers. Violators of public norms were likely subject to private and informal forms of correction and punishment.

Gradually, however, official acts and public laws came to play a larger role in policing public interaction. Modernization eventually brought perceived threats to social order, including offensive or "corrupting" public language. Some nineteenth–century state laws thus prohibited speakers from even approaching listeners with the "intent to harass, disturb, or offend." Other laws forbade calling women "strumpets" or otherwise publicly questioning a person's honor or integrity. Early efforts to regulate public interaction focused in part on codifying public manners and appropriate forms of public exchange. Local authorities also sought to cleanse public expression through discretionary enforcement of early permit schemes. Beggars, solicitors, proselytizers, and others who were deemed indecent, offensive, or who engaged in what was deemed "blasphemous" expression were simply denied permits to speak and arrested (or worse) if they proceeded. Discriminatory taxes were imposed on certain speakers to deter their exercise of public liberties. Breach of peace and disorderly conduct laws were used to impose a sense of decorum on embodied and other forms of public expression. Finally, police officers would routinely order public speakers who transgressed supposed bounds of decency and decorum to simply "move along."

As noted in Chapter 2, however, many of these early laws and forms of discretionary policing were invalidated in the 1930s and 1940s. Early public breathing space for embodied forms of expression was opened primarily as a result of litigation by the Jehovah's Witnesses. In a number of Supreme Court cases, Witnesses successfully challenged laws granting unfettered discretion to public officials as unconstitutional "prior restraints" upon expression and interferences with free speech and free press. The Court also invalidated several poorly disguised discriminatory license fees and taxes on public expressive activity typically engaged in by Jehovah's Witnesses and other proselytizers.[31] Finally, invoking Thomas Paine and other radical thinkers, the Court struck down laws flatly banning the distribution of handbills, leaflets, and other literature in public places and door to door.

---

[31] William Kaplan, *State and Salvation: The Jehovah's Witnesses and Their Fight for Civil Rights* (1989).

In the course of invalidating early restrictions on embodied expression, the Supreme Court emphasized that face-to-face interaction had been a "potent force in various religious movements down through the years."[32] Indeed, the Court described the Witnesses' embodied expression as part of "the best tradition of free discussion."[33] It also emphasized the connection between public leafleting and important democratic functions such as the collection of signatures for political campaigns. The Court was not at all persuaded by the government's insistent plea that embodied expression tended to disturb the public peace. It pointedly responded: "The authors of the First Amendment knew that novel and unconventional ideas might disturb the complacent, but they chose to encourage a freedom which they believed to be essential if vigorous enlightenment was ever to triumph over slothful ignorance."[34]

In most of these cases, the speakers had remained polite and had not, as the Court noted in *Chaplinsky v. New Hampshire* (1942), communicated any "profane, indecent, or abusive" remarks. But robust protection for embodied expression would require some breathing space for even "profane, indecent, or abusive" appeals. In 1942, the Court upheld the conviction of a Witness who had called the town marshal a "God-damned racketeer" and "a damned Fascist" under a New Hampshire law making it a crime to address "any offensive, derisive, or annoying word to anyone who is lawfully in any street or public place . . . or to call him by an offensive or derisive name."[35] That decision has been interpreted to allow authorities to prohibit so-called "fighting words" – epithets that by themselves cause injury or that are likely to cause a reasonable person to engage in a brawl. Later cases have essentially rejected the notion that speech that causes psychological injury may be punished for that reason alone. Although the "fighting words" doctrine has never been officially abandoned, *Chaplinsky* was the last case in which the Supreme Court upheld a conviction on such grounds. As noted in Chapter 2, the trend thereafter was toward expanding the breathing space for even the most offensive public expression – including its intimate or embodied forms.

This liberalization of public expression did not signal the end of public decorum. It did, however, create a robust, wide-open, and, for some, less pleasant public arena in which offensive and disturbing public expression was sometimes thrust upon unwilling recipients. During the Civil Rights

---

[32] Murdock v. Pennsylvania, 319 U.S. 105, 108–09 (1943).
[33] Martin v. Struthers, 319 U.S. 141, 145 (1943).
[34] *Id.* at 143.
[35] Chaplinsky v. New Hampshire, 315 U.S. 568 (1942).

Era and its aftermath, the Court continued to insist on broad public tolerance for even disturbing and offensive expression. It repeatedly held that authorities could not silence public speakers based upon audience offense or the mere possibility of violence.[36] The Court also invalidated regulations and punishments of contentious forms of speech like political hyperbole and rhetoric.[37] Perhaps most importantly insofar as embodied expression is concerned, by the 1970s the Court had made clear that while in *public* places audiences enjoy no generalized right to privacy or repose.[38] People may insist, said the Court, on some protection from indecent and other messages thrust upon them while at home, where it may be difficult or impossible to avoid. But once they leave that sanctuary, the Court strongly indicated that they must generally tolerate offensive and disturbing expression and resort to self-help measures such as averting the eyes.

To be sure, these developments did not enshrine a principle of "anything goes" in terms of embodied expression or public speech more generally. Authorities still possessed the basic authority to regulate harmful and unlawful conduct, as well as to restrict the "time, place, and manner" of public expression. But early inroads made by the Jehovah's Witnesses and others into embodied places created critical breathing space for fundamental embodied activities like leafleting, solicitation, and proselytizing. Owing to the efforts of the Witnesses and other early public speakers, breathing space was also opened for communicating even highly offensive and disturbing messages from close personal distances. Early inroads into the personal space of public audiences allowed public speakers to reap the critical First Amendment benefits of proximity and immediacy and to use public places for critical democratic purposes.

CONTEMPORARY LIMITS ON ACCESS TO EMBODIED PLACE

Over the past several decades, various social, architectural, and legal forces have conspired to move speakers, in Edward Hall's words, "outside the circle of involvement." In landscape and in law, we have gradually moved toward the codification of "social" distance, at least for certain

---

[36] Edwards v. South Carolina, 372 U.S. 229 (1963); Cox v. Louisiana, 379 U.S. 536 (1965).
[37] Watts v. United States, 394 U.S. 705 (1969).
[38] Cohen v. California, 403 U.S. 15 (1971).

types of speakers and speech. This will, as social science research strongly suggests, make many of us more comfortable in public places. But the First Amendment costs of granting this sort of personal protection to public audiences will be substantial.

Social, Architectural, and Other Environmental Restrictions

As we shall see across the expressive topography, forces other then law have a profound effect on the exercise of public expressive liberties. Some of the loss of access to embodied places can be traced to a variety of social, architectural, and environmental circumstances associated with modernity. Let us begin with a brief consideration of these restrictions.

It is axiomatic that in order for embodied expression to occur, speakers must be able to reach public audiences under conditions conducive to proximate and immediate interaction. The location and nature of public audiences has changed rather dramatically since the Jehovah's Witnesses first opened embodied places to expressive activity. An increasingly mobile populace is, of course, more difficult to locate and engage. Moreover, when they are finally at rest, modern audiences are increasingly distracted, in particular by the now-ubiquitous personal computing devices they have transported into public places (Chapter 9). The "narrowcasting" people do in private places has recently gone public. In sum, today's audiences appear on the expressive topography as constantly moving targets that are generally distracted and disinclined to see or hear embodied appeals.

Serious obstacles to interpersonal communication have actually been *built into* the architectures on the expressive topography. As noted in Chapter 2, most urban and suburban areas have been planned and constructed in a manner that fails to encourage or facilitate spontaneous interaction among a diverse range of citizens. In many places where such exchanges might still occur, public expression is often expressly prohibited. For example, as discussed in Chapter 5, except in a handful of states shopping mall owners and business districts may and typically do ban expressive activity. The presence of unwanted persons such as the homeless is even enforced through such innovations as "bum proof" benches and other architectural changes to public buildings and places.[39]

---

[39] *See* Mike Davis, *City of Quartz* (1990) (describing the "bum proof bench" and other socio-spatial strategies used by Los Angeles); Mitchell Duneier, *Sidewalk* 128–32 (1999) (describing architectural changes to Pennsylvania Station in the 1990s).

The choice of many to live in exclusive neighborhoods like "gated" communities further limits opportunities for citizen interaction. This trend, which has been growing in popularity since the 1980s, expands the sphere of residential "personal space" to include even the streets, parks, and sidewalks of the neighborhood.[40] Modern urban areas often exhibit similar "gated" features; these, too, effectively expand the "privacy" and tranquility of residents to the detriment of anyone who might wish to make an embodied appeal or statement. In many urban and suburban areas, it seems that any activity that might interfere with preferred forms of tranquil consumption are not welcome. Activities like pamphleteering, begging, and soliciting are often discouraged or prohibited simply by virtue of the built environment itself.

In sum, certain basic features and characteristics of the modern built environment and our modernized society generally reduce the breathing space for face-to-face appeals. Opportunities for engaging others from personal distances have decreased with each social and physical expansion of audiences' "personal space" bubbles.

Legal Restrictions

Some of the restrictions discussed above are the inevitable result of progress and modernity. But we must add to these environmental forces a variety of not-so-inevitable legal restrictions on embodied appeals. In the relatively few public places that remain available to embodied speakers, new legal restrictions have imposed additional obstacles to interactions within personal space. Access restrictions have been imposed on a variety of speakers – beggars, sidewalk counselors, solicitors, proselytizers, petitioners, and pollsters – who today still rely primarily upon embodied expression and appeals. While some of these limits on speech out of doors have been successfully challenged by public speakers, others remain in force. Further, and of more general concern, the courts have retreated somewhat from the once-settled proposition that audiences enjoy no general right to "privacy" in public places. Access to embodied places thus cannot be taken for granted – at least not by all speakers.

Beggar-Free Zones

The National Law Center on Homelessness and Poverty has been tracking and cataloguing legislation relating to homelessness since

---

[40] Margaret Kohn, *Brave New Neighborhoods: The Privatization of Public Space* (2004).

1991.[41] In general, the Center has noted that as homelessness has increased each year so too have efforts to ban and criminalize activities like sleeping, loitering, erecting structures, and asking for alms in public places.

Restricting public begging or "panhandling" is one of the most common official responses to the problem of homelessness in this country. For years, begging and other public activity by the homeless were regulated by arresting and prosecuting violators under "vagrancy" and "loitering" laws. As noted above, these and other "public order" laws were commonly used to regulate a variety of unwanted and "offensive" embodied public expression. The homeless and destitute were also regularly displaced through more informal discretionary police "sweeps" and orders to "move along."[42] These and other mechanisms effectively restricted or banned embodied and other appeals by the homeless and other beggars.

Although bans and restrictions on public loitering and begging have been around for some time, focus and reliance upon such laws became far more acute starting in the early 1990s. At that time, municipalities began in earnest to address what many viewed as intolerable "disorder" in public places, especially urban centers. Public officials like then-mayor Rudolph Giuliani of New York City called for a general cleansing of public places based on the "broken windows" theory of public order maintenance. This approach, made famous in a 1982 article in *The Atlantic Monthly* by James Q. Wilson and George L. Kelling, was based on the premise that disorder and crime were inextricably linked.[43] If a window in a building went unrepaired, the theory held, soon all of the windows in that building would be broken. Eventually, according to Wilson and Kelling, the entire neighborhood would succumb to decay and dilapidation. Many urban officials treated panhandling, like the broken window, as a symptom of urban decay and disorder.

To make public places "safer" and more orderly, and to address the fear some people have of confronting panhandlers and other such "public nuisances," officials took various steps to restrict or deny beggars' access to public places. In addition to the enforcement of public order laws and tactics like urban sweeps, the National Law Center studies demonstrate that laws expressly criminalizing "panhandling" have now been enacted across the nation. Among these laws, measures imposing "beggar-free

---

[41] National Law Center on Homelessness & Poverty, "Punishing Poverty: The Criminalization of Homelessness, Litigation, and Recommendations for Solutions ii (2003).

[42] Egon Bittner, "The Police on Skid Row: A Study of Peace Keeping," reprinted in Bittner, *Aspects of Police Work* (1990).

[43] James Q. Wilson & George L. Kelling, "Broken Windows," *Atlantic Monthly* (Mar. 1982); *see also* George L. Kelling & Catherine M. Coles, *Fixing Broken Windows* (1996).

zones" are among the most prevalent. Such laws typically ban embodied appeals for assistance in designated public areas like beaches, sidewalks near banks, and areas near sidewalk cafes – essentially anywhere the consuming or recreating general public is likely to be.

New zones are constantly being designated, typically in response to panhandling activity in a particular area. For example, the Minneapolis City Council approved an ordinance that banned all verbal requests for money within 10 feet of crosswalks, convenience stores, and liquor stores. Begging was also banned within 50 feet of entrances and exits to parks or sporting arenas, and within 80 feet of a bank or ATM. In addition, the Minneapolis ordinance banned begging at night and in groups of two or more people. Similarly, in response to complaints from tourists the Atlanta City Council enacted a measure in 2005 that prohibited begging near most of the city's tourist attractions. The ordinance made it illegal to ask strangers for food or money near downtown museums and, ironically, the Martin Luther King, Jr. National Historic Site. Under the Atlanta ordinance, violators were to be given a warning on their first offense, a referral to a city resource center on the occasion of their second, and a one-month jail sentence for a third offense. Municipalities that see measures like these invalidated in the courts typically attempt to narrow or alter the law rather than abandon the effort.

Some states and localities have gone so far as to enact what appear to be *blanket* prohibitions on begging in *all* public places. For example, some states adhere to a common law rule that prohibits begging in any public place by any person who is "able to work."[44] Other laws and regulations prohibit "loitering for the purpose of begging" in any public place. Still other measures prohibit only "aggressive" panhandling, which is typically defined as following, harassing, or accosting others while making an appeal for assistance.[45] Many of these broad statutes and regulations have never been challenged in court. Some are undoubtedly subject to vagueness and other constitutional challenges. Some are not now actively being enforced – although they remain in state codes or municipal regulations.

New proposals for dealing with the seemingly intractable problem of public begging continue to be proposed and enacted. In 2005, the Chief of Police for Minneapolis proposed that panhandlers be required to obtain a *license* to beg and to wear photo identification while in public.[46]

---

[44] *See* Tracy A. Bateman, "Laws regulating begging, panhandling, or similar activity by poor or homeless persons," 7 A.L.R. 5th 455 (2006).
[45] *See* Hershcoff & Cohen, *supra* note 25 at 896 n. 5.
[46] The proposal was not ultimately adopted.

In 2006, New York's highest court upheld a Rochester ordinance providing that "no person on a sidewalk or alongside a roadway shall solicit from any occupant of a motor vehicle that is on a street or other public place."[47] The stated governmental interests in expanding protection from panhandlers to the area inside the vehicle were road safety and traffic flow. That logic did not apply to firefighters collecting charitable donations from motorists, who were apparently never cited under the law. Laws and regulations on the subjects of homelessness and begging have become increasingly draconian. If they could legally do so, some municipalities would apparently simply ban the homeless and other destitute persons from some public places altogether.[48]

As these laws and other measures indicate, courts and local officials have had a difficult time dealing with the public policy and constitutional issues raised by public panhandling. New York City's experience is instructive in several respects. The city initially enacted and enforced a limited ban on begging in the subway system. That ban was upheld by a federal appeals court, which seemed to go out of its way to characterize begging as "much more conduct than speech"; "nothing less than a menace to the common good"; and an "assault" on passengers in the subway system.[49] Three years later, however, a different panel of the same federal appellate court invalidated a New York City ban on begging in *all* public places.[50] Notably, that court characterized begging as *fully protected* expression.

The constitutional uncertainty stems in large measure from the fact that the Supreme Court has never decided whether begging is in fact protected speech under the First Amendment. The Court has held in a trilogy of cases that soliciting charitable donations is protected expression.[51] Some lower courts, relying on these cases, have found that panhandling similarly conveys a message and is entitled to First Amendment protection. Other courts have disagreed.[52] Academic commentary has

---

[47] People v. Barton, 8 N.Y.3d 70, 861 N.E.2d 75 (N.Y. 2006).

[48] A recently enacted Los Angeles ordinance would have criminalized sleeping or lying down in public places under certain circumstances, thus making it a crime for the homeless to simply be *present* in certain public places. The Ninth Circuit invalidated the ordinance on the ground that it violated the Eighth Amendment's ban on "cruel and unusual punishment." Jones v. City of Los Angeles, 444 F.3d 1118 (9th Cir. 2006). A handful of municipalities have passed ordinances that purport to ban the *feeding* of the homeless in public parks and other public places.

[49] Young v. New York City Transit Auth., 903 F.2d 146 (2d Cir. 1990).

[50] Loper v. New York City Police Dept., 999 F.2d 699 (2d Cir. 1993).

[51] *See* Riley v. National Fed'n of the Blind, 487 U.S. 781 (1988); Secretary of State of Md. v. Joseph H. Munson Co., Inc., 467 U.S. 947 (1984); Village of Schaumburg v. Citizens for a Better Env't, 444 U.S. 620 (1980).

[52] *See* Hershkoff & Cohen, *supra* note 25 at 896–97 n. 6.

been similarly divided, although most scholars seem to favor First Amendment protection for at least peaceful public panhandling. The First Amendment status of panhandling is discussed further later in this chapter. In any event, the uncertain constitutional status of panhandling will likely only encourage further efforts to limit this form of public appeal.

New York's experience has been somewhat enlightening in another sense. As it turns out, the appeals court decision invalidating the ban on all public begging was not the end of the matter. The law was actually invalidated only as applied in New York City itself. Officers in other parts of the state continued to enforce the law, charging more than 2,400 people with unlawful begging over the course of the past decade or so.[53] More disturbing still, despite the court's ruling police continued to enforce the ban *within* New York City itself. Indeed, twelve years after the appeals court decision a federal judge found that the New York City Police Department was arresting or issuing summonses to hundreds of people citywide and that prosecutions were still ongoing. Remarkably, even after that judge ordered police to cease and desist enforcing the panhandling law, they did not do so. In the two years following the judge's order, New York City police officers issued 791 additional summonses for public begging. Notwithstanding this unlawful behavior, the court refused to hold the police department in contempt on the ground that it had taken some minimal steps to notify its officers of the law's invalidity.[54] The experience in New York is one indication of the strong commitment municipal and law enforcement officials have to restricting public appeals for assistance by the destitute and homeless.

For some people, embodied appeals by beggars or panhandlers are among the most disconcerting of public interactions. For the beggar, however, the "message" to be delivered is one that requires both proximity and immediacy. A variety of laws, ordinances, regulations, and enforcement policies that target the "nuisance" of public begging effectively prevent beggars from attempting to reap those critical benefits.

Abortion Clinic "Buffer Zones" and "Bubbles"

As discussed in more detail in the next chapter, during the past few decades abortion clinics have been among the most contested places on our expressive topography. In the late 1980s and early 1990s, abortion

---

[53] Fernanda Santos, "Loitering Case Is Dismissed As Unlawful," *N.Y. Times*, May 31, 2007, B3.
[54] Cara Buckley, "Judge Criticizes Police Dept. For Illegal Loitering Arrests," *N.Y. Times*, June 1, 2007, B2.

Figure 3.2. Planned Parenthood Sidewalk Protest.
Source: Photograph by Christopher Murad.

opponents resorted to violence and vandalism at or near clinics as well as in other places.[55] There were several incidents of arson, assault, chemical attacks, harassment, and bomb threats involving the clinics and abortion providers. Abortion opponents also used more legitimate repertoires of contention, some in fact borrowed from the civil rights movement. These included pickets, blockades, and sit-ins. These and other acts of civil disobedience were ultimately intended to shut down the clinics.

During contests and protests at abortion clinics, two types of speakers are generally present. Small groups of protesters and demonstrators assemble, shout slogans, and display signs equating abortion with murder. As noted earlier, there are also typically a few "sidewalk counselors," whose mission is to approach women at or near the clinic and persuade them, through a variety of means, not to terminate their pregnancies (Figure 3.2). The counselors, as discussed, rely heavily upon access to the embodied spaces of clinic patrons. The basic idea is to establish personal rapport with the woman. As one set of counseling literature states: "Sidewalk counseling is a highly intense verbal interaction between you and a mother who is about to deliver her unborn child over to death. Your goal is to persuade her to keep her baby."

The volatile and sometimes violent situation at abortion clinics across the country eventually led to efforts at both the state and federal levels to guarantee access to health care facilities providing abortion services. Some violent protesters were prosecuted under state criminal laws.

---

[55] *See* National Abortion Federation, *Incidents of Violence & Disruption Against Abortion Providers* (1993).

In addition, in 1993, Congress enacted the Freedom of Access to Clinic Entrances Act (FACE), which prohibits injuring, interfering with, or intimidating anyone providing or obtaining reproductive health services or intentionally destroying clinic property.[56] Violators are subject to civil and criminal penalties. The FACE statute has survived several First Amendment challenges.

In addition to the protections under FACE, judicial injunctions and various state enactments have established "buffer zones" and "bubbles" to protect clinic properties and patrons. For purposes of the discussion that follows, "buffer zones" typically limit the areas at or near clinics where protesters are permitted to assemble and speak. Their essential purpose is to preserve rights of ingress and egress for patients and clinic workers, although they may protect the psychological repose of these groups as well. These zones are discussed in the next chapter, which examines access to *contested* places. "Bubbles" tend to be smaller zones that are specifically designed to limit speakers' access to the embodied places of clinic patrons. In this context, "bubbles" effectively legalize the sociological concept of "personal space" by defining its parameters with respect to the audience of abortion clinic patrons. In addition to protecting clinic patrons from physical assault, the "bubbles" also protect women against adverse psychological effects thought to be associated with clinic protest activity.

The Supreme Court has examined buffer and bubble provisions in a trilogy of cases. In *Madsen v. Women's Health Center, Inc.* (1994), the Court upheld an injunctive 36-foot "buffer zone" encompassing the public sidewalks and streets around the clinic.[57] This was the second injunction issued by the state court, after protesters refused to comply with a prior injunction ordering them not to block access to the clinic. As a result of the 36-foot buffer, protesters were not able to get closer than 10 to 12 feet from cars approaching or leaving the clinic. Although the Court upheld the "buffer zone," it invalidated several other injunctive provisions – including a ban on all displays of "images observable" from within the clinic and a prohibition on "uninvited" physical approaches within 300 feet of the clinic entrance.

The Court examined a second set of injunctive restrictions on protests at abortion clinics in *Schenck v. Pro-Choice Network* (1997).[58] The

---

[56] 18 U.S.C. § 248. In 2003, the Supreme Court held that antiabortion protesters could not be punished under the Racketeer Influenced and Corrupt Organization Act, a federal extortion law. *See* Scheidler v. National Organization for Women, 537 U.S. 393 (2003).
[57] 512 U.S. 753 (1994).
[58] 519 U.S. 357 (1997).

injunction in *Schenck* prohibited antiabortion demonstrators from protesting within 15 feet of abortion clinic entrances and driveways, and within 15 feet of vehicles and patients entering or leaving a clinic. These were called "fixed" and "floating" buffer zones, respectively. The second zone was "floating" because the counselor, once told by the patron that counseling was not welcome, was required to move alongside the patient or car while maintaining the appropriate distance. In effect, the "floating" zone erected a protective "bubble" around the clinic patron – even while she was on the public streets and sidewalks. The Court upheld the "fixed" buffer zone, for essentially the reasons it had stated in *Madsen*. The "floating" zone or bubble, however, was deemed by the Court to be both overbroad and too difficult to administer. In effect, said the Court, the floating buffer would have prohibited traditional forms of expression like handbilling. The floating buffer or bubble also would have required that some protesters back into busy streets to maintain the requisite distance from patients. As written, the injunction may also have prohibited even very small assemblies on the public sidewalks near the clinic.

Such was the landscape respecting abortion clinics when the Court decided the final case in the trio, *Hill v. Colorado* (2000).[59] In *Hill*, the Court reviewed a Colorado statute that made it unlawful (within 100 feet of the entrance to any health care facility) for anyone to knowingly come closer than 8 feet from any person without their consent "for the purpose of passing a leaflet or handbill to, displaying a sign to, or engaging in oral protest, education, or counseling with such other person." In assessing the Colorado law, the Court took note of lower court findings that protesters had in the past yelled, thrust signs at the women approaching the clinics, and displayed pictures of bloodied fetuses. It also noted, however, that none of the sidewalk counselors had themselves engaged in any physically confrontational or abusive activity.

The *Hill* Court first rejected the contention that the eight-foot "bubble" restriction was an effort to suppress any antiabortion message. Although the law expressly restricted approaches and embodied appeals for the limited and express purpose of "engaging in oral protest, education, or counseling[,]" the majority treated the measure as a content-neutral regulation of the manner and place of expression. While acknowledging that the 8-foot "bubble" would inhibit (if not entirely prevent) leafleting and handbilling, the Court, over strong dissents from Justices Kennedy and Scalia, nevertheless upheld the restriction as necessary to protect clinic patrons from the physical and emotional harm

[59] 530 U.S. 703 (2000).

associated with being approached by an unwelcome speaker. The Court also recognized the clinic patrons' right or interest in avoiding the "unwanted" communications of sidewalk counselors who, it should be noted, conveyed their messages in "traditional public forums" like sidewalks and streets. In a passage with serious implications for access to embodied places across the expressive topography, the Court characterized the counselors' intrusion into patrons' personal space as a violation of "the broader right to be let alone" – an offshoot of the constitutional right to "privacy."[60]

Hill's recognition of a public "right to be let alone" was remarkable. As noted earlier, the Court had previously said that an interest in avoiding unwanted expression may exist only where "substantial privacy interests are being invaded in an essentially intolerable manner."[61] But prior to *Hill*, the Court had never held that this standard had been met in any case involving public expression in traditional public forums. According to the Court, however, clinic patrons were in some sense "captive" to the counselors' expression while moving along public sidewalks near the clinics. They were, the Court observed, in a physically and psychologically vulnerable state. Under the circumstances, said the Court, the law imposed an "exceedingly modest" restriction on counselors' free speech rights.[62]

Like proliferating restrictions on begging, abortion clinic "buffer" and "bubble" provisions are examples of the creeping codification of what Hall referred to as "social" distance. The thrust of the abortion clinic trilogy is that personal contact and close communication at contested places such as clinics ought to be *generally* treated as threatening. As discussed below, the true threat to public expression from these cases exists not in their narrow holdings, but rather in the "public privacy" rationale they partly rest upon. If women at clinics possess such a right or interest, then so too might racial minorities, funeral attendees, victims,

---

[60] *Id.* at 717. Steven Heyman argues in his recent book that the sidewalk counselor's message violates the patrons' right to privacy because it "disrespects the dignity and autonomy of the unwilling listener and constitutes a serious intrusion into her personal life." Steven J. Heyman, *Free Speech & Human Dignity* 152 (2008). But Professor Heyman gives inadequate weight to both the speaker's location and the expressive benefits associated with embodied appeals. Like the Court in *Hill*, he fails to cite any precedent establishing a "right to privacy" on the public streets and sidewalks. Ultimately, Professor Heyman's support for *Hill* seems to result in substantial part from his view that sidewalk counseling is a form of "low value" expression. *See id.* at 153 (indicating that sidewalk counselors were not seeking to convey any "general or public message" but to "influence the personal choices of women entering the clinic").

[61] *Cohen*, 403 U.S. at 21.

[62] *Hill*, 530 U.S. at 729.

and other persons or groups likely to experience psychological distress as a result of being approached by an unwanted or uninvited speaker. Once expanded beyond the traditional context of unwanted speech that enters the home, just how broadly will the public "right to be let alone" extend?

Peddlers, Proselytizers, Pamphleteers, and Solicitors
Although they are not highly publicized, are sometimes buried in municipal codes, and appear to be enforced somewhat sporadically and unevenly, additional restrictions on a variety of other forms of embodied expression are quite common. These include restrictions on petition-gathering, solicitation, and the distribution of literature.

As discussed in Chapter 5, in most states petition gatherers are not permitted to operate in or near shopping malls and other quasi-public places. Permit schemes and other ordinances further restrict various forms of leafleting, peddling, and soliciting. In an effort to make public places "safe" and orderly for preferred commercial and recreational uses, municipalities often limit or ban soliciting and other forms of embodied expression.[63] Police may also prevent speakers from distributing literature in places where such activity is fully protected by the First Amendment – on the grounds of a state capital, on university campuses, in public parks, and on public streets.[64] Many ordinances and discretionary actions are never challenged in court or reported to the media. Thus, the actual extent of this particular kind of suppression of embodied speech cannot be precisely determined.

When contests do arise, however, courts are likely to defer to governmental concerns regarding orderly pedestrian traffic flow and, in the case of solicitation, protection of the public from fraudulent appeals. In *Heffron v. International Society for Krishna Consciousness, Inc.* (1981), the Supreme Court upheld a rule instituted at the Minnesota State Fair that prohibited the sale or distribution of printed or written material except from booths rented to applicants on a first-come, first-served basis.[65] Hare Krishnas challenged the rule as interfering with expression and with the practice of Sankirtan, which enjoins members to go into public places to distribute or sell religious literature and solicit religious donations. The Court, after determining that the fairgrounds were a "non-public forum," upheld the rule as a reasonable time, place, and manner requirement.

---

[63] *See, e.g.*, Duneier, *supra* note 39 at 231–52 (1999) (discussing limits on solicitation in New York City "Business Improvement Districts").
[64] *See id.* at 272–77.
[65] 452 U.S. 640 (1981).

Officials were justifiably concerned, the Court said, with the "widespread disorder" that might occur if solicitors were allowed to wander the fairgrounds and distribute their materials face-to-face.[66] Officials were also entitled, the Court held, to combat potentially fraudulent solicitation by forcing solicitors to speak from remote booths rather than within the personal space of fair-goers. In this context, as in others, the strong implication is that embodied appeals are generally threatening to public order and public audiences.

The Court has also upheld solicitation bans imposed by transit authorities in airport terminals.[67] Once again, as discussed in Chapter 5, the Court determined that the terminals were "non-public forums." The Court again deferred to the government's interests in orderly pedestrian traffic flow and the concern that harried passengers might be vulnerable to fraud or duress. Solicitors were limited under transit authority regulations to the sidewalk areas outside the terminals, where airport visitors quickly rushed past or otherwise avoided them. The Court did, however, invalidated a flat ban on the "sale *or distribution* of literature" in the terminals. According to the Court, distribution of literature did not raise the same disruptive concerns as face-to-face solicitation. Reflecting the early inroads of the Jehovah's Witnesses, the Court observed that the right to distribute flyers and other literature "lies at the heart of the liberties guaranteed by the Speech and Press Clauses of the First Amendment."[68]

Nevertheless, these and other precedents have been relied upon by municipalities and other governmental institutions to support various restrictions on embodied appeals. In airport terminals and other public places, authorities exercise broad discretion to ban the sale of literature and to establish "speech-free zones" and "free speech zones."[69] Peddling is also generally subject to detailed and often restrictive regulations, including permit requirements and spatial limits, in cities, towns, and suburbs across the United States. Indeed, almost anywhere there is likely to be a crowd, restrictions on embodied expressive activities have been enacted in the name of facilitating pedestrian traffic flow and preventing fraud.

---

[66] *Id.* at 654.
[67] Int'l Soc'y for Krishna Consciousness, Inc. v. Lee, 505 U.S. 672 (1992); Lee v. Int'l Society for Krishna Consciousness, Inc., 505 U.S. 830 (1992).
[68] ISKCON v. Lee, 505 U.S. at 679.
[69] *See, e.g.,* ISKCON Miami, Inc. v. Metropolitan Dade County, 147 F.3d 1282 (11th Cir. 1998) (upholding regulations prohibiting solicitation and sales of literature in public places of airport, including on sidewalks and in parking lots, and upholding grant of discretion to airport director to establish free speech zones).

Despite the Supreme Court's support for public pamphleteering and other forms of literature distribution, municipalities continue to enact and sometimes enforce bans on even this most traditional form of embodied expression. For example, Susan Mendelson, a member of Jews for Jesus, was recently escorted by police out of a public park in Oyster Bay, New York, after she attempted to distribute free religious literature there and sought to speak to those present about her beliefs. The town had enacted an ordinance requiring that any person who wished to distribute literature or otherwise address another person in any park or beach area first obtain a "special permit" from the town. Citing the "venerable" tradition of distributing literature in public places, including the pre-revolutionary distribution of Thomas Paine's *Common Sense*, a local judge invalidated the permit requirement as an unconstitutional prior restraint on expression.[70]

Cities across the country are constantly seeking to revitalize urban areas. Many believe that revitalization will only occur if pamphleteers, solicitors, and other speakers who are thought to depress the area or disturb the desired atmosphere are displaced. In the 1990s, for example, downtown Las Vegas was suffering from a sharp economic downturn. Emulating other cities across the United States, Las Vegas decided to create a "pedestrian friendly zone." The city contracted with a private entity to revitalize a five-block area to be known as "the "Freemont Street Experience" (Figure 3.3). Five blocks of Freemont Street were closed to automotive traffic. The street and abutting sidewalks were torn up and repaved, creating a large promenade. The area was designed to serve as both a pedestrian thoroughfare and a commercial and entertainment complex intended to attract tourists and members of the public.

Based upon complaints from businesses and citizens, the City Council enacted a flat ban on all solicitation – including panhandling, peddling, and pamphleteering – within the five-block area. The city naturally claimed that the ban served interests in orderly traffic flow and prevention of fraudulent solicitation. But the mayor of Las Vegas, perhaps better reflecting the Council's true motivation, publicly endorsed pedestrians' "right to be left alone." A federal appeals court eventually invalidated the ban on the grounds that it was content-based and prohibited far more expression than necessary to serve the city's stated interests (outright bans rarely survive First Amendment scrutiny). A month later, however, the Las Vegas City Council enacted a narrower ordinance that banned only solicitation for the purpose of the "immediate" obtaining of money, charity, business or

---

[70] People v. Mendelson, 00602/2006 (Nassau, 4th Dist.) (April 4, 2007).

Figure 3.3. The "Freemont Street Experience".
Source: Photograph by Chris Metcalf.

patronage. The ordinance, the Council contended, should be upheld because it allowed nonprofit speakers to solicit donations, while preventing only *businesses* from soliciting in the Freemont Street area.[71]

As Ms. Mendelson's case and the history of the "Freemont Street Experience" show, protection of the fundamental right to distribute literature in public cannot necessarily be assumed in all municipalities. Fortunately, in light of the critical inroads into embodied space made by

---

[71] That ordinance, too, was successfully challenged in court. Undaunted, the City Council quickly considered and enacted a new ordinance restricting certain embodied appeals.

the Jehovah's Witnesses in the 1930s and 1940s, courts can generally be counted on to invalidate such laws. Still, speakers must be vigilant and must sometimes litigate to defend this fundamental public liberty. Peddlers and solicitors, by contrast, continue to face substantial restrictions on their ability to communicate commercial information from personal distances. Municipal interests in maintaining pleasant shopping environments and serene pedestrian thoroughfares, public order, traffic flow, and the avoidance of fraud and duress purportedly associated with embodied public expression are generally deemed sufficient to validate typical peddling and solicitation regulations.

Polling Places

Embodied places near polling stations are critical to the free flow of political information. Campaigns seek to sway undecided voters and to extend the time and reach of the campaign. Pollsters seek access to voters in order to collect information on voting and voting habits. The government has competing and important interests in protecting the orderly administration of elections and the election process, increasing voter participation, and providing unobstructed access to the polls.

Limitations on activities like solicitation, distributing campaign material, and peddling near polling places have generally been upheld against First Amendment challenges. In *Burson v. Freeman* (1992), the Supreme Court upheld a broad Tennessee law restricting *all forms* of political campaigning, including the distribution of leaflets, the display of posters, and the wearing by pedestrians of lapel buttons, within 100 feet of polling places.[72] The Tennessee zone banned political expression even in some "traditional" public forums like streets and parks. Owing to its focus on campaign speech, the Court subjected the law to the strictest judicial scrutiny. It found the state's interests in maintaining access to polling places and orderly administration of elections to be compelling. The Court also refused to second-guess the contours of the 100-foot zone. It noted that most states had adopted *some* spatial restriction on access to polling places, and many had adopted the same measurements. Finally, the 100-foot safety zone was not, said the Court, so large as to *completely* block out political messages.

"Campaign free zones" at polling sites are now commonplace during primary and general elections. Despite the important state interests involved, these zones can have a substantial effect on public democracy in

---

[72] 504 U.S. 191 (1992).

general, and on embodied forms of expression in particular. As Justice Stevens noted in his dissent in *Burson*:

Campaign free zones are noteworthy for their broad, antiseptic sweep. The Tennessee zone encompasses at least 30,000 square feet around each polling place; in some States, such as Kentucky and Wisconsin, the radius of the restricted zone is 500 feet–silencing an area of over 750,000 square feet. Even under the most sanguine scenario of participatory democracy, it is difficult to imagine voter turnout so complete as to require the clearing of hundreds of thousands of square feet simply to ensure that the path to the polling place door remains open and that the curtain that protects the secrecy of the ballot box remains closed.[73]

Polling place restrictions thus often extend well beyond ensuring orderly access to the polls. As Justice Stevens suggested, campaign-free zones appear to assume that *all* campaign activity near a polling place is a form of public nuisance. The laws, he said, tend to "confuse sanctity with silence."[74]

In addition to broad limits on "retail" campaigning near polling places, since the 1980s legislatures have enacted and state officials have enforced a host of restrictions on the practice of "exit polling." Exit polling typically involves a pollster located near a polling place interviewing voters immediately after they have cast their ballots. Many of the polling restrictions were initially enacted owing to anger over the 1980 presidential election, which was "called" for Ronald Reagan at a time when polls on the West Coast remained open. Many blamed the networks and their broadcasting of election poll results for Jimmy Carter's defeat. Exit polls continue to generate political controversy. Most notably, in the 2000 presidential election the state of Florida was "called" for Al Gore based primarily upon exit poll results.

Despite the significant controversy it has entailed, exit polling is a form of political expression protected by the First Amendment. Proximity and immediacy are critical to pollsters, who seek to provide a window into the public's mindset on election day. Some research has shown that in places where a 100-foot polling-free zone was in effect, polling error rates are

---

[73] *Id.* at 218 (Stevens, J., dissenting).
[74] *Id.* They may also have a tendency to disadvantage nonincumbents. *See* Note, "Defoliating the Grassroots: Election Day Restrictions on Political Speech," 77 *Geo. L. J.* 2137, 2158–60 (1989) (collecting authorities).

more than double the rates in places where pollsters can stand within 25 feet of a polling place.

Thus far, the media have been generally successful in challenging restrictions on exit polling.[75] The challenges have tended to focus on high-profile and contested districts. For example, restrictions in Florida, Nevada, and Ohio were invalidated by federal courts as recently as 2006. Still, many such laws remain in effect and are enforced during elections. For example, South Dakota was recently sued by several news organizations when it announced that it would enforce a 100-foot polling-free zone during the 2008 presidential primaries. Some states also rely on antiloitering and general proscriptions on personal contacts with voters to restrict exit polling and other embodied appeals near polling places.

All of this regulatory activity continues despite the lack of evidence that pollsters hinder voters or otherwise interfere with elections. A district court judge in Miami found that of the 5,090 voter complaints submitted by Florida voters in the 2006 congressional elections, *none* regarded exit polling.[76]

Petitioning Public Officials

Limits on access to *voters* are not the only, or even most serious, threat to core embodied political expression. With few exceptions, it is generally very difficult, and in many cases now impossible, to engage our *public officials* from personal or conversational distances.

Particularly since September 11, 2001, security "bubbles" around public officials have expanded and have sometimes been aggressively enforced. In some cases, limiting the public's access to political leaders is a necessary safety precaution. It is a crime, for example, to enter a specified zone around the President of the United States without authorization.[77] Still, as images of President Bush being mobbed by crowds of Albanians, or of presidential candidates working extensive public "rope lines" show, we ought to be mindful of the danger of selective enforcement of such protective policies.

In recent years, officials appear to have reached a level of hypersensitivity with regard to embodied political petitioning. The case of Steven Howards is illustrative. Mr. Howards, an environmental consultant from Colorado, visited a local outdoor shopping mall with his son.

---

[75] *See, e.g.,* Burson, 504 U.S. at 222–23 (Stevens, J., dissenting) (collecting cases).
[76] CBS Broadcasting, Inc. v. Cobb, 470 F.Supp.2d 1365, 1367 (S.D. Fla. 2006).
[77] *See* 18 U.S.C. § 1752 (a)(1)(ii) (making it a federal crime to knowingly enter and remain in a restricted area the President is visiting).

Mr. Howards claims that when he noticed that Vice President Dick Cheney was in the area, he approached to within two feet of Mr. Cheney and stated in a calm voice "I think your policies in Iraq are reprehensible."[78] Mr. Howards was promptly arrested by federal Secret Service agents and local law enforcement officials. The "threat" in this instance was apparently the mere entry of the Vice President's personal space.[79]

Whatever the unique concerns may be with regard to presidential and vice-presidential security, it is certainly far from clear that *all* public officials should travel in security bubbles whenever in public. During the 2004 Republican National Convention, Mayor Michael Bloomberg, who was then embroiled in a dispute with organized labor, was protected from protesters by a 15-foot security bubble.[80] If public officials at every level of government were to adopt such measures, no citizen would be able to petition any public official or politician from within his or her "personal space." The idea that the public *generally* poses a threat to public officials is a pernicious one in a democracy. The First Amendment right to "petition" officials for "redress of grievances" should extend in at least some cases to the embodied spaces of political leaders or would-be leaders.

In sum, as a result of social, architectural, and legal limits on embodied expression speakers increasingly find that they have the right to offend, provoke, and petition others only from some "safe" (social) distance. In many public places, audiences, including public officials, have a *de facto* and in some cases *de jure* "right to be let alone." The codification of social distances and spaces on the expressive topography has affected a variety of traditional expressive forms (pamphleteering, soliciting, proselytizing, campaigning, and petitioning) and a range of expressive content regarding important matters of public concern from religion to politics.

PRESERVING ACCESS TO EMBODIED PLACE

The contemporary limits discussed above have exacerbated a long-standing tension in this country regarding embodied expression. Culturally, Americans place a high value upon and jealously guard their

---

[78] Kirk Johnson, "Man Sues Secret Service Agent Over Arrest After Approaching Cheney and Denouncing War," *N.Y. Times*, October 4, 2006.

[79] The agents involved have since publicly disagreed as to whether Mr. Howards posed any actual threat to the vice president.

[80] *See* Julia Preston, "Court Backs Police Dept. in Curbs on Labor Tactics," *N.Y. Times*, August 26, 2004, at B7.

"personal space." Constitutionally, the First Amendment has been interpreted as conferring a right to make even offensive and disturbing appeals within this space. The discomfort and offense that may accompany such expression are, the Supreme Court has said, "in truth necessary side effects of the broader enduring values which the process of open debate permits us to achieve."[81] If we wish to preserve the expressive and democratic values associated with embodied places, we must acknowledge and address this fundamental tension. This will require some basic changes in attitudes and behaviors, physical landscapes, and legal interpretations.

Attitudes and Behaviors

Preserving breathing space for intimate appeals will require adjusting private and official attitudes toward this kind of expression. As sociologists have long observed, face-to-face or close-range communication is often uncomfortable, upsetting, and disruptive. Today, of course, new "virtual" forms of communication offer an increasing variety of escapes from this sort of social discomfort. In some sense, the Web is enabling Americans' cultural preference for personal space and communicative "privacy." Yet even with the expressive migration to virtual spaces, we cannot simply avoid public places or public speakers. Nor should we want to.

Although there are no figures or studies to confirm the observation, tolerance for embodied expression appears to be declining from what were undoubtedly already low levels. Unfortunately, officials have reflected this attitude in their own statements, policies, and rulings. In some cases, officials have publicly advocated the public's "right to be let alone" – even in quintessential public forums like streets and parks. In response to complaints of annoyance or offense, local public officials have acted promptly to codify social space limitations on activities such as pamphleteering and solicitation. The Supreme Court's own precedents lend credence to the idea that in-person solicitation is generally associated with fraud and public disruption.

One of the values the Web provides is instantaneous public feedback on public events, including expressive contests. Although these comments are hardly a basis for drawing firm conclusions, they do provide a sense of current public sentiment. Comments made on the Web in response to videotaped confrontations, like the one mentioned at the

---

[81] Cohen v. California, 403 U.S. 15 (1971).

beginning of this chapter between "Reverend Billy" and the New York City police, indicate that public opinion tends to run decidedly against embodied expression. In response to Reverend Billy's arrest for simply reading the text of the First Amendment in close proximity to officers, many comments invoked the "right" not to hear the speech. Others, convinced of the lawfulness of the arrest, commented that having to arrest such speakers was a "waste of scarce resources." Some even opined that Reverend Billy deserved some "jailhouse justice." Few commenters paused to ask whether the officers ought to have been more tolerant. Only a few comments generally supported Reverend Billy's expressive activity or criticized his arrest.

Increased toleration, if not full embrace, of embodied appeals is absolutely essential for several reasons. As some of the examples in this chapter show, society's "poorly financed causes" and "little people" still critically need access to embodied places. There are, as noted, a number of circumstances in which there are no viable substitutes for embodied appeals. Petition gatherers, sidewalk counselors, exit pollsters, and product hawkers all depend upon the ability to reach people in tangible public places. One cannot simply assume that these or other speakers can find audiences as readily online. Beyond these speaker-specific concerns, in-person interaction among strangers is vital to civic life and public democracy. It is remarkable how little the public seems to appreciate the historical pedigree of this traditional form of public democracy.

The law obviously cannot enforce tolerance and understanding of this sort. It cannot require that people acknowledge and appreciate the victories of the Jehovah's Witnesses, who first carved breathing space on the expressive topography for close interpersonal exchanges. But there are behavioral modifications that might help preserve this part of our expressive culture. It may sound rather quaint, but we can stop rushing past every speaker we meet on the public sidewalk, in the public squares of our cities and towns, and in our parks as if they pose a threat to our safety or are a public nuisance. We can take a few minutes and listen to the arguments of petition gatherers, solicitors, politicians, and even panhandlers who seek to make personal connections in public places. Of course, we can only do these things if we are willing every now and then to remove our earplugs and disengage from the personal computing devices that are now a ubiquitous public distraction. As discussed in Chapter 9, increased "absent presence" or "present absence" in public places is a serious threat to *all* forms of public expression, but especially to embodied appeals. Admittedly, assuming the response to Reverend Billy is representative of public opinion, negative attitudes toward embodied expression are deeply entrenched. Simple modifications to attitudes and behaviors are not likely to substantially narrow the gap between social preferences and First Amendment rights. But they are a start in that direction.

Finally, a word regarding the behavior of would-be embodied speakers is appropriate. As aggressive begging, harassing forms of solicitation, and the history of abortion clinic contests amply demonstrate, speakers must be mindful of the public backlash likely to follow this sort of embodied interaction. This sort of behavior has undoubtedly led to some of the more damaging recent limitations on access to embodied place. More generally, speakers must be aware of the manner in which their putative audiences regard and protect their "personal space." Knowledge of the sociology of close interaction can be helpful in this regard. Although it can be exceedingly difficult to do in busy public venues, speakers must seek to tailor embodied approaches accordingly. Physically thrusting speech at an already skeptical and generally unwilling audience will only further entrench negative public attitudes toward embodied expression.

Landscape and Architecture

One of the recurring themes in this book is that our built environment substantially limits opportunities for public contention and exchange. As noted earlier, the architectures and other physical characteristics of contemporary urban and suburban places do not generally facilitate embodied encounters. In addition to reconsidering attitudes regarding embodied expression and altering certain public behaviors, we will also need to rethink basic spatial choices that have favored separation and tranquility over somewhat messier forms of human interaction like embodied expression.

Chapter 2 briefly discussed ongoing efforts by new urbanists and other public place activists to alter landscapes and architectures in ways that will promote public life and community. Some of the proposed changes, including broadening sidewalks and providing for more common meeting spaces, may indeed facilitate the sort of spontaneous appeals embodied speakers tend to rely upon. While one certainly cannot force audiences to stop and listen, public planning that encourages presence and interaction can increase the breathing space necessary for embodied expression.

If embodied expression is to survive, we will also need to reverse the trends toward privatization and commercialization of public spaces. This topic is discussed in much greater detail in Chapter 6. As the "Freemont Street Experience" in Las Vegas shows, officials are increasingly eager to privatize slumping areas and to exclude "problematic" speakers from refurbished public spaces. Owing to the fact that embodied speakers rely disproportionately on access to public streets and sidewalks, this loss of space can have a substantial effect on them. Chapter 6 will discuss the constitutional argument against public space privatization and "demotion" of traditional public forums like streets and parks. For now it is sufficient to note that efforts to make public places more appealing for recreational and commercial purposes often drastically reduce opportunities for embodied appeals to strangers.

Public spaces are a form of commons, which means of course that they ought to be open to everyone. The built environment can be as effective as expressive zoning and other legal measures at excluding embodied expression from public places. Public planners ought to seriously consider the innovations proposed by new urbanists and others. Officials (and courts, as necessary) ought to ensure that public projects and other landscape alterations do not simply codify majority preferences for public tranquility, pleasant shopping, "privacy," and repose.

The De-Codification of Social Distance

The various limitations on embodied appeals discussed in this chapter represent an effort to codify social distance (according to Hall's typology, approximately 4–12 feet) as a First Amendment benchmarks. If embodied appeals are to be preserved and protected, social space must generally be de-codified and personal distance recognized as a more appropriate context for embodied interaction.

One of the questions rarely, if ever, asked with regard to regulation of embodied expression is what role laws and regulations *ought* to play. Although legal buffers and bubbles have been enthusiastically embraced by officials and courts, there is at least some social science evidence indicating that audiences view offensive forms of public expression as a personal and social problem rather than a legal one.[82] Even those who are most vulnerable to street offense and harassment – minorities and women – do not seem to expect or *want* lawmakers to address the matter. One radical proposal, then, is for lawmakers and public officials to allow the people themselves to regulate offensive forms of expression on the

---

[82] *See* Laura Beth Nielsen, *License to Harass: Law, Hierarchy, and Offensive Public Speech* (2004).

expressive topography. When and if speakers engage in threatening or other unlawful conduct, there are ample laws under which to prosecute and punish them.

Given apparent majority preferences and the inevitable tensions that flare up on the expressive topography when speakers seek access to embodied places, this proposal is not likely to gain much traction. Legislators (and sometimes judges) will likely continue to seek codification, through zones, buffers, and bubbles, of social distance. They do so, however, without a firm grasp of the sociology of face-to-face interaction. They do not seem to appreciate and understand the critical expressive values of proximity and immediacy, and the important democratic functions associated with embodied expression. As a result, they generally over-value peace and tranquility, and under-value the discomfort and contention that embodied expression can produce. Buffers and bubbles ought to be measures of last, not first, resort. When and if they are adopted, they ought to be as narrowly constructed and tailored as possible. As in other places on the expressive topography, courts should be especially vigilant in ensuring that this is the case.

The details of expressive zoning, in terms of designated feet and the existence of alternative avenues of communication, are unfortunately only part of the problem in this context. Deeper doctrinal and constitutional uncertainties affect the analysis of embodied expression. The Supreme Court, as noted, has contributed to the notion that embodied expression is generally dangerous to the public. Far more troubling, however, is the extent to which the abortion clinic trilogy, and the *Hill* case in particular, are in considerable tension with a number of long-standing First Amendment principles and doctrines relating to embodied appeals. That tension may affect prospects for embodied expression across the expressive topography. The critique that follows is not meant to deny the psychological vulnerability of abortion clinic patrons. The concerns at this point are more general; they relate to future applications of the principles established in this particular context. Bad cases, as the saying goes, can make bad law.

There is, first, a substantial question regarding the supposed "neutrality" of the enactment in *Hill*, which regulated only expression near abortion clinics and only "oral protest, education, or counseling" in such places. This seemed, as Justice Kennedy forcefully argued in dissent, a "textbook example" of a law targeting expressive content.[83] Here as elsewhere on the expressive topography, place is simply not

---

[83] *Hill*, 530 U.S. at 766 (Kennedy, J., dissenting).

as "neutral" as the Court's ordinary time, place, and manner analysis suggests. By buffering and protecting clinics and clinic patrons in this fashion, the legislature was indeed disfavoring a particular message. Whether other officials will be permitted to do the same, with the same level of judicial deference, will now depend on whether courts can distinguish the law upheld in *Hill*.

The abortion trilogy undervalued place and embodied expression in more general terms. The "buffers" and "bubbles" were established in "quintessential" public forums – streets and sidewalks – where expressive rights are supposed to be at their zenith. In terms of proximity and immediacy, the sidewalks near abortion clinics are critical places. The act which is being opposed – abortion – is one that is clearly imminent. If the counselors' message is to be even minimally effective, it must be received in these places. As Justice Kennedy stated in dissent: "It is the location where the Court should expend its utmost effort to vindicate free speech, not to burden or suppress it."[84] As even the majority seemed to acknowledge, "buffers" and "bubbles" limit speakers' rights to engage in even the most fundamental and traditional embodied expressive activities like leafleting or pamphleteering. The *Hill* Court naively suggested that since speakers were only prohibited from *approaching* patrons, they could still distribute literature and speak to any patron who happened to come near them. This ignores both the sociology of close communication, which shows that the natural inclination is to maintain spatial separation from strangers, and the reality of embodied expression – which depends upon making receipt of public messages as simple and easy as possible.

Finally, the Supreme Court's apparent recognition of a public "right to be let alone" is in tension with literally decades of First Amendment jurisprudence. Indeed, prior to *Hill* no such right or interest had ever been recognized. This new right to public privacy now "lies about like a loaded weapon."[85] Indeed, some courts have already applied or alluded to *Hill*'s notion of public privacy in sustaining restrictions on expression near places other than abortion clinics – at busy public intersections, on highways near homes, on subways, in public library lobbies, and at public monuments.[86] If allowed to expand, this creeping captivity principle will

---

[84] *Id.* at 789.
[85] Korematsu v. United States, 323 U.S. 214, 246 (1944) (Jackson, J., dissenting).
[86] *See* Frye v. Kan. City Police Dep't, 375 F.3d 785 (8th Cir. 2004) (upholding restrictions on display of aborted fetus signs at a busy intersection); Texas v. Knights of the Ku Klux Klan, 58 F.3d 1075 (5th Cir. 1995) (rejecting a Klan application to participate in the "adopt-a-highway" program); ACLU v. Mineta, 319 F. Supp. 2d 69 (D.D.C. 2004) (limiting advertisements in subway system); Gay Guardian Newspaper v. Ohoopee Reg'l Library Sys., 235 F. Supp. 2d 1362 (S.D. Ga. 2002) (involving a free literature table in library lobby);

substantially limit opportunities for interpersonal communication in public places across the expressive topography.

As noted earlier, First Amendment uncertainty also continues to encourage efforts to prohibit or severely restrict public begging or panhandling. It is hoped that the Supreme Court will one day expressly hold that public begging is protected expression; indeed the proliferation of ever more restrictive homelessness policies may eventually force its hand. Even if it does not do so, lower courts should themselves recognize the expressive aspect of this embodied appeal. Beggars, perhaps more than any other group of public speakers, are the rightful constitutional beneficiaries of early gains by the Jehovah's Witnesses.

On the merits, the legal scholars Hershkoff and Cohen have advanced perhaps the most convincing arguments for full First Amendment protection of peaceful public begging.[87] They defend peaceful panhandling under First Amendment enlightenment, self-government, and self-realization theories or principles. The authors argue that begging conveys information to society about poverty and the lives of the poor, influences governance decisions regarding subsistence measures, and contributes to the beggars' self-realization by allowing them to express that they are destitute and in need of assistance. As well, with regard specifically to the First Amendment values of embodied place and proximate expression, Hershkoff and Cohen argue that begging has a "relational aspect" that assists the poor in making identity claims and breaking down the wall between the marginalized and the rest of society.[88]

Still, of the many forms of uncomfortable and offensive public expression that occur in public places each day, it is primarily the appeals of the destitute that are subjected to systematic regulation and prohibition. If, as the Supreme Court has held, dancing topless and burning a flag are presumptively expressive, then surely verbally asking for assistance in a public place must be protected speech. Putting aside more intrusive and harassing forms of "aggressive" panhandling, public begging ought to receive First Amendment protection.

Of course, allowing these and other speakers access to the personal spaces of public audiences will upset certain sensibilities. This has led to some broad proposals to literally codify separation in public places. The legal scholar Robert Ellickson once proposed that we regulate what he

---

Wash. Tour Guides Ass'n v. Nat'l Park Serv., 808 F. Supp. 877 (D.D.C. 1992) (upholding regulation of solicitation at national monuments).
[87] Hershkoff & Cohen, *supra* note 25 at 898–904.
[88] *Id.* at 910–16.

called "chronic" panhandling (and other "chronic" public behaviors by
the destitute like bench squatting) by *zoning* public spaces for certain
behaviors.[89] Treating public space as a commons, Ellickson noted that
such behaviors often discourage other citizens from using public places.
Ellickson's proposal goes to the heart of the issues in this chapter – indeed
in the book as a whole. For if officials were free to literally zone embodied
appeals out of public space entirely, who doubts but that they would do
so? Indeed, have they not already started down this path?

Ellickson proposed that municipal communities establish red, yellow,
and green "zones" in which different types of public behavior (and
expression) would be permitted. Red zones would be small areas (roughly
5% of city space) where what Ellickson called "rowdy" street behavior
would be tolerated. In large yellow zones (90% of the urban landscape),
communities would enforce rules such that the majority of the citizens
would feel "comfortable" using the space. Chronic (although not episodic) panhandling would be flatly prohibited there. Finally, green zones
would be "places of refuge for the unusually sensitive: the frail elderly,
parents with toddlers, unaccompanied grade school children, bench sitters reading poetry."[90] In green zones, very little, if any, activity by the
homeless – expressive or otherwise – would be allowed.

Although Ellickson himself billed this scheme as a mental experiment,
it actually accurately describes vast portions of the expressive topography.
Embodied expression, whatever the claim or message, is indeed now
viewed as something of a "chronic nuisance" by many public officials and
perhaps most of the public. The problem with a zoning scheme that
prefers "bench sitters reading poetry" to beggars and other embodied
speakers is rather obvious: It ignores both the expressive values and
democratic functions associated with public places in general and personal space in particular.[91] Placing those who rely upon begging, or
solicitation, or proselytizing into small red zones effectively denies these
speakers access to any meaningful public audience.[92] Allowing them
into yellow spaces only insofar as their behavior does not make anyone
else "uncomfortable" flouts fundamental premises of First Amendment
theory and jurisprudence regarding the value of "robust" and often

---

[89] Robert Ellickson, "Controlling Chroninc Misconduct in City Spaces: Of Panhandlers, Skid
Rows, and Public Space Zoning," 105 *Yale L. J.* 1165 (1996).
[90] *Id.* at 1221.
[91] *See* Mitchell, supra note 30 at 211–218 (critiquing Ellickson on social justice grounds).
[92] For a critique of Ellickson's proposal from liberal, romantic, and democratic perspectives, *see*
Kohn, *supra* note 40 at 172–84.

uncomfortable exchanges. As Justice Douglas, writing for the Court, once said: "[Speech] may indeed best serve its high purpose when it induces a condition of unrest, creates dissatisfaction with conditions as they are, or even stirs people to anger."[93] If embodied expression is to be preserved and robustly protected, this is a lesson that must be re-learned – by the public, courts, and our public officials.

---

[93] Terminiello v. Chicago, 337 U.S. 1, 4 (1949).

4   CONTESTED PLACES

Speakers often rely upon access to specific places to facilitate, amplify, and convey particular messages. We shall call these *contested* places. Sites of contest and exchange have existed from the very first assemblies of the "people out of doors." The nature and identity of contested places typically highlight the significant social and political issues of particular eras. Over time, sites of contest have shifted from the private homes of prominent individuals in the precolonial era, to jails, courthouses and lunch counters in the Civil Rights Era, to abortion clinics and, most recently, cemeteries in more contemporary eras. In this fashion and others, the expressive topography is inscribed with cycles of political and social contention.

Owing to the variety of critical functions these places serve in terms of public liberties, access to contested places is highly sought after. Contested places are perhaps the most potent venues on the expressive topography. They provide access to general and specific audiences, are often inextricably tied to the content of speakers' messages, and are often powerfully symbolic of the social or political contest itself. Today, expressive zoning, certain types of public policing, and a variety of other restrictions on access to contested places substantially inhibit the conveyance of place-specific viewpoints. The assumption, generally although not uniformly accepted by courts, is that speakers' rights are adequately preserved so long as they can speak *someplace*. That assumption ignores the considerable expressive power of contested places. Simply put, places are not fungible. Although no one has a right to demand access to a public place regardless of circumstances, the Supreme Court observed long ago that "[one] is not to have the exercise of his liberty of expression in appropriate places abridged on the plea that it may be exercised in some other place."[1]

---

[1] Schneider v. State, 308 U.S. 147, 163 (1939) (emphasis added).

ANTECEDENTS – "OBVIOUS CENTERS OF PROTEST"

As noted in Chapter 2, on the early expressive topography public contention was often directed at discrete private places. In the eighteenth and nineteenth centuries, the people assembled in public areas and then proceeded to focus their collective ire on the private home or business property of public officers and other alleged miscreants. These, in effect, were the first contested places. Access to these places was not constrained by either legal rules or public policing, neither of which yet existed. The "mob" itself largely determined the limits of public contention. During this early era, the state was still in its infancy. As states developed and became more powerful, the people gradually shifted the focus of contention to the state itself and to more public venues and places including the streets.[2]

Gradually, public properties – statehouses, capitols, courts, and other symbolic places – became sites of political contest and exchange (Figure 4.1). In the modern era, repertoires of contention focusing on place were perhaps most prominent during the Civil Rights Era. Not all of the action was in or about the streets. Racial segregation was an extensive and distinctly *spatial* regime that expressly separated people by place – separate restrooms, separate dining facilities, segregated courthouses.[3] To contest this racial-spatial segregation, protesters sought access to legally and culturally forbidden public and private places. Place was often used to reach and affect specific audiences such as lawmakers, jailors, or judges. "Unauthorized" spatial presence was also used as a repertoire of contention owing to its symbolic connection to messages of equality. In many instances, of course, protesters hoped that by contesting places they would generate wider public and media attention. In addition to images of police brutality in public streets, spatial contests succeeded in riveting local and more general audiences.

In several cases during the Civil Rights Era, the Supreme Court implicitly recognized the expressive significance of access to contested places. For example, in 1966 the Court reversed the convictions of five young African-American men who staged a silent protest of a public library's "whites only" policy in the library's reading room.[4] The protesters chose this particular place not because it offered access to a

---

[2] *See* Sidney Tarrow, *Power in Movement* 29–32 (2d ed. 1998); Charles Tilly, *Social Movements, 1768–2004* (2004).
[3] David Delaney, *Race, Place and the Law, 1836–1948* (1998).
[4] Brown v. Louisiana, 383 U.S. 131 (1966).

Figure 4.1. Civil Rights Marchers at the Lincoln Memorial (August 1963).
Source: National Archives and Records Administration.

public audience, but because it effectively symbolized the objected-to public apartheid. Although four dissenting justices were aghast that the Court had granted protesters the right to use public property "as a stage to express dissident ideas," the majority noted that the protesters had not interfered in any way with the ordinary functions of the library. Their protest, the Court observed, was "compatible" with the contested place they had chosen.

Protesters' rights of access to targeted audiences near highly symbolic places of governance were also affirmed. In one case, the Court reversed the breach of peace convictions of 187 black students who assembled near the South Carolina State House to protest laws establishing racial segregation.[5] In another, more than 2,000 students engaged in a peaceful march near a public courthouse to protest the arrest of 23 students being held inside. The Court invalidated the convictions of several participants in the march under

---

[5] Edwards v. South Carolina, 372 U.S. 229 (1963).

a Louisiana law prohibiting all "pickets or parades in or near a building housing a court of the State of Louisiana."[6] The Court also overturned the convictions of 85 demonstrators who had gathered peacefully in front of the Chicago mayor's residence to urge desegregation of the public schools.[7]

These precedents were critical to the civil rights movement. Access was permitted to contested places even though it caused some public disruption and a violent audience reaction seemed under the circumstances to be a real possibility. Police officers were denied the authority to disperse the crowds or remove them from the vicinity of contested places based solely on the *possibility* that a disturbance might result. Indeed the Court appeared to establish, without ever expressly saying so, that police had an obligation to preserve the speakers' rights to expression in these and other public places – even in the face of "hostile" audiences.

Although access to contested places was allowed in many cases, civil rights protesters were sometimes denied their choice of place. In a sharply divided decision, for example, the Court upheld the convictions of 32 university student protesters who stood near a county jail to peacefully protest the arrest (for trying to integrate public theatres) of their classmates.[8] The Court emphasized that protestors did not have a constitutional right to convey their message "whenever and however and wherever they please."[9] Justice Black, one of the dissenters who had objected in the public library case to the idea that public places could be used as "stages" for dissent, wrote an opinion stressing that the driveway the students had been standing on was reserved for official jail business. In a statement inconsistent with the substance and tenor of many opinions of the era, he added: "The State, no less than a private owner of property, has power to preserve the property under its control for the use to which it was lawfully dedicated."[10] Thus, even during the Civil Rights Era, the conception of place-as-property sometimes influenced the Court.

In sharp contrast, the dissenters saw this as a case involving marginalized and powerless interests strategically using place to convey a message of protest to public officials – in a location that was central to their message. Justice Douglas wrote:

> The Court errs in treating this case as if it were an ordinary trespass case or an ordinary picketing case. The jailhouse, like an executive

---

[6] Cox v. Louisiana, 379 U.S. 536 (1965).
[7] Gregory v. Chicago, 394 U.S. 111 (1969).
[8] Adderley v. Florida, 385 U.S. 39 (1966).
[9] *Id.* at 48.
[10] *Id.* at 47.

mansion, a legislative chamber, a courthouse, or the statehouse itself is one of the seats of government, whether it be the Tower of London, the Bastille, or a small county jail. And when it houses political prisoners or those whom many think are unjustly held, it is *an obvious center of protest*.[11]

According to Justice Douglas, the students' activity was an exercise of a fundamental public liberty – the right to petition government for a redress of grievances. This was not a right, he said, that could be extinguished by the state through its status as "owner" of the jailhouse.

As noted in Chapter 2, places of *private* segregation were also successfully contested by civil rights protesters. In a series of sharply divided decisions, the Supreme Court refused to allow private lunch counter owners to eject patrons on the basis of their race.[12] Given their sharp divisions, these cases did not establish any broad right of access to private contested places. It was sufficient for the cause of civil rights that owners were not permitted to oust the protesters under local trespass laws. Photographs of protesters sitting peacefully, but defiantly, at lunch counters and in other public accommodations produced some of the most powerful imagery of the Civil Rights Era (Figure 4.2).

The contested place decisions of the Civil Rights Era embraced two general, and seemingly conflicting, propositions concerning access to public places. On the one hand, it seemed that so long as expression was basically "compatible" with the place in question it was to be permitted. On the other hand, although it expanded space for public contention the Court did not go so far as to say that speakers were entitled to choose the location of a public contest. Indeed, Justice Black seemed to endorse the contrary proposition in the jail case, when he said government had the same right as a private property owner to exclude speakers from contested places. As the 1960s came to a close, it was apparent that the Court's "public forum" doctrine was in some disarray. As Chapter 2 explained, these tensions would be addressed and to some extent resolved in later decisions.

In general, however, during the Civil Rights Era the Supreme Court appeared to recognize the intersection between speakers' messages of equality and the specific places they had chosen to contest. The public library, statehouse, courthouse, mayoral residence, and lunch counter were all potent symbols of racism, segregation, and oppression. Some of these places also housed audiences – lawmakers, judges, and executive

---

[11] *Id.* at 49 (Douglas, J., dissenting) (emphasis added).
[12] Lombard v. Louisiana, 373 U.S. 267 (1963); Bell v. Maryland, 378 U.S. 226 (1964).

Figure 4.2. Sit-In at a Woolworth's Lunch Counter (1960).
Source: Library of Congress, *New York World-Telegram* and the *Sun Newspaper*
Photograph Collection.

officials – speakers critically needed to reach. Access to these "obvious centers of protest" helped shape the debate in America regarding segregation and civil rights.

PLACES OF CONTEST, EXPRESSION, AND EXCHANGE

Although social scientists have often engaged place in descriptive terms, for instance in studies of social movements and public politics, they have not generally considered speakers' strategic choice of place to be a subject worthy of independent study.[13] Yet as the civil rights spatial contests show, social movements do not rely upon mass displays alone; rather, they *diversify* their spatial presence by contesting a variety of local places. That diversification can tell us something about the social movement itself and about the condition of the expressive topography.

[13] *See* William Sewell, "Space in Contentious Politics," in Aminzade, McAdam, Perry, Sewell, Tarrow, & Tilly, eds., *Silence and Voice in the Study of Contentious Politics* 51 (2001) (noting that "most studies bring in spatial considerations only episodically, when they seem important either for adequate description of contentious political events or for explaining why particular events occurred or unfolded as they did").

Contested places on the expressive topography have been a critical aspect of the nation's public politics – both before and after the Civil Rights Era. This remains true today, although as we shall see the sites of contest have changed. To better understand how and why particular places remain so important to public contention we must first examine more closely the various expressive functions served by contested places.

Choice of Place and Expressive Functions

Contested places are often chosen strategically to serve several distinct expressive functions. First, location or place may provide access to a particular audience. As some of the civil rights examples show, government buildings where targeted public officials work often serve this function. Second, the place itself may be significant to the content of the speaker's message. Protest at an abortion clinic, for example, is more effective for the pro-life activist than protest in a public park. Places facilitate and enhance messages by providing visual, tangible, and symbolic context "on location." Simply put, the "visual" is often an important part of the message. Third, as the segregated public facilities during the Civil Rights Era show, a chosen place may be symbolic of the very object of protest. Contesting place can thus bring wider attention to issues of public concern, through the power of location and media coverage of the spatial contest. When speakers seek access to "contested" places, they are typically pursuing one or more of these primary expressive functions. In addition, they may also choose particular places for ceremonial and "topophilic" reasons – as locales that engender solidarity with others or evoke emotional bonds and reactions.

Speakers naturally seek access to places on the expressive topography where specific target audiences can be found within eyesight and earshot. They go there to confront, cajole, and even sometimes to harass the intended audience. For example, for weeks during the summer of 2005 Cindy Sheehan stood on a public road not far from President Bush's "Summer White House" in Crawford, Texas. Sheehan chose a place where the President could not readily avoid her message. She sought to petition the President – to ask, in a proximate and public venue, why her son had given his life in the Iraq War. Sheehan never received an audience with President Bush. Tellingly, when she (and the media) left Crawford, local officials promptly enacted a ban on *all* roadside gatherings.

As noted, contested places can also be expressive in the sense that they relate intimately to and thus facilitate and amplify speakers' messages. The Supreme Court has recognized that place can profoundly affect speakers' messages in this sense. In *City of Ladue v. Gilleo*, the Court invalidated a law that banned the display of signs from residences.[14] Acknowledging the unique importance of message placement, the Court stated:

> Displaying a sign from one's own residence often carries a message quite distinct from placing the same sign someplace else, or conveying the same text or picture by other means. . . . A sign advocating 'Peace in the Gulf' in the front lawn of a retired general or decorated war veteran may provoke a different reaction than the same sign in a 10-year-old child's bedroom window or the same message on a bumper sticker of a passing automobile. An espousal of socialism may carry different implications when displayed on the grounds of a stately mansion than when pasted on a factory wall or an ambulatory sandwich board.[15]

Examples of this use of place abound. In 2006, for example, a group of eighteen elderly women who later became known as the "Granny Peace Brigade" (Figure 4.3) stood outside the Armed Forces Recruitment Center in New York City's Times Square. The Grannies sought to register their objection to the war by staging a protest near the recruitment center itself. The women, some of whom moved only with the assistance of canes and walkers, were arrested, tried, and ultimately acquitted of breaching the public peace. The judge found it highly implausible that the Grannies had physically blocked access to the recruitment center, as authorities had alleged. Although they avoided imprisonment, the Grannies' arrest effectively terminated the contest.

Finally, access to a contested place is sometimes sought owing to the connection between that particular place and a pressing matter of public concern. As the political scientist William Sewell has noted: "The meanings of places are crucially important to contentious politics both as contexts and as stakes. Sometimes the normative meanings and uses of places are themselves a significant focus of social movement activity."[16] Places may effectively and sometimes powerfully symbolize a range of ideas – power (the White House); loss or grief (Ground Zero); equality

---

[14] 512 U.S. 43 (1994).
[15] *Id.* at 56.
[16] *See* Sewell, *supra* note 13 at 51–88.

Figure 4.3. Members of the Granny Peace Brigade.
Source: Photograph by Clementine Choubrac.

(the Lincoln Memorial); or militarization (the Pentagon). A particular social or political contest may *inhere* in a place – it may "express" that contest without words. For example, Cindy Sheehan's use of the public roads in Crawford, Texas raised awareness not only of her own petition but of substantial public objection to the Iraq war itself. Her targeted vigil near the Summer White House, which was ultimately joined by hundreds of sympathetic protesters, celebrities, and counter-protesters, highlighted public dissent and frustration far more effectively than had countless other larger public displays in public streets and parks.

In sum, just as proximity to *audience* is often important to the speaker, so too is proximity to a certain *place* often critical to public expression. Here, as elsewhere on the expressive topography, place intersects with expression in several distinct ways. Pragmatically, speakers contest places to secure access to audiences. But beyond this critical function, contested places also facilitate message conveyance and can be highly and powerfully symbolic.

Places of Last Resort

Contesting place is a deeply rooted tradition of public protest and petition in this country. In addition to the iconic civil rights examples, in the 1960s and 1970s Vietnam War protesters targeted not only the Capitol and the White House but the Pentagon and other places that symbolized the nation's militarization. During the same period, college and university students commandeered administrative buildings. In the 1980s, students erected shantytowns near administrative offices as a protest of South African apartheid. Preserving access to contested places on the expressive topography is critical both to the preservation of breathing space for speech out of doors and the future of public democracy.

To fully appreciate the importance of contested places to public contention and politics, however, we must view the expressive topography as an interconnected *system* of places. Indeed, one of the principal weaknesses of First Amendment doctrines and analyses of place is that they tend to treat places as isolated locations rather than part of an expressive topography. An accurate accounting of the First Amendment and democratic values of contested places must consider not only the specific contested place itself, but its relation to the remainder of the topography. Thus, familiarity with the conditions on the balance of the expressive topography may help us understand speakers' contemporary choices regarding which places to contest.

Owing to trends and phenomena such as citizen mobility, spatial privatization, public planning, and various legal restrictions on public assembly and expression, contested places have become ever more critical to public contention. As discussed in Chapter 2, a variety of forces and events have generally reduced both the space for public contention and the accessibility of public audiences. Thus, for example, people no longer occupy town squares in great numbers. Moreover, most urban and suburban spaces do not facilitate chance encounters or audience accessibility. As discussed in the next chapter, speakers are not generally permitted access to places of modernity like malls and airport terminals. Unable in many cases to reach audiences that spend increasing amounts of time in their cars, in speech-free transportation and commercial hubs, and in private places, speakers may naturally resort to more targeted contention. In some instances, speakers may be choosing their spatial targets out of a sense of desperation. For at least some speakers and causes, a contested place may in fact be a *place of last resort*.

Of course, the First Amendment does not guarantee any speaker the right to access and occupy any place she happens to consider critical to or symbolic of her message. Protesters cannot insist, for example, upon taking their political contests inside nuclear sites or into the hallways of the Pentagon. Neither, however, should officials or courts unthinkingly deny access to specific places based upon the supposition that speakers can always speak in some other place. Increasingly, that supposition may simply be false.

CONTEMPORARY PLACES OF CONTEST AND EXCHANGE

Today's centers of protest are often not "obvious" at all. Places of contest and exchange are scattered across the contemporary expressive topography. As we shall see, the most hotly contested *issues* include abortion, war, militarization, homelessness, and environmental preservation. Fully aware of the power of specific places to facilitate audience accessibility and attention, amplify these and other messages, and symbolize contests, the people continue to rely upon localized forms of spatial contention. Contemporary activists have adopted many of the spatial repertoires of the civil rights movement, including demonstrations, blockades, and sit-ins at various places.

In fact, localized spatial contests appear to be proliferating. In the past few decades, a remarkable variety of specific places on the expressive topography have been sites of public expression and contention. Contemporary contests have focused on a range of places: abortion clinics, official residences, private residences, court buildings, churches, military academies, national forest lands, businesses, ports, military installations, national political conventions, national parks, and even cemeteries. Some of these contests have targeted state policies, properties, or officials. In others, however, today's public speakers, adopting a repertoire from the colonial era, have contested *private* places connected in some fashion to issues of general public concern. In some instances, places have been chosen for audience accessibility; in others place has informed and amplified particular messages; and in still others contested places have served ceremonial or "topophilic" functions.

There are a number of possible explanations for this diverse and active spatial contestation. As always, there are deep cultural and political divisions on issues of public concern in this country. People involved and invested in such divisions continue to seek public outlets for contention and exchange. Assembling with others near a contested site is one such outlet – in some cases, as noted earlier, it may be the *only* viable public outlet for certain speakers. This reality has taken speakers, as we shall see, to places like abortion clinics and residential neighborhoods.

Sometimes speakers who do in fact have other options decide that a localized spatial contest is the best available repertoire for airing a matter of public concern. Mass events that focus on the state may actually be far less effective. As discussed in Chapter 6, mass protests and demonstrations have become rather predictable, institutionalized events. Political sociologists and scientists have noted that the various controls placed upon such public events, including permit requirements, advance negotiation with police regarding location and other details, and restrictions on movement have rendered many protests and demonstrations ineffective repertoires of public contention. In light of the expressive functions of contested places, a more localized protest might be considered a more effective option. Such a display, moreover, does not require mass numbers, complex negotiation, or detailed organization.

Another explanation for continuing spatial contestation might be that public contention itself has fallen prey to media and more general communicative saturation. In the mainstream media, *controversy* tends to attract airtime and coverage. Public speakers may (rightly) calculate that one way to raise public consciousness is to engage in contentious displays at key locales. This may explain, for example, why two men recently chained themselves to the front door of a Victoria's Secret store on Manhattan's Upper West Side as a protest of the company's use of nonrecycled paper. Before dismissing this sort of display as a frivolous appeal for public attention, one should consider two things: First, the protest garnered substantial media attention and, second, after witnessing the display at least some of the bystanders were reported to have misgivings about patronizing the store.

Finally, as we shall see in certain instances public frustration with increasingly inaccessible or inattentive public officials has led to targeted spatial contests. Thus, when officials refuse to answer the public's letters and other appeals, the people may seek them out at official or private residences. Similarly, when the vice president refuses to appear willingly before dissenting citizens, they may try to petition him at events such as the West Point commencement ceremony. And when President Bush fails to publicly and adequately explain to families of lost soldiers the reasons for the invasion of Iraq, citizens assemble on the roadside near his home seeking a public reckoning. As during the Civil Rights Era, citizens' political frustrations account for many of our most notable contemporary spatial contests.

Of course, one cannot discount the possibility that some spatial contests may in fact merely be publicity stunts or frivolous appeals for public attention. Some undoubtedly are just that. This does not mean, however, that the displays are not entitled to First Amendment protection. In any event, most public spatial contests do not seem to meet this description. Contesting place requires a serious commitment of time and resources.

Moreover, as the "Grannies" and other public speakers have discovered, it may even result in arrest and prosecution.

CONTEMPORARY RESTRICTIONS ON TARGETED SPATIAL CONTENTION

For those who are serious about contesting place, or who may substantially rely upon it to convey a particular message, there are many contemporary challenges to this form of public expression and contention. By the early 1980s, the legal and physical landscape posed several distinct challenges to people wishing to contest place. As noted in Chapter 2, within the governing First Amendment framework, government officials gained considerable discretion to restrict public contention generally and access to contested places in particular. By far the most common contemporary tactic used by governments to keep speakers at some distance from contested places is *expressive zoning*. Speech-free "buffer zones" have been established at numerous potential places of contest and exchange. In addition, permit schemes and more informal "institutional free speech policies" impose more general limits or bans on access to contested places. General public order laws such as prohibitions on traffic obstruction and breach of peace may also be used to separate speakers from targeted places. Finally, modifications of public spaces and architectures, particularly after September 11, 2001, have imposed some additional limits on access to contested places.

The Legal Transformation of the Expressive Topography

In hindsight, the Civil Rights Era was probably a high water mark in terms of access to contested places. During the 1970s and 1980s, changes to the two principal doctrines of place – public forum and time, place, and manner – generally expanded the authority of officials to regulate access to public places and to displace speakers. As we shall see, these changes particularly disadvantaged speakers who rely on spatial contestation.

During this transition period, the Supreme Court did decide a handful of spatial contest cases. It held that noisy demonstrations near public school buildings could be banned while classes were in session.[17] The

---

[17] Grayned v. Rockford, 408 U.S. 104 (1972).

Court also invalidated a federal law that barred all public displays outside the Supreme Court building itself, as well as a District of Columbia law barring displays "critical" of foreign governments within 500 feet of any foreign embassy.[18]

These were not particularly challenging cases. Students can hardly be expected to learn where protesters are allowed to assemble outside their classrooms during instructional hours. Fundamentally, this sort of contest is not "compatible" with the place at issue. The federal law barring public displays outside the Supreme Court imposed an *absolute ban* on expression in "traditional" public forums like sidewalks. And the District law expressly discriminated against messages "critical" of government. In short, these contested place cases could be resolved by applying long-settled First Amendment principles.

The transformation of the expressive topography, particularly with regard to contested places, was effected by more general means. As discussed in Chapter 2, by the early 1990s the Supreme Court had (1) abandoned the "compatibility" standard under which many civil rights protesters had gained access to contested places; (2) breathed new life into the principle that "[t]he State, no less than a private owner of property, has power to preserve the property under its control for the use to which it was lawfully dedicated";[19] (3) established a rigid categorization of places under the "public forum" doctrine; and (4) signaled that courts should give broad deference to time, place, and manner restrictions. Officials have taken extensive advantage of these fundamental transformations to regulate and restrict a variety of spatial contests.

Expressive Zoning

Expressive zoning – the act of restricting First Amendment activities to specific places or within certain boundaries – has been present on the expressive topography at least since the IWW "free speech fights" of the early twentieth century (*see* Chapter 2). In Chapter 7, we will see how this tactic has been used at critical democratic moments like national party conventions. In Chapter 8, we will examine expressive zoning on

---

[18] United States v. Grace, 461 U.S. 171 (1983); Boos v. Barry, 485 U.S. 312 (1988). In *Boos*, the Court held that the statute was content-based and not sufficiently tailored to survive judicial scrutiny. The Court left in place, however, a prohibition on congregations of three or more persons within the restricted zone, which could be enforced if police believed the assembly posed a threat to the safety or normal functioning of the embassy.
[19] *Adderly*, 385 U.S. at 47.

university and college campuses. Today, expressive zoning is one of the most common tactics for regulating public expression and public contention across the expressive topography.

Expressive zoning has had a particularly substantial impact on speakers who wish to contest specific places. It has been deployed to protect certain places – and, more specifically, the targeted audiences in these places – from public dissent and contention. The discussion here focuses on expressive zoning at some notable but representative contested places – abortion clinics, residences, and cemeteries. In this section I will describe in general terms the manner in which expressive zoning has been used at these contested places. Critical analysis of these spatial restrictions will follow later, in the prescriptive part of the chapter.

Abortion Clinic "Buffer Zones"

As discussed in the preceding chapter, in the 1980s and 1990s pro-life activists and protesters appeared at abortion clinics to contest what they considered to be the taking of human life there. In terms of expressive functions, clinics are both pragmatically useful, given the audience protesters seek to reach, and important to conveyance and amplification of the speakers' message. Some protesters used peaceful repertoires of contention, like sit-ins and blockades, which were borrowed from the civil rights movement. As political sociologists have observed, these repertoires are "modular," meaning that they are used across social, historical, and political contexts.[20]

But as noted in the previous chapter, some protesters and "sidewalk counselors" also resorted to violence, including assaults and property damage, in an effort to close down the clinics. The government's primary response to this violence and disruption was to erect very precise "buffer zones" around clinic properties and clinic staff residences. This was done, according to officials, to preserve women's access to health care services and to protect clinic personnel.

Expressive zoning is a much more sophisticated, orderly, and peaceful means of shielding places and audiences from conflict than the force and violence sometimes used by police in the 1960s and 1970s. But drawing buffer zone lines is a rather tricky endeavor, especially given the expressive functions typically served by contested places. Obviously, ingress and egress to places must be preserved. But to realize the expressive functions of these places, speakers need to be both near enough to the place itself to

---

[20] Tarrow, *supra* note 2 at 97.

Figure 4.4. Planned Parenthood Prayer and Protest, St. Louis, Missouri (January 2008) (Planned Parenthood Building Pictured Beyond the Gate). *Source*: Photograph by Kevin Dern.

connect it to their cause and close enough to target audiences to convey their message. The dimensions of many buffer zones, when combined with the local topography, do not always permit speakers to effectively contest abortion clinics (Figure 4.4).

In two cases in the 1990s, the Supreme Court upheld abortion clinic buffer zones of 36 and 15 feet.[21] In *Madsen v. Women's Health Center* (1994), the Court upheld injunctive restrictions against demonstrating within 36 feet of the clinic (to the extent that the 36-foot buffer did not include private property), making loud noises within earshot of the clinic, and making loud noises within 300 feet of an employee's residence. The Court rejected injunctive provisions banning the display of images, approaching patients within 300 feet of the clinic, and peacefully picketing within 300 feet of an employee's residence. In *Schenck v. Pro-Choice Network of Western New York* (1997), the Court upheld another injunction, this one prohibiting demonstrators from speaking within 15 feet of clinic entrances. Jurisdictions across the United States have generally adopted zones closer to the more expansive limits approved by the Court in *Madsen*. Massachusetts, for example, recently expanded its statutory "buffer zone" from 18 feet to 35 feet.

As of the early 1990s, expressive zoning began to appear with some regularity across the expressive topography. The abortion clinic decisions suggested to officials that they could legitimately limit the contesting

---

[21] Madsen v. Women's Health Center, Inc., 512 U.S. 753 (1994); Schenck v. Pro-Choice Network of Western New York, 519 U.S. 357 (1997).

of place, thereby quelling public outbreaks of social and political contention, by simply drawing spatial boundaries around clinics and other
contested places. As we shall see, "buffer zones" have since appeared in
many other locations on the expressive topography.

Residential Privacy Zones

As abortion clinic protests show, speakers sometimes seek access to
audiences in places where messages are guaranteed to reach their targets
and cannot be easily avoided. The residence has become a rather frequently targeted contested place.[22] During recent years, antiabortion,
animal rights, gun control, civil rights, and other activists have focused
contests over matters of public concern on both private and official residences. Contesting residences has raised new concerns regarding individual privacy and repose, and has engendered some new limits on public
expression and contention.

Protests at or near individual residences are another "modular" repertoire of contention. One can actually trace such displays as far back as
the eighteenth century, when people directed their ire at the individual
household of public officials and other alleged miscreants. In the 1960s,
civil rights protestors also frequently picketed the residences of public
officials.[23] As noted earlier, in one Civil Rights Era case the Supreme
Court upheld the right of protesters to engage in peaceful demonstrations
against municipal segregation policies outside the home of Chicago's
mayor.

Residences can serve all of the primary expressive functions of contested
places. Most obviously, contests relating to residences focus on a particular
target audience – the occupant of the home. Spatial contests that focus on
residences also amplify protesters' messages; they facilitate message conveyance through assembly "on location" and in some cases enhanced
media coverage. Official residences sometimes serve to more generally
symbolize matters of public concern. Even *private* residences might serve
this function as to particular issues and within particular communities.

Contests focused on residences pit speakers' First Amendment
interests in access to place against homeowners' interests in privacy and
repose. The Supreme Court most recently addressed this conflict in
Frisby v. Schultz (1988).[24] In *Frisby*, assemblies in a small community

---

[22] *See* Hazel A. Landwehr, "Unfriendly Persuasion: Enjoining Residential Picketing," 43 *Duke L. J.* 148 (1993).
[23] Note, "Picketing the Homes of Public Officials," 34 *U. Chi. L. Rev.* 106 (1966).
[24] 487 U.S. 474 (1988).

outside Milwaukee ranging from 11 to 40 people picketed the residence of a physician who performed abortions. The demonstrators shouted slogans and on occasion trespassed onto the physician's property. The Court upheld a municipal ordinance, enacted directly in response to this activity, which prohibited picketing "before or about the residence or dwelling of any individual." Although it was broadly worded, the Court interpreted the ordinance as banning only "focused" or "targeted" picketing of a specific residence rather than extending to *all* pickets on the neighborhood's public streets and sidewalks.

The majority opinion in *Schultz* staunchly defended ideals of suburban tranquility and residential privacy, reasoning at one point that "even a solitary picket can invade residential privacy."[25] Suburban homeowners, the Court said, are entitled to protection from focused residential picketing, which the majority opinion frequently referred to as an "offensive" and "disturbing" means of public assembly and expression. The Court downplayed the expressive significance of contesting place. Indeed it was reluctant to recognize any First Amendment interest in access to place not directly associated with communicating with a *public* audience. Thus, the Court distinguished traditional methods of public expression, such as residential leafleting, from focused or targeted picketing on the ground that the former targeted a public audience rather than an individual *place* like the home or a specific audience.[26]

Frisby's holding was limited to the "targeted" form of residential picketing. The Court did not address broader or more systematic legal restrictions on public contention near private or official residences. In particular, it did not address the use of *expressive zoning* as a means of regulating residential picketing. Thus, unlike the abortion clinic cases, *Frisby* did not establish any clear spatial lines or boundaries for other officials or courts to follow.

Nevertheless, based upon the combination of *Frisby* and the abortion clinic "buffer zone" cases, many municipalities and some courts have enacted or imposed residential privacy zones. Some of these residential buffers track the ordinance in *Frisby*, banning picketing "near, about, or

---

[25] *Id.* at 487.

[26] The decision would seem to be in some to tension with Gregory v. Chicago, 394 U.S. 111 (1969). There the Court held that protesters could not be convicted under a disorderly conduct statute for peacefully protesting the mayor's home. *Gregory* might be the product of a unique historical context, one in which breathing space for public contention was generally being expanded to accommodate the civil rights movement. As well, protesters converging on an official residence are engaged in core political speech and are presenting a quintessential petition for governmental redress. Thus, the balance between expressive liberties and interests in public order and privacy might be said to differ substantially in the two contexts.

Figure 4.5. Pasadena, Texas Residential Protest.
Source: Photograph by Bob Price.

adjacent to" a person's residence. Presumably, only "targeted" picketing may constitutionally be prohibited under such ordinances. Other laws and injunctions have established more specific residential privacy zones, in which public picketing and other expressive activity are not permitted. These zones range in size from 50 to as many as 300 feet. In some localities, officials have considered imposing *absolute bans* on protesting near residences.

As in *Frisby*, recent residential privacy zones have typically been enacted in response to specific public events and controversies. Thus, for example, in response to protests by animal rights activists near the homes of university researchers, Salt Lake City recently enacted a ban on all demonstrations within 100 feet of any home. The ordinance was challenged by antipoverty activists, who contended it would ban expression even near the governor's mansion. Where tensions have been particularly high, municipalities have acted on an emergency basis to impose bans on picketing or protesting near residences. The Pasadena, Texas City Council promptly considered such a ban after a well-publicized incident in which a man shot and killed two people who had burglarized a neighbor's home. After gun control and other activists engaged in protests outside the shooter's home, the city council approved a ban on protests near residences (Figure 4.5).

As speakers continue to contest residential places, ordinances and injunctions imposing residential privacy buffer zones will likely

Figure 4.6. Westboro Baptist Church Funeral Protest, Topeka, Kansas (2005).

continue to proliferate. Homeowners are obviously entitled to some degree of privacy and tranquility. But here, as elsewhere on the expressive topography, a *balance* is involved. In fashioning the suburban portion of our expressive topography, legislators and courts must distinct carefully consider not only the privacy and repose of homeowners, but also the distinct expressive functions of residences as contested places.

Funereal Protest Zones

Easily the most challenging – from both moral and First Amendment perspectives – contemporary example of spatial contestation has been the spate of recent public protests near *cemeteries* during military funerals.[27] For the past few years, members of the Westboro Baptist Church, which is composed of a small group of family members based in Kansas, have been picketing and demonstrating near cemeteries across the country. Church members typically stand on the public sidewalks and streets near the funeral procession carrying banners with messages like "Thank God for 9/11" and "Thank God for Dead Soldiers" (Figure 4.6). The church embraces a literal interpretation of the Bible. Its members believe that God strikes down the "wicked." In the funeral protests, the Church seeks to draw a connection between military deaths in the Iraq and Afghanistan Wars and America's supposed "tolerance" of homosexuality.

The Westboro protesters are generally careful to comply with local laws, to remain on the public streets and sidewalks, and to refrain from violence. Following the repertoires of abortion clinic and residential

---

[27] *See* Mathis Rutledge, "A Time to Mourn: Balancing the Right of Free Speech Against the Right of Privacy in Funeral Picketing," 67 *Md. L. Rev.* 295 (2008).

protesters, Westboro's members use the cemeteries as contested places.[28] By assembling "on location," they seek not only to reach a targeted audience but also to generate publicity in order to reach a much larger public audience. By all accounts, the church has been very successful in doing so; prior to the recent cemetery protests few had probably ever heard of the Westboro Baptist Church or been exposed to its message.[29] Today, as a result of media interviews and other attention, most are at least aware of the church's activities.

As in other contexts, the fact that the message in these protests is indescribably offensive does not deprive it of First Amendment protection. A flat ban on this sort of expressive activity, which like the abortion clinic and residential protests occurs in "traditional" public forums like public sidewalks and streets, would not be constitutional. Recognizing as much, officials have enacted time, place, and manner restrictions on these protests. The laws generally seek to shield mourners from these demonstrations through expressive zoning – by establishing buffer zones around cemeteries and imposing certain time and manner restrictions.

In 2006, Congress enacted the "Respect for America's Fallen Heroes Act," which prohibits all public expression within 300 feet of any road or path leading to a federal cemetery, from sixty minutes before until sixty minutes after the funeral ceremony.[30] Since 2005, thirty-eight states and countless localities have enacted funeral protest statutes.[31] Although the specific provisions of these state laws vary, they typically contain some form of "fixed" buffer zone prohibiting "picketing" and other "protest activities" within a certain number of feet of any funeral site.

The sizes of the buffer zones vary. At one extreme, Montana prohibits protests and other expressive activity within 1,500 feet – six city blocks – of any funeral site. South Dakota and Mississippi prohibit public displays within 1,000 feet of a funeral site. Roughly half of the state laws impose a 500-foot restriction on pickets and protests near funeral sites – a buffer roughly equal to one and a half football fields. Ohio's law imposes a 300-foot buffer zone. The Illinois and Utah legislatures have enacted 200-foot buffer zones. Arkansas restricts public pickets and other displays within 150 feet of funeral sites. At the opposite extreme, three states – Maryland,

---

[28] Church members have conveyed the same message at other places, including Walter Reed Army Medical Center.

[29] The Church first gained public notoriety when it protested at the funeral of Matthew Shepard, a homosexual who had been beaten to death in Laramie, Wyoming.

[30] 38 U.S.C. § 2413 (2006).

[31] See Robert F. McCarthy, "The Incompatibility of Free Speech and Funerals: A Grayned-Based Approach for Funeral Protest Statutes," 68 *Ohio St. L. J.* 1469, 1486 n. 94 (2007) (citing and discussing state funeral protest statutes).

New York, and Vermont – prohibit picketing and protesting within 100 feet of a funeral site. Some states, like Florida and Missouri, have set no specific spatial limits, instead banning protests *"in front of or about* any location at which a funeral is held."

In addition to fixed buffer zones, about half of the state laws also establish "floating" buffers that ban expressive activity at or near the *processional*, as it moves toward the funeral site. Many of the laws contain prohibitions on "interfering" with a funeral procession. Most of the state laws also contain "grace periods" that limit speech for certain time periods before, during, and after the funeral ceremony. Some laws prohibit specific expressive content, such as the display or communication of "fighting words." Nearly all of the funeral protest measures impose criminal sanctions for violations.

Municipal laws also vary, but they too typically impose "fixed" and "floating" buffer zones. Clay County, Tennessee's ordinance is one of the most restrictive in the nation. The ordinance bars demonstrations within *5,000 feet* of any funeral service. In one instance, this limited protesters to a place on the outskirts of town and near the county sanitation department. The Clay County ordinance also requires that demonstrators obtain a permit from the mayor and protest only in approved areas. Most of the city and county ordinances are less restrictive; they employ place and time restrictions similar to those in the federal and state laws discussed above.

Courts have just begun to address the constitutionality of these measures.[32] In September 2006, a federal judge in Kentucky issued a preliminary injunction barring enforcement of that state's law, which prohibits picketing with 300 feet of a funeral site. The court found the law to be "neutral" with regard to the content of any "picket," despite language in the law's preamble suggesting that it was enacted in response to "certain despicable individuals" and their expressive activity near funerals. It also found the law to be supported by a significant state interest, namely protecting citizens' "privacy interests" in avoiding offensive and unwelcome communications.[33] The court concluded, however, that plaintiffs were likely to succeed in demonstrating that the law, which prohibited picketing on some *private* property and limited more expression than the narrower restrictions upheld in *Frisby* and the abortion clinic cases, was not adequately tailored.

---

[32] In the first decision, issued more than a decade ago, a federal district court invalidated as unconstitutionally vague the predecessor to the current Kansas law, which prohibited "picketing before or about" any funeral site "before or after" a funeral service. Phelps v. Hamilton, 840 F. Supp. 1442 (D. Kan. 1993).

[33] McQueary v. Stumbo, 453 F. Supp.2d 975 (E.D. Ky. 2006).

In another recent case, a federal appeals court reversed a lower court's refusal to issue an injunction against Missouri's funeral protest law, which is named after a fallen soldier and criminalizes "picketing or other protest activities in front of or about" a funeral site.[34] The court specifically observed that "[Westboro Baptist Church] presents a viable argument that those who protest or picket at or near a military funeral wish to reach an audience which can only be addressed at such occasion and to convey to and through such an audience a particular message."[35] The court concluded that the Westboro protesters would likely succeed in demonstrating that the state's interest in protecting mourners is outweighed by their expressive interests and that the law is not narrowly tailored.[36]

Not all courts have been similarly persuaded. A federal court upheld Ohio's funeral buffer zone, which prohibited picketing and other protest activities within 300 feet of any funeral or funeral procession.[37] Plaintiffs conceded that the statute was content-neutral. The court concluded, as had the court in the Kentucky case, that the state had a substantial interest in protecting "captive" mourners from unwanted and "offensive" expression. Although the court found a statutory "floating" buffer that applied to the funeral procession insufficiently tailored, it held that the 300-foot "fixed" buffer zone suppressed no more expression than necessary to serve the state's interests.

Expressive zoning is not the only restriction the Westboro Baptist Church protesters must be concerned about. A jury recently awarded the father of a slain soldier whose funeral was picketed by Church members nearly $11 million in damages for invasion of privacy and intentional infliction of emotional distress.[38] In assessing that verdict, which is presently on appeal, it ought to be noted that the protesters were engaged at the time in otherwise lawful protest activity in a "quintessential" public forum. As in other protests, Church members did not enter the cemetery grounds to convey their message.

Litigation concerning the funeral protest zones is still in its infancy. One can already see, however, how cases like *Madsen*, *Schenck*, and *Frisby* have influenced legislative and judicial thinking regarding contests at

---

[34] Mo. Rev. Stat. § 578.502 (2006).
[35] Phelps-Roper v. Nixon, 509 F.3d 480 (8th Cir. 2007).
[36] *Id.* The court relied specifically on its decision in Olmer v. Lincoln, 192 F.3d 1176 (8th Cir. 1999), which held that the government did not have a compelling interest in protecting individuals from focused picketing near churches.
[37] Phelps-Roper v. Taft, 2007 U.S. Dist. LEXIS 20831 (N.D. Ohio, March 23, 2007).
[38] The amount has since been reduced to $5 million.

funeral sites. Legislators have swiftly and predictably turned to spatial restrictions to combat "offensive" and unwanted expression near these contested sites, where psychologically vulnerable audiences are present. Courts have found that the laws, which have been enacted in direct response to the Westboro protests and expressly restrict "pickets and other protest activities," are *neutral* with regard to content or message and allow speakers "ample" alternative places from which to reach public audiences. Perhaps most importantly, courts have begun to recognize a "privacy" interest possessed by "unwilling" audiences near these contested places. The tort verdict against the Westboro protesters, if upheld, will serve to fortify that interest.

These three representative instances of expressive zoning at contested places – abortion clinics, residences, and funeral sites – raise some of the most challenging free speech issues on the expressive topography. What are the appropriate First Amendment limits for contesting place? *Where* does one have a right to avoid unwanted expression and to be let alone? To what extent can governments protect places, and the people who visit or occupy them, from public contention and dissent?

Permit Requirements and Institutional Free Speech Policies

Injunctive and legislative restrictions are not the only limits on spatial contestation. As discussed in greater detail in Chapter 6, today nearly all public displays are governed by detailed permit schemes that require the time, place, and manner of displays to be preapproved. Whether the contested place is a local arena, a national park, or a government building, speakers must be aware of the many prerequisites for public expression.

Permit requirements can negatively affect the contesting of place. The National Parks Service regulations, which govern public displays near the White House and Capitol, are representative.[39] Under these regulations, a permit can be denied for a variety of reasons. The reasons include an inability to accommodate the display in a particular location "considering such things as damage to park resources or facilities, *impairment of a protected area's atmosphere of peace and tranquility*, interference with program activities, or impairment of public use facilities."[40] Many public contests are, of course, specifically intended to disrupt this "atmosphere of peace and tranquility."

---

[39] *See* 36 C.F.R. § 2.51.
[40] *Id* (emphasis added).

In addition, regulatory schemes often establish places, areas, or "zones" in which public displays are permitted to occur. For example, a court recently upheld the conviction of 34 people arrested for demonstrating on the plaza outside the Supreme Court – a "speech free zone" for protesters (but apparently not for the media, which often report from the same area). The protesters wanted the Court to force the government to close the detention facility at Guantanamo Bay, Cuba. Further, as discussed in Chapter 6, planners have recently proposed to limit protests near the United States Capitol building to what activists derisively refer to as a "protest pit." Predesignated "free speech areas," some of which may be hundreds of yards from a contested place, are sometimes identified on maps incorporated in permit regulations. Some regulatory schemes allow for "floating permits" that permit displays in several areas, while others strictly limit protesters to the free speech zones or areas.[41] In addition to spatial restrictions, regulatory provisions may inhibit spatial and other public contests by, for example, limiting the number of persons who may gather in a particular place.

These are merely the formal regulatory requirements for engaging in public displays near places. Today, the areas near most public and quasi-public facilities are governed by yet another regulatory layer. Many, if not most, public facilities have adopted "institutional free speech policies." The policies tend to serve the same general purpose as more formal regulations and are often just as detailed. Among other things, the institutional free speech policies designate certain limited areas for public displays and protests. Depending on the local landscape, institutional free speech policy provisions may relegate a speaker to isolated areas far away from contested places.

Thick layers of zoning govern public contention at or near public facilities and institutions. Insofar as speakers wish to use particular places to facilitate messages, reach specific audiences, or connect with particular places, they must navigate this complex and sometimes inhospitable spatial regime.

General Laws Limiting Public Displays of Contention

Expressive zoning and permitting are just two of the regulatory mechanisms used to limit contention at targeted places. General public order laws prohibiting breach of peace and disorderly conduct may also be enforced in

---

[41] *See, e.g.*, United States v. Baugh, 187 F.3d 1037 (9th Cir. 1999); Galvin v. Hay, 374 F.3d 739 (9th Cir. 2004).

a manner that prevents speakers from accessing contested places. Laws that ban public displays in certain places on "safety" or "security" grounds can also substantially limit or even prohibit spatial contestation.

Police exercise a tremendous amount of discretion in enforcing general public order laws. For example, as noted earlier the "Granny Peace Brigade" was removed from the public sidewalk near a military recruitment center in New York City on the ground that the elderly protesters, many of whom walked only with assistance, were blocking access to the center. Ultimately, the allegedly obstructive protesters were acquitted. But their protest was effectively terminated by the arrest and prosecution. This example may be enough to deter other protesters, as the next group that assembles near the recruitment center may similarly risk arrest and prosecution. Of course, it is impossible to know whether the Grannies' case was commonplace or an anomalous abuse of discretion.

Cindy Sheehan's odyssey in Crawford, Texas represents another example of the manner in which general laws can affect access to contested places. Sheehan was not arrested for her roadside display. There was at the time no specific law preventing it, and Sheehan and others assembled on the side of the road at what came to be popularly known as "Camp Casey" (named for Sheehan's son) did not breach the peace. Soon after Sheehan decamped, however, Crawford officials enacted an ordinance banning *all* roadside protest activity on public safety grounds. By enacting and enforcing that law, officials have removed another contested place from the expressive topography.

Of course, these two recent examples hardly demonstrate a pattern. The point is that general public order and safety laws allow sufficient enforcement discretion to be of particular concern to those who wish to contest places. Especially today, when public "security" is often an overriding concern of officials, speakers may find that their access to certain contested places is limited or altogether prohibited. Under current First Amendment standards, reactionary laws and ordinances, like the one enacted in Crawford, stand a good chance of being upheld as "neutral" public safety measures.

Fortress USA

As is true elsewhere on the expressive topography, limits on public expression and contention arise from nonlegal sources as well. In recent years, local and national officials have altered the architectures and landscapes of public places in ways that may limit spatial contestation.

Anyone who lives in or has visited a metropolis since September 11, 2001 has undoubtedly noted some of these changes. Jersey barriers, French barriers, checkpoints, fences, bollards, "No-Gos," parked trucks, weighted barrels, planters, and other physical transformations have been implemented to make public places more "secure." Described as the "architecture of fear" or "Fortress USA" by detractors, and "secure urban design" by supporters, these physical barriers may or may not actually be effective at preventing the targeted terrorist activity. They are, however, sometimes quite effective at preventing speakers from coming within close distance of structures and buildings that are sites of social and political contestation. Barriers and other security mechanisms occupy public space, disrupt movement, decrease opportunities for spontaneous interaction, and separate people from buildings and places. These architectural barriers are sometimes used to establish "hard" and "soft" zones around buildings and to effect public sidewalk and street closures. Thus, the power of the built environment is such that even without enactment of a single law or regulation, speakers can be kept hundreds of feet from places with which they have or desire to have an expressive connection.

The fortressing or securing of public space has had a particularly substantial effect on access to contested places of governance – "obvious centers of protest." Today capitols across the United States employ physical barriers as a first line of "defense" against public access, with surveillance, identity and security checks, and a host of other screening protocols fortifying the spatial barriers. Governors, mayors, and other elected officials have had large fences installed around official residences. Highly symbolic places, such as the Washington Monument and the Lincoln Memorial, have also been surrounded by barriers in recent years. Several streets near the White House have been closed by the Secret Service to all vehicle and pedestrian traffic.

New architecture is also being affected by spatial fortressing or "secure urban design." Today "security consultants" often substantially influence building designs. In addition to large barrier walls, consultants often advise that buildings be set back some substantial distance from the street, perhaps hundreds of feet, and contain few or no windows on lower floors. Thus, even if a small assembly could get close to such a structure, its message would not likely be seen or heard by anyone inside.

Providing security for what may indeed be potential terrorist targets is of course essential. But here as in other contexts, the dominant narrative of "security" is subtly but profoundly affecting the democratic functions of public places and the exercise of expressive liberties. Public architecture, as much as public laws, can make us less free.

PRESERVING PROXIMITY TO CONTESTED PLACES

There are some measures that, if taken, would help to ensure continued access to contested places on the expressive topography. The largest role with regard to this particular portion of the expressive topography must be played by courts and local officials. Both must approach the difficult balancing of interests in spatial contests with great sensitivity and care. When officials, as they often do, respond to local outrage or cries for public tranquility, courts must ensure adequate breathing space for spatial contestation. Public planners and architects must also be good stewards of the expressive topography; they must resist in particular the urge to build public fortresses impenetrable by not only feared terrorists but public speakers as well. Finally, public protesters must take care to contest places tactically and responsibly.

The Constitutional Tradition of Contesting Place

As noted earlier, we ought to remember that the act of contesting place has deep constitutional roots. Colonial Americans focused public contention on particular homes and businesses. During the Civil Rights Era, speech and spatiality intersected at statehouses, courthouses, jails, libraries, and lunch counters. Indeed throughout our history, the people have robustly contested places.

Particularly since the 1960s, there has been a rather marked change in official and judicial *attitudes* regarding the repertoire of contesting place. Local officials, spurred by Supreme Court and other judicial opinions emphasizing the "offensive," "unwanted," and "disruptive" nature of contesting place, have barely acknowledged its place in our constitutional tradition. Targeting places and audiences seems to have become a form of "low value" expression, akin to "indecent" speech or controversial symbolic acts like flag burning. Indeed, in one case, a California state appellate court forcefully opined that peaceful residential picketing on the public streets and sidewalks is "highly offensive conduct" and "a disfavored activity not entitled to a high level of First Amendment protection."[42]

---

[42] City of San Jose v. Superior Court, 38 Cal. Rptr.2d 205, 209–10 (Ct. App. 1995).

The act of contesting place is indeed often offensive, unwanted, and disruptive. But these are, from the speaker's perspective, some of the great virtues of spatial contestation. Public expression and expressive forms do not lose constitutional protection because they are offensive, unwanted, or disruptive of daily routines or expectations. Indeed, the Court has consistently said that First Amendment doctrines, principles, and theories apply not with less but rather with *greater* force to such expression. Courts and officials ought to recognize that targeted pickets on public sidewalks and streets are as fundamental to public liberties, and as deeply inscribed in our expressive history, as things like pamphleteering and leafleting.

Valuing Expressive and Topophilic Interests

Related to this recognition of tradition, officials and courts ought also to expressly recognize the full panoply of First Amendment interests speakers have in access to contested places. Recall that in *Frisby*, the Supreme Court expressly and unfavorably compared spatially focused expression near residences, which it said was intended for a *specific* audience, with expression that is intended for a more *general* public audience.

There are several problems with this distinction. First, it fundamentally mischaracterizes the expressive functions of contested places. In *Frisby*, the protesters likely were seeking to engage the neighborhood as a whole, and an even broader public audience, in their protest regarding abortion. Second, the amount of protection expression receives does not turn on the number of persons in the audience. The protesters were communicating on a matter of deep public concern; their message ought to receive the same level of constitutional protection regardless of whether one or one hundred people witnessed or heard it. Third, particularly in light of its constitutional tradition, there is no basis for treating activities such as leafleting as "high value" public speech and spatial contestation as its "low value" cousin. Fourth, and finally, protesters may appear at contested places like residences precisely because they cannot reach – through leafleting or otherwise – an appropriate audience in other places on the expressive topography. In sum, assuming that the content of the message itself is lawful, there is no principled basis for refusing to grant spatial contestation *full* First Amendment protection.

The audience question raised in *Frisby* requires consideration of a related First Amendment issue. If speakers who assemble and wish to speak at a contested place where *no* audience is present are denied access, do they have a First Amendment claim? In other words, are the topohilic or largely ceremonial functions of contested places also cognizable under the First Amendment? The Supreme Court has never addressed this question. Most of the time, of course, speakers use contested places to communicate with at least targeted and often more general audiences as well. But suppose, for example, that protesters were to assemble deep in a national forest outside sight or sound of any audience, to protest the policies of the federal Forest Service.[43] Is this spatial contest protected by the First Amendment?

Free speech values relating to self-autonomy and self-expression strongly suggest that it ought to be. The concept of contested place indicates that *where* something is said can be as or more important as *what* is said, *when* speech occurs, or *how* it is communicated. Choice of place in such instances relates to the shared meaning, for the participants, of the gathering or ceremony in a specific location. The gathering on-site is a form of communication, at least among all those present. Again, presence or absence of a target audience ought not to be determinative of First Amendment public liberties.

Thus, in addition to recognizing the constitutional tradition of contesting place, courts and officials ought to fully recognize the expressive values and functions of contested places. Newly fashioned rules and exceptions purportedly based on audience size or presence mischaracterize and nullify some of the expressive functions associated with contested places. Topophilic or ceremonial assemblies, although rare, also ought to be recognized as expressive events.

Questioning Spatial Neutrality

Chapter 1 explained why place ought not to be *presumptively* considered a neutral regulatory device. As responses to spatial contests indicate, place is often a means to some regulatory end very closely related to the content of a speaker's message or its particular form. Indeed, perhaps nowhere on the expressive topography is the dubiousness of spatial "neutrality" more apparent than in contested places. In many cases involving contested place, a far greater degree of skepticism than currently applied by courts is warranted.

One of the serious limitations of the time, place, and manner doctrine is that so long as governments can *justify* spatial restrictions with reference

---

[43] This occurred in United States v. Griefen, 200 F.3d 1256 (9th Cir. 2000).

to content-neutral reasons, these limits are typically upheld. It is, of course, the rare ordinance that cannot be justified with regard to order, safety, security, or repose. But where place is contested, there are several reasons to doubt that neutral justifications predominate.

One basis for enhanced skepticism of the neutrality of spatial restrictions involving contested places is the intimate connection between choice of place and message. In most cases, officials are quite well aware of that connection. Denial of access to place in this context may well terminate the protest itself. Or it may neutralize the message by substantially separating speakers from critical locations. Limits on access to contested places are in this sense distinguishable from run-of-the-mill time, place, and manner regulations. In seeking to protect the security or tranquility of the place itself, at least part of the governmental concern lies in protecting the target audience – women visiting abortion clinics, residents in their homes, or mourners at funerals, for example – from the *expression* itself. To the targeted audiences, the expression is offensive, hurtful, and unwanted.

Suppose, for instance, that in *Frisby* a convicted sex offender rather than a physician who performed abortions happened to live in the targeted residence. Is it not likely that speakers would have been permitted to draw that fact to the attention of their neighbors by peacefully picketing near the home? Or suppose that rather than the Westboro protesters' anti-homosexuality message, groups of veterans had stood outside the cemeteries to express respect for the fallen soldiers and support for their families. Is it likely that Congress, thirty-eight states, and many localities would have enacted funereal buffer zones?

In some instances, the language of the law itself makes it nearly impossible to credit the legislature's claim of neutral justification. This is particularly the case in the funeral context. The Kentucky funeral protest law actually states that it was enacted in response to the acts of "certain despicable individuals" who protested funerals. Other recently enacted funeral protest laws are named in honor of fallen soldiers. Funeral buffers generally prohibit "picketing *or other protest activities*," a phrase that would seem to apply primarily if not exclusively to negative or critical demonstrations and messages. Groups seeking to *honor* soldiers and their families have not been arrested or prosecuted under these laws. For example, a group of veterans known as the "Patriot Guard Riders" has appeared at many of the picketed funerals. The Riders seek to shield grieving families from the Westboro Baptist Church protesters by standing on the side of the road across from the protest holding United States flags and, when necessary, revving their motorcycle engines to drown out Church members' speech. On what basis is this group exempted?

Moreover all of the expressive zones imposed in response to recent spatial contests have been reactions to and the direct result of the speech of particular groups. The "buffers" near abortion clinics were responses to the contentious acts of Operation Rescue, which clinic patrons and employees often deride as "harassment." Residential zones have in nearly every case been enacted on the heels of specific instances of targeted expression. The funereal buffer zones are, again, perhaps the clearest example. These laws, which quickly blanketed the expressive topography, were often enacted in haste precisely to prevent Westboro Baptist Church members from protesting near funerals in the state or locality.

Finally, as a general matter, zones and other boundaries may be "vocal" in ways that can distort messages. Displacing and immobilizing only certain public assemblies and displays raises the specter of discriminatory treatment. Even if a "buffer zone" is not marked by barricades and fences, sorting public speakers in this fashion treats them – as a class – as potentially dangerous. The potential vocality of a spatial restriction or regulation does not alone suggest that it is content based: but it is a factor officials and courts ought to be aware of as they consider whether spatial arrangements are being imposed for reasons that have nothing to do with distaste for the message or the messengers.

In short, expressive zones are no ordinary time, place, and manner regulations. "Buffer zones" are particularized, tactical responses to certain speakers, messages, and forms of communication that many find deeply offensive. Although the Supreme Court has been reluctant to label injunctions that apply only to particular wrongdoers "content-based," when viewed as a pattern or practice the nonneutrality of at least some of the restrictions imposed near contested places is rather apparent. At the least, courts should carefully inquire and investigate – using facts on the ground and, where available, legislative history – the neutrality of these measures.

Audience "Privacy" and "Captivity"

Particularly since the Court's abortion clinic decisions, officials have invoked interests relating to "privacy" and "captivity" to support restrictions on access to contested places. Like the *embodied* places discussed in the previous chapter, contested places highlight a thorny First Amendment issue regarding protection of audiences from unwanted and offensive speech. As we saw, in embodied places messages are communicated from close range, raising the possibility that the recipient will suffer psychological or even physical harm. With regard to contested places, the question is whether an audience at a particular site – a clinic or hospital, a residence, a church, or a funeral site – is entitled to similar protection from otherwise lawful expression targeting a particular place.[44]

What is peculiar in both instances is that audiences have recently been granted a degree of privacy – a "right to be let alone" – with regard to expression *conveyed from a public place* like a sidewalk or street. As the Supreme Court has said, these are "quintessential" expressive forums that have "immemorially" been dedicated to public assembly, communication, and debate. As discussed in the previous chapter, prior to the decision in *Hill*, where the Supreme Court upheld the 8-foot protective "bubble" near abortion clinics, the Court had steadfastly refused to recognize a constitutional interest in (or right to) public "privacy." Thus, whether on the sidewalk, the road, in a public courthouse, or elsewhere on the expressive topography, it has generally been incumbent upon the listener to avoid unwanted communication.

The Court has held that a speaker's message may be suppressed only where "*substantial* privacy interests are being invaded in an *essentially intolerable* manner."[45] There is of course considerable room for interpretation in this standard, both with regard to what interests are "substantial" and which means of expression are "intolerable." There are sound reasons to continue to limit this "privacy interest" to the home, as the Court has historically done. As the three representative examples discussed above show, the combination of an expanded conception of public "privacy" and diminishing tolerance for targeted and unwanted public expression has begun to erode access to contested places. Indeed, in the contested place context we are seeing a subtle and slippery expansion of the *right* to avoid unwanted and offensive public expression targeted at particular places.[46]

Although the abortion clinic cases are certainly troubling in this regard, the funereal protest cases pose perhaps the greatest danger of an expansion of this privacy/captivity principle. One is not "captive," at least not as that term has been interpreted to date, to expression that is delivered on the public ways and which an audience is able to quickly walk by or drive

---

[44] I am assuming the expression does not constitute legally proscribable content such as "fighting words" or "true threats." None of the examples or incidents discussed in this chapter involved such content. Speech in contested places is generally not delivered face-to-face, as required under the fighting words doctrine. While some of the expression discussed above undoubtedly highly offensive to the recipient, it did not include threats of physical or other harm.

[45] Cohen v. California, 403 U.S. 15, 21 (1971) (emphasis added).

[46] With regard to the operation of "slippery slope" extensions in constitutional law, *see generally* Eugene Volokh, "The Mechanisms of the Slippery Slope," 116 *Harv. L. Rev.* 1026 (2003).

away from. No one would suggest that a speaker can insist upon access to a private funeral (or a church or medical facility) in order to deliver a targeted message. The First Amendment does not protect this sort of invasive "thrusting" of expression. Nor should speakers be permitted, through loud volume or other means, to interfere with the funeral ceremony (or church service, or convalescence of patients). But speakers who have targeted contested places like funeral sites have confined their contention to public sidewalks and streets. They have been visible and audible to audiences, but have not intruded upon or otherwise interfered with ceremonies or services.[47] And they have not approached or entered embodied spaces. The buffer zones at funeral sites thus have not been erected to prevent unlawful interference or face-to-face harassment. They have been established so that audiences do not have to be exposed in public places to uncomfortable, hurtful, and offensive messages.

Of course, the most delicate balancing is required when the contested place is someone's home. There a recognized and substantial privacy interest certainly does exist. Even in *Frisby*, however, the Supreme Court was careful not to sanction a ban on "residential protests" generally. The Court could of course have extended greater protection to residential contests, by requiring that trespass laws, limits on assembly size, and noise ordinances be relied upon to regulate "targeted" picketing. But the fact remains that the Court upheld only the narrowest restriction, one that prohibited focusing *constant* attention on an individual's private residence but did not preclude speakers from being seen or heard there altogether. By contrast, there is nothing narrow or preservative about the residential and other buffer zones that some municipalities have adopted since *Frisby* was decided. Depending on a neighborhood's topography, residential privacy zones of 100 to 300 feet will in some cases effectively prevent access to contested residences. That would amount to recognition of a right to residential privacy beyond that contemplated in *Frisby*.

One cannot lightly dismiss the hurt feelings and even psychological harm that may accompany targeted messages like those recently conveyed at military funerals and abortion clinics. But there are broader concerns with expanding notions of privacy and captivity. Each recognition of new

---

[47] Many who oppose funeral protests appear to assume that they disrupt the procession or interfere with mourning. *See* Steven J. Heyman, *Free Speech & Human Dignity* 155 (2008) (arguing that funeral protests intrude into "private life" by interfering with a family's ability to mourn in peace). As with the sidewalk counselor, it is important to keep in mind that the funeral protester is located in a traditional public forum. In any event, actual disruptions or intrusions could be addressed without the substantial displacement effected under recent measures, through laws prohibiting trespass, or noise ordinances, or other public order laws.

audience rights or interests – "privacy," "dignity," the "right to mourn," or the "right to worship" – will further erode or eliminate access to contested places on the expressive topography.[48] Given the generally poor condition of the expressive topography, this is breathing space that ought not to be sacrificed – even to ideals of proper manners, basic civility, or morality.

Choice of Place and Tailoring

Under the time, place, and manner standard, a content-neutral displacement will be upheld so long as it leaves open "ample" and "adequate" alternatives for expression. In theory at least, a speaker is not to be denied access to an otherwise appropriate place on the ground that she may speak in some other place. In actual fact, however, displacements are rather routinely upheld based upon this very principle. Indeed, so long as government does not seek to *eliminate* the speaker's message, or make it impossible to convey, a spatial restriction is very likely to be upheld under prevailing First Amendment standards.

Like other speakers, those displaced from areas near contested sites can always convey their messages elsewhere – through pamphlets, on the Web, or by other means. But in the case of contested places, the speaker loses much – indeed perhaps everything in expressive terms – when forced from her chosen location. If the speaker seeks a particular audience found *only* in the contested place, substantial displacement operates more as suppression than regulation. Thus, where a particular place is being contested, greater sensitivity and attention to the tailoring of expressive zones and other spatial boundaries are warranted.

Many of the expressive zones established to quell contention at contested places are more problematic than courts and officials seem to recognize. For example, although protesters generally remain within sight and sound of abortion clinics, buffer zones near the clinics can substantially separate speakers from the places they seek to contest (*see* Figure 4.4). The zones also generally keep speakers well out of range of intended audiences for purposes of proselytizing, pamphleteering, and other proximate expression. When, as discussed in Chapter 3, legislatures and courts add "bubble" protections for women and staff members at these clinics, traditional means of face-to-face expression are effectively banned at abortion clinics.

---

[48] *See* Rutledge, *supra* note 27 at 309–11 (discussing church and funeral buffer zones and arguing for both a right to worship and a right to mourn).

Of course, like other public speakers abortion clinic protesters do not have a constitutional right to the most effective place on the expressive topography from which to convey their message. But remember that the primary – and of course entirely legitimate – reason for the "buffer zones" is to *preserve access* to health care facilities. A 36-foot zone seems substantially overbroad in light of this limited purpose. Indeed, even a 15-foot zone would seem to provide more "buffer" than generally needed to comfortably enter and leave a facility. Of course, one must consider the actions of protesters at specific clinics as well as any architectural limits of the site. Where violence or interference is prevalent, officials and courts may reasonably conclude that a more substantial buffer is warranted. But that does not mean they ought to apply a presumption that every contested clinic *must* have a sizable buffer. Nor does it eliminate the need to revisit the original boundaries in light of local events and circumstances. In sum, courts and officials ought not to simply assume that a large buffer is appropriate in all contested places regardless of circumstance.

As *Frisby* at least implicitly recognizes, absolute *bans* on spatial contestation, which again generally occurs on public streets and sidewalks, are constitutionally invalid. But the outer limit of residential privacy zones – 300 feet – would also appear to be of dubious constitutionality. As noted earlier, in the abortion clinic context the Court invalidated an injunctive 300-foot buffer zone that had been set around the residences of clinic staff. Nevertheless, courts have in fact *upheld* residential privacy zones of this size.[49] Outside the extremes, of course, much may turn upon things like lot sizes and other physical characteristics in a particular neighborhood. Depending on such local circumstances, a 100-, 200-, or 300-foot privacy zone could place speakers well outside of eyesight and earshot of the contested residence. Thus, again, a tailoring inquiry ought to proceed on a place-by-place basis rather than by reference to boundaries previously approved by courts or officials in different contexts.

As noted, courts have only begun to address the tailoring of funereal protest laws. Clay County, Tennessee's 5,000-foot buffer is a patently unconstitutional effort to ban this form of protest. Buffer zones that extend for more than 1,000 feet, or several city blocks, are also probably invalid as effective bans. It may also be the case that these funereal protest laws will interfere with other protests that simply happen to occur within the restricted zones. As abhorrent as the Westboro Baptist Church

---

[49] For example, 300-foot residential buffer zones were upheld in Klein v. San Diego County, 463 F.3d 1029 (9th Cir. 2006) and City of San Jose v. Superior Court, 38 Cal. Rptr.2d 205 (Ct. App. 1995).

protesters' message may be, suppressing it (and in its wake, other protests) through displacement is unconstitutional. Although they cannot
choose the best place for their display, so long as they remain in traditional
public forums and do not interfere with the funeral procession or disrupt
the funeral service, even the Westboro Baptist Church protesters have a
First Amendment right to be seen and heard.

Spatial Stewardship and the Architecture of Fear

The preservation of breathing space for spatial contests is not solely the
responsibility of judges. Public officials, who after all act as "trustees" and
stewards of our public places, must resist the urge to "securitize" places to
such an extent that spatial contention is no longer possible.

Capacious regulatory and other language allowing parks officials to
deny permits where expressive activity might "impair an atmosphere of
peace and tranquility" is an invitation to virtually unbridled discretion.
Moreover, administrators must resist the urge to locate designated "free
speech zones" in places that substantially separate speakers from likely
contested sites or which do not otherwise facilitate public expression.
Speakers ought not to be forced to assemble and demonstrate in tall
weeds, at the bottom of a distant hill, or in otherwise inhospitable and
ineffective locations.

As stewards of public places, administrators should work with protesters and demonstrators to accommodate access to contested places and
to offer viable substitutes and alternatives when the desired proximity is
not achievable. Police and prosecutors should also be aware of the
intentionality of contesting place. They too ought to preserve choice of
place to the extent consistent with genuine concerns for public order and
safety. Surely there are greater threats to public security than the "Granny
Peace Brigade."

Those responsible for the character of our *built* environment also have
an obligation to consider the manner in which expression intersects with
contested places. Fences, barriers, and bollards have recently been situated near any place that might conceivably be a target of violence – which
is to say, nearly *everyplace*. This architecture of fear has spread very
rapidly across the expressive topography. Thankfully, most such barriers
are not permanent. Architects, concerned mostly with the *aesthetics* of the
built environment, have been working to develop "friendlier" versions of
the Jersey and French barrier. This will improve public settings; but
replacing old barriers with new ones shaped like benches or canisters

will of course do nothing to resolve the increasing separation of people from places.

Fortunately, architects and planners are already experimenting with designs that will *eliminate* spatial barriers, while still protecting places from truck bombs and other substantial terrorist threats. One such design consists of a platform that will collapse under the weight of a truck but easily support the weight of pedestrians. This is no trivial matter insofar as public freedoms are concerned. One of the themes of this book is that the design of physical places is highly relevant to the scope of public expressive liberties. That design may ultimately determine whether the people are able to effectively contest particular places.

Contesting Place – Speakers' Tactics

As was true with regard to the embodied places discussed in Chapter 3, speakers themselves bear some responsibility for preserving access to contested places. By its nature, spatially focused expression is disruptive, disturbing, and offensive to many. Of course, as noted, these character-istics may also be among the principal benefits of this particular form of public expression.

Speakers must realize that violence, trespass, harassment, blockades, and other unlawful activity will provide authorities with a basis for enacting, and judges with grounds for upholding, "buffer zones" and other restrictions on access to contested places. Civil rights protesters demonstrated that spatial contention can be disruptive and effective without being violent or unlawful. They were not only early architects of the expressive topography, but conscientious stewards of it. Civil rights protesters used new repertoires of contention to draw attention to places. They showed that choice of place was an important *strategic* concern.

For reasons discussed earlier, recent protests have centered on some rather nonobvious places of contest. Residences, medical facilities, churches, military academies, and cemeteries have now joined capitols, courthouses, and other government buildings as contested places on the expressive topography. Given their unusual and in many cases private nature, these sites may require an added amount of restraint and disci-pline. A little self-regulation may go a long way toward preserving access to these and other places for future contests. It is now clear, for example, that the conduct of certain protesters at abortion clinics during the 1980s not only produced bad legal precedents, but also altered the expressive landscape at similar contests in other places on the expressive topography.

Recent spatial contests, including those near funeral sites, have had the same effect.

Speakers and social movements should be as strategically invested in choice of place as they are in other repertoires of contention. They should, where possible, coordinate policies with regard to choice of place and public contention at or near those places. Sometimes, of course, choice of place is not a matter subject to any centralized control. Rogue speakers like the Westboro Baptist Church protesters strike out on their own to further individual goals. Perhaps the only recourse other speakers may have in such cases is to lobby officials not to aggravate the matter by drawing further attention to such speakers with restrictive laws; these laws only give them greater cause to publicly complain. In the end, there is little conscientious public speakers can do to lower the collective costs of this sort of expressive autonomy. Sadly, if the funeral buffer laws are upheld, portions of the expressive topography will be unavailable to *all* speakers regardless of what they wish to communicate. Assuming that the laws are neutrally enforced, speakers may be prohibited from conveying even supportive messages like "Pray for the souls of our fallen men and women" or "Pray for an end to the War in Iraq."

Contesting place requires a delicate and sophisticated approach that is often difficult for impassioned speakers to execute. Speakers must continue to press for access to symbolic and expressive contested locations. At the same time, they must exercise restraint at times of high emotion and conflict. The First Amendment is not merely a grant of expressive liberties; it sometimes obligates speakers to self-govern by self-regulating. Like laws, regulations, and physical architectures, speakers leave their own distinct footprints on the expressive topography.

5   NON-PLACES

The Mall of America in Bloomington, Minnesota occupies 4.2 million square feet. The consumer mecca draws 37.5 million visitors a year. It houses, among many other things, the nation's largest amusement park, a public school, a branch of a private university, and a police substation operated by the city. Public financing substantially aided the construction of the Mall, whose operators proudly compare certain public areas to "city streets" and the "town square." The Mall, they boast, is "a city within a city." Yet when a small group of antifur protesters gathered near the Mall's entrance, holding placards and peacefully distributing leaflets expressing opposition to the cruel treatment of animals, they were arrested by Mall security officers and charged with trespass. The Minnesota Supreme Court ultimately upheld their convictions.[1] In the Mall City, the people do not enjoy any expressive liberties.

Malls are not the only contemporary places at which the public assembles in substantial numbers but expressive activity is generally forbidden. As people began to move in great numbers to the suburbs and to travel about the country (and the world), the question arose whether their expressive liberties were as mobile. Did the First Amendment apply in places like airports, transportation hubs, subway platforms, and other contemporary places? Applying the public forum doctrine, courts have generally answered in the negative. Indeed, as the Supreme Court has interpreted this doctrine, "new" public places simply cannot be treated as "quintessential" public forums – regardless of their architectural features or actual uses. Owing to the fact that they have not "immemorially" been open to expressive activity, new structures erected on the expressive topography are presumptively "non-public" forums – places in which people possess few, if any, expressive liberties. Finally, as elsewhere on the

---

[1] State v. Wicklund, 589 N.W.2d 793 (Minn. 1999).

expressive topography, landscape and architectural transformations like "gated communities" and other "secure" properties pose additional obstacles to the exercise of expressive liberties. Here, as elsewhere, substantial gaps in the expressive topography have resulted from both constitutional interpretation and the built environment itself.

This chapter examines *non-places*, or dead spaces, on the expressive topography. The existence and proliferation of non-places has substantially reduced the breathing space for public expression. After situating non-place in a broader sociological perspective, the chapter critiques the primary constitutional doctrines and principles that have resulted in the stifling of expressive liberties in such places. It then examines two general proposals: First, introducing expression to at least a limited extent into current non-places, and, second, locating alternative places that might compensate for the loss of breathing space produced by non-places.

THE EROSION OF PUBLIC PLACE

As noted in Chapter 2, the contemporary expressive topography has been shaped by a variety of conditions related to modernity, including increased mobility, mass communication, suburbanization, and the rise of consumer culture. Sociologists, anthropologists, and geographers have long lamented the general and systematic erosion of place produced by these and other conditions.[2] Their principal claim is that conditions of modernity have led to a deadening spatial homogenization. Shopping malls, airports, shops, hotels, and other public and quasi-public places seem to be the same, no matter where one goes. At this point, most people view such places in exclusively functional terms – as culturally insignificant spaces except insofar as they may be useful for shopping, or travel, or some other personal convenience.

This homogenization and erosion of place is problematic because people connect to the world and one another through and in places. In this and other senses "place," which is personalized and experienced, differs from "space," which is essentially undifferentiated physical mass.[3] Stated differently, space *becomes* place when people socialize in it and form

---

[2] A good summary can be found in Tim Cresswell, *Place: A Short Introduction* 43–45 (2004).
[3] Of course, there are many different conceptions of "place" and "space." This chapter (and this work more generally) treats place as something experienced and characterized by topophilic connections. In other words, the book examines what might be called "anthropological" place. Under this conception, non-place is a type of undifferentiated space.

attachments with and connections to it. The existence of what the geographer Yi-Fu Tuan has called "topophilia," or connection to place, is critical to our daily lives, socialization, and culture.[4] The circumstances of modernity – or, as some might prefer, "hyper-modernity" or "super-modernity" – make it very difficult to generate attachments to places and, consequently, to develop a diverse and fulfilling public culture in places. This has led to what Edward Relph has called a sense of "placelessness," or the absence of authentic relationships to place.[5]

Social scientists have sometimes referred to modern homogenous public and quasi-public spaces as "non-places." The anthropologist Marc Augé compares "place" and "non-place" in this manner: "If a place can be defined as relational, historical and concerned with identity, then a space which cannot be defined as relational, or historical, or concerned with identity will be a non-place."[6] According to Augé, the proliferation of non-places has radically transformed public space:

> The multiplication of what we may call empirical non-places is characteristic of the contemporary world. Spaces of circulation (freeways, airways), consumption (department stores, supermarkets), and communication (telephones, faxes, television, cable networks) are taking up more room all over the earth today. They are spaces where people coexist or cohabit without living together.[7]

Non-places are generally rootless and disconnected locations marked by, and facilitative of, mass mobility and travel. Augé identified these basic characteristics in the new vocabulary that has developed to describe our contemporary environment:

> Thus we can contrast the realities of *transit* (transit camps or pas-sengers in transit) with those of residence or dwelling; the *interchange* (where nobody crosses anyone else's path) with the *crossroads* (where people meet); the *passenger* (defined by his *destination*) with the *traveller* (who strolls along his *route* []), the *housing estate* . . . where people do not live together and which is never situated in the centre of anything (big estates characterize the so-called peripheral zones or

---

[4] Yi-Fu Tuan, *Topophilia: A Study of Environmental Perception, Attitudes, and Values* (1974). See also J.E. Malpas, *Place and Experience: A Philosophical Topography* (1999); Robert Sack, *Homo Geographicus* (1997).
[5] Edward Relph, *Place and Placelessness* (1976).
[6] Marc Augé, *Non-Places: Introduction to an Anthropology of Supermodernity* 77–78 (1995).
[7] Marc Auge, *An Anthropology for Contemporaneous Worlds* (Amy Jacobs, transl.) 110 (1999).

outskirts), with the *monument* where people share and commemorate; *communication* (with its codes, images and strategies) with *language* (which is spoken).[8]

Augé's observations encapsulate one of the major challenges not only for our public topography, but for the contemporary *expressive* topography. Increasingly, expanses of the expressive topography are becoming *non-public*, both in the sense of legal ownership and insofar as public connection and interaction are concerned. Conditions of mobility, consumption, and the increasing desire for personal separation from others have created dead spaces (insofar as expression is concerned) like malls, urban megastructures, airport terminals, transit hubs, vast interstate highways on which travel is interrupted only by the occasional rest stop or hotel, and secluded communities.

These non-places occupy a substantial amount of physical space. In contrast to *embodied* (Chapter 3) and *contested* (Chapter 4) places, which are critical to public expressive liberties but occupy a relatively small amount of physical space, non-places represent a significant and expanding portion of the expressive topography. Forty years ago, for example, shopping centers were relatively rare. Today there are more than 48,000 shopping centers in the United States, covering more than 6 billion square feet of retail space.[9] The number of centers of more than 1 million square feet is increasing. The number of adults shopping in these places has risen to over 190 million per month.[10] People also spend substantial amounts of time in these places. Recent figures indicate that the typical person made 3.1 visits per month to shopping malls, and remained on the premises more than 80 minutes each trip.[11]

If they were available in some aggregate form, the figures with regard to airport and other transportation terminals would likely be as or even more substantial. The nation's airports and related transportation facilities occupy vast land areas and accommodate hundreds of millions of

---

[8] Auge, *Non-Places, supra* note 6 at 107–08.
[9] *See The Scope of the Shopping Center Industry in the United States 2006: Basic Facts and Economic Impacts* (2006) (published by the International Council of Shopping Centers). According to conversations with industry personnel, these figures may in fact *underestimate* the space currently occupied by shopping centers in the United States.
[10] *Id.*
[11] *See* Veronica V. Soriano, "Converting Browsers into Spenders: Mall Shoppers Spend More Time and Money," 13(2)*Research Review* (2006) available at http://www.icsc.org/srch/rsrch/researchquarterly/current/rr2006132/Converting%20Browsers%20into%20Spen ders.pdf# xml=http://icscsearch.icsc.org/texis/search/pdfhi.txt?query=time+spent+shoping &pr=IcscLive&prox=page&rorder=500&rprox=500&rdfreq=500&rwfreq=500&rlead=500 &sufs= 0&order=r&cq=&id= 44b854b111.

passengers annually. Further, a driving tour of the United States would undoubtedly confirm the proliferation and expansiveness of "gated" and other privatized communities. Indeed, as evidenced by places like Celebration, Florida, a Walt Disney production, the old "company town" (discussed below) may even be making something of a comeback.[12] As Margaret Kohn has demonstrated, the proliferation of non-places is not just a suburban phenomenon.[13] Downtown "business improvement districts," which bring the logic and landscape of the suburban mall to urban areas, can just as readily transform public spaces into non-places.[14]

Social scientists have noted how shopping centers, business improvement districts, and other controlled environments lessen opportunities for interaction and generally inhibit meaningful communication. Augé notes, for example, that a person in an airport terminal "communicates wordlessly, through gestures, with an abstract, unmediated commerce."[15] Individuals in shopping malls, airport terminals, and other places of modernity interact mostly with *texts* – directions, instructions given by machines, their daily newspaper – rather than with each other. Rather than function as vibrant interactive places, non-places sever person and place, leaving only a "solitary contractuality."[16] Non-places thus facilitate and encourage "cocooning" – a retreating into the self.[17] An expressive topography filled with non-places would be, in Augé's words, "a world [] surrendered to solitary individuality, to the fleeting, the temporary and ephemeral."[18]

The shopping center, perhaps the quintessential non-place, has been subjected to withering criticism by scholars and critics in a variety of disciplines.[19] Although many of the complaints are aesthetic in nature, a common lament is that although they are the heirs apparent to public squares and other traditional public forums, these places of modernity exhibit no public soul or society. As the architect Margaret Crawford has noted:

The malls looked inward, turning their back on the public street. Set in the middle of nowhere, these consumer landscapes reflected

---

[12] See Martin Stoltz, "In Utah, a 'Company Town' Means Just That," *N.Y. Times*, July 24, 2007, A14.
[13] Margaret Kohn, *Brave New Neighborhoods: The Privatization of Public Space* (2004).
[14] See *id.* at 81–88 (discussing "business improvement districts").
[15] Augé, *Non-Places, supra* note 6 at 78.
[16] *Id.* at 94.
[17] *Id.* at 119.
[18] *Id.*
[19] See, e.g., Robert Sack, *Place, Consumption and Modernity* (1992); William Severini Kowinski, *The Malling of America: An Inside Look at the Great Consumer Paradise* (1985).

the profound distrust of the street as a public arena visible in the work of such dissimilar urbanists as Frank Lloyd Wright and Le Corbusier.[20]

The simulated downtowns in shopping centers (and, now, in many transportation terminals) have "compressed and intensified space;" they have created "a fantasy urbanism devoid of the city's negative aspects: weather, traffic, and poor people."[21] Gated communities are, of course, the ultimate escape from others. As Margaret Kohn has observed, the business improvement district similarly "allows consumers to enjoy the traditionally urban pleasures of proximity to diverse strangers in a setting where any risk of threat, disruption, disorientation, or discomfort has been removed."[22] In sum, many if not most places of modernity are not genuinely *public* places at all.

The proliferation of non-places raises serious concerns, particularly with respect to diminished opportunities for genuine public exchange, contestation, and interaction. Although constitutional doctrine obviously did not create any of these places, as we shall see it substantially contributed to their present condition. This, then, is another context in which constitutional law has combined with social and architectural circumstances to significantly transform the expressive topography.

PROPERTY RULES AND PLACES OF MODERNITY

As a general matter, the United States Constitution does not constrain the acts of private persons. Under the principles of the "state action" doctrine, private property owners are not normally affected by First Amendment or other constitutional limitations. No one, for example, has a First Amendment right to speak in another's home, in a private community, on a private college or university campus, or inside a private office building.[23] Although speech cannot occur lest it occur in some place, the Constitution does not generally guarantee the existence of or access to expressive places. Nowhere on the expressive topography is it more apparent that

---

[20] Margaret Crawford, "The World in a Shopping Mall," in Michael Sorkin (ed.), *Variations On a Theme Park: The New American City and the End of Public Space* 21 (1992).

[21] *Id.* at 22.

[22] Kohn, *supra* note 13 at 84.

[23] For a general consideration of the scope of expressive rights on private properties, *see* Warren Freedman, *Freedom of Speech on Private Property* (1988).

property rules often dictate the scope or existence of expressive liberties than in non-places.[24]

Suppose, for example, that a private owner invites the general public to visit a place of business. Suppose also that the construction of this place is funded by the government, has many of the physical characteristics of public spaces, including streets, sidewalks, and public squares, and is occupied by police, post office, and other governmental institutions. Should the First Amendment apply in this "city within a city"? Suppose the government actually owns and operates such a structure, for example, a metropolitan airport or other transit hub. Does the First Amendment require some breathing space for expressive liberties within? Does the Constitution prohibit wholesale privatization and exclusion of the public from entire communities, even those constructed with the approval and assistance of public authorities?

The Supreme Court has essentially answered all of these questions in the negative, under the "state action" and "public forum" doctrines. First Amendment liberties have essentially been trumped in these and other circumstances by both private and governmental rights to control access to property. Before we turn to proposals for reversing the loss of breathing space occasioned by non-places, let us first revisit the process by which these substantial gaps on the expressive topography were originally created. There are important implications in this history for the future contours and condition of our expressive topography.

Company Towns and Shopping Centers

In *Marsh v. Alabama* (1946), the Supreme Court held that a privately owned and operated "company town" owned by the Gulf Shipbuilding Corporation could not flatly prohibit Jehovah's Witnesses from distributing literature on the streets of the town's business district by invoking state trespass laws.[25] In all critical respects this town operated as, and indeed appeared to be, a municipal entity. The property itself consisted of residential buildings, streets, a system of sewers, a sewage disposal plant and a "business block" on which most of the town's businesses were located.

---

[24] *See* Louis Michael Seidman, "The Dale Problem: Property and Speech Under the Regulatory State" (2008) (available at http://ssrn.com/abstract=1082114).

[25] 326 U.S. 501 (1946). Company towns "developed primarily in the Deep South to meet economic conditions, especially those which existed following the Civil War." Lloyd Corp. v. Tanner, 407 U.S. 551, 566 (1972). In these places corporations essentially assumed the role of local government, including the provision of customary services and utilities.

Legal title, however, was held by a private company. Legally speaking, then, this was *private* property as to which the owner would ordinarily possess the right to exclude others. Private title notwithstanding, the Court held that running a town was in the nature of a "public function." The Court ruled that where an owner was effectively acting as a sovereign, and performing sovereign functions, the fact that legal title was held by a private entity was not a sufficient basis upon which to rest a prohibition on all public expression. In such cases, ordinary property rules had to yield to First Amendment liberties. This was another early victory by the Jehovah's Witnesses that created space for speech out of doors. As we shall see, however, it was not a lasting victory.

Marsh is often cited as a precedent involving the constitutional principle of "state action." At bottom, however, the decision actually rested upon a critical balance of public and private rights. As the Court stated, "the more an owner, for his advantage, opens up his property for use by the public in general, the more do his rights become circumscribed by the statutory and constitutional rights of those who use it."[26] In the case of the company town, the right of the Jehovah's Witnesses (and others) to exercise expressive liberties was held to have *outweighed* the property owner's right to exclude based on property principles like title and trespass.

Marsh was decided in 1946, well before shopping centers sprouted like weeds in American suburbia. During the subsequent two decades, shopping centers proliferated across the suburban landscape. In many ways the new malls were very similar to the old company towns. They were essentially business districts located under a single roof. Even before the birth of the "megamall," shopping centers covered acres upon acres of land. They contained multilevel building complexes, parking facilities, sidewalks, indoor plazas, benches, escalators, bridges, gardens, and recreational facilities like skating rinks. Even then, shopping centers were quintessentially "cities within cities." Indeed by the early 1970s, suburban shopping centers had become one of the primary gathering places for millions of Americans.

The Supreme Court's first decision regarding shopping center speech rights reflected these architectural and social realities. Two decades after *Marsh*, the Court held in *Amalgamated Food Employees Union v. Logan Valley Plaza* (1968) that nonemployee union members had a First Amendment right to peacefully picket a grocery store located in the Logan Valley Mall.[27] The picketers sought to convey their message in a parcel pickup area located in the parking lot abutting the store. The Court started

---

[26] *Marsh*, 326 U.S. at 509.
[27] 391 U.S. 308 (1968).

"from the premise that peaceful picketing carried out in a location open generally to the public is, absent other factors involving the purpose or manner of the picketing, protected by the First Amendment."[28] As in *Marsh*, the nature and character of the shopping center itself, rather than possession of title, was critical to the Court's analysis. The Court specifically noted that the shopping center served as "the community business block" and was "freely accessible and open to the people in the area and those passing through."[29] It was, the Court held, the "functional equivalent" of the business district in *Marsh*.[30]

Speaking for the Court, Justice Marshall emphasized the geopolitics of the modern shopping mall:

> The economic development of the United States in the last 20 years reinforces our opinion of the correctness of the approach taken in *Marsh*. The largescale movement of this country's population from the cities to the suburbs has been accompanied by the advent of the suburban shopping center, typically a cluster of individual retail units on a single large privately owned tract. It has been estimated that by the end of 1966 there were between 10,000 and 11,000 shopping centers in the United States and Canada, accounting for approximately 37% of total retail sales in those two countries.
>
> These figures illustrate the substantial consequences for workers seeking to challenge substandard working conditions, consumers protesting shoddy or overpriced merchandise, and minority groups seeking nondiscriminatory hiring policies that a contrary decision here would have. Business enterprises located in downtown areas would be subject to on-the-spot public criticism for their practices, but businesses situated in the suburbs could largely immunize themselves from similar criticism by creating a cordon sanitaire of parking lots around their stores. Neither precedent nor policy compels a result so at variance with the goal of free expression and communication that is the heart of the First Amendment.[31]

Ultimately, the *Logan Valley* Court was careful to cabin its holding. For example, the Court did not hold that the areas inside a shopping center were the "functional equivalent" of streets, sidewalks, and public squares for First Amendment purposes. The Court decided only that the

---

[28] *Id.* at 313.
[29] *Id.* at 319.
[30] *Id.*
[31] *Id.*

shopping center owners could not wholly exclude speakers from the premises under state trespass laws, where the speakers sought proximity to a specific *contested* place (Chapter 4) and were exercising First Amendment rights "in a manner and for a purpose generally consonant with the use to which the property was actually put."[32] This meant that although the owners of the property might limit expression in terms of time, place, or manner, they could not *ban* the exercise of expressive liberties altogether.

Had the Supreme Court ended its examination with *Logan Valley*, the contemporary expressive topography would have a very different character. So long as the expressive activity was *compatible* with the place, speakers presumably would possess a First Amendment right to convey messages at the nation's malls and shopping centers. This would include not just the right to contest place, but presumably also many forms of embodied expression (Chapter 3) as well. But a mere four years after *Logan Valley*, the Court abruptly reversed course. In *Lloyd Corporation v. Tanner* (1972), the Court upheld the exclusion from a large suburban mall of several Vietnam War protesters who sought to distribute handbills inside the mall.[33] The Lloyd Center Mall occupied over 50 acres of land, housed more than sixty businesses, and was bounded by four public streets. Its security guards, who wore uniforms similar to those worn by city police, were given full police power by the city government and were licensed to carry handguns. The shopping center owners had embedded small signs in the sidewalk stating that the spaces within the complex were not public ways, and that permission to use them could be revoked at any time by the owner.

Despite its resemblance to a municipal business district, the Court viewed the Lloyd Center Mall as *private* property designed principally to serve "utilitarian and esthetic functions."[34] It relied upon the testimony of an architectural expert regarding the shopping center's primary function:

> In order to make shopping easy and pleasant, and to help realize the goal of maximum sales (for the Center) the shops are grouped about special pedestrian ways or malls. Here the shopper is isolated from the noise, fumes, confusion and distraction which he normally finds along city streets, and *a controlled, carefree environment is provided.*[35]

---

[32] *Id.* at 319–20.
[33] 407 U.S. 551 (1972).
[34] *Id.* at 553.
[35] *Id.* (*emphasis added*).

Given this principal function, the Court held that a private shopping center owner was entitled to exclude *anyone* who did not use the property for these intended commercial purposes, free from any "attenuated doctrine of dedication of private property to public use."[36] According to the Court, to order private shopping center owners to allow even traditional handbilling would constitute an infringement of their Fifth and Fourteenth Amendment rights to "private" property.

Despite its apparent breadth, *Lloyd Corp.* purported to only narrowly distinguish *Logan Valley*. The Court emphasized that the labor picketers' expression in *Logan Valley* had related specifically to one of the shopping center's tenants and, thus, there was no realistic alternative forum in which the picketers could convey their message. The Vietnam protesters in *Lloyd*, by contrast, sought to reach a more general public audience. In contrast to the residential picketers discussed in the previous chapter, whose First Amendment rights were somewhat diminished by their failure to seek a general audience, the Vietnam protesters suffered a disadvantage precisely because they sought a *broad* public audience. Their message had nothing to do with the shopping center's businesses or business practices. According to the Court, the war protesters had access to plenty of alternative forums, including the public streets and sidewalks bordering the shopping center.

In an impassioned dissent, Justice Marshall extolled the "preferred" status of First Amendment rights as compared to rights to private property. He noted that the Lloyd Center Mall bore an even closer resemblance to the "company town" than the Logan Valley Shopping Center. Justice Marshall and his fellow dissenters, now clearly fighting an uphill battle, once again emphasized the mall's social and political significance: "For many Portland citizens," they said, "Lloyd Center will so completely satisfy their wants that they will have no reason to go elsewhere for goods or services. *If speech is to reach these people, it must reach them in Lloyd Center.*"[37]

Despite its considerable effort to distinguish *Logan Valley*, the Court signaled rather unmistakably that speakers' access to shopping centers rested on precarious constitutional ground. Four years later, the ground collapsed. In *Hudgens v. NLRB* (1976), the Court expressly overruled *Logan Valley*.[38] In *Hudgens*, four labor union members had peacefully

---

[36] *Id.* at 569.
[37] *Id.* at 580 (Marshall, J., dissenting) (emphasis added).
[38] Hudgens v. NLRB, 424 U.S. 507 (1976). Indeed, the Court went so far as to say that *Lloyd* had itself sounded the death knell for *Logan Valley. See Hudgens*, 424 U.S. at 518

picketed a retail store of the Butler Shoe Company, located within the North DeKalb Shopping Center in suburban Atlanta. The pickets were objecting to practices at Butler's warehouse, which was located elsewhere. After they were threatened with arrest the picketers departed. The union filed an unfair labor practice charge against Hudgens, the owner of the shopping center, alleging interference with rights protected under the federal labor laws.

Hudgens might have been decided on statutory grounds or even by distinguishing Logan Valley. But the Court was now prepared to hold that shopping centers, as a class, were not the functional equivalent of company towns or business districts for First Amendment purposes. Indeed the Court flatly refused to recognize any public right to use these "private" properties, no matter how compatible with their primary functions, if the owner chose to invoke its property right to exclude. "It matters not," the majority stated, "that some Members of the Court may continue to believe that the Logan Valley case was rightly decided."[39] Nor did it matter, as it had in Logan Valley, that the picketers' message was at least partially related to the "contested" place of the shopping center.[40] The First Amendment, said the Court, simply "has no part to play" with regard to privately owned shopping centers.[41]

The turn toward a "preferred" status for private property rights was now complete. A constitutional balance once struck in favor of preserving physical breathing space for at least some expressive activities in modern shopping centers was recalibrated to permit private property owners to monopolize areas frequented by the general public (at the owners' request). A Court that, as noted in the previous chapter, had once supported civil rights protesters' access to private lunch counters now moved to defend owners' rights to preserve a "controlled, carefree environment" in malls and shopping centers. As noted in Chapter 2, this turn was entirely consistent with the Supreme Court's more general efforts starting in the 1970s to impose order on the expressive topography – through, in particular, development of the "public forum" and "time, place, and manner" doctrines.

("[W]e make clear now, if it was not clear before, that the rationale of Logan Valley did not survive the Court's decision in the Lloyd case").

[39] Hudgens, 424 U.S. at 518.

[40] In contrast to Logan Valley, the picketers did not seek access to the specific place in contest. They sought to protest working conditions, albeit at an off-site warehouse, associated with the company doing business in the shopping center. The apparent intent was to reach both the specific audience inside the business as well as the general public patronizing the center.

[41] Hudgens, 424 U.S. at 521.

Again, this shrinkage did not merely affect the suburban expressive topography. Recall that Justice Marshall had expressed concern in *Logan Valley* that under a private rights regime, downtown businesses would have been subjected to protest whereas suburban mall owners would have been protected from such contention. *Hudgens* essentially casts a protective bubble around *both* kinds of businesses (and other places as well). At least insofar as they are privately run, business improvement and development districts may now also possess the power to exclude unwanted speakers.[42]

As broadly as it swept, *Hudgens* left a significant question unresolved. The Constitution merely establishes a *floor* for individual liberties. States are free, under their own constitutions, to provide more expansive protection for the liberties contained in the Bill of Rights. In a 1980 decision, the Supreme Court unanimously held that the states could grant individuals the freedom to enter privately owned malls for expressive purposes, and that such compelled access did not violate the owners' First and Fifth Amendment rights.[43] As discussed below, very few states have taken this step toward replenishing the expressive topography. By and large, contemporary shopping centers remain non-places – both socially and insofar as expressive liberties are concerned.

Places of Modernity

The battle over malls and shopping centers was part of a much larger contest over access to private and quasi-public places during the 1960s and 1970s. People did not just move out of the city centers and into suburbs. As noted earlier, they became mobile in a far more general sense. As the pace of life quickened, people began to spend increasing amounts of time in airports, bus terminals, railway stations, and other transitional places of modernity.

Some of these places were privately owned; thus, absent state constitutional or common law rules to the contrary they were, like the nation's malls, off limits to speakers under the property rules discussed above. Other transportation nodes and hubs, like airport terminals and rail

---

[42] Kohn, *supra* note 13, at 87–88.

[43] PruneYard Shopping Center v. Robins, 474 U.S. 74 (1980). For a discussion of the takings implications of PruneYard, *see* Lillian R. BeVier, "Give and Take: Public Use as Due Compensation in PruneYard," 64 *U. Chi. L. Rev.* 71 (1997). For a comprehensive critique of the PruneYard decision, *see* Gregory C. Sisk, "Uprooting the Pruneyard," 38 *Rutgers L. J.* 1145 (2007).

stations, are owned and administered by governmental entities. As do shopping centers, these places vary in terms of their size, services, physical layout, and commercial offerings.

From the speaker's perspective, of course, all of these places are effective platforms for reaching large numbers of people where they typically gather. Although lower courts had expressed mixed views, the Supreme Court did not address the First Amendment status of municipal airport terminals until the early 1990s. By this time, two significant developments had occurred in terms of First Amendment jurisprudence. First, as the shopping center saga showed, the Court had abandoned the idea that speech "compatible" with a certain place was generally welcome and protected there. Second, as discussed in Chapter 2, the Court had developed a categorical approach to place that purported to divide all public space into just three categories of "public forums" – "traditional," "designated," and "non-public."

In two companion cases – *International Society for Krishna Consciousness v. Lee* (1992) and *Lee v. International Society for Krishna Consciousness* (1992) – shifting majorities of the Court sustained an airport authority's ban on the solicitation of money inside airport terminals, but narrowly invalidated a flat ban on the distribution of literature there.[44] The aspects of these cases relating to *embodied* expression, in particular in-person solicitation, were examined in Chapter 3. There was, however, something far more significant at stake in these cases than the right to leaflet in or near airport terminals. One of the questions the Court had to answer was whether an airport terminal was a traditional, designated, or non-public forum for purposes of the First Amendment. That decision, and more specifically the logic by which the Court reached it, had tremendous implications for the future of expressive liberties in places of modernity.

A majority of the justices held that airport terminals were to be *categorically* treated as *non-public* forums. This means that rules and policies regarding speech in such places merely have to be "reasonable" and neutral as to the speaker's viewpoint to survive First Amendment scrutiny.[45] In terms of categorization, Chief Justice Rehnquist

---

[44] Int'l Soc'y for Krishna Consciousness, Inc. v. Lee, 505 U.S. 672 (1992); Lee v. Int'l Society for Krishna Consciousness, Inc., 505 U.S. 830 (1992). In her opinion invalidating the ban on leafleting, Justice O'Connor emphasized that under the time, place, and manner doctrine airport authorities could relegate leafleting to "a relatively uncongested part of the airport terminals." 505 U.S. at 692 (O'Connor, J., concurring).

[45] *See, e.g.,* Greer v. Spock, 424 U.S. 828, 838 (1976) (upholding rule banning leafleting on portions of military base without prior approval of base commander).

explained that the "tradition of airport activity does not demonstrate that airports have historically been made available for speech activity."[46] The Court noted that unlike public streets, sidewalks, and parks, which are considered "traditional" public forums, airport terminals are actually products of modernity. Reflecting the increased mobility of the people, these structures did not appear in great numbers until well into the twentieth century.[47] For the majority it necessarily followed that these places had not been open to public expression "time out of mind" – the very essence of a "traditional" public forum like a public street or park. Nor, said the Court, were airport terminals "designated" forums for expressive activity. The Court noted that managers of publicly owned terminals had not generally allowed expression there – except perhaps in some cases under threat of court order.[48] Finally, the Court observed that the primary function and purpose of airport terminals was "the facilitation of passenger air travel, not the promotion of expression."[49] Thus, in these as in other non-public forums, terminal operators are entitled to impose broad restrictions on expression so long as they are reasonable and do not distinguish among speakers based upon their viewpoint.

The *Lee* cases highlighted both the general disarray of the Court's public forum doctrine and the failure of its approach to respond to social and architectural changes, matters to which I return below. The majority did not expressly consider the substantial effect its categorization method and conclusion would likely have on the contemporary expressive topography. In a concurrence, Justice Kennedy observed that the Court's narrow focus on the "tradition" and the "primary function" of a place left "almost no scope for the development of new public forums."[50] Echoing Justice Marshall in the shopping center cases, Justice Kennedy criticized the public forum doctrine as having "no relevance in times of fast-changing technology and increasing insularity."[51] He emphasized the broader significance of the Court's decision for the expressive topography:

> In a country where most citizens travel by automobile, and parks all too often become locales for crime rather than social intercourse, our

[46] ISKCON v. Lee, 505 U.S. at 680.
[47] *Id.* at 680.
[48] *Id.* at 680–81.
[49] *Id.* at 682.
[50] *Id.* at 695 (Kennedy, J., concurring).
[51] *Id.* at 697.

failure to recognize the possibility that new types of government property may be appropriate forums for speech will lead to a serious curtailment of our expressive activity. One of the places left in our mobile society that is suitable for discourse is a metropolitan airport. It is of particular importance to recognize that such spaces are public forums because in these days an airport is one of the few government-owned spaces where many persons have extensive contact with other members of the public. Given that private spaces of similar character are not subject to the dictates of the First Amendment, it is critical that we preserve these areas for protected speech.[52]

Justice Kennedy, it will be recalled, was one of the few justices to appreciate the significance of embodied places to abortion clinic counselors and protesters (Chapter 3). Here too he recognized that the Court's approach threatened to erode the expressive topography, this time by creating substantial gaps where expressive culture could not take root.

Lee's categorical approach treats airport terminals – and, presumably, other transportation hubs such as train stations – as nonpublic forums regardless of the variety of functions these places serve or their individual physical characteristics. Further, although as precedents the *Lee* cases only determined the fate of public airport terminals, the Court's methodology essentially precludes *any* modern public place from ever gaining the status of "traditional" or "quintessential" public forum. Thus, for example, places like interstate rest stops, built to accommodate a modern and mobile public, have been held to be nonpublic forums because they too are "modern creations."[53] Significantly, as Justice Kennedy observed, under the Court's approach there can be no further broad expansions of the expressive topography. New places, or those not yet constructed, obviously cannot have been "immemorially" open to public debate and discussion. Absent a governmental decision to *designate* places of modernity as open expressive forums – a very unlikely occurrence, as the airport terminal cases show – all such places will remain gaps or non-places on the expressive topography.

Privatizing Community

As noted, non-places are not merely products of First Amendment and other constitutional doctrines. Social and political events have also created

---

[52] *Id.* at 698 (citations omitted).
[53] Jacobsen v. Bonine, 123 F.3d 1272 (9th Cir. 1997).

substantial dead space on the expressive topography. As discussed in the next chapter, privatization of even quintessential public places has become a growing concern. Owing to budgetary constraints and aesthetic agendas, some municipalities have proposed to sell off places like public parks to the highest bidder and, in certain instances, to "demote" traditional public forums like streets by privatizing them or limiting public access. Such policies limit or extinguish First Amendment liberties in these places.

Further, privatization of entire communities has been on the rise in the past few decades. The number of people in this country living in gated communities or secure developments has grown tremendously. In the 1970s, there were approximately 2,000 gated communities in the United States. By the year 2000, there were over 50,000. According to the Census Bureau's 2001 American Housing Survey, more than 7 million households – about 6 percent of the national total – were then located in developments behind gates, walls, and fences. The figure has since leveled off, although it has remained relatively constant. While gated communities are generally favored by white and affluent Americans, persons living in various other types of secure enclaves cut across ethnic and socio-economic strata.[54]

Social scientists generally lament this social separation, often attributing it to a general climate of fear of others. In addition to its social implications, there are also substantial expressive concerns associated with this trend. The combination of gated and other spatial enclaves and the proliferation of private, unincorporated communities in the United States has done serious damage to the expressive topography. The sheer loss of public space is merely one important aspect of this damage. In the streets of gated, unincorporated, and other secluded communities, there essentially are no First Amendment liberties. Public access is often severely limited. The state is generally absent, having been replaced by the now-ubiquitous "homeowner's association."[55] More generally, privatized communities are not – or at least have not yet proven to be – particularly civic-minded or social places.[56] Indeed, as the anthropologist Setha Low has observed, one of the common reasons people have moved to such places is to *avoid* the ethnic and cultural diversity of truly public places.[57] This undermines the fundamental democratic functions of public places.

---

[54] For an ethnographic account of those who choose to live in such communities, *see* Setha Low, *Behind the Gates: Life, Security, and the Pursuit of Happiness in Fortress America* (2003).
[55] *See* Kohn, *supra* note 13 at 117–25 (discussing residential community associations and other forms of local, private governance).
[56] *See* Edward J. Blakely & Mary Gail Snyder, *Fortress America: Gated Communities in the United States* (1999).
[57] Low, *supra* note 54.

The Constitution does not prohibit a society from privatizing its communities. But when this occurs, First Amendment liberties do not necessarily extend to the newly "privatized" spaces. As a result of the proliferation of non-places, a person may readily avoid not merely the presence but the identity claims and other messages of *strangers* – in the neighborhood, at local shopping centers, and as she waits for an airplane or train. Non-place gaps on the expressive topography are vast – and they have been growing at a steady pace.

THE CONSTITUTION OF NON-PLACE

The dominance of property rules and concepts has essentially defeated the very notion that vast public, quasi-public, and potentially public properties are or could be *places* on an expressive topography. What has happened to shopping centers and other places of modernity constitutionally is symptomatic of the manner in which our expressive topography has been generally eroded over the past four or five decades. There is at present little, if any, hope that the principal constitutional doctrines that have transformed places of modernity into non-places will be substantially revised, or that these doctrines will suddenly require facilitation of public expression or creation of public space. Nevertheless, in light of the extraordinary effects they have had on the expressive topography, it bears emphasizing just how contested the major premises of the doctrines that have literally *constituted* non-places actually are. There may, as argued below, be some hope for creating space through state constitutions and common law, as well as through the peoples' own resilience in locating alternative expressive and communal places.

The Problematic Public-Private Distinction

The "state action" doctrine has facilitated a significant trend toward privatization of an array of governmental functions and services. Unless the state actually owns something or exercises near-absolute dominion over it, the action will not likely be deemed to have been exercised in the sovereign's name. This is not the space for a broad debate regarding the normative implications of privatization.[58] It suffices to say that privatization is not always and in every instance problematic – at least so long as

---

[58] For a defense of public spaces as public goods, *see* Kohn, *supra* note 13 at 193–205.

we can expect some efficiency returns and so long as there are safeguards to correct and remedy "private" misconduct.[59]

When it comes to public space, however, privatization can be extremely problematic. No private entity has any independent incentive to facilitate public expressive liberties or preserve them. A regime premised largely upon possession of *title* to property cannot and will not be capable of sustaining a diverse and robust expressive topography. Indeed one of the most remarkable things about the contemporary expressive topography is just how little truly *public* space remains a part of it. As Justice Kennedy suggested in *Lee*, this is precisely what makes "new" places so critical to expressive liberties. Legal scholars, in particular, tend to debate privatization in relatively abstract terms. To understand it in this context, however, one must appreciate and acknowledge the *overall* condition of the expressive topography. When considered in that context, the privatization of public and quasi-public places, either through ownership transfers or constitutional property rules, is especially problematic.

One of the principal suppositions in the resolution of the shopping center saga was that the government is under no obligation to ensure adequate breathing space for public expression. Indeed under one interpretation of current doctrine, there would seem to be nothing to prevent the government from either selling all public spaces to private owners or flatly prohibiting expression in *all* public places.[60] Gated and other privatized communities are evidence of the creeping acceptance of this state of affairs. As they are privately owned and operated, these communities and districts need not permit expression by "the public" on neighborhood streets and sidewalks. Governments are not in any sense required to force these communities to remain open to public activity and expression; among other limitations, it is not clear that they could enforce such a mandate without compensating the community.[61]

As emphasized in Chapter 6, the very notion that there are "quintessential" public forums in which public expression has traditionally been permitted arises from mere *dictum* in *Hague v. CIO* (1939). Even if Hague's dictum means that officials must preserve access to *old* places

---

[59] The state action doctrine is a notorious mess. Critiques of the doctrine are numerous. For proposals to either substantially revise or do away with the doctrine altogether, *see* Gillian E. Metzger, "Privatization as Delegation," 103 *Colum. L. Rev.* 1367 (2003); Erwin Chemerinsky, "Rethinking State Action," 80 *Nw. U. L. Rev.* 503 (1985).

[60] This is a troubling implication, even for those who generally do not support a facilitative interpretation of constitutional liberties. *See, e.g.*, Charles Fried, *Modern Liberty and the Limits of Government* 105 (2007).

[61] The Takings Clause of the Fifth Amendment may require compensation in the event authorities commandeer private property for a public use. U.S. Const., amend. V.

like public streets, this bare recognition does not necessarily impose on the government any obligation to provide or ensure access to any *new* places devoted to public expression. In this and other ways, the rejection of a "facilitative" or "enhancement" approach to First Amendment liberties has led to the proliferation of non-places and the general denuding of the expressive topography.[62]

In addition to the gaps created by the absence of any duty to create breathing space for public expression, the notoriously slippery line between what is "public" and what is "private" has created substantial gaps of its own. Consider the case of shopping center properties. Under current "state action" doctrine, owners of *quasi-public* places are permitted to flatly prohibit expressive activity on their premises. There is no longer any balancing of First Amendment liberties and private ownership interests. Title counts for everything. This is so even if the property in question is the "functional equivalent" of a public place that had traditionally supported expressive liberties.

The categorical application of a "public-private" distinction to shopping centers and other properties is problematic. As this book shows in various contexts, places are highly variable in the sense that their properties and functions can change over time. The shopping center was still in a relatively early stage of development when the Court removed it from the expressive topography in the mid-1970s. It is doubtful that anyone could have anticipated, as long ago as the 1960s, modern urban megastructures that contain hundreds of businesses, scores of recreational options, and even permanent housing. It is equally doubtful that the modern "city within a city" was within the Court's conceptual vision when it considered access to shopping centers in the 1960s and 1970s. Forty years ago shopping centers barely dotted the retail landscape of America. There are at least five times as many shopping centers today as there were four decades ago. Today 190 million people visit a shopping center each month, and many visit multiple times. The Court was also not anticipating the rise of the "business development district" and other means of privatizing densely populated urban spaces.

Many of today's shopping centers are much more than collections of commercial establishments under a single roof. As one observer wryly noted in the mid-1980s:

---

[62] For a discussion of the distinction between "enhancement" and "distortion" models of the First Amendment, *see* Lillian R. Bevier, "Rehabilitating Public Forum Doctrine: In Defense of Categories," 101 *Sup. Ct. Rev.* 79 (1992).

You can get anything from diamonds to yogurt in the mall; you can attend college classes, register to vote, go to the library, see topless dancers and male strippers, give blood, bet, score, jog and meditate, and get a room or a condo and live there. Someday it may be possible – if it isn't already – to be born, go from preschool through college, get a job, date, marry, have children, fool around, get a divorce, advance through a career or two, receive your medical care, even get arrested, tried, and jailed; live a relatively full life of culture and entertainment, and eventually die and be given funeral rites without ever leaving a particular mall complex – because every one of those possibilities exists now in some shopping center somewhere.[63]

Hyperbole aside, the contemporary shopping center is a quasi-public place of great significance to millions of Americans. Indeed, for many only the home and workplace may be more socially important places. Among other things, people shop, play, exercise, and even worship in contemporary shopping centers.

What is more, several governmental functions and services can now be found inside some of these centers. A survey conducted by one legal scholar in the late 1990s found that many shopping centers support a variety of governmental functions – United States postal stations, community centers, police substations and precincts, early voting centers, libraries, and schools.[64] In some properties, retail stores share space with government agencies like the Department of Labor and the Division of Motor Vehicles and officials like city treasurers, state auditors, and even a United States congressional representative. One shopping center located in Knoxville, Tennessee leases space to both the city and county in order to provide the convenience of essential governmental services right on the premises (and of course to attract consumers). The city invites citizens to visit "City Hall at the Mall" – to pay property taxes, renew drivers' licenses, conduct post office business, and apply for marriage licenses there. These properties are no more "private" than the company town; indeed if anything they are far less so.

Shopping centers are "public" endeavors in other respects as well. Many simply would not exist without substantial governmental assistance. Substantial public funds may be used to aid in construction of these new indoor downtowns. Public bonds may be issued to finance site preparation, including parking ramps and access roads. Roadways around the mall may

[63] Kowinski, *supra* note 19 at 21–22.
[64] Mark C. Alexander, "Attention, Shoppers: The First Amendment in the Modern Shopping Mall," 41 *Ariz. L. Rev.* 1 (1999).

need to be altered or repaired – all at public expense. Like other businesses, shopping centers reap substantial benefits from localities desperate for more retail dollars, jobs for citizens, and future tax revenue. In short, governments need shopping centers, and shopping centers need them.

Although title to these places may be privately held, the character of many is recognizably "public." And yet they remain, under the authority of *Hudgens* and state action doctrine, generally beyond constitutional reach. The fate of the fur protesters at the Mall of America, mentioned at the beginning of the chapter, demonstrates the incongruity in this approach. Construction of the Mall, which as noted draws some 37 million visitors annually, was substantially financed with public funds. Among other things, inside the Mall one can find a public school, a branch of a private university, and a police substation. City police officers patrol the Mall and are considered "on-duty" under the supervision of the police department. The Mall has a community booth for the publicizing of community events. The League of Women Voters registers people to vote there. The Mall has hosted numerous public events, including the World's Largest Marriage Workshop, the World's Largest Sleepover, and a reception for the President of Botswana. As also mentioned, the Mall's public areas are touted by its proprietors as "city streets" and "town squares" (Figure 5.1).

Figure 5.1. Inside the Mall of America.
Source: Photograph by Jeffrey Long.

Despite all of this, the Minnesota Supreme Court, applying state action rules identical in relevant respects to those the Supreme Court has announced, held that there was insufficient state involvement to invoke the free speech guarantees of the state constitution. There was, it said, a "lack of evidence connecting the 'power, property and prestige" of the State of Minnesota or the City of Bloomington with the actions of [the Mall] management[.]"[65] The court noted that it was not convinced by the testimony of an architecture expert that malls are "simulation[s] of traditional towns."[66] Nor was it persuaded by an urban studies expert who opined that suburban communities do not take pains to create public space "because it's assumed the mall is effectively going to be that."[67] The same expert observed that "the reduction of public space 'reduces levels of civility overall for everyone.' "[68]

Although it would not likely have made any difference, had a First Amendment expert been called to testify she might have opined that physical grassroots organizing for poorly financed causes depends upon access to the considerable audiences found at places like shopping centers. Data indicate that more and more people are going to the malls for the purpose of general browsing or for events *unrelated* to making purchases. If this is so, one wonders why all expression unrelated to the owner's business, including small and peaceful protests, is somehow deemed incompatible with the space. The reason, of course, is that expression and other public-oriented activity is thought to interfere with the private owner's vision of a peaceful, uninterrupted, and undisturbed "mall experience." Shopping center owners go to great lengths to control the environment and focus the shopper. Some have even expelled patrons for wearing items of clothing – like t-shirts and in one case a colored bandanna – thought to violate rigid dress and no-expression policies.

The foregoing considerations – the actual function of shopping centers, the need for public space, the effect a vibrant expressive topography has on

---

[65] *Wicklund*, 598 N.W.2d at 802. If a state nexus could not be found at the Mall, one can appreciate the degree to which centers across the country can and often do offer public services yet remain constitutionally "private." To be sure, as discussed below some courts have interpreted the state action doctrine somewhat more broadly than the Minnesota Supreme Court. A distinct few, again interpreting state constitutional law, have even dispensed with the requirement in the shopping center context. But the Minnesota Supreme Court's decision is not at all unusual or out of the mainstream. Any speaker may challenge the notion that a shopping center is "private" for First Amendment or state constitutional purposes. But the likelihood of success is very small indeed.

[66] Jennifer Niles Coffin, Note, "The United Mall of America: Free Speech, State Constitutions, and the Growing Fortress of Private Property," 33 *U. Mich. J.L. Ref.* 615, 640 (2000).

[67] *Id.* at 641.

[68] *Id.*

public civility, the importance of a public domain to self-governance – are all distinctly relevant to public *places*. But they matter not at all when the issue is simply one of *properties* and who owns them. Although they expressly invite the public to come in great numbers, private shopping center owners generally may rely upon their title to condition access upon the public's agreement not to engage in any expressive activity. Mall owners are thereby permitted to monopolize these quasi-public places. Students may not, as the Supreme Court once famously said, shed their constitutional rights at the schoolhouse door – but patrons at most of the nation's quasi-public shopping centers certainly do.

These observations do not automatically lead to the conclusion that every property owner who extends an invitation to the public forfeits the exclusionary benefits of title. Private hospital or clinic waiting rooms, for example, are sites where substantial portions of the public often go to obtain medical services. But these places are not the "functional equivalent" of the public square or city hall. They do not share space with or support governmental services or officials. Given their specific functions, most forms of expression would not be "compatible" with such places. The mere presence of invitees thus cannot be determinative.

The general point is that we ought not to so quickly accept that certain quasi-public properties are constitutionally "private." As suggested below, in some cases courts might more rigorously examine whether the state is sufficiently "present" to warrant at least some First Amendment breathing space. If we do not begin to reconsider the public-private distinction, there is a substantial risk that more and more of our expressive topography will be transformed into non-places.

Spatial Categorization and Ossification

As the state action doctrine was eliminating access to shopping centers and other "private" properties, the public forum doctrine was doing similar work with regard to some plainly *public* places of modernity. Like malls and shopping centers, many airports and other publicly owned and administered transportation facilities serve multiple functions. Many host a variety of public and private services similar to those present in contemporary shopping centers. As Justice Kennedy observed in *Lee*, these are among the few publicly owned places where speakers can still reach large public audiences. Similar to shopping centers, they represent what little remains of a vanishing public sphere.

According to the Supreme Court, however, these too are *categorically* to be treated as non-places insofar as the First Amendment is concerned. Indeed, in a single stroke the Court removed most public places of modernity from the expressive topography. Recall that the Court held in *Lee* that airport terminals could not be considered "traditional" public forums primarily because they had not been around long enough to claim this status – they had not "time out of mind" been open to expression. By definition, of course, no *modern* place will be able to claim such a history.

This book contains a variety of criticisms of the public forum doctrine. Indeed, as discussed in Chapter 1, it rejects many of the doctrine's major premises.[69] One of the specific criticisms is that the blunt instrument of forum categorization removes expressive activity from entire classes of properties. As others have noted, public forum doctrine rests upon a "myopic focus on formalistic labels" that purports to distinguish "public" from "non-public" forums.[70] As *Lee* itself demonstrates, the process whereby places are categorized as "traditional," "designated," or "non-public" forums distracts courts from considering the range of First Amendment values and practices such places affect.[71] More generally, the categorical approach elides the social and expressive significance of public places.

The treatment of places of modernity demonstrates that public forum doctrine is, as the First Amendment scholar Calvin Massey has said, "historically ossified."[72] The doctrine relies upon outdated notions of

---

[69] Criticism of the public forum doctrine has been unsparing, and has come from many quarters. Representative critiques can be found in Calvin Massey, "Public Fora, Neutral Governments, and the Prism of Property," 50 *Hastings L. J.* 309, 310 (1999); Steven G. Gey, "Reopening the Public Forum – From Sidewalks to Cyberspace," 58 *Ohio St. L. J.* 1535, 1577 (1998); Laurence Tribe, *Constitutional Law* 993 (2d ed. 1988); Robert C. Post, "Between Governance and Management: The History and Theory of the Public Forum," 34 *U.C.L.A. L. Rev.* 1713, 1715–16 (1987); Geoffrey R. Stone, "Content-Neutral Restrictions," 54 *U. Chi. L. Rev.* 46, 93 (1987); Keith Werhan, "The Supreme Court's Public Forum Doctrine and the Return of Formalism," 7 *Cardozo L. Rev.* 335, 341 (1986); C. Thomas Dienes, "The Trashing of the Public Forum: Problems in First Amendment Analysis," 55 *Geo. Wash. L. Rev.* 109, 110 (1986); Daniel A. Farber & John E. Nowak, "The Misleading Nature of Public Forum Analysis: Content and Context in First Amendment Adjudication," 70 *Va. L. Rev.* 1219, 1234 (1984); Ronald A. Cass, "First Amendment Access to Government Facilities," 65 *Va. L. Rev.* 1287, 1308–09 (1979); David Goldberger, "Judicial Scrutiny in Public Forum Cases: Misplaced Trust in the Judgment of Public Officials," 32 *Buffalo L. Rev.* 175, 183 (1983); Kenneth Karst, "Public Enterprise and the Public Forum: A Comment on *Southeastern Promotions, Ltd. v. Conrad*," 37 *Ohio St. L. J.* 247 (1976).

[70] Stone, *supra* note 69 at 93.

[71] *See* Werhan, *supra* note 69 at 341 (contending that the doctrine "produces incoherent results untouched by the interplay of considerations that should inform . . . decisionmaking under the first amendment"); Gey, *supra* note 69 at 1536–37 (noting the rigidity of forum analysis); Farber & Nowak, *supra* note 69 at 1224.

[72] Massey, *supra* note 69 at 310.

where speakers and audiences are co-present.[73] It fails to account for societal mobility, changes that have occurred elsewhere on the expressive topography, and local architectural transformations. Remarkably, during the course of more than six decades public streets, (most) public side-walks, and public parks are the *only* forums that have been recognized under the public forum doctrine as fully open to public debate and dis-cussion. Owing to its reliance on tradition and historical practice – a form of "spatial originalism" – forum doctrine will not allow for any meaningful expansion of the expressive topography.

The *Lee* Court also placed substantial emphasis on the primary and original intended *function* of the airport terminal. The primary function of an airport terminal, the Court said in *Lee*, is to facilitate travel. That is undoubtedly so. But as Justice Kennedy and others have noted, applica-tion of a "primary function" test leads to some absurd results. The pri-mary function of a sidewalk is to facilitate pedestrian movement; and yet expression is protected there. That a public place facilitates one function dose not mean it can serve no other. Further, whether or not a place was originally built for expressive or some other purpose tells us little or nothing about that place's role on the *contemporary* expressive topogra-phy. The focus on original purpose does not allow for consideration of architectural and other transformations of these and other places of modernity. Like the shopping center, the airport terminal has changed dramatically over the past six decades. Finally, treating airport terminals as an undifferentiated *class of property* assumes that all terminals are alike. But just as no two shopping centers are precisely the same, airports are highly variable in certain respects. A small regional hub is not the same as a metropolitan international airport. Yet public forum doctrine insists that they are identical for purposes of the First Amendment.

Absent the requisite history, tradition, and original function, the only way airport terminals or other places of modernity will be deemed open to expressive activity is if public officials expressly "designate" them for such purpose. This, as one can well imagine, will be the rare exception to the rule of exclusion. Public forum doctrine has been accurately described as "a declaration of deference to forum administrators."[74] Recall that one of the very reasons cited in *Lee* for the exclusion of expression from airport terminals was the historical resistance of public administrators. To leave

---

[73] For a discussion of the importance of co-presence, *see* William H. Sewell, Jr., "Space in Contentious Politics," in Ronald Aminzade, Jack A. Goldstone, Doug McAdam, Elizabeth J. Perry, William H. Sewell, Jr., Sidney Tarrow, & Charles Tilly, *Silence and Voice in the Study of Contentious Politics* 57–59 (2001).

[74] Massey, *supra* note 69 at 319.

the matter up to the administrators of places of modernity is effectively to decide against breathing space for expressive liberties in new or modern places on the expressive topography.[75]

Although it has not garnered any significant support among the justices, Justice Kennedy has offered an alternative to this sort of rigid categorization and deference. He suggested in *Lee*:

> If the objective physical characteristics of the property at issue and the actual public access and uses which have been permitted by the government indicate that expressive activity would be *appropriate and compatible* with those uses, the property is a public forum. The most important considerations in this analysis are whether the property shares physical similarities with more traditional public forums, whether the government has permitted or acquiesced in broad public access to the property, and whether expressive activity would tend to interfere in a significant way with the uses to which the government has as a factual matter dedicated the property.[76]

Justice Kennedy's approach makes several important adjustments. It resurrects the "compatibility" standard the Court applied during the Civil Rights Era and briefly flirted with in some early public forum cases. "Appropriateness" and "compatibility" are obviously far more speech-facilitate standards than the requirement that the place have been "born" a public forum or that there be clear evidence that the government intended to create an expressive forum. Justice Kennedy's proposed standard asks more of courts than the forum doctrine, in particular that they carefully examine the "physical characteristics" of the type of place at issue – both for the purpose of comparison to more traditional forums and to ensure the compatibility of expression with the place's other functions. It makes the government's preferred uses for the place only one, rather than the predominant, consideration in deciding whether expression ought to be

---

[75] Property categorization does have its defenders. Labeling classes of property, some suggest, provides more clarity to speakers and proprietors in terms of where expression is publicly permitted. It places decisions in that regard in the hands of officials more politically accountable, and perhaps more knowledgeable, than federal judges. *See* Bevier, *supra* note 62 at 102–12 (explaining forum categories as consistent with the "distortion" model of the First Amendment); Post, *supra* note 69 at 1833 (positing that a "line between governance and management corresponds to the distinction between the public and nonpublic forum"). But those same officials are naturally biased in favor of peace, tranquility, order, security, and other interests usually at odds with expressive ones. They gain little, if anything, from allowing speakers to distribute information or engage in other forms of public expression on "their" properties.

[76] Lee v. ISKCON, 505 U.S. at 698 (Kennedy, J., concurring) (emphasis supplied).

permitted. Under this standard, Justice Kennedy would have held that airport terminals are public forums. If Justice Kennedy's approach had prevailed, not only airports but at least some *future* places of modernity would also likely be included on the expressive topography.

Despite its merits, however, there is one substantial weakness in Justice Kennedy's approach. Insofar as it remains categorical in orientation, it does not go far enough. Either *all* airports would be public forums under this standard or *none* would be. Like present public forum doctrine, this fails to appreciate that places exhibit unique characteristics. An entire class of place should not be ruled within or outside the expressive topography on the basis of a single design model plucked from among the cases in the Supreme Court's *certiorari* pool. The distinctiveness of place requires that courts take into consideration the special characteristics of places before determining whether they are to be expressive forums. In this respect, the approach taken by Justice Souter in *Lee* is preferable. Justice Souter asserted that "[t]he inquiry may and must relate to the *particular property* at issue."[77] A public forum, he asserted, is "any piece of public property that is 'suitable for discourse' in its physical character, where expressive activity is 'compatible' with the use to which it has actually been put."[78]

Unfortunately, to date the more spatially sensitive approaches of Justices Kennedy and Souter have not prevailed on the Court. Nor are they likely to find much traction, at least absent a significant change in the Court's makeup. The categorical treatment of public places of modernity under public forum doctrine has created substantial additional gaps or non-places on the contemporary expressive topography. More seriously, the Court's approach to these places, which emphasizes history and tradition, has ossified the expressive topography. Its approach has placed prospects for future replenishment of public breathing space for expression squarely in the hands of public officials, who will generally favor a host of other functions to expressive ones.

NEGATING NON-PLACE

What, if any, promising and realistic possibilities exist for countering or even negating the proliferation of non-places? There are two main possibilities which, separately or in combination, could replace at least some

---

[77] *Id.* at 710 (Souter, J., concurring) (emphasis added).
[78] *Id.* at 711.

of the expressive breathing space that has recently been lost to non-place. The first depends upon state courts and local lawmakers creating additional breathing space in places of modernity. The Supreme Court's state action and public forum rulings merely establish a constitutional floor. State and local officials can, and in some cases already have, gone further. The second solution is for the people themselves to not only resist the urge to live in "secure" enclaves like gated communities, but to actually seek out alternative public and quasi-public places where interaction and expression can occur. Indeed many people have already located and used such "third places" – places between work and home – to fill some of the non-place voids on the expressive topography.

Adding Expressive Space Above the Constitutional Floor

With regard to certain matters of constitutionality the Supreme Court has the last word. Fortunately, this is not the case when it comes to creating breathing space for expressive liberties. State courts can, and in some cases have, interpreted their own constitutions to require owners of even private properties to allow speech on the premises. Further, with regard to places within their jurisdictions, including those that are privately owned, states and localities exercise substantial police powers. Local governments have various options available to them for opening places of modernity to at least some expressive activity.

As noted earlier, some time after it had ruled that speakers had no First Amendment right to access "private" shopping centers, the Supreme Court invited state courts to decide whether their own charters ought to be interpreted to require owners to admit expression there. In *PruneYard Shopping Center v. Robins* (1980), the Court held that "a state's organic and general law can independently furnish a basis for protecting individual rights of speech and assembly."[79] The Court held that neither the Fifth Amendment's Takings Clause nor the First Amendment itself barred such interpretations.

Most state courts have not interpreted state constitutions to require that speakers be granted access to quasi-public places like shopping centers and universities.[80] But a handful of the states' highest courts have indeed

[79] 447 U.S. at 81.
[80] *See* Fiesta Mall Venture v. Mecham Recall Committee, 159 Ariz. 371 767 P.2d 719 (Ariz. Ct. App. 1988); Cologne v. Westfarms Associates, 192 Conn. 48, 469 A.2d 1201 (1984); Citizens for Ethical Govt., Inc. v. Gwinnett Place Associates, 260 Ga. 245, 392 S.E.2d 8 (1990); Estes v. Kapiolani Women's and Children's Med. Ctr., 71 Haw. 190, 787 P.2d 216 (1990); Illinois v. DiGuida, 604 N.E.2d 336, 340 (Ill. 1992); State v. Lacey, 465 N.W.2d 537, 540 (Iowa 1991); Woodland v. Michigan Citizens Lobby, 378 N.W.2d 337, 348

expanded speakers' access to such places. A few courts have simply dispensed with the state action requirement altogether for purposes of interpreting state constitutional liberties. These courts have held that large shopping centers and other quasi-public places must permit speakers to exercise at least some expressive liberties on the premises even though the state is not closely connected to the premises. Courts in New Jersey and California have taken the broadest approach. California law currently requires that large multistore shopping centers allow leafletters, signature gatherers, and other speakers on the premises.[81] New Jersey has a similar constitutional rule, which applies to private universities in the state as well.[82]

The basic theory in these cases, which dates back to the *Marsh* "company town" decision, is that by inviting the public to gather in such places for a variety of purposes the owners have essentially invited "normal" expressive activity as well.[83] The New Jersey Supreme Court reasoned that because shopping center owners "have intentionally transformed their property into a public square or market, a public gathering place, a downtown business district, a community," they could not rescind their implied invitation insofar as speakers were concerned. "[I]n necessitous circumstances," said the court, "private property rights must yield to societal interests and needs."[84] The New Jersey and California courts have thus essentially rejected the rigid, title-based "state action" doctrine announced by the Supreme Court in *Hudgens*.

Unlike the Supreme Court, the New Jersey and California courts recognized the necessity of preserving breathing space for expressive liberties in places of modernity. Echoing statements made by Justice

(Mich. 1985); State v. Wicklund, 589 N.W.2d 793 (Minn. 1999); Schad Alliance v. Smith Haven Mall, 488 N.E.2d 1211, 1213 (N.Y. 1985); State v. Felmet, 302 N.C. 173, 273 S.E.2d 708 (1981); Eastwood Mall, Inc. v. Slanco, 626 N.E.2d 59, 61–62 (Ohio 1994); Stranahan v. Fred Meyer, Inc., 153 Or. App. 442, 958 P.2d 854 (1998); Charleston Joint Venture v. McPherson, 308 S.C. 145, 417 S.E.2d 544 (1992); Republican Party v. Dietz, 940 S.W.2d 86, 89–90 (Tex. 1997); South Center Joint Venture v. National Democratic Party Policy Comm., 113 Wash. 2d 413, 780 P.2d 1282 (1989); Jacobs v. Major, 407 N.W.2d 832, 841 (Wis. 1987). State approaches are discussed in John A. Ragosta, "Free Speech Access to Shopping Malls Under State Constitutions: Analysis and Rejection," 37 *Syracuse L. Rev.* 1 (1986) and Stanley H. Friedelbaum, "Private Property, Public Property: Shopping Centers and Expressive Freedom in the States," 62 *Albany L. Rev.* 1229 (1999).

81 *See* Robins v. PruneYard Shopping Center, *supra*. The California Supreme Court recently reaffirmed *PruneYard. See* Fashion Valley Mall v. NLRB.

82 New Jersey Coalition Against War in the Middle East v. J.M.B. Realty Corp., 650 A.2d 757 (N.J. 1994).

83 The New Jersey Supreme Court's holding was limited to "leafletting and associated free speech: the speech that normally and necessarily accompanies leafleting. . . . It does not include bullhorns, megaphones, or even a soapbox; it does not include placards, pickets, parades, and demonstrations; it does not include anything other than normal speech." *Id.* at 782.

84 *Id.* at 777.

Marshall two decades earlier and by Justice Kennedy more recently, the New Jersey Supreme Court stated:

> If free speech is to mean anything in the future, it must be exercised at these centers. Our constitutional right encompasses more than leafletting and associated speech on sidewalks located in empty downtown business districts. It means communicating with the people in the new commercial and social centers; *if the people have left for the shopping centers, our constitutional right includes the right to go there too, to follow them, and to talk to them. We do not believe that those who adopted a constitutional provision granting a right of free speech wanted it to diminish in importance as society changed, to be dependent on the unrelated accidents of economic transformation, or to be silenced because of a new way of doing business.*[85]

The right recognized by the New Jersey and California Supreme Courts was not a license to follow and harass public citizens. Nor was it a right to engage in *all* forms of public expression, including assemblies that would disrupt the usual functioning of the place. Reasonable time, place, and manner regulations can be and are imposed by mall proprietors in these states. The right recognized was simply the opportunity, in a place where speakers were likely to find a public audience, to peacefully and nondisruptively engage others regarding matters of public concern.

Courts in other jurisdictions have allowed for somewhat more limited speaker access to "private" places. For example, Pennsylvania courts have interpreted the state constitution to require private property owners to permit expressive activity only if the owner has generally opened the property to public expression and debate.[86] Although few, if any, shopping centers would meet this standard, it is possible that the standard would require some private *universities* to allow public access for expressive purposes. Colorado law requires private owners to admit speakers only if the government is specially intertwined with the private mall. The courts there have adopted a somewhat less demanding version of the "state action" requirement.[87] Finally, Massachusetts law requires that large privately owned shopping centers allow speakers on the

---

[85] *Id.* at 779 (emphasis added).
[86] Pennsylvania Socialist Workers 1982 Campaign v. Connecticut General Life Ins. Co., 512 Pa. 23, 515 A.2d 1331 (1986).
[87] Block v. Westminster Mall Co., 819 P.2d 55, 58 (Colo. 1991). The mall at issue in *Block* featured a highly visible governmental presence, including a police substation, military recruiting offices, and county voter-registration drives.

premises for certain limited purposes, namely to gather signatures to qualify a candidate for the ballot or to place an initiative measure on the ballot.[88] This limited obligation arises, according to the Massachusetts Supreme Judicial Court, from the election provisions of the Massachusetts constitution rather than from its free speech guarantee.

Many state courts may be reluctant to grant a *constitutional* right of access to privately owned places, or may be constrained by precedent from doing so. But state courts need not rely solely upon constitutional interpretations and rulings to create additional breathing space on the expressive topography. As some legal scholars have argued, access for speakers could also be required under common law property theories.[89] As these scholars note, state courts have developed several doctrines in derogation of private property owners' rights. These include the implied warranty of habitability, the promotion of free alienability of the tenant's interest, and the defense of retaliatory eviction. Thus, courts applying state trespass laws might balance the speaker's interests in accessing new public forums with the property owner's interests in exclusion. If a speaker is able to convince a court that the place is indeed the "functional equivalent" of a public forum and that the specific expressive activity is appropriate in that place, then access ought not to be denied based upon the law of trespass.[90] This approach, which thus far has not been applied to shopping centers, would of necessity require a place-by-place determination regarding a right of expressive entry.

State legislatures could also create additional physical space for expressive activities in quasi-public places. Some time ago, the legal scholar Curtis Berger suggested that states empower municipalities to use predevelopment conditions to extract a form of "public easement" for limited expressive activities on private properties.[91] With regard to developed properties, Professor Berger argued that legislatures themselves could simply require owners to maintain some form of expressive space on their properties. They could also establish a general principle of access by, for example, decriminalizing peaceful and nondisruptive expressive entries at certain properties. As Professor Berger has noted, there are many regulatory precedents for such measures, including

---

[88] Batchelder v. Allied Stores Int'l, 388 Mass. 83, 445 N.E.2d 590 (1983). *But see* Commonwealth v. Hood, 389 Mass. 581, 452 N.E.2d 188 (1983) (holding that *Batchelder* does not extend to nonelectoral activities).

[89] *See* Curtis J. Berger, "*Pruneyard* Revisited: Political Activity on Private Lands," 66 *N.Y.U. L. Rev.* 633, 662 (1991). *See also* Neil Hecht, "From Seisin to Sit-In: Evolving Property Concepts," 44 *B.U. L. Rev.* 435 (1964).

[90] Berger, *supra* note 89 at 666–67.

[91] *Id.* at 673–74.

warranties of habitability, pollution emission standards, and antidiscrimination laws.[92]

These alternative means of creating physical space for public expression are not as far-fetched as they may sound. As the political scientist Benjamin Barber has noted, cities have used tax incentives and building permit requirements "to induce developers to offer public sculptures, park space, and a livable, environmentally-accommodating architecture along with new retail and corporate space."[93] Why, then, not a speaker's corner, a performance stage, or some other space for expressive activity? The answer cannot be that shopping centers and other places of modernity are simply incompatible with all forms of noncommercial interaction and expression. Some such activity is already taking place in many shopping centers and airport terminals.

The real question is whether such places can be conceived and operated as both commercial *and* civic at once. Today there are several public-minded groups committed to transforming places of modernity like shopping centers into more "public" places, thus "allowing customers to re-conceive themselves as neighbors and citizens as well."[94] In his work Professor Barber has discussed the Agora Coalition in New Jersey, a team of architects, planners, social scientists, developers, and state government officials currently collaborating to establish "mall-town squares" in the state and across the Northeast. In the spirit of Jane Jacobs and William Whyte, the coalition espouses architectural and other revisions that will transform big-box commercial malls into more public places. As Barber notes:

> [W]ell-conceived public space invites loafing, public gatherings, playfulness, hanging out, communication, people watching, and spontaneous interaction. Such space requires ample seating with a pleasant sense of social proximity, multiple foci for casual

---

[92] *Id.* at 677. One potential obstacle to both the common law and regulatory methods of creating expressive breathing space is the Fifth Amendment's protection against regulatory takings. As Professor Berger convincingly argues, however, unlike the true private property owner mall proprietors have already partially yielded their exclusionary rights by inviting the general public to be on the premises. *See id.* at 682–83. Nor would these proposals violate the First Amendment rights of owners not to be compelled to speak, or patrons' right to be free from unwanted expression. The owner is no more forced to speak than is the town that permits a parade to proceed. And the patron is in a public place, where protection from captivity generally does not apply.

[93] Benjamin R. Barber, "Malled, Mauled, and Overhauled: Arresting Suburban Sprawl Sprawl by Transforming Suburban Malls into Usable Civic Space," in Marcel Henaff & Tracy B. Strong (eds), *Public Space and Democracy* (2001).

[94] *Id.* at 213.

Figure 5.2. Brea Mall, Brea, CA.

entertainment, spontaneous opportunities for encountering friends
and strangers, and activities that attract diverse demographic populations and allow them to interact around something more than
shopping.[95]

Most mall space is sterile and inert; this, it fails to serve any of these
communal functions (see Figure 5.2). There is plenty of space with which
to experiment. As Barber notes, suburban malls have been overbuilt,
some estimate by 30 percent or more.

The idea espoused here is not to turn shopping centers or other places
of modernity into raucous streets or town halls. (Parades and bullhorns, to
take just two obvious examples, certainly have no place there.) It is, rather,
to think creatively about how to add at least *some* expressive activity to the
mix of uses to which these places are presently put, such that they can
serve fundamental civic and democratic functions in addition to dominant commercial ones. This will give rise to serious architectural and
other spatial challenges best addressed by groups such as the Agora

[95] *Id.* at 214. *See also* William H. Whyte, *The Social Life of Small Urban Spaces* (1980).

Coalition, which can access ideas from a diversity of disciplines. Opening non-places to expression will, of course, require that "security" concerns be acknowledged and addressed. But these should not prevent all consideration of allowing expression into such spaces. The general public is already invited to access malls, airports and other public and quasi-public spaces. To suggest that speakers present some unique threat to public safety diminishes the First Amendment tradition of public speech itself. It buys into the notion, expressed in embodied and contested place contexts, that speech out of doors is *inherently* dangerous.

These challenges are hardly insurmountable, assuming the will to make changes to our public and quasi-public spaces. When presented with proper incentives, proprietors have already shown some real spatial ingenuity. To take just one example, in designing the new JetBlue terminal at John F. Kennedy International Airport in New York, officials consulted not only architects but a *dance choreographer* as well. They wanted a place, not a property – one which the public would experience and in which people would smoothly and efficiently go from one location to the next. That sort of ingenuity could be put to civic as well as commercial ends.

In sum, there are several methods – constitutional interpretation, common law judging, enforcement of local zoning conditions, legislative regulation, and local activism – that could reverse the spread of non-place and create some additional physical breathing space on the expressive topography. All of these things would dilute private property rights to a degree. But as the New Jersey Supreme Court said, "in necessitous circumstances private property rights must yield to societal interests and needs."[96] The alternative is to accept that vast areas on the contemporary expressive topography are in essence democratically defunct.

The "Third Place" and the Search for Expressive Community

Even assuming that some of the foregoing changes were to occur, a substantial void in terms of places of sociability and personal connectedness would remain. Opening a few more square feet of mall or airport terminal space, however welcome, would not begin to refurbish the space we have lost to social, architectural, and legal circumstances. We may yet be able to rescue these locations from the worst aspects of non-place. But they will probably never be fully vibrant expressive places.

[96] *J.M.B. Realty*, 650 A.2d at 14.

As increasing numbers of Americans have moved into secure and secluded communities, the prospects for meaningful interaction with strangers in public places have further diminished. As Max Lerner put it well in advance of the radical transformation of our contemporary expressive topography: "The critical question is not whether the small town can be rehabilitated in the image of its earlier strength and growth – for clearly it cannot – but whether American life will be able to evolve any other integral community to replace it."[97] That was a pertinent question in the middle of the twentieth century, when the people moved *en masse* to the suburbs and the malls. In today's climate of fear and insecurity, the answer to Lerner's question is every bit as critical.

The sociologist Ray Oldenburg has identified a certain type of place with which many of us are already familiar, and which might serve to fill at least a portion of the gaps in our expressive topography. Oldenburg has long been a proponent of what he calls the "great variety of public places that host the regular, voluntary, informal, and happily anticipated gatherings of individuals beyond the realms of home and work."[98] His principal thesis is that "third places" like cafes, coffee shops, bars, community centers, general stores, and other public hangouts – places that are neither home (first place) nor work (second place) – can fill some of the emptiness of public life occasioned by the current lack of activity in "interstitial" places like streets, sidewalks, and parks.[99]

Oldenburg ascribes a variety of functions to third places, including "mixing" or uniting neighborhoods, sorting persons with similar and dissimilar interests, serving as staging areas in times of crisis, providing a space for "public characters" attuned to community events, encouraging diversity and inclusion, and serving as political and intellectual forums.[100] Echoes of the agendas of Jane Jacobs and the New Urbanists are readily apparent in this list of functions. Of these functions the potential *political* benefits are obviously most germane to my project, although many of the social possibilities also relate to the development and preservation of expressive community.

As Oldenburg notes, the coffee house and tavern are deeply linked to grassroots political activism. As discussed in Chapter 2, third places

---

[97] Max Lerner, *America As A Civilization* 3 (1957).
[98] Ray Oldenburg, *The Great Good Place* 16 (1989).
[99] *Id.*
[100] *Id* at xvii–xxvi.

have been critical to American public politics at least since the Revolutionary period.[101] Benjamin Franklin used to meet with informal tavern groups to discuss the political issues of the day. In the eighteenth century, gristmills, inns, gunshops, printers' offices, and taverns all served as community centers and vibrant exchange points. Alexander Hamilton once described the tavern as "a genuine social solvent with a very mixed company of different nations and religions."[102]

The point is not to wax nostalgic. Lerner's caution that we cannot recreate the past is well taken. Today's taverns and coffee houses cannot serve precisely the same political functions as their forebears. For one thing, today's politicians do not typically frequent the same places as their constituents. Increased scrutiny of certain forms of political lobbying render it increasingly unlikely that local officials will buy rounds at the local public house. Today, Oldenburg laments, we construct "civic centers that are concentration camps for bureaucrats."[103] For a host of reasons, including the advent of new communications media and limits on public embodied communication (Chapter 3), face-to-face electoral politics is rapidly receding across the expressive topography.

This does not mean the people cannot use third places like taverns and community centers for political debate, discussion of public issues, poetry readings, and other forms of public expression. Many already do. But many more are isolated shut-ins or residents of "communities" in name only. As nostalgic as Oldenburg is for the corner soda fountain and the town square, he recognizes the difficulty of getting the people out of doors again. In comparison to those in other countries, he notes, American citizens seem to "glorify our freedom *not* to associate."[104]

For those who do seek more connectedness and community, many places are already available. These are not our modern malls, many of which Oldenburg aptly described as "a drifting amalgam of non-persons."[105] The best contemporary hope insofar as "third places" are concerned is the flourishing of local coffee shops and cafes. One can find these (typically several in fact) on every urban block and in every suburban and even many rural neighborhoods. Indeed as spatial distance, mobility, and the rootlessness sometimes brought about by new

---

[101] Oldenburg notes that in certain totalitarian regimes these places were considered so dangerous to the state that governments actually ordered them shuddered. *Id.* at 67.

[102] *Quoted in* Carl Bridenbaugh & Jesse Bridenbaugh, *Rebels and Gentlemen* 21 (1962).

[103] Victor Gruen, *The Heart of Our Cities* 106 (1964).

[104] Oldenburg, *supra* note 98 at 10.

[105] *Id.* at 122.

technologies have increased, many have discovered the communal potential of such places.[106]

The best among these places, in terms of possibilities for citizen exchange, are not the large, impersonal chains – which in certain respects have come to resemble mini-malls. They are the unique community locales where people come to meet with others, to work, and to simply "hang out." In these third places, one will find performance stages, poetry readings, and other civic functions and organized programs. As do shopping centers, these places bring people together outside the home – but this time without the overbearing emphasis on consumption. It would not be difficult, if the people so desired and if management was willing, to turn some of these places into even more robust expressive communities.

In order to do this, however, people will be required to break or at least occasionally break from a habit that is constraining public interaction across the expressive topography. As discussed in Chapter 9, the "networking" of public places enables people to remain connected to personal computing devices *wherever* they may be located. In many communities, particularly those in urban areas, the people have already appeared in great numbers in cafes, coffee houses, taverns, and other contemporary "third places." But they have carried with them a variety of mobile computing devices that tend to encourage personal isolation. The resulting "absent presence," a phenomenon discussed in greater detail in Chapter 9, tends to interfere with personal interaction and exchange. In short, we are in danger of transforming potential third places like cafes into non-places where, as Augé noted, we "cocoon" and communicate with machines rather than one another.

In sum, the *potential* for vibrant and fulfilling third places exists. To be sure, even coupled with local legal and other efforts to create breathing space for civic and expressive activity, these places are only a partial antidote to non-place and "placelessness." Still, they are some evidence of the basic desire to create or evolve what Lerner called "integral community."

---

[106] *See* Glenn Reynolds, *An Army of Davids: How Markets and Technology Empower Ordinary People to Beat Big Media, Big Government, and Other Goliaths* 30–35 (2006) (extolling the virtues of coffee houses as "third places").

6 INSCRIBED PLACES

Almost seventy years ago, the Supreme Court ushered "place" into First Amendment jurisprudence with this statement: "Wherever the title of streets and parks may rest, they have immemorially been held in trust for the use of the public and time out of mind have been used for the purposes of assembly, communicating thoughts between citizens and discussing public questions."[1] As we saw in Chapter 2, since colonial times, "quintessential" public spaces – streets, squares, and parks – have indeed been integral to the exercise of public liberties. Over time, these places have literally and figuratively been *inscribed* with our history, politics, and values. All of our social and political movements, for example, have relied upon access to such places. By virtue of their prominence and their special relation to public democracy, some of these inscribed places – for example, the National Mall in Washington, D.C. and Central Park in New York City – have become *sacred* places. Access to inscribed and sacred places is symbolic of an enduring commitment to public liberties and public democracy. Among all the places on the expressive topography, none serve the democratic functions of place – identity, participation, and transparency – more directly than do these places. If First Amendment liberties are to survive in this country, then *at least* public streets, sidewalks, parks, squares, and commons must remain open to press, petition, assembly, and expression.

What has happened to our inscribed and sacred places over the past half-century or so is something of a national disgrace. A variety of forces and factors have combined to substantially restrict First Amendment liberties in such places. The people did not simply abandon the public squares and other arenas once critical to speech out of doors. Detailed permit schemes, pecuniary burdens on public speakers, and aggressive policing strategies have chilled and suppressed public expression in these

---

[1] Hague v. CIO, 307 U.S. 496, 515 (1939).

places. Privatization of public places, physical and in some cases legal modification of urban and suburban places, and aesthetic projects have all collectively reduced the amount of available democratic space. Access claims in these places raise some particularly thorny – and to this day unresolved – First Amendment questions, including whether the government is obligated to *facilitate* the exercise of public liberties (rather than simply to refrain from unconstitutional interference with them), and whether there is anything we might legitimately refer to as a "right to place" for the exercise of First Amendment liberties. This chapter considers these and other questions raised by the treatment of inscribed and sacred places on the expressive topography.

"TIME OUT OF MIND": THE HAGUE DICTUM

Until nearly the middle of the twentieth century, the people had no recognized and enforceable constitutional right of access to public places like streets, sidewalks, parks, and squares. As the colonial experience described in Chapter 2 showed, early access to public places was controlled largely by elite members of a community. While elites often willingly invited the people into the streets, there was no claim of right to be there. Neither state constitutions nor the First Amendment – which had not yet been made applicable to local authorities – supported any claim of right to public space. The prevailing early view was that government could deny access to such places in the same manner as any private homeowner could exclude unwanted persons from the home. Indeed, relying on this ownership analogy, in 1895 Oliver Wendell Holmes, Jr., then sitting on the Massachusetts Supreme Judicial Court, upheld the conviction of a man who had delivered a speech on Boston Common without first obtaining official permission.[2] Despite the First Amendment's abhorrence of prior restraints, Holmes saw nothing remarkable about vesting *absolute* discretion in authorities with respect to access to Boston Commons. Under the then-prevailing view, public places like this were merely properties, and they were owned by governments.

Applying similar logic, in 1897 the Supreme Court affirmed Holmes's decision, and expressly adopted the ownership principle as constitutional law. The government's right to exclude the people from public places, the Court said, "necessarily includes the authority to determine under what

[2] Davis v. Massachusetts, 162 Mass. 510, 511, 39 N.E. 113 (1895).

circumstances such use may be availed of, as the greater power contains the lesser."[3] Thus, although the First Amendment expressly guaranteed rights of public assembly, petition, press, and expression, for much of our nation's history there was no designated public place in which the people had a right to exercise these liberties. Under the ownership principle, the people could legitimately be treated as ordinary trespassers – even in the public streets and parks.

It would be nearly four decades before the public streets, sidewalks, and parks would become part of – indeed, the very foundation for – our expressive topography. In *Hague v. CIO* (1939), the Supreme Court reviewed an ordinance that required a permit for any assembly on public property. Under the ordinance, officials could refuse a permit request only to prevent riots, disturbances, or disorderly assemblage. The *Hague* Court, while still embracing the place-as-property metaphor, for the first time questioned its *ownership* principle. In dicta – not part of the holding of the case – the Supreme Court announced:

> Wherever the title of streets and parks may rest, they have immemorially been held in trust for the use of the public and time out of mind have been used for the purposes of assembly, communicating thoughts between citizens and discussing public questions. Such use of the streets and public places has from ancient times been a part of the privileges, immunities, rights and liberties of citizens.[4]

This was critical dicta insofar as public liberties were concerned. The Court acknowledged the historical – "immemorial," "time out of mind," and "from ancient times" – intersection between expressive liberties and public places. In doing so, the Court implicitly recognized that the people out of doors, beginning with prerevolutionary "mobs" and "riots," had always depended upon the ability to assemble with others in public places and express their views.[5] The Court also acknowledged in this passage one of the primary democratic functions of public places, namely their use *for the purpose of* discussing matters of public concern. Finally, *Hague* implied that the government had a responsibility, as "trustee" of the public streets and parks, to both maintain such places and permit access to them for expressive purposes.

---

[3] Davis v. Massachusetts,167 U.S. 43, 48 (1897).
[4] *Hague*, 307 U.S. at 515.
[5] *See* Gordon S. Wood, *The Radicalism of the American Revolution* 213–14 (1991) (discussing revolutionary "mob" activity in the streets).

This was a defining moment for First Amendment liberties. *Hague* implied that the people had an enforceable *right* to be in particular places for expressive purposes. This would be critical to the success of the civil rights movement two decades later. As discussed in Chapter 2, Supreme Court decisions in the 1960s carved invaluable public space for peaceful civil rights protests. Indeed, the legal scholar Harry Kalven, Jr. read *Hague* as establishing a democratic "easement" for the people in public parks and streets, one that even permitted them to "commandeer" certain public places for expressive purposes. Social movements of the 1960s and 1970s relied to some extent on this "easement," as did the ordinary street corner orator. In the 1980s, the Supreme Court indicated that in what it then called "quintessential" public places – streets, parks, and (most) sidewalks – the peoples' expressive liberties were to be most robust. Although it might deny access to *other* public places, or close other forums once opened to expression, "quintessential" public places seemingly had to remain open to the people.

As critical as these developments would turn out to be for speech out of doors *Hague* had left some critical issues unresolved. Most significantly, the *terms* of the public "trust" it had established were not clear. The Court made clear that expressive liberties would sometimes have to yield to interests in public order, comfort, and convenience. As Kalven's "easement" metaphor suggested, there was no absolute right to use the public streets and parks for expressive purposes. What was missing was a sense of the *procedural* rules that would govern the exercise of public liberties in such "quintessential" expressive forums – what Kalven and Alexander Meikeljohn later characterized as the Robert's *Rules of Order* for public expression.[6] These rules would be developed over the next several decades, and are of course known to us today as the "time, place, and manner" doctrine. As we have already seen, these rules grant government rather broad discretion to displace, inconvenience, and otherwise regulate public expression – across the expressive topography.

Hague broke new and critical constitutional ground. It jettisoned an ownership principle that had allowed government to treat public streets and parks as its own personal "back yard." It established the broad outlines of what would later become the contemporary expressive topography. And it promised that our nation's history of public expression and contention would live on – at least in some public places. But the *Hague* Court did not abandon the notion that place was merely property; government had simply been demoted, in a sense, from "owner" to "trustee." As we shall see, the

---

[6] Alexander Meikeljohn, *Political Freedom* 24–28 (1960).

manner in which that "trust" has been administered has dictated the course of First Amendment liberties in the most "quintessential" and sacred of public places on the expressive topography.

INSCRIPTION, PUBLIC LIBERTIES, AND PUBLIC DEMOCRACY

According to the Supreme Court, the public streets, parks, and sidewalks must be open to discussion on matters of public concern in large measure because they have *traditionally* been so. As Chapter 5 showed, this narrow time-based justification has inherent and systemic flaws. Among other things, it has allowed for the proliferation of *non-places* or dead spaces on the expressive topography, particularly as modern and super-modern places have come on line. In the case of public streets, parks, and sidewalks, heavy reliance upon "tradition" obscures other, more important reasons for treating such places as critical to public expression. The public streets, parks, squares, and other common areas remain an integral part of our public life. People seek both literally and figuratively to "write" their concerns and histories onto such places. Public places like streets, parks, and squares are thus continuously *inscribed* with democratic moments, public politics, and in some cases public memories. Owing to their special histories and functions, some of these places are *sacred* venues insofar as public democracy is concerned.

Spatial Inscription

In their studies of place and space, anthropologists and geographers have acknowledged "the depth and complexity with which people construct meaningful relationships with their surroundings."[7] Some have referred to this phenomenon as "inscription," or the manner in which "people form meaningful relationships with the locales they occupy, how they attach meaning to space, and transform 'space' into 'place.' "[8] A rich literature spanning several disciplines examines "how experience is embedded in place and how space holds memories that implicate people and events."[9]

---

[7] Setha M. Low & Denise Lawrence-Zúñiga, "Locating Culture," in Setha M. Low & Denise Lawrence-Zúñiga eds., *The Anthropology of Space and Place: Locating Culture* 18 (2003).
[8] *Id.* at 13.
[9] *Id.*

This phenomenon can occur in public as well as private places. Insofar as public expression is concerned, we might think of the idea of spatial inscription as having both literal and experiential elements. Graffiti and signage, for example, are methods of literally *writing* one's identity, message, and experience on public places. Experientially, inscription refers to the notion that certain places serve as "centers of human significance and emotional attachment."[10]

Public places are felt and experienced by the people who occupy and use them. Some places act as mnemonics for recalling social and political events. For example, as noted in Chapter 4, by highlighting and facilitating certain messages *contested* places serve a particular version of this function. Inscription is a more generalized and permanent form of this phenomenon. Inscribed places do not typically speak to or of distinct messages; rather, they represent a more general inscription of public experiences, including expressive ones, in public places.

It may seem somewhat strange to think of streets, parks, and sidewalks as deeply inscribed public places. After all, these are merely "bricks and mortar." On the surface, such places seem inert and unconnected to larger or deeper concerns. Their function, generally speaking, is to facilitate public recreation, transport, and movement. But as the urban critic Jane Jacobs so eloquently explained, these places literally *define* our neighborhoods, communities, and polities.[11] In them, public life is tangibly and transparently acted out and experienced. Without places like streets, parks, sidewalks, and squares our "public lives and public" identities would essentially be reduced to virtual venues. Thus, it is imperative that the people continue to be permitted to "write" experiences, contests, and histories in and on public places. This is so not merely because "tradition" supports some minimal access to these places, but rather so that new traditions and experiences can be written in our most public venues.

The process of inscription takes on special significance in certain public places. Indeed, some inscribed places are so critical to public life and public democracy that we may justifiably refer to and treat them as *sacred* places. Although they are few in number, sacred places have an outsize influence on public life and public expression. These places serve as mass cultural repositories. They symbolize a grand ethos of public

---

[10] *See, e.g.*, Christopher Tilley, *A Phenomenology of Landscape: Places, Paths and Monuments* (1994); Eric Hirsch, "Introduction," in Eric Hirsch & Michael O'Hanlon eds., *The Anthropology of Landscape: Perspectives on Place and Space* (1995).

[11] Jane Jacobs, *The Death and Life of Great American Cities* (1961).

Figure 6.1. Civil Rights March on the National Mall, Washington, D.C. (1963).
Source: National Archives and Records Administration.

liberty. Sacred places *belong* to the people in an even stronger sense than do other inscribed places.

Among our nation's sacred places are the National Mall in Washington, D.C. (Figure 6.1) and Central Park in New York City. The National Mall is a living symbol of the civil rights movement and other demonstrations that have taken place there. As Justice Marshall once noted, "Lafayette Park and the Mall have served as the sites for some of the most rousing political demonstrations in the Nation's history."[12] For many, the national Mall evokes memories of Martin Luther King, Jr.'s *I Have a Dream* speech. For others, antiwar, abortion, or social justice demonstrations are deeply inscribed there. In Central Park, protesters and demonstrators have gathered on the Great Lawn and elsewhere to present a variety of social and political grievances, as well as to worship and engage in various forms of public recreation. The park is both centrally located and central to both local and, in some sense, national histories.[13]

Sacred places come in smaller sizes as well. For example, Union Square Park in New York City has been a venue for public parades, demonstrations, and other gatherings since the late nineteenth century.

---

[12] Clark v. Cmty. for Creative Non-Violence, 468 U.S. 288, 303 (1984) (Marshall, J., dissenting).
[13] *See* Roy Rosenzweig & Elizabeth Blackmar, *The Park and the People: A History of Central Park* (1992).

Public events there have included the first Labor Day parade, held in 1882, and a 1927 rally for Sacco and Vanzetti. Communists rallied in the park in the 1930s. Since the 1960s, civil rights activists have relied on it to make public displays. There are sacred places like this in communities across the nation, from Berkeley to Boston.[14] Such places represent a bond with expressive culture and public democracy that is different in kind and character from other places on the expressive topography.

As we shall see, there is often more at stake in contests over inscribed places, particularly sacred ones, than the scope of First Amendment liberties. As observed in Chapter 2, since colonial times the sharing of public space by elites and the less powerful has been fraught with tension. Many of today's contests, as did yesterday's, pit elites who wish to limit access and use of public space owing to aesthetic and other reasons against a public determined to retain some access and opportunities for spatial inscription.[15] Thus, contests over inscribed and sacred places are often about "ownership" of public places and the character of public life in a community.

PUBLIC TRUST, PUBLIC SPACE, AND PUBLIC ORDER MANAGEMENT

From the perspective of the public speaker, the legacy of *Hague*'s dictum, in particular its implications for spatial inscription, has been decidedly mixed. The Supreme Court has continued to emphasize that public expression ought to be as robust as possible in "quintessential" public forums like public streets and parks. It has defended broad conceptual "breathing space" in these forums. Thus, for example, the Court has held that speakers must be permitted to express themselves in these forum even if the audience is deeply offended by what they say. The First Amendment does not permit a "heckler's veto" over even combustible public expression. Courts also continue to insist that a speaker's liberties in "traditional" public forums are broader than elsewhere on the expressive topography. They thus pay at least lip service to Harry Kalven's notion that the people have an "easement" in such places for expressive purposes.

---

[14] *See* Don Mitchell, "The End of Public Space? People's Park, Definitions of the Public, and Democracy," 85 *Annals of the Association of American Geographers* (March 1995).
[15] *See* Setha M. Low, *On the Plaza: The Politics of Public Space and Culture* (2000) (describing the conflict surrounding renovation of the Parque Central, one of the oldest places in San Jose, Costa Rica).

Beneath the surface, however, the commitment to robust public liberties in our most public places has been substantially mitigated over time – both by the diminution of "traditional" expressive space itself, as discussed later in this chapter, and the development of what social scientists have called a "public order management system" for public expression and contention.[16] Today nearly every gathering of the people out of doors must be approved in advance by officials. Further, speech in even "quintessential" public forums is quite literally not "free" – speakers must often pay for its exercise. Finally, owing to a system of negotiated policing and management of public contention, large-scale expressive assemblies have become mostly scripted affairs. A cadre of consultants, lawyers, and government officials carefully plan, in advance, every conceivable detail involving public displays.

The Price of Admission: Permitting and Charging For Public Expression

As noted earlier, *Hague* left for future development the details of the "public trust" applicable to public places. Over the past six decades, a detailed and rather complex legal regime has developed with regard to the exercise of public liberties in "quintessential" or, as this chapter refers to them, "inscribed" public places. Political sociologists have noted the gradual development of a systematic "public order management system" that is now applicable to all forms of public assembly and contention in such places.[17] This system includes, among other things, detailed permitting and other procedural requirements for public displays.

Two years after *Hague*, the Supreme Court held in *Cox v. New Hampshire* (1941) that governments could demand that speakers obtain a permit to speak in public places.[18] *Cox* also upheld, with little discussion, the imposition of a license fee of up to $300 to recoup the "actual costs" associated with public speech activity. Several Supreme Court cases during the same era established that in making permit decisions, officials could not be guided by their personal views with respect to the content of the message the speaker wished to convey. Such "unbridled discretion,"

---

[16] C. McPhail, D. Schweingruber, & J. McCarthy, "Policing Protest in the United States: 1960–1995," in Donatella Della Porta & H. Reiter, eds., *Policing Protest: The Control of Mass Demonstrations in Western Democracies* (1998).

[17] McPhail *et al.* define the public order management system as "the organizations charged with managing public disorder problems, their policies and programs, their individual and collective policing actions, and their enabling technologies." McPhail *et al.*, *supra* note 16 at 49.

[18] 312 U.S. 569 (1941).

the Court held, amounts to a forbidden "prior restraint" on expression. Thus, in issuing permits, officials must be guided by neutral and objective criteria. Precedents also established that although it could charge a fee to recoup the costs of cleanup, government could not institute a flat ban on leafleting owing to concerns about public litter and its attendant expense. The Court held that the litterer, not the speaker, ought to be penalized.

Based upon the general principles announced in *Cox*, governments have imposed a host of detailed requirements for the public exercise of First Amendment liberties. Permits or licenses are now routinely required for public events and public expression of various forms. The requirement that a speaker obtain permission from the government before speaking is undoubtedly a literal form of "prior restraint." These sorts of restrictions are heavily disfavored under the First Amendment; indeed they are presumptively unconstitutional. Nevertheless, the Supreme Court has held that so long as permit requirements are not expressly based on the content of the speaker's proposed message and contain objective criteria for granting or denying the application, they do not raise the same concerns as other prior restraints. They are to be treated, as the Court has recently held, as ordinary time, place, and manner regulations.[19]

A typical local permitting ordinance begins with a description of the types of events subject to the permit requirement. For example, an ordinance may state that any assembly that may impede traffic, or consists of a certain designated number of participants, or requires the placement of temporary structures on public property, requires a permit. Depending on the place, a very small number of participants may trigger permit requirements. Special provisions typically apply to large events like parades or demonstrations.

Over the years, it has essentially become the case that the people may not *legally* assemble and speak in most inscribed places without first obtaining a permit. A few examples will illustrate the extent to which public displays are regulated in many localities. Some ordinances require permits for displays or other forms of public expression by even a *single person*. Thus, a solitary peace activist holding a "fallen soldier vigil" outside the county courthouse in Flemington, New Jersey was recently arrested for failing to obtain a permit under an ordinance applicable to "any parade, march, ceremony, show, exhibition, pageant or procession of any kind, or any similar display in or upon any street, park or other public place." An abortion-rights activist in Harrisburg, Pennsylvania was arrested for holding a "Dad for Choice" sign on a sidewalk along the

---

[19] *See* Thomas v. Chicago Park Dist., 534 U.S. 316, 322 (2002).

town's main square under an ordinance that requires a permit for public events involving *nineteen or fewer* persons. Permit triggering numbers vary by locality and specific context. For example, under rules recently proposed by the New York City Police Department, a permit would be required when *thirty or more* "vehicles, bicycles or other devices moved by human power, or ridden or herded animals" proceed together on any public street or roadway. (A prior proposal would have required a permit for gatherings of *two or more* persons.).[20]

Under most permit schemes, speakers must provide some advance notice of their intent to assemble and speak. Organizers typically must apply for a permit a certain number of days in advance of their event. Different categories of events are often subject to varying advance notification requirements. Although times vary, 48-hour advance application periods are fairly common and have generally been upheld by courts. Some permit schemes waive advance notice requirements for so-called "spontaneous events" – typically defined as those held in response to rapidly breaking public events, affairs, or issues. Permit ordinances also generally set forth the time period in which a permit application must be processed, as well as procedures for appeal of permit denials.

Parade routes are, of course, a particular concern in terms of public order and safety. A permit for a particular route may be denied on grounds of safety, traffic congestion, or for any other reason unrelated to the content of the proposed demonstration. Decisions to deny permits for particular routes may substantially affect, or in some cases even prohibit, access to *contested* places (Chapter 4). This was the case, for example, at the 2004 Republican National Convention in New York City, where demonstrators who had hoped to parade past the convention site were instead diverted to more distant streets on the grounds of "security."

Permits for parades may be necessary so that two groups do not seek to parade down the same thoroughfare at the same time. But restrictions on parades have been imposed for other reasons as well. For example, New York City recently imposed a prohibition on all "new" parades – those that had not been permitted prior to 2001 – along the entire length of Fifth Avenue. Fifth Avenue is thus arguably a sacred venue insofar as public contention and public expression are concerned. This avenue has been the site for parades and processions by suffragettes, Vietnam War protesters, and of course the famous St. Patrick's Day parade. The city's

---

[20] The New York City proposal was enacted to address monthly "Critical Mass" bicycle protests in the city, which draw attention to urban congestion and encourage alternative modes of transportation by riding through city streets in disruptive patterns.

justification for the limitation was that Fifth Avenue had been "over-saturated" with public events (there had been as many as fifteen parades per year, many during the more seasonable months of the year). Not all new events are forbidden on Fifth Avenue, however. Under the permit scheme, the mayor may issue a "special permit" for parades or events relating to "occasions of extraordinary public interest," defined as "celebrations organized by the City honoring the armed forces; sports achievements or championships; world leaders and extraordinary achievements of historic significance."[21] In other words, under the regulation a "new" protest group or social movement would automatically be denied a permit for an event on Fifth Avenue, but the New York Giants could be granted a "special" permit for a victory parade down Fifth Avenue.

Detailed permit requirements have long been enforced in the nation's parks, including some of the most sacred places on the expressive topography. As social scientists and legal scholars have noted, the ordinances described above are rather simple as compared with the regime applicable to public places like the National Mall.[22] Multiple government institutions, including the National Park Service, the Secret Service, and the District of Columbia Police, have jurisdiction over various areas on the Mall. In general, to hold a parade or other assembly on the Mall consisting of more than twenty-five persons speakers must apply for a permit 14 days in advance. A separate permit scheme applies to demonstrations that exceed the limits set for Lafayette Park (3,000 people) or the sidewalk in front of the White House (750 people). An entire section of the Code of Federal Regulations sets forth elaborate rules for public activity in places under the jurisdiction of the National Park Service. Thus, putative protesters and demonstrators must review and comply with a variety of legal rules and regulations in order to lawfully demonstrate on the National Mall.

In an increasing number of contexts, speakers may not be able to obtain a permit for a preferred location. As elsewhere on the expressive topography, protesters who wish to make a public display in an inscribed place must be cognizant of predetermined "free speech areas" that limit where expression can occur. This is particularly the case in public parks and near public monuments. For example, a First Amendment area in

---

[21] New York City Administrative Code §10–110(a)(4); Rules of the City of New York § 19–01. *See* Int'l Action Ctr. v. City of New York, 522 F. Supp.2d 679, 684–91 (S.D.N.Y. 2007) (upholding limits on new parades, but invalidating exercise of unbridled discretion by mayor in granting special permits).

[22] *See* Don Mitchell & Lynn A. Staeheli, "Permitting Protest: Parsing the Fine Geography of Dissent in America," 29.4 *International Journal of Urban and Regional Research*, 796–813 (December 2005).

Figure 6.2. "First Amendment Area," Muir Woods, CA.
Source: Photograph by Justin Baugh.

California's Muir Woods (Figure 6.2), a preserve that covers more than 500 acres, has been designated by a sign that reads as follows: "This area has been set aside for individuals or groups exercising their constitutional first amendment rights. The National Park Service neither encourages nor discourages, or otherwise endorses, these activities and receives no funds in relation to these activities." This particular form of expressive zoning purports to limit expression, even in "quintessential" public forums, to what are typically relatively small approved areas.

The permit or license is merely one of several pre-speech requirements applicable in inscribed places.[23] Permit application and license *fees* that are directly related to the actual costs of administering the permit scheme are now routinely charged to speakers. The total fees charged for initiating and engaging in public liberties have been mounting for decades. Based presumably upon the very brief consideration of permit fees in *Cox*, governments now routinely impose a number of user fees or taxes for things like the costs of police overtime services; use of health equipment and portable toilets; and use of traffic cones and structures like pens and barricades. Some municipalities require that speakers pay cleanup costs *in advance*, with any unused portion of the fee reimbursed after cleanup. The various "user fees" are calculated differently depending on the jurisdiction. In some jurisdictions, a large protest or demonstration may require the deposit of thousands of dollars in advance. Some municipal permit

---

[23] *See* Eric Neisser, "Charging for Free Speech: User Fees and Insurance in the Marketplace of Ideas," 74 *Geo. L. J.* 257, 268–272 (1986); Kevin Francis O'Neill, "Disentangling the Law of Public Protest," 45 *Loy. L. Rev.* 411 (1999); David Goldberger, "A Reconsideration of Cox v. New Hampshire: Can Demonstrators Be Required to Pay the Costs of Using America's Public Forums?", 62 *Tex. L. Rev.* 403 (1983); Vince Blasi, "Prior Restraints on Demonstrations," 68 *Mich. L. Rev.* 1481 (1969).

codes contain an "indigency" exception, sometimes with fairly complex eligibility requirements, under which application and service fees can be waived. But not all municipalities make such an exception, and those that do often have ambiguous guidelines for granting the waiver.

The imposition of user fees for police and other services can have a substantial effect on the exercise of First Amendment liberties in inscribed and sacred places. Many groups would likely be deterred by such fees. For example, "second-line" clubs, an outgrowth of late-nineteenth century freedmen's benevolent societies, have traditionally paraded in New Orleans on Sundays. In response to a few violent incidents at second line parades, the New Orleans Police Department recently *tripled* the fees it charges to escort the parades, to $3,760 per event. The clubs filed a lawsuit challenging the fees, which they claim will destroy a decades-long tradition. Similarly, advocates for farm workers were recently charged $1,500 by the city of Camden, New Jersey, for expenses associated with a public march. Were they to be challenged, some of these fee requirements might be invalidated in the courts. But bringing such a case will itself cost time and money. For these and other reasons, some speakers may be reluctant to mount a First Amendment challenge.

In addition to user fees, many municipalities also require that speakers obtain general liability insurance prior to a parade, demonstration, or other public event. The requirement is generally intended to protect the municipality from tort claims arising from permit-authorized activities. In addition, or sometimes in the alternative, some municipalities require applicants to sign a "hold-harmless" or indemnification agreement to protect the municipality from liability and litigation defense costs. Some of these agreements even require that speakers pay the cost of a municipality's defense for any injuries caused by audiences' *reactions* to expression, or for expenses directly related to the permitted expression such as loss of business.

In addition to requiring that protesters procure liability insurance to cover their own losses, some municipalities require speakers to post indemnity bonds. Some also require that speakers agree to reimburse the city for damage to city property, and to refrain from suing the city for any injuries to participants. As with user fees, in some municipalities certain of these requirements may be waived upon demonstration of the event sponsor's indigency. Some municipalities also claim to apply insurance and indemnification requirements only to "special events," like concerts, and not to "political" demonstrations. Of course, issues of vagueness quickly arise as officials attempt to determine which events are "special" and which are "political."

The public "trust" established by the *Hague* dictum did not specify whether or when the government could require a license or impose a tax for the exercise of public liberties on public streets and in public parks. *Cox* upheld a permit requirement for a street parade and (almost as an aside) held that government could recoup "actual" expenses associated with the event. The decision was vague with regard to what charges would be appropriate. Could a municipality charge any fee, even if it effectively suppressed expression? Could it charge the speaker for police services and cleanup costs? Could insurance and indemnification be required? Municipalities across the country appear to assume an affirmative answer to most if not all of these questions. As a result, speakers seeking access to inscribed places must now not only navigate complex permit schemes; they must in many instances come prepared to pay for the privilege of engaging in public expression.

The Institutionalization of Public Protest and Contention

Permit schemes are only one layer of a complex bureaucratic apparatus that now affect speech out of doors the exercise of public liberties in inscribed (and sacred) places. As a result of these and other limitations, the nature and character of what political sociologists refer to as "public contention" has changed dramatically since the 1960s. In a word, public expression and contention in inscribed places have been largely *institutionalized*.

As the political sociologists David Meyer and Sidney Tarrow have explained, the process of institutionalization has three components.[24] First, collective action becomes routinized to the extent that public protest and official reaction to it follow a familiar script. Second, those who go along with this program are included while those who reject it and insist on engaging in more disruptive forms of collective action are essentially shunned, marginalized, and excluded. Finally, cooptation occurs when challengers alter their public claims such that they do not disrupt the routines of daily public life. As a result of this process, public activity that was once "out of doors" – in the sense of being outside the political mainstream – becomes a routine and expected part of institutional politics.

The process of institutionalization has fundamentally changed the manner in which the people present claims and contentions in public places

---

[24] *See* David S. Meyer & Sidney Tarrow , "A Movement Society," in David S. Meyer & Sidney Tarrow, eds., *The Social Movement Society* 21 (1998).

like streets, sidewalks, and parks.[25] Permit schemes are merely one aspect of a comprehensive *"public order management system"* that substantially affects and ultimately institutionalizes the exercise of First Amendment liberties in public places.[26] Among other things, this system involves changes in methods of protest policing in localities across the United States.[27]

As noted in Chapter 2, public policing tactics have changed dramatically since the 1960s. Political sociologists have charted the steady movement from policies and practices of "escalated force" to a system of "negotiated management."[28] Escalated force policing involved little or no concern on the part of police for First Amendment liberties, a general intolerance with regard to public disruption, and violent police responses to public contention. The police response to demonstrators' behavior at the 1968 Democratic National Convention in Chicago is a paradigmatic example of escalated force policing.[29] During the convention, police responded to even peaceful exercises of expressive liberties with escalating violence. Protesters were clubbed and other forms of violence were used as a first resort. By contrast, as its name implies, "negotiated management" entails police and protesters actively negotiating the terms of public contention prior to a public event. The police routinely communicate with protesters about their plans, arrest them only as a *last* resort, and use minimal if any force. The overarching aim of "negotiated management," from the perspective of the police and public officials, is to achieve predictability and public order during public protests and other events.

The granting of a permit application typically signals merely the beginning of the negotiation process.[30] For larger public events, activists and organizations typically designate one or more representatives to negotiate the terms of the event. This designation is possible owing to the increased professionalization of protest movements – a development that itself has contributed to protest institutionalization.[31] Many activist groups now incorporate and formally "register" with local and other

[25] John McCarthy & Clark McPhail, "The Instituitionalization of Protest in the United States," in David S. Meyer & Sidney Tarrow, eds., *The Social Movement Society* 93–95 (1998) (discussing abortion protests by Operation Rescue and Klan rallies).

[26] *See* McCarthy & McPhail, *supra* note 25; Donatella della Porta & Herbert Reiter, *Policing Protest: The Control of Mass Demonstrations in Western Democracies* (1998).

[27] *See* McCarthy & McPhail, *supra* note 25 at 104–08 (describing process of "institutional isomorphism" by which public order management systems diffused starting in the 1960s).

[28] *See id.* at 96–100 (describing changes along five "dimensions").

[29] For an account and analysis of the Chicago Democratic National Convention protests, and police responses, *see* Jerome H. Skolnick, *The Politics of Protest* (1969).

[30] McCarthy & McPhail, *supra* note 25 at 92–93.

[31] *See* Meyer & Tarrow, *supra* note 24 at 14–15; McCarthy & McPhail, *supra* note 25 at 100–01.

government officials. Given their concerns regarding protest costs and liability, many organizers now have a vested interest in negotiation and predictability.

In recent years, professional protest "consultants" have also routinely been employed to negotiate permits, meet with police, and generally represent the interests of protest groups. For larger public displays, it is not uncommon for lawyers – for both activists and municipalities – to attend pre-event negotiation meetings. Depending on the size of the event, numerous government agencies as well as commercial interests may also be involved in these negotiations. Authorities at all levels of government now have detailed manuals and policies relating to protest planning and policing. They strongly encourage and sometimes require protest groups to designate "marshals" who will be points of contact during public events. This imposes a hierarchy of command within the group and provides a central point of contact between police and event organizers during the event.

Typical terms of negotiation include, among other things, the route of the event, the time, the number of participants, and the manner of protest or contention. Speakers often negotiate even the terms of arrests – including the charges and the detention location – in advance of the event. Thus, in many cases, the entire public event is stage-managed from its inception, with protesters willingly negotiating every detail with officials except, of course, the actual content of their message.

Pre-event planning, advanced negotiation, and ritualized arrests *normalize* what the political scientist Sidney Tarrow has called "the major non-electoral expression of civil politics."[32] As Tarrow has noted, "police practices designed and perfected since the 1960s routinize protest and remove much of its sting."[33] More than this, events that begin as protests against the *status quo* often end up as mere symbols of it. Under the public order management system, in particular its negotiated management component, speakers cooperate with the very symbols of authority they are often protesting. They do so, it should be noted, in an environment in which their bargaining power is quite weak. After all, the protesters need the permit in order to lawfully assemble and speak.

Public displays thus often become tightly scripted affairs, with pre-determined routes and results. Under these circumstances, the power that inheres in *disrupting* ordinary routines, including garnering the attention of mainstream media interested primarily in covering contention and

[32] Sidney Tarrow, *Power in Movement* 100 (1998).
[33] *Id.* at 98.

disruption, all but vanishes. The emphasis on preemptive planning and public order has undoubtedly reduced violence and injury at public events – particularly at the hands of police officers no longer operating under the "escalated force" model. But this form of public order management has imposed order at a substantial cost to public expression and public democracy.

The *Hague* dictum purported to reject the ownership principle and to place the public streets and parks under the protection of a public trust. Layer upon layer of permit and other time, place, and manner regulations, coupled with the rise of the public order management system, have resulted in a system in which public protest occurs more or less at the discretion of and on terms largely dictated by public officials. Public forms of self-governance occur only on condition that permission is sought and granted, predetermined spatial zones are used, fees or taxes are paid (or waived), and the specific terms of contention are negotiated and agreed upon.

OWNERSHIP OF INSCRIBED PLACES: COMMERCIALIZATION, PRIVATIZATION, AND BEAUTIFICATION

Legal restrictions and public policing methods pose serious challenges to the exercise of First Amendment liberties in inscribed and sacred places. As emphasized throughout this book, however, architectural, environmental, and social forces also substantially affect the scope of First Amendment freedoms on the expressive topography. The *res* or property committed to *Hague*'s public trust has changed dramatically since 1939. Owing to commercialization, privatization, and what might be called "aesthetic" projects, inscribed public space has diminished substantially and continues to erode. With little regard for First Amendment liberties or public democracy, the functions of public places have been altered, titles to public places transferred, and "improvements" to public properties made. These developments and improvements have substantially reduced the breathing space for expressive liberties in traditional public venues.

The "Malling" of Public Places

As noted in Chapter 2, countless observers, from Jane Jacobs to more recent public space critics, have chronicled the slow but steady destruction of what we might call the "public realm." Critics contend that in both urban and suburban areas, local officials and planners have sapped public places of vitality and democratic function. By the 1990s, for example, the architect Michael Sorkin detected "an ill wind blowing through our cities, an atmosphere that has the potential to irretrievably alter the character of cities as the preeminent sites of democracy and pleasure."[34]

Critics have complained, in particular, that public planners tend to emphasize commerce over democratic function, order over cacophony, and homogeneity over dissent and difference. Many public places, among them our "quintessential" or inscribed expressive forums, have gradually become more and more like giant shopping malls. Architects, urban planners, geographers and others have long lamented this "Disneyification" and commercialization of public space.[35]

This transformation, which some critics have referred to as "the malling of America," has indeed profoundly affected the very conception of the public realm. *Consumption* is the driving force and vision behind many recent changes to public space. Commercialization has created a public realm in which First Amendment elements of disorder and dissent are generally discouraged and suppressed in favor of relaxed browsing and consuming. As Sorkin succinctly put it, "there are no demonstrations in Disneyland."[36]

Privatizing Public Space

This atmosphere was created, Sorkin and others have contended, in part through the privatization of formerly public places.[37] In particular, large chunks of formerly public space, including streets and sidewalks, have sometimes been sold to the highest bidder. This effectively "demotes" a public forum by prohibiting or severely restricting public access. The trend continues to this day, as struggling cities seek to reduce expenses associated with large public spaces like parks. Rather than rethink and revitalize these spaces, officials sometimes sell them to land-hungry private developers. As a result, public squares and commons have literally disappeared, or have been altered such that access is tightly restricted to potential purchasers of goods for sale there.

In some areas of the country, inscribed places such as streets and sidewalks have disappeared or been radically displaced. In some cases,

---

[34] *See* Michael Sorkin (ed.), *Variations on a Theme Park: The New American City and the End of Public Space* xv (1992).
[35] *Id.*
[36] *Id.*
[37] On the many forms of privatization of public space and their effects on democracy, *see* Margaret Kohn, *Brave New Neighborhoods: The Privatization of Public Space* (2004).

inscribed places have been replaced by new, quasi-private bridges, sky-ways, and underground tunnels.[38] In these places, people can avoid not only the elements but an array of public speakers as well. In Houston, Texas, for example, there are nearly *seven miles* of underground tunnels connecting more than seventy buildings. On hot summer days, the nation's fourth-largest city can seem like a ghost town. Nearly all of this underground space, which is heavily traveled by the public, is *privately* owned. Speakers who have for so long depended on the above-ground public streets and sidewalks have no First Amendment liberties in the "private" city below.

More generally, in the course of the past two or three decades, public places – from large urban centers to remote suburban and exurban areas – have been visibly and functionally transformed into simulated theme parks. The intimacy, vibrancy, contact, and contestation of the public realm have been replaced by physical separation, inaccessibility, inertness, and a form of order largely enforced through the built environment itself. Public life itself has been fundamentally altered by these and similar changes. The "messy vitality" of the public streets, parks, and squares has given way to a "filtered, prettified, homogenous substitute."[39] In short, place has increasingly become less *public* – both in terms of its title and its character.

Even in the space that ostensibly remains "public," speakers are not necessarily guaranteed access. By a variety of means, governments can and do effectively "privatize" inscribed places. Limiting access to private events held within public forums, granting officials "exclusive use" permits, and issuing permits to private parties who purport to exercise the power to exclude the public all result in limiting public access to traditional public speech forums.[40] Private permits for things like sports and fashion events can effectively close large portions of even *sacred* places like the National Mall and Central Park to public use, sometimes for weeks at a time.

This privatization-by-permit occurs even at the most critical of demo-cratic moments. During the 2004 presidential campaign, for example, special use permits became a mechanism for cleansing campaign events held not only in rented halls, but also in inscribed places like public squares and parks, of all dissent and contrary opinion. Campaign committees simply secured local permits, and then excluded any person who disagreed or might have been expected to disagree with their candidate. President

---

George W. Bush's campaign routinely used this mechanism to exclude persons who wore apparel or displayed signs critical of the candidate.

Property "Improvements" and First Amendment Liberties

The expressive topography is always an evolving work in progress. Public spaces are constantly being modified in response to economic conditions, community demands, security concerns, and land use management policies. Inscribed and even sacred places are subject to developments and "improvements" that can have as profound an impact on the exercise of First Amendment liberties as do permit requirements, commercialization, and privatization.

The National Mall, one of our most sacred speech forums, has been markedly affected in this manner. The demand for monument space is fast eroding the public space available for expressive displays on the Mall. The World War II memorial, for example, dedicated in 2004, occupies more than *seven acres* of land between the Washington Monument and the Lincoln Memorial. Part of the monument now sits on space in which crowds listened to Martin Luther King, Jr.'s "I Have A Dream" speech.

The National Park Service has recently proposed a substantial plan for the future development of the National Mall. Plans for several new memorials and increased security measures may shrink this critical part of the expressive topography further, rendering the Mall little more than a static museum display. Congress has imposed several moratoria on Mall construction – with the understanding, of course, that it may override the ban on construction any time it chooses. Predictably, since the latest moratorium several new monuments have been constructed. Several more permanent displays – including a 4-acre Martin Luther King, Jr. memorial and 7.5-acre Ronald Reagan tribute – are presently being considered. At this pace, there may be as many as *fifty* additional memorials on the Mall by the middle of the century.

Judging by some of the statements made by those charged with the Mall's future, the plan seems to be to reduce and limit the people's presence and interaction with one another in this sacred place. For example, one recent proposal involves designating a specific venue or area for public demonstrations and protests at the foot of the Capitol. Activists have referred to this as a government approved "protest pit." In addition to objecting to the designation and dimensions of the "pit," activists have noted that the Capitol is not always the strategic target of their protest messages. In general, then, a current debate has arisen between those who view public protest as *inscribed* on the Mall and sacred to this space and those who view it as somewhat incongruous with the "urban civic square" envisioned by some planners. As an indication of the latter view, one administrator ominously stated that he envisions a Mall that would be "just like Disneyland."[41]

Finally, in terms of property improvements and modifications that can substantially affect First Amendment liberties in inscribed and sacred places, we must also consider efforts by officials to maintain the appearance of and "beautify" public places like parks, commons, and squares. The general notion that speakers' access can be denied, even to sacred places, on the ground of "aesthetic harm" finds some constitutional support in a 1984 Supreme Court case – *Clark v. Community for Creative Non-Violence* (1984). In *Clark*, the Court upheld a denial by the National Park Service of a permit application by homeless activists who wanted to sleep overnight on the National Mall and in nearby Lafayette Park.[42] The activists hoped to demonstrate the plight of the homeless by camping at the very seat of government power; in effect, they sought to treat the Capitol and the White House as *contested* places (*see* Chapter 4). The Supreme Court, however, ultimately deferred to the agency's determination that allowing overnight camping would substantially damage the lawns of the Mall and Lafayette Park.

Relying on this precedent, officials have refused access to even the most sacred places on the expressive topography on the ground that assemblies and other displays would "harm the lawn" or cause other aesthetic damage. During the 2004 Republican National Convention, for example, New York City denied antiwar protest permits for Central Park on the ground that they violated an informal (and apparently selectively enforced) regulation limiting assemblies on the Great Lawn to no more than 50,000 people (Figure 6.3). The City spent over $18 million in 1997 to restore the park and the lawn, and has since steadfastly maintained that it is entitled to protect that investment by, among other things, limiting public assemblies. As a result of a recent settlement of a lawsuit filed by some of the protesters who were denied a permit to demonstrate on the Great Lawn in 2004, the City has agreed to increase the size of permitted assemblies to 75,000 people – pending a study (funded by the city) to determine the optimal and sustainable use of the Great Lawn. As a result of this (perhaps temporary) concession to public democracy, at this time

---

[41] *See* Andrew Ferguson, "The Mess on the Mall," *The Weekly Standard*, 010 (45) (August 15/22, 2005).
[42] Clark v. Community for Creative Non-Violence, 468 U.S. 288 (1984).

Figure 6.3. The Great Lawn, Central Park, New York City.
Source: Photograph by Matthew Chan.

the largest stationary rally or demonstration possible in New York City probably cannot exceed 75,000 persons. By way of comparison, a February, 2003 antiwar protest rally in Rome, Italy was reported to have involved approximately *three million* participants.

Insofar as they tend to impose "private" and generally elite aesthetic ideals on public places, aesthetic improvements are generally consistent with the commercialization and privatization agendas noted earlier. Rather than pursuing more populist goals, officials in many instances are treating public places as they might their own private garden or lawn. This attitude extends to public "beautification" efforts as well. Thus, for example, officials have recently proposed to alter the landscape of Union Square Park in New York City to "beautify" it and to make it more suitable for peaceful recreation like bench sitting (Figure 6.4). As noted earlier, this park has been the site of countless rallies and demonstrations regarding matters of great public concern. The proposed modifications, which include generally limiting the amount of open space in the park, may fundamentally alter public life and public liberties there. In particular, activists have expressed concerns that substantial rallies, demonstrations, and assemblies will no longer be possible once the proposed modifications are completed.

Figure 6.4. Audience Watching a Public Demonstration During Construction,
Union Square Park, New York City (June 2008).
Source: Photograph by Jessica Alfieri.

Hague suggested that governments would henceforth hold public places like streets, parks, and squares "in trust" for the benefit of the people. In administering that trust, officials have increasingly favored the majority beneficiaries' desire for commerce, recreation, order, and aesthetics over that of "minority" uses such as protests and demonstrations. The rise of "aesthetic" concerns is particularly troubling. Certainly, everyone benefits from pristine public parks. Yet only very recently have exercises of First Amendment liberties been treated as a threat to places like Central Park, necessitating precise limits on assemblies there and elsewhere. Particularly given the more general erosion of the expressive topography, it is troubling that even our inscribed and sacred places are being treated as the functional equivalent of botanic gardens and private back yards. As *Hague*'s dictum suggested, these places have been "immemorially" open to assembly and discussion of matters of public concern.

HONORING HAGUE

If the promise of *Hague*'s dictum is to be realized and the tradition of public expression it embraced continued, the practice of spatial inscription must be protected and preserved. This will require revisiting some fundamental First Amendment principles and doctrines. It will require

that the people, public officials, and the courts prevent the further privatization, demotion, and erosion of inscribed places. Finally, honoring *Hague*
will require reconsideration of current attitudes and trends affecting public
architecture, public planning, and public "improvements."

Taxing Public Liberties: Permits, Payments, and Free Speech "Facilitation"

The idea that speakers ought to pay for the privilege of speaking in public
places is an affront to the First Amendment. Taxing speech is anathema to
our nation's expressive history, jurisprudence, and culture. Yet as noted
above, most jurisdictions charge some fee for public demonstrations and
other events. Public officials naturally want to minimize the expense of
policing and cleaning up after public events. But the piling on of fees for
permit applications, cleanup costs, and indemnity has taken us well
beyond the Supreme Court's rather cryptic validation of reimbursement
costs in *Cox v. New Hampshire* (1941). New proposals for shifting costs to
public speakers continue to be floated. Just a few years ago, for example,
the Governor of Minnesota, Tim Pawlenty, proposed that protesters be
required to pay "restitution" for costs associated with their arrests
(regardless of ultimate disposition).

It is time that we carefully reconsider the variety of prior restraints being
imposed on the exercise of First Amendment liberties in our inscribed and
sacred public places. In particular, courts ought to review permit and various
financial restrictions on public expression with far greater skepticism. As
noted, these elements of the "public order management system" can substantially chill and even mute expression in inscribed and sacred places. As
prior restraints, permit schemes would ordinarily be treated as presumptively invalid. In extreme cases, courts have invalidated certain provisions in
draconian permit schemes and disallowed particular fees. For the most part,
however, officials continue to impose and courts to uphold such restrictions,
largely on the basis of the Supreme Court's decision in *Cox*.

There are, as we shall see, considerable reasons to reject *Cox*'s rationale for allowing the prior licensing of public speech and the imposition of
fees and taxes. These arguments do not necessarily require wholesale
abandonment of permit schemes and fees. That outcome would of course
preserve maximum breathing space for expressive liberties, but with
unknown costs in terms of public order and safety. The arguments ought,
however, to at least result in greater skepticism and scrutiny of what are
now typical permitting terms and financial requirements.

Warnings regarding the pernicious effect permit schemes have on public expression were sounded long ago but, unfortunately, never heeded. Years ago, the legal scholar C. Edwin Baker wrote a little-noticed but very plausible argument against the basic "public order" rationale for licensing public expression.[43] Before describing the argument, some context is critical. Baker was mounting a broader challenge to the use of the "reasonableness" standard in First Amendment cases. His "test case" was the requirement that speakers obtain a permit in advance of public parades. Baker firmly believed *Cox* to have been wrongly decided; indeed, he argued that the decision was based on a number of false premises.[44] Moreover, Baker approached the permit question from an "absolutist" First Amendment perspective. He argued that the animating theory for public assemblies ought to be self-actualization, not the "marketplace" of ideas principle. Under the marketplace theory, the liberty of many participants could in fact be "abridged" so long as the *general idea* ultimately found its way into the marketplace. Individuals, Baker argued, have a *personal* right of participation, one that is not satisfied solely because some in the group are allowed to make their point.

Baker emphasized that the permit requirement inhibits dissent, spontaneity, and disruption – three elements that, as discussed in the next chapter, are critical to the self-actualizing protester. In essence, Baker was offering an early critique of what would soon become the "public order management system." His analysis was animated by an enlightened view of the power of public protest and assembly – a power, he noted, that mainstream interests have every reason to want to regulate and even suppress. Thus, Baker noted that to assemble was not merely to communicate but also to

> generate and exercise power, to do things, to engage in activities that are valued in themselves, to engage in activities that often give the people involved an exhilarating sense of power and self-actualization, and to engage in the extraordinary as a way to challenge and change the ordinary and routine.[45]

Thus, the problem with assessing the "reasonableness" of permits, Baker argued, is that First Amendment liberties of assembly and expression exist precisely so that the people can engage in activities that are *unreasonable*

---

[43] C. Edwin Baker, "Unreasoned Reasonableness: Mandatory Parade Permits and Time, Place, and Manner Regulations," 78 *Nw. U. L. Rev.* 937 (1983).
[44] *Id.* at 1001.
[45] *Id.* at 948.

from the perspective of the "existing order."[46] Permits are grounded upon a systemic bias against what used to be called "mobs" (*see* Chapter 2). In a sense, permits are directed at assembly *itself*. Although few assemblies are vicious mobs bent on public destruction, our constitutional framework for public expression in inscribed places is essentially based on such worst-case scenarios. In general, Baker argued, the costs of individual liberty tend to be overestimated and its benefits substantially underestimated. Permit requirements are one manifestation of that skewed balance.

But aren't mandatory permits necessary to preserve public peace, order, and tranquility? We generally assume so. To be sure, mandatory permits aid in policing events, avoiding scheduling conflicts, and ensuring the orderly flow of traffic. Baker posited that the choice is not one between mandatory permits and anarchistic circumstances, but rather one between mandatory and *voluntary* permit schemes. In most cases, Baker argued, organizers would voluntarily seek a permit out of self-interest – in order to ensure space and their own safety. Police would thus not lose the information they need to prepare for larger assemblies. In the case of smaller assemblies, such as the individual protester subject to some modern-day permit requirements, Baker argued that permits are not needed to ensure order or appropriate levels of policing.

Professor Baker went on to argue that the costs of a voluntary system, including that a few assemblies would fail to voluntarily seek a permit, would be substantially outweighed by the benefits to speakers and protesters. Certain types of expressive conduct would no longer be prohibited; ideological conformity would no longer be formally imposed; and rather predictable and in some sense unavoidable abuses of discretion would be avoided.[47] Perhaps most importantly, authorities could no longer hold out denial of a permit as a possible punishment for failure to negotiate or accede to official demands. Speakers, Baker argued, would become a *constituency* rather than a potential adversary of municipal authorities, thus equalizing the parties' negotiating positions.

Of course, we cannot know for sure whether Baker was correct. No municipality appears to have ever implemented a voluntary permit system. As it has been interpreted, *Cox* provides absolutely no incentive to do so. But even if Baker's argument does not convince officials and courts that the fundamental rationale underlying permit requirements is unsound, there is nevertheless much to take from his argument.

---

[46] *Id.* at 949.
[47] *Id.* at 1013–14.

First, it is undeniable that permit schemes are fundamentally at odds with public dissent and the general purposes of public assembly. Indeed, the entire "public order management system" is anathema to public contention. An appreciation of the expressive interests involved in public displays of contention should cast doubt upon at least some of the mounting limitations imposed upon speech out of doors in inscribed and sacred public places. Second, Baker's argument highlights the fact that whether one supports mandatory permits often comes down essentially to normative considerations about what is "normal," how much disruption is tolerable, and how much order ought to be enforced. Biases against the unorthodox and "unreasonable" ought not to sway opinions regarding limits on public displays. Third, in terms of typical permit requirements, localities should at the very least repeal mandatory permit requirements for small assemblies and enact broad exemptions for spontaneous displays. As Baker argued, the justifications for imposing "order" on large gatherings are surely lacking as applied to the lone dissenter and the small assembly. Just as surely, permit schemes ought to reserve adequate breathing space in which citizens can react to fast-breaking news cycles and events.

The variety of financial preconditions for public expression rests on even weaker constitutional ground than the basic permit requirement. Simply put, free speech ought to be *free*. Since 1941, the Supreme Court has given only the slightest attention to the matter of what essentially amounts to the taxing of public expression. As noted above, conditions on the ground suggest that it may well be time for the Court to address the matter more specifically and forthrightly.

Several First Amendment scholars have been highly critical of permit fees, policing fees, insurance and indemnity requirements, and other financial burdens placed on public expression and assembly. For example, David Goldberger has argued that pecuniary restrictions ought to be subject to the *same* constitutional standards as nonpecuniary ones.[48] Thus, he argued, financial conditions should be subject to ordinary time, place, and manner scrutiny. This would necessarily mean that any "flat ban" imposed as a result of speaker impecuniousness would be unconstitutional. According to Goldberger, most permit fees, police fees, cleanup fees, and insurance requirements would also be invalid under ordinary First Amendment time, place, and manner standards.

Taking a different approach, Eric Neisser has argued that fees are generally akin to disfavored "taxes on knowledge."[49] Thus, he argued,

---

[48] Goldberger, *supra* note 23.
[49] Neisser, *supra* note 23.

expressive license fees should receive *greater* scrutiny than ordinary speech regulations. Neisser argued that fees and insurance requirements are not only contrary to well-established constitutional principles, but inconsistent as well with both user fee and economic theories. Public expression, he argued, provides publicly distributed "positive externalities" that are not taken into account in establishing financial conditions. Moreover, Neisser has argued, certain insurance and indemnity provisions violate the principle that speakers cannot be forced to absorb costs associated with wrongdoing they neither intended nor approved.[50]

The so-called "indigency" exemptions, which have been included in many permit schemes, do not cure the problem. Even if formally exempted, low-income and unsophisticated groups may not participate – for fear of failing to meet the exemption, concern regarding public disclosure of financial condition, or perhaps for lack of knowledge regarding the basic legal requirements for mounting public displays. Moreover, courts and officials ought not to overlook the substantial administrative difficulties associated with many typical financial restrictions on expression. Who actually qualifies as "indigent"? What sort of information must be provided to prove the exempted status? Might the required disclosures themselves chill public expression? At the very least, these and other uncertainties counsel in favor of the broadest interpretation of so-called "indigency" exemptions – to inhibit the least amount of public expression and to guard against discrimination against unpopular speakers.

The Supreme Court has held that municipalities cannot *vary* the amounts charged to speakers based upon factors such as the content of expression, the nature of the event, or the public response to the speaker's message.[51] Although important, this limitation fails to account for certain cost and expense realities relating to modern-day public assembly and protest. For one thing, premium and coverage amounts for public displays are likely to be set at the *upper* limits. Typically, this will impose the greatest burden on small assemblies. Further, as a function of private risk assessment, "unknown" or unfamiliar groups will likely pay more in the insurance market. This will often impose a heavier financial burden on *ad hoc* and dissident groups. Thus, whether or not officials expressly vary fees, public speakers will inevitably experience variable financial and expressive burdens. Private insurers are, of course, not generally

---

[50] Even Vincent Blasi, who generally was of the view that there are *some* valid justifications for imposing fees to recoup expenses for public expression, drew the line at insurance and indemnity requirements. Blasi, *supra* note 23.

[51] Forsyth County v. Nationalist Movement, 505 U.S. 123 (1992).

sensitized to expressive concerns. This situation raises the disturbing prospect that state action will impose private market biases on constitutionally protected activity.

The various indemnity and bonding requirements now routinely found in permit schemes exist for two possible reasons – either to inhibit public expression or to allocate the costs of public expression and contention. The former purpose would obviously be constitutionally illegitimate. So we must assume that this is a matter of cost allocation. As noted, the Supreme Court has said very little about financial prerequisites for public expression since it indicated in *Cox* that the "actual costs" associated with this activity could be charged to speakers. Localities have seemingly interpreted *Cox* as suggesting more broadly that the speaker can be forced to "pay her own way."

To hold otherwise, some might insist, is to demand that the government *subsidize* or *facilitate* the exercise of constitutional rights. This raises one of the oldest debates regarding constitutional liberties: Does the government have any affirmative obligation to facilitate the exercise of constitutional rights? Generally speaking, the answer to that question is "no."[52] Yet in the free speech area, certain post-*Cox* precedents indicate that governments, in part as a condition of the trust relationship imposed by *Hague*, must at least ensure that speakers have some physical breathing space for public expression. The public forum doctrine itself provides for at least some minimal provision of public space for speech out of doors. Further, as noted, the Supreme Court has held that officials cannot flatly ban the distribution of literature on the ground that the activity induces littering; if there are expenses associated with this activity, the taxpayers must foot the bill. Nor, the Court has held, can the mere possibility that some listeners might respond violently to public expression serve as justification for suppressing speech; in that situation, it seems, police may be obligated to defend the public speaker from the angry mob.[53] Authorities would thus appear to have at least some minimal affirmative obligation to facilitate public expression.

Indeed, *Hague*'s promise would essentially be meaningless if officials were not required to maintain at least some physical breathing space for speech out of doors. After all, the mere *existence* of rights to assembly, expression, petition, and press presupposes some public space for their exercise. "Quintessential" or inscribed public places have, "time out of mind," been such places, especially for poorly financed causes. Notably,

---

[52] David P. Currie, "Positive and Negative Constitutional Rights," 53 *U. Chi. L. Rev.* 864 (1986). *See also* Susan Bandes, "The Negative Constitution: A Critique," 88 *Mich. L. Rev.* 2271 (1990) (critiquing the distinction between positive and negative liberties).

[53] *See, e.g.,* Cox v. Louisiana, 379 U.S. 536 (1965).

for much of our history these places served critical expressive and democratic functions free of any advance charge.

There is still another fundamental reason why the First Amendment in some circumstances obligates government to facilitate or subsidize the exercise of public liberties. *Cox* did not address the situation in which a speaker could not afford the imposed fee or liability insurance, and no indigency exemption was provided for. If the Constitution does not obligate government to facilitate the exercise of constitutional rights, then the indigent speaker necessarily has no valid First Amendment claim. If she cannot pay her own way, the government is not required to assist her. But surely if one accepts the legitimacy of charging for the privilege of speaking, that privilege cannot be granted or denied based on the ability to pay. Some equal protection precedents hold that wealth cannot be used to burden or deny certain fundamental rights.[54] Although the Supreme Court has never expressly extended this rationale to First Amendment liberties, there are very strong arguments that it should. Even if a speaker is able to pay, moreover, she ought not to have to essentially bankrupt herself in the process.

There is an inherent equality issue lurking here, one that perhaps allows us to avoid the First Amendment facilitation conundrum. The problem with the imposition of fees, insurance, and indemnity requirements is to some degree that no other class of citizen is required to meet similar requirements. No other public activity is burdened *in advance* with fees targeting the activity itself, as opposed to being supported through more general tax schemes. Under the permit schemes, only public expression is being burdened on the mere *prediction* that expense or disruption associated with this activity may occur. And only the public speaker is being forced in some situations to incur liability for acts she neither intended nor committed. Speakers ought not to be forced to pay for their freedom – any more than a pedestrian or driver ought to be charged each time she uses the sidewalks and streets.

Permit requirements and financial preconditions on the exercise of public liberties are quintessential prior restraints. They threaten even the smallest spontaneous displays, allow officials to favor Super Bowl parades over budding social movements, and leave speakers vulnerable to both varying official conceptions of "indigency" and the terms and conditions of private insurance markets. Perhaps most seriously, these requirements disparately affect the least advantaged public speakers – those who rely most upon access to inscribed and sacred places. Even if we are to accept

---

[54] Currie, *supra* note 52 at 882–85.

that speakers must in some instances pay their own way, local officials ought to exercise greater care in enacting and courts ought to scrutinize with far more skepticism the myriad limitations on modern-day protests and other public displays.

✦

Privatization and Spatial Demotion

As noted earlier, complicated permit schemes and onerous pecuniary restrictions are not the only threats to the exercise of public liberties in inscribed and sacred places. The "privatization" of these places, as well as various architectural and aesthetic modifications, can also have a substantial impact on First Amendment liberties.

Various forms of spatial privatization threaten public liberties by, as Professor Kevin O'Neill has observed, effectively *demoting* places from inscribed and expressive to private and "non-public." As noted, officials sometimes effectively privatize public places, including portions of sacred sites like the National Mall and Central Park, by providing special use permits to private commercial interests. Sometimes these permits exclude the public from inscribed and sacred places for several weeks at a time. Of course, commerce is also inscribed on our public streets and in public parks. It is not the mere granting of the permit, however, but its *scope* that is problematic. Parades and demonstrations do not occupy streets and parks for more than several hours at a time. By contrast, permits for Super Bowl extravaganzas and "fashion weeks" commandeer public space for days and weeks at a time. Officials ought to take special care that these permits not pose long-term barriers to the people's use of inscribed places like public parks.

As noted, political campaigns have also secured use permits for public squares and other inscribed places.[55] In some instances, the campaigns have then sought to exclude anyone from these public places who does not share the candidate's point of view. Generally, the organizer of a public event is entitled to exercise expressive autonomy in shaping the message of the assembly.[56] That situation is distinct, however, from saying that a speaker can transform a "traditional" public forum into a "non-public" forum by virtue of a use permit. A permit for use of public space does not

---

[55] *See* O'Neill *supra* note 40.
[56] *See* Hurley v. Irish-American Gay, Lesbian and Bisexual Group of Boston, 515 U.S. 557 (1995) (holding that an Irish-American group may constitutionally prevent a group of gay and lesbian persons from marching in its parade).

entitle a campaign to silence all dissenters who are in the area. All persons lawfully in such places have a right to speak there – whether or not they agree with the permit-holder's specific message. Indeed, one of the primary functions of "quintessential" public forums is to create space for a clash of opinions on matters of public concern. Thus, if a campaign or other speaker wishes to preserve the right to exclude all others, it ought to rent private space.[57]

Public planning and land use policies also result in spatial privatization and public forum demotion. The sale of large swaths of municipally owned land to private interests can remove what once were inscribed places from the expressive topography. In one recent high-profile example, Salt Lake City sold an *entire block* on Main Street to the Mormon Church.[58] The site, known as "Soapbox Corner," was a quintessentially inscribed place. It had been the site of numerous protests and demonstrations over the years. The City initially retained an easement for public access and passage. It later sold the easement to the church, effectively eliminating any public rights of access and expression.[59] The letter of the First Amendment does not prevent the sale of property to which the government holds title. Its spirit, however, ought to dissuade public officials from engaging in this sort of wholesale demotion. There are precious few "Soapbox Corners" left on the expressive topography.

While the First Amendment does not literally prohibit the sale of public properties, it does limit the effects of certain spatial conversions and alterations. Specifically, municipalities ought not to be allowed to dilute expressive liberties by conversion, transformation, and demotion of established inscribed places. Indeed, the Supreme Court expressly rejected this strategy in *United States v. Grace* (1990).[60] In *Grace*, Congress attempted to demote the sidewalks around the Supreme Court from "traditional" to "non-public" forums. A federal law banned all leafleting and signage on those sidewalks. The Court rejected the argument that the sidewalks could be effectively demoted by legislative decree, and invalidated the sweeping prohibition on expression. To be sure, part of the Court's rationale was that inscribed and contested places near the Court building are pregnant with symbolism. But the principle that government

---

[57] Of course, this would undermine the campaign's effort to create the illusion of unanimous public support for its candidate and platform. The short answer is that the First Amendment does not protect such an interest.
[58] *See* Kohn, *supra* note 37 at 93–95.
[59] Utah Gospel Mission v. Salt Lake City Corp., 425 F.3d 1249 (19th Cir. 2005).
[60] 497 U.S. 720 (1990).

may not deny public liberties by spatial conversion ought to be one of more general application.

There have been a few successful challenges to this particular means of spatial demotion. For example, a federal appeals court held that a sidewalk constructed on private property in Las Vegas, which essentially replaced a public walkway, was not in fact a "non-public" forum.[61] The same court recently held that Las Vegas's transformation of a several-block down-town area into a pedestrian mall did not alter its status as a "traditional" public forum.[62] But there have been defeats as well. For example, a court upheld the demotion-by-transformation of a 600-foot public street in Denver. City officials transformed the once-public street into an open-air, glass-covered, pedestrian walkway providing access to a government-owned performing arts complex.[63] The court held that after transfor-mation of this public space, the people had only the minimal rights of access accorded in "non-public" forums. If municipalities are permitted to transform public liberties by transforming public places in this manner, we shall see a continued erosion of the expressive topography.

Finally, and far more typically, officials sell public places to private developers to fill municipal coffers and to put newly privatized land to its most economically profitable use.[64] These commercial and residential projects often effectively *erase* streets, sidewalks, and in some cases even park lands from the expressive topography. The private analogs that remain are designed mostly for residential and recreational uses. Municipalities should carefully consider the cost of these projects in terms of public expression and public life. Conditions on large-scale develop-ments ought to include preservation of a substantial portion of public space, including express easements for public access and public events.[65] In order to preserve public space for the exercise of First Amendment liberties, "fortress" developments that broadly prohibit public access ought to be rejected in favor of more mixed public-private uses.

---

[61] *See* Venetian Casino Resort v. Local Joint Executive Board of Las Vegas, 257 F.3d 937 (9th Cir. 2001), *cert. denied*, 535 U.S. 905 (2002). *See also* Allen Lichtenstein & Gary Peck, "Sidewalk Democracy: Free Speech, Public Space, and the Constitution," 8 *Nevada Lawyer* 18 (May 2000) (describing legal battle over Las Vegas sidewalks).
[62] ACLU of Nevada v. City of Las Vegas, 333 F.3d 1092 (9th Cir.), *cert. denied*, 540 U.S. 1110 (2002).
[63] Hawkins v. City and County of Denver, 170 F.3d 1281 (10th Cir. 1999).
[64] *See* Setha Low & Neil Smith, eds., *The Politics of Public Space* (2006).
[65] Similar proposals for public space set-asides were made as far back as the New Deal. Then, as now, the real estate lobby opposed them – and largely won the battle. *See* Dolores Hayden, "Building the American Way: Public Subsidy, Private Space," in Low & Smith, *supra* note 64, Ch. 3.

Architecture

Again the expressive topography is as much affected by physical altera-tions as it is by legal ones. We ought to be more sensitive to the effect on First Amendment liberties of the expansive "public improvement" and "beautification" projects across the expressive topography. Of course, public officials have the authority to pursue aesthetic ends and the public benefits associated with more attractive public areas. But they must be aware that even planters and playgrounds can alter the prospects for speech out of doors. More broadly, public improvements and architec-tural changes can threaten the inscriptive process itself – even in our most sacred public places.

The influence of aesthetic interests over public space has not, of course, all been negative. Parks and other public spaces have sometimes been restored as a result of improvement projects.[66] Central Park is an excellent example. The park was not at all welcoming, or even safe, during the 1960s, 1970s, and much of the 1980s. Today it is one of the most pleasant public places in the city, if not the world. But what does this sacred place actually welcome? Without open spaces that can accommodate sizeable protests and assemblies, the park seems most welcoming to urban professionals who want to sunbathe or play soccer. Many suburban town squares and com-mons, taking their cue from this vision of urban living, are also increasingly incompatible with public assembly and expression. In terms of commerce and recreation, these are indeed more comfortable and aesthetically pleasing places to be. But in most cases they do not, unfortunately, preserve much in the way of physical breathing space for First Amendment liberties.

The architectures planned and created by urban and suburban offi-cials often fail to facilitate spatial inscription. Jane Jacobs wrote in the 1960s of the role that parks and even sidewalks play in creating and shaping our communal public life. As discussed in Chapter 2, she argued that the urban planning policies of the time were diminishing public interaction and sapping communities of their vibrancy. Driving, sprawl, and other environmental forces have greatly diminished the sort of public interaction that leads to spatial inscription. In response to these and other forces, today "new urbanists" are taking up Jacobs' cause. They are encouraging planners to build cities and towns that blend not only property uses but people as well. New urbanists are seeking to increase

---

[66] Setha Low, Dana Taplin, & Suzanne Scheld, *Rethinking Urban Parks: Public Space and Cultural Diversity* (2005).

social capital by literally redesigning neighborhoods and entire regions in ways that encourage encounters between diverse citizens in a public setting. Their specific proposals focus on community walkability, connectivity, diversity (of citizenry and place), density, and neighborhood structure – in other words, the very things that can lead to spatial inscription. The new urbanist agenda is not without flaws, particularly in terms of some of its recent executions. But it does at least encourage the building of spaces and architectures that could, if adopted, create public meeting grounds, replace public space that has been lost to development, beautification, and demotion, and produce a more vibrant public sphere.

One may not think that these proposals have much to do with the exercise of expressive liberties. But here, again, speech and spatiality are intimately connected. The architecture that new urbanists encourage, and the uses of public space they propose, do at least create greater *opportunities* for public encounters, interactions, and inscriptions. If we are to preserve speech out of doors and our public expressive culture, we must first get people out of their cars, off the roads, out of the skyways and tunnels, and back into their communities. To accomplish this, we will have to rethink some of our basic public architectures.

Activism

As in other places on the expressive topography, the people obviously cannot rely on courts, public officials, city planners, and private developers to preserve First Amendment liberties in inscribed and sacred places. Citizen activism with respect to these places can take many different forms. Chief among these are spatial activism and preservation programs, public participation, and even certain mild forms of civil disobedience.

On the spatial activism front, there are currently several organizations devoted to improving public places and encouraging what this chapter has called "inscription." Some organizations consisting of both academics from the social sciences and citizen-activists focus on public spaces generally – the "commons." Some groups focus on more specific places, like the National Mall, while still others devote their time and energy to public squares or parks more generally. Some of this spatial activism is animated by the core principles of new urbanism. But most of it appears to be motivated by the simple desire to preserve public places as communal sites capable of facilitating connection and inscription. These activists can boast some successes – both in terms of creating more citizen-friendly public places and stemming the tide of public space erosion. Without modifying their basic proposals, spatial activists could broaden their appeal by articulating a more explicit connection between speech and spatiality. Respect for First Amendment liberties is itself a rationale for preserving public places.

Of course, spatial activism and any preservation it may produce will matter very little if the people do not *use* public places. In the United States, the number of citizens who participate in public displays has historically been rather small.[67] It is simply impossible to know whether the people would use revitalized public spaces for expressive purposes. It is at least possible that making public presence and public places more attractive – and in particular more facilitative of public interaction – might serve both the new urbanists' agenda and the goal of preserving basic expressive liberties in public places.

Finally, those committed to preserving First Amendment liberties in inscribed and sacred places may have to resort on occasion to acts of civil disobedience. As noted earlier and discussed in the next chapter, the "public order management system" has drained public expression of much of its spontaneity, vibrancy, disruption, and effectiveness. Nonviolent forms of civil disobedience can help preserve some of these things. In this regard, note that perhaps the most effective recent public display of contention involved Mexican-American immigrants and their supporters, who literally poured into the streets across the United States during the summer of 2006. Significantly, they assembled and protested in many cases *without* first obtaining the requisite permits, or paying required fees, or obtaining liability insurance. The immigration protests were peaceful but also quite effective. They seemed to spark a serious dialogue on immigration policy in the United States, one that continues to this day. These demonstrations, and others held in response to social and political events, showed that peaceful but disruptive protests are still an effective means of putting issues on the public agenda. By essentially ignoring institutional constraints on public contention in inscribed places like streets and parks, the protesters were able to make identity claims on behalf of an entire class of marginalized persons. In doing so, of course, some of these protesters risked arrest and detention. As in the past, these are risks protesters must be willing on occasion to accept if speech out of doors is to be preserved.

Preserving access to inscribed and sacred places on the expressive topography is a monumental task. Honoring *Hague*'s essential promise

---

[67] *See* Matthew Crozat, "Are the Times A-Changin'? Assessing the Acceptance of Protest in Western Democracies," in Meyer & Tarrow, *supra* note 24, Ch. 3.

will require judicial, official, and citizen intervention. It will require that the public interest be redefined to include the preservation of physical breathing space for First Amendment liberties, particularly in our "quintessential" public forums. Should we continue on our present path, we will have some very nice places to sit, stroll, and shop; but these places will have little or no inscriptive character.

7   MILITARIZED PLACES

The people out of doors are never more actively engaged than at critical democratic moments such as national party conventions, election campaigns, presidential inaugurals, meetings of world leaders, and mass protests. At these events protesters seek to reach attending audiences and, more importantly, to generate substantial media exposure for their causes. Critical democratic moments tend to attract large public crowds, government officials, and dignitaries. As a result, they raise substantial security concerns. Indeed, at no time is the balance between security and liberty on the expressive topography more tenuous than at moments of such high public energy, sharp dissent, and profound contention.

Previous chapters examined the expressive significance – largely from the speaker's perspective – of a variety of places on the expressive topography. This chapter examines the transformation of public places when governments react – or in some instances overreacts – to perceived threats to public order and security. At recent critical democratic moments, authorities have sharply limited public contention by transforming portions of the expressive topography into *militarized* places. "Militarization" is the control of public places and public expression through repressive measures like expressive zoning, surveillance, infiltration of protest groups, mass arrests, and use of force. The process is both more focused, and more repressive, than the "public order management system" described in Chapter 6. The object of militarization is to impose a distinct kind of order on places during certain public events.[1] Imposition of that order can suppress or severely curtail the repertoires of contention speakers rely upon to disseminate their messages. It can profoundly affect speech out of doors and public politics.

---

[1] *See* Steve Herbert, *Policing Space: Territoriality and the Los Angeles Police Department* 18–20 (1997).

Spatial militarization highlights many of the central themes of this book. In particular, the militarization of "quintessential" public venues at critical moments of public democracy negatively affects the primary democratic functions of public places – identity, participation, and transparency – discussed in Chapter 2. Given its distinct timing and features, the costs of militarization may in fact be substantially greater; militarization may affect not only the vibrancy of the expressive topography at critical moments but the prospects for future social movements as well.

PUBLIC POLICING AT CRITICAL DEMOCRATIC MOMENTS

Although one might look as far back as the debacle of the 1968 Democratic National Convention in Chicago, which is discussed below, militarization at recent democratic events is primarily a response to the public disorder that occurred during World Trade Organization (WTO) meetings in Seattle in November 1999. The official reaction to events in Seattle, coupled with the generalized fear of terrorism caused by the attacks of September 11, 2001, has given rise to a new form of public protest policing at high-profile democratic events.

"The Battle in Seattle"

In late November 1999, protesters gathered in Seattle to demonstrate against the WTO at its annual Ministerial. According to various after-event reports, local authorities believed they were prepared to maintain order at this critical democratic event while allowing peaceful public protests and demonstrations.[2] Pursuant to the "negotiated management" regulatory model described in Chapter 6, authorities met in advance with leaders of certain protest groups to determine demonstration routes and establish basic ground rules for the week-long event. Police had gathered intelligence with respect to groups thought to pose

---

[2] For accounts of these events, *see* American Civil Liberties Union, *Out of Control: Seattle's Flawed Response to Protests Against the World Trade Organization* (June 2000); Seattle City Council, *Report of the WTO Accountability Review Committee* (September 14, 2000); Preparations and Planning Panel, *Report to the Seattle City Council WTO Accountability Review Committee* (August 24, 2000); The Seattle Police Department, *The Seattle Police Department After Action Report* (April 4, 2000); Alexander Cockburn & Jeffrey St. Clair, *Five Days That Shook the World: Seattle and Beyond* (2000).

some threat of violence. They had designated a few small areas or "free speech zones" near the Convention Center for where delegates were to meet demonstrations and other expressive activities. Finally, they had established a "flying squad" that could move quickly to arrest any law-breaking demonstrators throughout the city.

As events would later demonstrate, however, Seattle officials had badly miscalculated in a number of respects. Demonstration areas were not clearly marked and had not been made known to protest leaders. In various forums, including on the Web, some activists had announced plans to "shut down" the WTO proceedings. Specifically, they planned to converge on the Convention Center and other contested venues from various directions, thereby choking traffic on nearby streets. It was thus clear from many public statements that some protesters were not planning to use designated protest zones. Yet police had no detailed plan for controlling the streets. They had an insufficient workforce, a weak central command, and no effective plan in place for dealing with violent or disruptive protesters. In short, officials were largely unprepared for what would turn out to be a decentralized, technologically sophisticated, and agile Web-based protest movement.

Ensuing public events would later become known as the "Battle in Seattle." While most of the 30,000–50,000 demonstrators peacefully engaged in marches, political theatre, and civil disobedience, a small number destroyed properties and occupied buildings. Some protesters outwitted the police and essentially shut down the WTO proceedings for a brief time. The police, lacking an effective central command, were unable to simultaneously control the few law-breakers and the large numbers of peaceful protesters blocking the streets. According to after-action reports by both the city and civil rights groups, many uses of force by officers were suspect or flatly contrary to official policies of engagement. Rather than using arrests to control peaceful protesters, police resorted to nonlethal force – in particular the use of chemical irritants – to disperse crowds. Some officers used more violent means to impose order. Worse, police officers, many not wearing official identification, pursued protesters into surrounding neighborhoods. This had the effect of increasing animus toward officers and encouraging even those who had previously not participated to engage in disruptive activity. According to the after-event reports, throughout these events, officers gave unclear and inadequate warnings to protesters before using force and making arrests.

The chaos in many parts of the city eventually led the mayor of Seattle to declare a "state of emergency." He called out the National Guard and issued several emergency orders. The most controversial of these orders created a "limited curfew zone" of more than twenty-five blocks sur-rounding the Convention Center. According to some on the scene, including officers charged with its enforcement, the zone effectively made it illegal for a time to express "anti-WTO" opinions in a large section of downtown Seattle. In litigation following the WTO protests, a federal appeals court upheld the use of the curfew zone (although the court remanded certain claims of discriminatory enforcement).[3]

The "Battle in Seattle" was an embarrassing failure for Seattle and its public officials. It was also an expensive one. The City of Seattle recently agreed to pay $1 million to peaceful protesters who had been wrongfully arrested during the protests. As we shall see, these events have occasioned more widespread costs in terms of the exercise of First Amendment lib-erties at critical democratic moments. After Seattle, and in particular after September 11, 2001, officials have approached many democratic events as security threats of the highest order. In some cases, they have treated public dissent itself as a threat to security.

Militarization

As Chapter 6 demonstrated, expressive activity on public streets, in public parks, and in other inscribed places is already limited by extensive permit schemes, detailed protocols required by "negotiated management" policing models, and myriad other restrictions. The process of spatial militarization adds to this existing layer of restrictions.

Militarization includes both the physical transformation of protest landscapes and systematic changes to public protest policing methods. In its physical aspects, militarization entails treating streets, parks, and other public demonstration areas as battle zones. As in any battle, the primary objective is to secure the physical area where the contentious activity will occur. Sometimes this entails strategically choosing the most "defensible" public space – perhaps one in which only limited protest and other expressive activity can physically occur. More generally, in cooperation with law enforcement, including in many cases federal Secret Service agents, officials have superimposed a military-style grid on "quintessential" or "inscribed" public places during critical demo-cratic moments.

---

[3] Menotti v. City of Seattle, 409 F.3d 1113 (9th Cir. 2005). The claims remanded were ultimately settled.

Prior to public events like conventions and world summits, "hard" and "soft" security zones are typically established. Access to "hard" zones is strictly policed; speakers are essentially forbidden to exercise First Amendment liberties there. Instead, speakers are relegated to areas within "soft" zones, which are typically located some distance from the target event, contested places, and intended audiences. Within the "soft" zones there are often further physical constraints. In some instances, officials have constructed architectures like pens and cages into which protest and other expression is physically channeled. Fences, barricades, and even military vehicles have sometimes marked the boundaries of "free speech areas." Thus, as it is militarized, the protest landscape is physically transformed.

Spatial zoning is attractive to officials in light of the order it imposes on public places and behaviors. Michel Foucault, whose works contain important insights regarding the disciplinary power of place, noted a critical distinction between architecture that was built to be seen and that which was built to impose discipline and control.[4] In his studies of institutions like prisons and asylums, Foucault observed that place can be used to serve the first need of government – to maintain order. Through spatiality, Foucault observed, "an exact geometry" may be used to combat things like disorder and dissent.[5] Foucault specifically anticipated the use of spatial tactics like expressive zoning to control public displays like protests and demonstrations. He observed that place could be ordered so as to "neutralize the effects of counter-power" – specifically, to counteract "*agitations, revolts, spontaneous organizations, coalitions.*"[6]

As Foucault noted, repression is not inherent in places and architectures. Rather, spatial tactics are *political strategies* that have been implemented at certain critical points in history. Heightened concerns over public disorder and, especially, the threat of terrorism have obviously increased tensions at democratic events.[7] Today every mass gathering is viewed as a threat to order; every place a crowd gathers is considered a potential terrorist target. In light of these concerns, officials have turned to

---

[4] See Michel Foucault, *Discipline and Punish: The Birth of the Prison* (Alan Sheridan trans., Vintage Books 1979) (1977). Steve Herbert has pointed to some limitations regarding the use of Foucauldian principles to analyze public policing. Herbert, *supra* note 1, at 17–18. While I agree that, in general, policing of territory is about more than power, in the case of militarization power is more directly at stake than in domestic relations and other types of community policing. Thus, Foucault is an appropriate lens through which to view policing tactics at the critical democratic moments discussed in this chapter.

[5] Foucault, *supra* note 4 at 174.

[6] *Id.* at 219 (emphasis added).

[7] Nick Suplina, "Crowd Control: The Troubling Mix of First Amendment Law, Political Demonstrations, and Terrorism," 73 *Geo. Wash. L. Rev.* 395 (2005).

spatial controls that inhibit movement, suppress contention, and facilitate surveillance. Physical architectures like zones and pens create a "docile body" through "enclosure and the organization of individuals in space."[8] According to Foucault, "[t]his is why discipline fixes; it arrests or regulates movements; it clears up confusion; it dissipates compact groupings of individuals wandering about the country in unpredictable ways; it establishes calculated distributions."[9] By reducing open public space to more manageable zones, militarization obviously helps officials preserve public order and safety.[10]

Militarized zoning is also attractive to officials because it reduces dependence on physical force. As noted in the previous chapter, escalated force policing has generally fallen out of favor. The use of force in Seattle was generally viewed as a tactical error by officers on the ground. Expressive zoning and other strategic manipulations of public space are much more subtle – if no less effective – means of disciplining contention than use of tear gas, mass arrests, and other forms of physical violence. So long as speakers comply with officially established boundaries, order can generally be maintained without resort to force or violence. Courts are encouraged to view such measures as ordinary time, place, and manner regulations. Officials can even maintain that they are engaged in a form of speech-*facilitative* public policing; after all, militarized zoning provides speakers with designated "free speech zones" and "assembly areas" in which to exercise First Amendment liberties.

Although the physical transformation of public places is a key aspect of militarization and its most concrete manifestation, broader changes to protest policing have also been implemented at recent critical democratic events. Such events are now typically designated "National Security Events" pursuant to federal statute and Department of Homeland Security directive.[11] As a result, the United States Secret Service generally oversees security matters at such events. At critical democratic moments, local and federal officials have increasingly resorted to law enforcement strategies and tactics commonly used to fight terrorism. These have included extended campaigns of overt and covert surveillance, infiltration

---

[8] *See* Denise L. Lawrence & Setha M. Low, "The Built Environment and Spatial Form," 19 *Ann. Rev. Anthro.* 453, 485 (1990) (discussing Foucault's theory of architecture as a mechanism of control).

[9] Foucault, *supra* note 4 at 219.

[10] The architecture of a militarized place is "a political 'technology' for working out the concerns of government – that is, control and power over individuals – through the spatial 'canalization' of everyday life." Foucault, *supra* note 4 at 198.

[11] 18 U.S.C. § 3056(e)(1). Such events are also typically designated "extraordinary events" under local codes as well. *See, e.g.,* Denver Mun. Code § 39–86.

of activist groups, mass arrests and detentions, new forms of physical restraint, intimidation tactics, and "preemptive" law enforcement techniques. Covert surveillance and other law enforcement activities have, of course, been used by officials at other points in our history to monitor and even repress public contention.[12] But like escalated force policing itself, these measures had fallen out of favor. Owing to heightened concerns regarding security, in particular since September 11, 2001, these tactics have now become *routine* aspects of public policing at critical democratic moments.

Since the "Battle in Seattle," officials have shifted their focus from facilitating safe public contention to keeping the public "safe" from contentious public displays. To understand the effects of militarization on speech out of doors, we must look beyond its physical manifestations – grids, zones, and pens – to the more general transformation of the environment in which public contention now occurs at critical democratic moments.

MILITARIZATION AT RECENT CRITICAL DEMOCRATIC MOMENTS

Both the physical and public policing elements of militarization have recently been evident at several types of public democratic events. The episodes discussed below demonstrate a distinct transformation in the social control of dissent at critical democratic moments.

National Political Conventions

Public contention at national political conventions is, of course, not a new phenomenon. At the 1968 Democratic National Convention in Chicago, protesters were denied permits to sleep in Lincoln Park and to hold demonstrations near the Amphitheater where the convention was to be held (although they had been offered permits for demonstration sites miles from the convention). When protesters marched on the Amphitheater, they were met with escalated force by thousands of police officers, who bombed crowds with tear gas and clubbed participants. The media recorded the

---

[12] For a general account of police surveillance activities, *see* Gary T. Marx, *Undercover: Police Surveillance in America* (1988). With regard to surveillance and political dissent, *see* Ward Churchill and Jim Vander Wall, T*he COINTELPRO Papers: Documents from the FBI's Secret Wars Against Dissent in the United States* (1990).

graphic violence, which occurred over the course of five days. Eventually, police put a barricade around the convention site and denied entry to anyone without credentials.

As in Seattle, after-action reports were highly critical of both the police response in Chicago and some of the more radical protesters. A Chicago grand jury later indicted eight police officers. Eight civilians were also indicted, resulting in the famous trial of the "Chicago 8." Changes in public policing followed. The display at the convention was a critical historical event leading to the abandonment of "escalated force" by police forces across the country and the adoption of the "negotiated management" model. But the events of 1968 had marked political conventions as potential threats to public order.

By comparison to 1968, subsequent conventions have generally been peaceful and orderly. This has been due in large part to the adoption and execution of negotiated management public policing methods. As events in Seattle demonstrated, however, negotiation with protesters is no guarantee that public order will be maintained. Following the "Battle in Seattle," officials turned to a more militaristic approach to national political party conventions. For example, military-style grids and zones were used at the 2000 Democratic National Convention in Los Angeles. Local and federal officials designated a "secured zone" around the Staples Center, where the convention was to take place. The zone cordoned off approximately 185 acres of land surrounding the convention site and was in effect 24 hours a day. Within the secured zone, officials designated an "Official Demonstration Area." The demonstration area kept protesters *260 yards* from the conventions site and the delegates. From this distance, protesters could obviously neither be seen nor heard by delegates.

After a federal district court concluded that no meaningful protest was possible from within the designated zone, officials were forced to move the protest area to a parking lot adjacent to the Staples Center.[13] During the convention, a disturbance occurred within the protest zone when some protesters threw rocks and other objects at police and attempted to scale the protest zone fence. Police on horseback and in riot gear cleared the area. Riots ensued on adjacent streets as police tried to corral the crowd. There were numerous injuries reported from the use of stun guns, tear gas, and pepper spray. Hundreds of lawsuits were filed by injured protesters; most of these claims were settled out of court.

---

[13] Serv. Employee Int'l Union v. City of Los Angeles, 114 F. Supp. 2d 966, 968–69 (C.D. Cal. 2000).

Figure 7.1. The "DZ" from Outside.

After the terrorist attacks of September 11, 2001, officials resorted to more restrictive tactics at national party conventions. As discussed at the beginning of Chapter 1, local and federal officials sharply limited public expression and contention at the 2004 Democratic National Convention in Boston. Prior to the convention, officials mapped out both "hard" and "soft" security zones. In the "hard" security zone, which comprised the Fleet Center where delegates would gather and certain immediately adjacent areas, protest activity was not permitted. Some space was provided for protest activity within the "soft" security zone, which encompassed areas somewhat further removed from the Convention Center. Specifically, officials constructed a "designated demonstration zone" (DZ) within the soft security zone (Figures 7.1, 7.2, and 7.3).

The DZ was a roughly rectangular space of approximately 26,000 to 28,000 square feet, or approximately 300 feet by 90 feet. A federal district court judge, who viewed the designated protest area, described it as follows:

> Most – at least two thirds – of the DZ lies under unused Green Line tracks. The tracks create a space redolent of the sensibility conveyed in Piranesi's etchings published as *Fanciful Images of Prisons*. It is a grim, mean, and oppressive space whose ominous roof is supported by a forest of girders that obstruct sight lines throughout as the tracks slope downwards towards the southern end.
>
> The DZ is surrounded by two rows of concrete jersey barriers. Atop each of the jersey barriers is an eight foot high chain link fence. A tightly woven mesh fabric, designed to prevent liquids and objects

Figure 7.2. The "DZ" Facing the Fleet Center.

from being thrown through the fence, covers the outer fence, limiting but not eliminating visibility. From the top of the outer fence to the train tracks overhead, at an angle of approximately forty-five degrees to horizontal, is a looser mesh netting, designed to prevent objects from being thrown at the delegates.

On the overhead Green Line tracks themselves is looped razor wire, designed to prevent persons from climbing onto the tracks where armed police and National Guardsman [sic] will be located . . . . The overall impression created by the DZ is that of *an internment camp.*[14]

---

[14] *See* Coal. to Protest the Democratic Nat'l Convention v. City of Boston, 327 F. Supp. 2d 61, 67 (D. Mass. 2004).

Figure 7.3. Security at the "DZ".

Other design elements of this "oppressive" architecture limited the number of protesters to no more than 1,000 (despite the fact that the city had originally assured that at least 4,000 could be accommodated); severely restricted the use of signs, posters, and other visual material; and prohibited the passing of leaflets to delegates - even those who approached the DZ. Police helicopters hovered above the structure. National Guardsmen and state police in black armor suits patrolled the area. The space, said the district court, "conveys the symbolic sense of a holding pen where potentially dangerous persons are separated from others."[15] Not surprisingly, protesters and demonstrators refused to use the DZ.[16]

The district court described the DZ as "a symbolic affront to the First Amendment."[17] Nevertheless, despite the negative view of the protest area taken by both the district court and, subsequently, a federal court of appeals the DZ survived First Amendment scrutiny.[18] The court of appeals reasoned that the DZ was the product of "content-neutral"

---

[15] *Id.* at 74–75.
[16] Pursuant to a court order, protesters were ultimately permitted to parade near the convention site.
[17] *Coal. To Protest the Democratic Nat'l Convention*, 327 F. Supp. 2d at 74–75.
[18] Bl(a)ck Tea Soc'y v. City of Boston, 378 F.3d 8 (1st Cir. 2004).

policies and protocols, and deferred to the government's interest in maintaining security at a political convention. The appeals court conceded that there was no "event-specific threat evidence."[19] It also acknowledged that the DZ essentially prohibited embodied expression, in that it "allowed no opportunity for physical interaction (such as the distribution of leaflets) and severely curtailed any chance for one-on-one conversation."[20] Finally, the court recognized that visual communication, as with signs or posters, was significantly hampered by the DZ's location and design. Nevertheless, the court found that adequate alternative channels of communication existed. It emphasized that demonstrators could convey their messages at such "high profile" events as national political conventions through television, the press, and the Internet.[21] The First Amendment, according to the court, did not require that protesters be allowed access to the embodied space of delegates or the contested place of the Fleet Center (*see* Chapters 3 and 4).

Militarization tactics were also used later that summer, at the 2004 Republican National Convention in New York City. Having failed to obtain a permit for demonstrations near Madison Square Garden (where the convention was to be held), protesters were eventually relegated to a place on the West Side Highway.[22] The protest area was far removed from the convention site and the delegates. Demonstrators were ultimately permitted to parade past the convention site. But they were denied a permit to rally in Central Park – in part because of concerns over possible damage to the lawn from an assembly of approximately 250,000 people (*see* Chapter 6). The courts upheld the denial of the demonstration permit – although a federal judge did refuse to allow police to search the bags and possessions of all demonstrators at random, absent information of a specific security threat. But the same judge allowed police to use closed, four-sided metal barriers or pens to contain protesters on city streets and sidewalks.[23] In addition to pens and other physical barricades, the police unveiled a new spatial technique at the Republican National Convention: Officers used large orange *nets* to divide and capture protesters. Many captured in these nets were not engaged in acts of civil disobedience or other wrongdoing.

[19] *Id.* at 13–14.
[20] *Id.* at 13.
[21] *Id.* at 14.
[22] Diane Cardwell, "Protesters Accept a Stage Distant From G.O.P. Ears," *N.Y. Times,* July 22, 2004, at B3. *See* Susan Rachel Nanes, "Constitutional Infringement Zones, Protest Pens and Demonstration Zones at the 2004 National Political Conventions," 66 *La. L. Rev.* 189 (2005).
[23] Stauber v. City of New York, 2004 WL 1593870, at *29 (S.D.N.Y. July 16, 2004).

In general, police officers in New York City adopted a preemptive strike approach during the convention. Mass arrests – more than 1,800 of them – were used to control public displays and contention. Many protests and demonstrations were dispersed before they became large enough to be seen or heard, much less substantial enough to affect the convention proceedings. Ultimately, charges against nearly *90 percent* of those arrested during the 2004 Republican National Convention were either dismissed or adjourned in contemplation of dismissal. Of those arrested, 550 were released before they were arraigned as a result of court orders finding that the city had failed to comply with a state mandate that prisoners be arraigned within 24 hours of arrest.

Additional details regarding militarization tactics used at the 2004 Republican National Convention have recently become available. A federal magistrate judge rejected the New York City Police Department's (NYPD) plea to keep confidential certain police intelligence documents produced in the period leading up to the convention. The documents reveal that starting 18 months prior to the convention, NYPD officers and detectives infiltrated political meetings held by activists and protesters, including church groups, street theater companies, antiwar organizations, and environmentalists. Officers and detectives posed as activists and protest sympathizers. Undercover detectives fanned out across the United States and to locations *across the globe*, to investigate everything from protest groups in California to graffiti artists in Germany. Police also carefully monitored email, listservs, and Web sites. New York City officials shared information about planned peaceful and lawful protest activities with police departments in cities across the country.

In conjunction with their preconvention surveillance, police created daily "RNC Intelligence Updates" and "Situation Reports."[24] In hundreds of pages of reports, officers highlighted activities like the following:

- A planned "Bands Against Bush" music show. NYPD officials observed that "the mixing of music and political rhetoric indicates sophisticated organizing skills with a specific agenda." Police departments and localities across the country were notified of this planned protest activity.
- Plans by a group known as "Axis of Eve" to use partial nudity as a "protest tactic." Without apparent irony, the intelligence report states: "The event is said to include the participation of roughly 100 women

---

[24] The reports are available at http://www.nytimes.com/ref/nyregion/RNC_intel_digests.html.

in thong type underwear and will be advertised heavily amongst the media for *maximum exposure.*

- The possible presence of graffiti artists riding "magic bikes" – customized bicycles equipped with spray paint dispensers and videotaping equipment.
- Performances by "The Living Theater" entourage, whose purpose according to one intelligence report "is to raise community awareness on political or social issues," and the "Surveillance Camera Players," who engage in street theatre protests concerning the use of public surveillance cameras.
- An Iowa group's plans to hold a film festival as a prelude to the RNC.
- Plans by the antiwar group "Not in Our Name" to conduct a poetry read in Central Park.
- Planned leafleting activity by a group called "United for Peace and Justice."
- A weekly vigil by "Grandmothers Against the War."
- A march across the Brooklyn Bridge by "Mothers Opposing Bush."
- A demonstration by devotees of the late country singer Johnny Cash, who were reportedly planning to dress in black and play Cash music.
- A "wet anti-Bush" T-shirt contest.
- A day-long Buddhist meditation.
- An indoor "anti-Bush" lecture at St. John the Divine church.

This police activity is a manifestation of what the legal scholars Jack Balkin and Sanford Levinson refer to as "the surveillance state."[25] As Professors Balkin and Levinson describe it, the surveillance state "is characterized by a significant increase in government investments in technology and government bureaucracies devoted to promoting domestic security and (as its name implies) gathering intelligence and surveillance using all of the devices that the digital revolution allows."[26]

As discussed below, under prevailing standards most if not all of the surveillance conducted by New York City officers and detectives likely did not violate the First Amendment.[27] In so indiscriminately choosing their subjects, however, officials may have given pause to those

---

[25] Jack M. Balkin & Sanford Levinson, "The Processes of Constitutional Change: From Partisan Retrenchment to the National Surveillance State," 75 *Fordham L. Rev.* 489 (2006).

[26] *Id.* at 520–21. *See also* Jack Balkin, "The Constitution in the National Surveillance State," *Minn. L. Rev.*, Vol. 93, No. 1 (2008).

[27] It is possible that some of the RNC surveillance activity may have violated a longstanding consent decree entered into by the police department which governs, among other things, surveillance of lawful public activities. This issue is discussed further in Chapter 9.

contemplating even the most peaceful and lawful forms of public dissent
and contention. This climate is in no sense limited to a few rogue police
departments across the country. For example, although it has thus far
received little attention, in 2007 the United States House of Representatives approved the "Violent Radicalization and Homegrown Terrorism
Prevention Act."[28] Among other things, the measure would establish a
ten-member investigative commission charged with rooting out
"homegrown terrorists" and "violent radicals." The definitions of these
terms are broad enough to encompass those who organize mass political
protests or assemble to demonstrate regarding matters of public concern
like the Iraq war or abortion.[29]

   At recent national political conventions, officials have used militarization techniques to transform not only the physical landscape but the
broader protest environment as well. As the NYPD "Situation Reports"
indicate, the act of protest itself is being treated at these events as a threat
to public order and security. More generally, public policies have begun to
embrace a disturbing – and false – equation of legitimate political protest
and terrorism.

Presidential Appearances and Inaugurals

The militarization of public places and protest policing has also been
evident during presidential appearances, campaign events, and inaugurals. Since 2001, officials in the Bush Administration have been routinely
shielded from protests, demonstrations, and dissenting viewpoints. Some
of the justification for this sort of protection relates to threats of terrorism
and other violence at public presidential appearances and events. It is
impossible to say whether some of the more repressive policies discussed
here will continue into the next administration. That will depend principally upon the next president's commitment to transparency and respect
for public dissent and contention.

   Militarization during campaign events and presidential appearances
has followed the same general pattern of zoning and displacing public
dissent seen at party conventions. During the last several years, commentators have noted a distinct trend of shielding federal officials and

---

[28] H.R. 1955.
[29] *See id.* (defining "homegrown terrorist" as any person who "intimidates or coerces the United
    States government, the civilian population . . . or any segment thereof, in furtherance of
    political or social belief").

political candidates from public dissent and disagreement.[30] For example, several protesters have been expelled from political events or refused entry for infractions as minor as wearing "anti-Bush" apparel and carrying signs critical of the administration.

In recent years, the Secret Service has routinely instructed local police to channel protesters into designated assembly and protest areas. In several instances, protesters have been arrested for refusing to confine their expressive activity to "free speech zones." In one instance, the "free speech area" consisted of a large baseball field surrounded by a six-foot high chain-link fence. The expressive zone was located far from the site of the presidential appearance. Once inside the zone, protesters were not permitted to leave until the event concluded. Reporters were generally not permitted to enter the zone. Meanwhile, as in other instances, several reports indicated that pro-Bush demonstrators were not confined to the zones and indeed were permitted to stand within eyeshot, earshot, and camera-shot of the president.[31] In another case, a protester at an airport at which President Bush's airplane landed was arrested when he refused to go to a designated "speech zone" to display a sign that said "No War for Oil." Although it was not clearly marked, the Secret Service maintained that a 100-yard area surrounding the airport constituted a "secured zone." Despite the fact that pro-administration individuals were assembled nearby and were not told by officers to leave the area, this protester's conviction was upheld over a First Amendment challenge.

Federal and local laws have been invoked in support of these arrests. The airport protester described above was convicted for violating a rarely invoked 1970 Secret Service Act provision that makes it a federal crime to "knowingly and willfully" enter an area restricted by the Secret Service.[32] In the age of suicide bombers, the judge concluded, the Secret Service could not be forced to take chances with regard to presidential safety. Other protesters venturing outside approved zones have been charged with trespass, disorderly conduct, and obstruction under state and local laws. Some of these charges have been thrown out by judges. In many

---

[30] *See* Timothy Zick, "Speech and Spatial Tactics," 84 *Tex. L. Rev.* 581 (2006); Mary M. Cheh, "Demonstrations, Security Zones, and First Amendment Protection of Special Places," 8 *U.D.C. L. Rev.* 53 (2004); American Civil Liberties Union Fact Sheet, "Free Speech Under Fire: The ACLU Challenge to 'Protest Zones'" (September 23, 2003); American Civil Liberties Union, "Freedom Under Fire: Dissent in Post-9/11 America" (May 8, 2003).

[31] The phenomenon is not limited to domestic appearances. When President Bush has traveled abroad, Secret Service officials have routinely insisted on virtual lock-downs of entire cities.

[32] 18 U.S. C. § 1752(a)(1)(ii). The provision was enacted in the wake of the 1960s Kennedy assassinations.

cases, however, charges have simply been dropped by authorities after the speaker's arrest and removal.

As a result of a lawsuit filed by a Texas couple ejected from a Fourth of July speech by President Bush for simply wearing "anti-Bush" T-shirts, we now know that suppression of protest at presidential appearances was an official federal policy. In the litigation, the Office of Presidential Advance produced a 2002 "Presidential Advance Manual" that essentially instructs presidential advance staffers in the art of "deterring potential protesters" from attending President Bush's public appearances.[33] The manual discusses pre-event measures to "minimize demonstrators" including limiting attendance to those with tickets and screening attendees for hidden protest signs (no "homemade" signs are allowed). If, despite these measures, protesters attend an event the manual instructs staff to ask local police "*to designate a protest area where demonstrators can be placed, preferably not in the view of the event site or motorcade route.*" If for some reason that is not possible, the manual suggests the strategic use of "rally squads" to shout them down. And if all else fails, the manual instructs that protesters should be thrown out of the event – although staffers are instructed not to fall into the "trap" of physical confrontation, which "most often" is desired by protesters.

The Secret Service is of course duty-bound to protect the president. In many cases, however, zones and other measures go well beyond keeping would-be terrorists from coming within potentially harmful range. The Presidential Advance Manual indicates a profound disrespect for public dissent and a lack of concern for public transparency. In the name of security, public events – including those that take place on public property – have been sanitized such that dissenting views can be neither seen nor heard. At critical democratic moments, simple acts or statements of dissent have resulted in arrest and prosecution.

Other critical democratic events involving the president have also been affected by militarization tactics and policies. Regardless of one's political affiliation, presidential inaugurals are generally a time of national celebration. As at any critical *public* democratic moment, however, some dissent is to be expected. Recent presidential inaugurals have also become militarized events. Consider this description of President Bush's first inaugural in 2001, which was held on the "sacred" space of the National Mall:

> [M]uch of the Mall was surrounded by a two-meter-high metal fence and entirely closed on inauguration day; six checkpoints complete

---

[33] The manual can be accessed at http://www.aclu.org/pdfs/freespeech/presidential_advance_manual.pdf.

with metal detectors were established for the few thousand ticketed guests allowed into the parade viewing area in front of the White House; police were stationed every two meters along the parade route with hundreds of other police in riot gear posted nearby; subway stations were closed; Secret Service snipers were deployed on rooftops; and several dozen buses stood ready to transport arrestees to mass arraignment sites away from the inauguration area.[34]

We should add to this physical description the presence of a number of "designated protest zones" along the inaugural route. In 2001, the National Park Service and the District of Columbia, which shared authority for the public space along the parade route, granted a blanket permit for the route to the Presidential Inauguration Committee.[35] Smaller protest groups were allowed access to designated places along the procession, while somewhat larger demonstrations were limited to certain official "protest zones" further removed from the inaugural route.

This, of course, all took place prior to the terrorist attacks in September 2001. At President Bush's 2005 inaugural, the National Park Service generally excluded the public from most sidewalks and open spaces between and around bleachers along the parade route. A limited number of antiwar protesters were permitted to gather along the parade route. But other protesters were limited to tiny areas behind bleachers and to fenced-in areas more than 100 feet from the parade route.[36] Prior to 2001, federal officials had designated presidential inaugurals "National Celebration Events." Subsequent inaugurals have, as noted earlier, been designated "National Special Security Events." In 2001, President Bush actually walked a portion of the parade route and mingled with the public. At his 2005 inaugural, the president remained in the limousine throughout the procession. By the second inaugural in 2005, concrete and other physical barriers were visible along the entire procession route, as were military vehicles and personnel. Journalists described the topography at this critical democratic event as a "steel cocoon."[37]

---

[34] Don Mitchell & Lynn A. Staeheli, "Permitting Protest: Parsing the Fine Geography of Dissent in America," 29(4) *International Journal of Urban and Regional Research* 807 (December 2005).

[35] *See id.*

[36] As of this writing, protesters continue to pursue First Amendment claims relating to these actions in federal court. A.N.S.W.E.R. Coalition v. Kempthorne, 537 F.Supp.2d 183 (D.D.C. 2008).

[37] David Johnston & Michael Janofsky, "A Steel Cocoon Is Woven For The Capital's Big Party," *N.Y. Times*, January 19, 2005, A16. Restricted zones have sprouted up throughout Washington, D.C. during critical democratic moments. During President Bush's 2006 State

World Conferences and Summits

After the events in Seattle, gatherings of world leaders – both in the United States and abroad – have also been affected by militarization. United States and foreign officials now go so far as to consider the strategic "defensibility" of proposed summit sites when choosing a location.[38] In 2004, for example, authorities chose Sea Island in Georgia as the site for the "G8" summit. The resort is located 60 miles south of Savannah, Georgia, where protesters and the media were essentially forced to stay during the summit. Thus, the local geography itself created a security zone that protected attendees from large-scale demonstrations and most indicia of public dissent.

Since September 11, 2001, increasingly elaborate security precautions have been taken in an effort to control dissent at summits, conferences, and meetings attended by world leaders. For example, police at a recent G8 summit in Germany erected a $17 million, 8-foot-high, 7.5-mile-long fence topped with barbed and razor wire to completely cut off the host resort from the general public. Officials banned protests within 200 yards of the fence. Both within and outside the United States, officials now routinely engage in both covert and overt surveillance in advance of world summits. Undercover detectives and federal agents maintain files on activists and protest organizations that may target a particular summit or conference. Police patrols are stepped up at event sites in advance of conferences, as is videotaping in areas near contested sites.

In 2001, police engaged in preemptive law enforcement tactics prior to demonstrations at meetings of the International Monetary Fund (IMF) and World Bank in Washington, D.C.[39] Based on information gathered from monitoring Web sites and infiltrating protest groups, officers arrived at activists' homes just as critical organizing activity was taking place. A few days before the demonstrations, police arrested several activists for possession of materials alleged to be intended for criminal purposes. Secret Service and other officials raided and searched a warehouse being used by demonstrators as a staging ground. Alleging several fire code violations, officials closed the building.

During the IMF meetings, officials established and enforced a large "no-protest zone" near the IMF conference site. As protesters peacefully

---

of the Union address, for example, protesters had to sue to gain access to Union Square, an area near the Capitol. Police claimed that the space was within a "security perimeter."
[38] Luis Fernandez, "Policing Space: Social Control and the Anti-Corporate Globalization Movement," No. 3(4) *The Canadian Journal of Police & Security Services* 242–43 (Winter 2005).
[39] Mitchell & Staeheli, *supra* note 34 at 808.

marched down streets and sidewalks, police assembled in riot gear and marched toward the assemblies. Six hundred protesters were arrested on charges of failing to disperse and parading without a permit. Similar measures were taken when the IMF and World Bank meetings returned to Washington, D.C. in 2002.

Militarization was also evident when several defense ministers and delegates gathered in 2005 for a meeting hosted by the United States Secretary of Defense in Colorado Springs, Colorado. A detailed security plan developed in advance of the event called for closing public streets and sidewalks and imposing a large "security zone" around the hotel where attendees were staying and meeting. The zone extended for several blocks in all directions around the event site. Although attendees, employees, and some members of the media were permitted to enter the secured zone after being screened, entry was denied to the general public. During the event, several hundred personnel from military and law enforcement agencies staffed the checkpoints of the security zone and patrolled the perimeter. Metal detectors and explosive-sniffing dogs were used throughout the event.

Despite all of these limitations, six peace activists requested to hold a one-hour peaceful protest within the security zone. Officials denied the request, offering instead to allow the protest outside one of the five checkpoints. The protesters initially refused the alternate site on the ground that attendees would not be able to see or hear them from this distance. They later relented and held a vigil several blocks from the meeting site. Given their location, neither the attendees nor the media saw or heard the protesters' message – although they did pass by on buses when entering the security zone. Largely in deference to officials' security concerns, and given the fact that the protesters were not *wholly* deprived of the ability to communicate their message, the courts upheld the prohibition on all expression within the broad security zone.[40]

Meetings of world leaders present unique and powerfully symbolic protest opportunities. Militarization has effectively prevented access to contested places, all forms of embodied expression, and access to media outlets at these critical democratic events. In the name of security, entire portions of public downtown areas have been closed to the public during these events. Expressive zones, shows of force, mass arrests, and detentions have been used to contain protesters committed enough to engage in contentious displays in such a militarized environment.

---

[40] *See* Citizens for Peace in Space v. City of Colorado Springs, 2005 WL 1769230 (D. Colo. July 25, 2005) (upholding a security zone that closed all public streets around the hotel), *aff'd*, 477 F.3d 1212 (10th Cir. 2007).

Antiwar and Other Political Demonstrations

As discussed in Chapter 6, public displays of contention like protests, parades, and demonstrations are already subject to a variety of restrictions and regulations. Permit schemes, limits on access to certain places, and a host of other time, place, and manner restrictions often reduce public demonstrations and protests to institutionalized and thus largely ineffective displays.

Recent large-scale demonstrations relating to the war in Iraq, abortion, Israel, immigration, and a variety of other matters of public concern show that mass public contention does in fact occur in the United States on a fairly regular basis. Today, however, protesters must contend not only with the restrictions of negotiated management and the general "public order management system" discussed in Chapter 6 but also with the additional restrictions of militarization. Beyond existing regulatory layers, protesters must be cognizant of measures like covert and overt police surveillance, pre-event infiltration, preemptive tactics, and of course expressive zones, pens, and other physical barriers.

Using the advance notice of negotiated management to their advantage, police now prepare for public events like mass protests as if going to battle. In 2003, for example, nearly a quarter of a million protesters in New York City planned to turn out to demonstrate near the United Nations building against plans to go to war in Iraq. Similar protests were then occurring across the globe. Prior to the demonstration, the FBI and other officials engaged in widespread surveillance and other intelligence activities targeting expected protest groups. With regard to specific contentious displays, the demonstrators were first denied a permit to march past the United Nations on the ground that the march was a "security risk." The city proposed an alternative route, one that would pass four blocks from the United Nations. But officials also sought to limit attendance at the march to no more than 10,000 protesters. Police closed off several streets to channel protesters away from the United Nations building. They drew up plans to accommodate any overflow crowd in four-sided pens, which provided very limited opportunity for movement or exit. During the actual march, police showed up *en masse*. They used horse charges and other methods of force to disperse crowds. Once again, many protesters filed civil rights lawsuits in which they alleged they were beaten or forcibly detained without cause.

Although "escalated force" is a disfavored policing method, it has apparently not been completely abandoned. For example, a public demonstration on behalf of immigrants in Los Angeles during 2006 "May

Day" celebrations was marred by extensive police violence. As captured by several video-cameras on the scene, in response to isolated instances of misconduct at MacArthur Park police officers indiscriminately wielded batons and fired 146 rubber bullets into a passive and confused crowd. More than 240 people, including 9 journalists covering the May Day rally, were injured. Eighteen police officers also sustained injuries. The mayor of Los Angeles described the events at MacArthur Park as "dark and tragic."

The Los Angeles Police Department issued a lengthy report on the MacArthur Park incident, in which it admitted that serious mistakes were made.[41] As in Seattle in 1999, planning for the 2006 May Day rally had been poor. Officers underestimated the rally's size – despite the fact that large May Day rallies had been held at MacArthur Park for decades. Pre-event planning meetings were requested, but not held. Requests by officers for additional resources were denied. Remarkably, critical units assigned to the event received no crowd control training in the 18 months leading up to the rally. Further, no media viewing area was established, despite a settlement agreement subsequent to the 2000 Democratic National Convention in Los Angeles expressly requiring such an area at future events. There was a severe breakdown in the chain of command. An "unlawful assembly" order was prematurely issued, interfering with the First Amendment rights of peaceful protesters. Instructions to disperse were issued a minute *after* police had started firing rubber bullets, and only in English (despite the fact that the crowds were comprised mostly of Spanish-speaking immigrants).

Large public demonstrations and other events must obviously be subject to careful policing and regulation in order to protect public safety and maintain order. Today, however, at most public events speakers should expect to encounter more than the ordinary public order management regime. In addition to the usual restrictions on public liberties, speakers will almost certainly encounter physical barriers, demonstrations of official force, mass arrests, and sometimes lengthy detentions. In many cases, they can also expect to be watched carefully and well in advance of the planned event. As the recent antiwar and May Day rally events show, militarization has apparently obscured some of the lessons that should have been learned as a result of the "Battle in Seattle."

---

[41] The text of the report is available at http://lapdonline.org/search_results/content_basic_view/35447. Contemporaneous videos of the May Day events are available at http://netzoo.net/videos-of-macarthur-park-mayday-police-violence/.

MILITARIZATION, REPRESSION, AND THE SOCIAL
CONTROL OF DISSENT

The militarization of public places and protest policing during critical democratic moments obviously affects the public exercise of First Amendment liberties. But militarization also raises broader concerns regarding public contention and public democracy. Before turning to specific expressive concerns, let us first consider militarization in this somewhat broader context.

Public policing and "public order management" are aspects of what social scientists sometimes call "the social control of dissent." Authorities sometimes control dissent through *repression*, which Charles Tilly has broadly defined as "any action by another group which raises the contender's cost of collective action."[42] As social scientists have noted, there are several distinct types of repression. In its most tangible and traditional forms, repression includes things like official harassment, physical intimidation, assault, arrest, and detainment. Many of these repressive actions are associated with the "escalated force" model of public protest policing. As noted, some of these actions have recently resurfaced as a result or function of militarization.

The political scientist Donatella della Porta has developed a typology that outlines five distinct dimensions relating to protest policing. Focusing largely on severity, she asks whether protest policing is (1) repressive versus tolerant (focusing on how many behaviors are restricted); (2) selective versus diffuse; (3) preventative versus reactive; (4) hard versus soft (based upon degree of force); and (5) "dirty" versus lawful.[43] Other social scientists have drawn different distinctions and generated their own typologies. For example, Jennifer Earl distinguishes between *coercive* repression, which involves shows and/or uses of force and other forms of standard police action like intimidation and violence, and *channeling*, which involves more indirect repression and is meant to affect the forms of protest, its timing, and/or flows of resources to protest groups.[44] Earl also distinguishes between covert repression, which is intended to be unknown

---

[42] Charles Tilly, *From Mobilization to Revolution* 100 (1978).
[43] Donatella della Porta, "Social Movements & the State: Thoughts on the Policing of Protest," in Doug McAdam, John D. McCarthy, & Mayer N. Zald, eds., *Comparative Perspectives on Social Movements*, 62–92 (1996).
[44] Jennifer Earl, "Tanks, Tear Gas, and Taxes: Toward a Theory of Movement Repression," *Sociological Theory*, 21(1), 44–68 (March 2003); Anthony Oberschall, *Social Conflict and Social Movements* (1973).

to protesters and the general public, and overt repression, which is intended to be obvious.[45] Militarization is a distinct form of repression. It combines many of the factors and elements that social scientists have identified in their typologies of repression. In terms of della Porta's typology, for example, although militarization can be highly repressive in certain situations (the DZ, for example), it does not generally result in suppression of *all* contention and expression. Militarization is highly selective. It has been used primarily at recent high-profile democratic events, although its use has expanded steadily since September 2001. Militarization is both preventative and reactive. In situations that allow for advance preparation, officials employ preemptive tactics including advance zoning and arrests. Where notice is less adequate or, in rare cases, is not available officials have adopted a more reactive approach. Militarization relies upon a combination of hard (physical constraints and violence) and soft (surveillance and infiltration) tactics. It is mostly lawful rather than "dirty." Using Earl's terminology, militarization represses by both "coercive" means (arrests, detentions, uses of force) and "channeling" (expressive zoning and strategic choice of place). It is both "covert" (surveillance) and "overt" (displays of riot gear, intimidation, and other shows of force).

Militarization's rather uneasy fit with current social science typologies and treatments of repression suggests that it is a subject worthy of independent study. In particular, social scientists ought to incorporate militarization into examinations of repression and the social control of dissent. The ultimate question, however, is what effect militarization may have on public politics and democracy.

Militarization complicates the terrain of public contention not just for scholars, but more importantly for activists. Protesters have learned in general terms what to expect when they participate in public displays at critical democratic moments. Most are now aware that large speech-free areas and even physical architectures like the DZ have survived scrutiny in the courts. They know to expect shows of force and intimidation. And they know that the possibility of arrest and detention has probably increased to some degree.

But protesters and activists are still learning, along with the general public, of the unique forms of repression that militarization brings prior to and during public events. Today, even lawful and peaceful protesters must assume they are being watched and that their groups have perhaps been infiltrated by undercover officers. Under negotiated management,

---

[45] *See* Earl, *supra* note 44.

arrests have often been orchestrated affairs. Protesters were routinely released after booking and citation. With militarization, the repercussions of civil disobedience are less clear, as the pattern of negotiated arrest, citation, and release has given way in some instances to mass arrests and lenghty detentions. Protesters must also be aware of record-keeping protocols under which arrest information may be retained by authorities. As a result of these changes, in a militarized environment, expressive behavior and peaceful forms of civil disobedience may be severely chilled at critical moments of public democracy.

In examining militarization at critical democratic moments, it is also important to consider its toll on *social movements*. According to one commonly accepted definition, a social movement is a sustained collective challenge based upon common purposes.[46] The civil rights movement is, of course, the paradigmatic example. Critical democratic events like national conventions, campaigns, world summits, and antiwar assemblies are fertile ground for both current and future social movements. Repertories of contention like rallies and demonstrations have always played a significant role in forming, energizing, and sustaining social movements.

Militarization presents sharp challenges to the continued use of public space for contentious politics. Social movements rely heavily upon the availability of physical breathing space for public displays. Transparent public displays are critical not only to the conveyance of particular messages, but to movement solidarity. Public assemblies communicate to others that a new social movement is forming, or that an already established movement is thriving. Public displays are also used to reach media outlets and, with their assistance, large public audiences. In certain rare cases, such displays may even influence public officials. In a militarized environment, however, the story often becomes the repression itself; the actual message may be garbled or even suppressed.[47] Neither public officials nor the general public will likely be swayed by protests in pens. We must also keep in mind that most people will only participate in public contention when the rewards of activism outweigh its potential costs. As the costs of public action increase and its benefits seem to decrease,

---

[46] Sidney Tarrow, *Power in Movement: Social Movements, Collective Action, and Politics* 19 (1994).

[47] Of course, even absent repression media attention and focus on substantive issues at critical democratic events, as elsewhere, are hardly guaranteed. *See* Jackie Smith, John D. McCarthy, Clark McPhail, & Boguslaw Augustyn, "From Protest to Agenda Building: Description Bias in Media Coverage of Protest Events in Washington, D.C.," 79(4) *Social Forces*, 1397–1423, (June 2001).

participation becomes less likely. Like other forms of repression, militarization drastically increases the costs of participation.

As political scientists and sociologists have observed, many factors affect the formation and maintenance of social movements. These include movement organization, broader political opportunities and constraints, and public support. Militarization will not likely determine, by itself, whether a social movement will form, thrive, or survive. It may, however, affect the frequency and character of public politics. The political scientist Sidney Tarrow has observed that people engage in contentious out-of-door politics "when patterns of political opportunities and constraints change and then, by strategically employing a repertoire of collective action, create new opportunities, which are used by others in widening cycles of contention."[48] By suppressing participation, militarization can marginalize protesters and dissent, prevent the formation of social capital, and inhibit critical information cascades. A repressive public landscape and protest environment may ultimately affect the patterns and cycles of social movements.

It is of course possible, as some social scientists have noted, that aggressive state repression will backfire, thus engendering greater movement solidarity and reducing goodwill toward the state.[49] That, indeed, may be one lesson to draw from the "Battle in Seattle." But given the security concerns that likely will continue to dictate strategy at critical democratic moments and events, it seems unlikely that officials will substantially alter, much less abandon, militarization for this reason alone. From the government's perspective, the benefits of militarization in terms of security and order appear to outweigh any monetary, political, or social costs.

In sum, as we consider the First Amendment issues raised by militarization we must keep in mind that the stakes are actually much higher. What is actually being planned and adjudicated is the set of conditions under which collective contentious politics will be permitted to take place at critical moments in the nation's public self-governance.

MAKING SPACE FOR PUBLIC POLITICS

With regard to the democratic and First Amendment functions of public places, militarization tends to suppress identity claims, decrease public

---

[48] Tarrow, *supra* note 46 at 19.
[49] *See* William A. Gamson, *The Strategy of Social Protest* [1975] (1990).

participation in collective contention, and lessen the transparency of public democracy. Particularly in light of the importance of public contention to collective politics and self-governance, in particular to social movements, we must ensure that there is adequate "breathing space" for public expression at critical democratic moments. As in other contexts, a number of actors – courts, officials, and protesters themselves – must participate in creating this critical space.

Judicial Review of Spatial Militarization

As explained below, generalized claims of expressive "chill" relating to militarization techniques are not likely to meet with success in the courts. As in other places on the expressive topography, the primary role for courts in this context will be to more skeptically review the *physical* transformation of the expressive topography that results from militarization. Specifically, courts ought to question the supposed neutrality of militarized places, acknowledge their unique vocality, and approach them with a spatial skepticism commensurate with their effect on expressive liberties and public democracy.

Neutrality

As emphasized throughout this book, within First Amendment doctrine much – too much – turns on whether the governmental tactic or regulation at issue is "neutral" with regard to the speaker's message. Under current doctrine, so long as governments can *justify* spatial militarization in "neutral" terms courts will be very reluctant to invalidate even the most repressive restrictions. Not surprisingly, "security" and "public order" generally suffice as neutral justifications.

The generally shallow constitutional analysis of militarized place, as exemplified in the treatment of Boston's infamous "Demonstration Zone," masks some of its more critical attributes. Scholars of place, influenced by critical thinkers like Michel Foucault and Henri Lefebvre, have long contested the assumed neutrality of place. Like contested places (Chapter 4), militarized places are hardly "neutral" - in either sociological or *constitutional* terms. A militarized place does far more than determine the place where expression may occur. It is the product of a unique transformative process, one initiated in response to discrete episodes of public contention and dissent. More specifically, three aspects of militarized places substantially undermine the presumption of neutrality that is often applied to them – the architects of militarized places, their physical architectures, and their extraordinary effect on certain contentious repertoires and messages.

Like other zoning schemes and plans, militarized places are, in Foucault's terms, "calculated distributions" of place. But unlike the run mine zoning regulation, expressive zones are far from ordinary calculations. Courts have historically relied upon certain principles to validate what we might call "ordinary" land use zoning.[50] First, zoning schemes are *comprehensive* plans. They implement a common community vision for cities and suburbs. Rather than target specific uses, these plans are exercises of the police power in pursuit of the general welfare. Second, ordinary zoning relies substantially on the skills of planning *experts* to conceptualize these community plans. The assumption was, and to some extent remains, "that the most important problems in land-use planning [are] not political but scientific and technical."[51] Thus, architects, engineers, and other professionals typically play some role in developing zoning plans. These professionals are presumed to be "neutral," at least with regard to specific uses. Third, increased specialization, it is assumed, ought to lead to a reduction in the scope of judicial review. The basic idea is that experts should receive substantial latitude from courts to manage rapidly changing local landscapes.

These progressive principles – comprehensiveness, expertise, and deference – may or may not counsel against interference with the regulation of slaughterhouses and subdivisions. On their own terms, however, these principles cannot be applied to zoning and other restrictions on the exercise of fundamental First Amendment liberties. Militarization is not part of any comprehensive plan. It is a targeted response – in Foucault's terms a *political technology* – by government to anticipated political unrest and public dissent. The "architects" of militarization are not engineers, scientists, land planners, or other neutral and disinterested experts. Those performing the spatial calculations – typically Secret Service and other law enforcement personnel – are not applying any neutral principles or measures. Indeed, they have typically been engaged in covert and overt surveillance of the very activities they intend to zone. The primary objectives of public space zoning in militarized contexts are law enforcement ones – security, separation, and surveillance. The zones are designed and enforced by officials with an inherent bias in favor of order

---

[50] *See* Eric R. Claeys, *"Euclid Lives? The Uneasy Legacy of Progressivism in Zoning,"* 73 *Fordham L. Rev.* 731 (2004); *see also* Village of Euclid v. Amber Realty Co., 272 U.S. 365 (1926) (upholding a comprehensive local zoning plan).

[51] Claeys, *supra* note 50 at 754.

and control. As they pursue those objectives, law enforcement personnel tend to view speakers and public contention as potential threats. Thus, where expressive rather than ordinary property uses are involved, inquiring whether fundamental expressive liberties have been preserved in militarized zones is hardly a form of judicial activism or overreaching.

The particular design features of militarized places also undermine their supposed neutrality. In some instances, as when officials ensure that "dissent" occurs in far-away zones while supporters are not similarly displaced, the edifice of neutrality disappears altogether. Even in the absence of such obvious forms of discrimination, the restrictive characteristics of militarized places – fences, gates, barriers, razor wire, snipers, military vehicles, riot officers – are designed to repress dissent or at least minimize its presence at key democratic events. Physical architectures like the DZ are tactically constructed with dissent and public contention specifically in mind. Inside the DZ, barriers separated speakers from audiences; mesh prevented anything, including pamphlets, from being passed outside the zone; covering, razor wire, and armed officers prevented any type of "escape." In some instances, the physical characteristics alone ought to at least give rise to an inference that a militarized place has been constructed with contentious and dissenting messages in mind.

Indeed, militarized places are not literally "neutral" with regard either to speakers or repertoires of expression. They tend to disparately affect expressive forms like assemblies and marches, which are relied upon mostly by dissenting activists and public agitators. Demonstrations and other forms of public contention at critical democratic moments are *attacks* on the *status quo*. To the affected speakers, disruption is not merely a political resource, but a significant part of the *message* they seek to convey at campaign events, inaugurals, party conventions, and anti-war rallies. That message is substantially distorted when demonstrators and protesters are made to passively file into pens, cages, and other "speech zones." If, as discussed in Chapter 6, ordinary public displays have been neutered by public order permit schemes and the like, militarization tends to snuff any remaining life out of collective politics at critical democratic moments. With militarization, public displays become *capitulations* to the *status quo*, rather than direct *challenges* to it. Meanwhile, supportive voices typically have no difficulty being heard or seen.

Militarized places have other effects which are also properly viewed as "non-neutral." As Foucault observed, certain places are designed "to permit an internal, articulated and detailed control – to render visible those who are inside it."[52] A militarized place will often "operate to transform individuals: to act on those it shelters, to provide a hold on their conduct, to carry the effects of power right to them, to make it possible to know them, to alter them."[53] In particular, militarized places reduce or eliminate the protections of public anonymity. Their distinct features make it easier for officials to observe public speakers, and to quickly intervene when speakers are deemed to have gone "too far."

Finally, from the dissenting speaker's perspective, militarization makes speech far more burdensome and thus far less appealing. Militarized places thus may have a substantial "chilling" effect on public dissent. The prospect of chill is magnified by the fact that spatial tactics like zones and pens operate directly on the body. If a speaker knows that stepping outside designated boundaries or zones can lead to punishment, she may be less inclined to step into them in the first place. If by entering a pen or barricade she forfeits her right to leave it, a protester may simply go home and skip the protest or display. Or, as at the Democratic National Convention in Boston, the architecture may itself be so unappealing, or so unsafe, that speakers simply refuse to enter it.

As First Amendment scholars well know, none of these features of militarized place would separately offend the narrow and rather technical line of "content-neutrality" the Supreme Court has articulated. Despite their disparate effects, for example, militarized places generally cannot be shown to target any particularized message or any particular speaker or group. Nevertheless, when these matters are considered in combination it is apparent that militarized places and tactics are at least closely correlated with the content and modes of expression they are generally designed to contain. As a result, heightened judicial skepticism with regard to spatial militarization is appropriate. If we cannot describe militarized places as content-based, we can at least acknowledge that they are "content-correlated." Calling a militarized place "content-correlated" would, as Justice Souter noted in a different First Amendment context, "not only describe it for what it is, but keep alert to a risk of content-based regulation that it poses."[54]

Vocality

There are additional reasons to be concerned about the content distortion militarized places can produce. Once transformed into a militarized place,

---

[52] Foucault, *supra* note 4 at 172. Foucault was particularly struck by the architecture of Jeremy Bentham's Panopticon, which he described as a "cruel, rather ingenious cage." *Id.* at 205
[53] *Id.*
[54] City of Los Angeles v. Alameda Books, Inc., 535 U.S. 425, 459 (2002) (Souter, J., dissenting).

an ordinary public place like a street becomes distinctly *expressive*. Whereas before it may have outwardly communicated little or nothing at all, serving instead as a potentially inscriptive space, after militarization the street, park, or square may well communicate something distinct. Courts ought to be alert to the possibility that spatial tactics can affect the *vocality* of public places.

As noted throughout this book, places do not merely facilitate communication. In some cases – for example, the contested places discussed in Chapter 4 and the "sacred" places discussed in Chapter 6 – the place *itself* may communicate through symbolism, metaphor, or historical reference. In very general terms, where one is "placed" in a society says something about relative status, knowledge, and power. Access to special events and policy-makers, first class accommodations, and gated communities "speak" to subjects like influence, wealth, and race.

Militarization likewise may convey something about speakers and their particular messages. As Foucault observed, officials sometimes use place to effect a sort of "binary division and branding" of individuals and groups.[55] As it separates speakers from both targeted and more general public audiences, a tactical place like a zone or pen can actually communicate something about those confined inside to persons on the outside. It may suggest that the people inside – dissidents and "troublemakers" – should be treated with caution and perhaps even avoided. Other accoutrements of militarized places, including architectural elements like razor wire, officers in camouflage and riot gear, and hovering helicopters may reinforce this message. In some cases, militarized places may actually *stigmatize* the speech and speakers they confine. Imagine, for example, what the DZ would have communicated had it actually been used.

In sum, militarized places not only distort or suppress the speakers' messages but may convey messages of their own. The vocality of a militarized place may undermine or distort public contention. This, too, sets militarization tactics and structures apart from ordinary time, place, and manner regulations. Here, as elsewhere on the expressive topography, speech and spatiality intersect in distinct ways that ought to be acknowledged and considered in any First Amendment analysis.

Spatial Skepticism

To help preserve adequate breathing space for speech out of doors during critical democratic moments, courts ought to review the

---

[55] Foucault, *supra* note 4 at 200–02.

"content-correlated" militarization of place with a greater degree of skepticism. This would entail, among other things, rejecting the idea that the mere *presence* of protesters is itself a security threat. Courts also ought to demand some justification for the lines, boundaries, and architectures of militarized places in light of *genuine* security concerns. Finally, they ought to very carefully scrutinize the supposed "adequacy" of proposed "alternative channels" of communication.

Courts are understandably reluctant to second-guess federal and state officials' "security" determinations. But this justification for militarization, which has been relied upon at every recent critical democratic event threatens to swallow general First Amendment principles regarding valid limits on public expression. There is no gainsaying that security is a substantial state interest. Understandably, no judge wants to be responsible for violence, disruption, and possibly death should "security" be breached. Some courts have very candidly acknowledged that particularly since September 11, 2001, they have weighed security concerns more heavily in the First Amendment balance. It is quite likely that they all do.

Courts must take special care to separate concerns regarding terrorism from those associated with public contention and dissent. In the absence of any actual showing by officials that particular protesters or planned public contention pose some credible danger, some courts have come dangerously close to accepting arguments of the "guilt-by-association" form. In upholding the DZ, for example, the lower and appellate courts relied expressly on the fact that protesters at *previous* conventions (specifically, the 2000 Democratic National Convention in Los Angeles) had committed some violent acts. Courts obviously cannot (and should not) second-guess every security determination made by law enforcement officials. But as evidence released in recent protest litigation indicates, officials have generally treated even lawful, peaceful protest as either an actionable security threat or a nuisance to be suppressed. Particularly in light of the effect militarization has on public democracy, it is critical that courts not simply accept every intonation of "security." At the very least, some *in camera* review of what the government claims is credible threat evidence ought to be required.

The lack of concrete information regarding the supposed threat posed by public protesters and contentious displays makes it difficult for courts to assess the lines and limits – or "tailoring" – of militarized places. Courts have sometimes invalidated tailoring choices made in militarized contexts. As noted earlier, in connection with the Democratic National Convention in 2000 a court invalidated a "free speech zone" located *260 yards* from the convention site. In situations like this, where the restriction is so obviously disproportionate to the government's stated concerns, one would certainly expect judicial invalidation. Recall, however, that the "DZ" survived First Amendment scrutiny. So did the closure of vast areas of seattle and Colorado Springs during meetings of world leaders in those cities. Large speech-free zones, which in some cases relocated public dissent as much as one-third of a mile from an intended audience, have either avoided scrutiny or been upheld by courts. These decisions are matters of line-drawing in the most literal sense. Courts ought not to consider themselves disqualified from addressing matters of distance or feet, even where a "security" justification is invoked.

In addressing tailoring issues in militarized places, it is critically important that courts consider what effect a 50-, 75-, or 100-foot zone will have on different types of public expression. At the least, courts ought to ensure that protesters can be seen and heard by intended audiences from wherever the militarization plan locates them. But there are other aspects of militarization that threaten fundamental expressive interests. In most cases, spatial militarization prevents *embodied* expression of any kind. Militarization also often prohibits access to *contested* places. There ought to be a presumption that any spatial tactic that imposes a flat ban on fundamental expressive activity like leafleting or bars all access to contested places is insufficiently tailored. The Supreme Court has held that speakers cannot be barred from engaging in embodied forms of expression on the streets and sidewalks, or even on citizens' doorsteps. To allow a ban on all forms of embodied expression at public political events like party conventions and world summits is contrary to core First Amendment values and traditions. Of course, in situations involving presidential appearances or the safety of other world leaders, the proposed presumption can be overcome by genuine concerns for security. But preventing speakers from reaching out to *public* audiences, and reaping the benefits of contested places through enforcement of quarter-mile and other substantial "buffers," ought to give rise to a presumption of improper tailoring.

Under prevailing First Amendment doctrine, courts must determine whether a time, place, and manner regulation leaves open "ample" and "adequate" alternative channels of communication. As interpreted and applied, most regulations readily satisfy these requirements. In most cases, a restriction with regard to a specific place will not prevent a speaker from communicating *elsewhere*. If, for example, a speaker cannot post signs in one place, she may typically hand out literature in another. As noted throughout this book, First Amendment doctrines of place generally presumes that one place is just as good as the next. Speakers, it is often said, are not entitled to the best or most effective place from which to convey a message.

Owing to this view that places are generally fungible, courts typically spend very little time contemplating the relative expressive merits of alternative venues. Thus, the Colorado Springs security plan described above was upheld on the ground that speakers were not *wholly* deprived of a place to speak; it was deemed sufficient that protesters were permitted to stand outside a security gate and display their message to media and conference attendees on passing buses. The DZ was upheld, in part, because the courts concluded that protesters could communicate their messages through the mainstream media present at the convention or through the Web. As these decisions show, if all that is required is the theoretical possibility that a message could be conveyed through some other channel, the "adequate alternatives" inquiry is utterly meaningless. It cannot be that simple access to a modem suffices to validate the suppression of public expression at the site of a national party convention. Further, the notion that the conventional media would be eager to report on protesters' messages if only they were asked evinces a fundamental misunderstanding of media coverage and bias; mainstream media are often less interested in the protesters' message than they are in covering the act of protest itself – which, of course, the DZ itself prevented.[56]

Spatial skepticism would require that the adequate alternatives inquiry be far more rigorous and spatially sensitive in militarized contexts. It is not enough that speakers have *some* place from which to convey their messages, whether that place is some distant venue or the virtual spaces of the Web. An "adequate" alternative must at least *approximate* the expressive place denied. Thus courts should ask, among other things: How facilitative of expression and contention is the alternative place, relative to the place speakers have been denied? How does the restriction affect access to contested and embodied places? How far is it from where the speakers originally desired to be? Does the displacement entail additional costs in terms of time or money? How are the alternative place's physical and other characteristics likely to affect the planned expressive activity? To what extent will the alternative place force speakers to alter their message or their chosen methods of communication? At a minimum, an *adequacy* determination should not be made without considering such things as the expense, location, qualities, and expressive effects of the suggested alternative place.

---

[56] *See generally* Smith, McCarthy, McPhail, & Augustyn, *supra* note 47.

There are ample reasons for heightened judicial skepticism of the physical militarization of public places during critical democratic moments. Without in any way disregarding genuine security concerns, courts can and should play an important role in ensuring that speakers have ample and adequate expressive breathing space at such times.

Policing the Police

As in other areas of the expressive topography, it is a mistake to rely too heavily on courts to create breathing space for First Amendment liberties in militarized places. Police tactics, including covert surveillance and variations on the escalated force model of protest policing, must also generally be regulated. This must occur primarily from *within* departments and through oversight by public officials.

Covert tactics like infiltration of activist groups and surveillance of public events are not generally forbidden by the First Amendment.[57] In some localities, however, police departments operate under consent decrees that limit surveillance of private and even some public activities. (These decrees are discussed in greater detail in Chapter 9.) In some cases, these limits were loosened somewhat after September 11, 2001. In light of militarization's possible effects on civil liberties and public democracy, it is imperative that departments follow these decrees to the letter. When they do not, of course, courts ought to enforce compliance through contempt proceedings.

Internal departmental controls and police training are also critical. As the response to the 2006 May Day rally in Los Angeles demonstrated, some departments have yet to fully internalize the lessons of the "Battle in Seattle." Education and preparation, including extensive civil rights training for officers, is critical to protecting public expression and public democracy. Too many officials, federal and local, appear to have adopted the attitude that dissent is itself a "threat" to be suppressed at critical democratic events. Many seem also to have forgotten that they have a duty under the First Amendment to protect and facilitate lawful contentious displays.

Finally, police departments ought to be mindful that militarization tactics can substantially backfire. They may reduce public goodwill toward authorities. Further, as events in Seattle and elsewhere have

---

[57] Laird v. Tatum, 408 U.S. 1 (1972). The concept of expressive "chill" is discussed further in Chapter 9.

shown, escalated force may also result in escalated disruption and public disorder as activists react to aggressive police tactics and militarization techniques. Localities and police departments also ought to consider the massive *expense* of militarization and escalated force policing methods. Mass arrests and other official actions at recent critical democratic events have resulted in the payment of millions of dollars in civil penalties and court costs. Militarization has thus far proven to be an extraordinarily expensive form of public order management.

Militarizing Protest

As the political scientist Michael Lipsky observed during the Civil Rights Era, protest is a *political resource*.[58] It remains the case today, as Lipsky then observed, that various constituencies of protest – members of the public, other activists, officials, and the media – must all be accounted for in any strategy of protest. Effective protests, in Lipsky's timeless formulation, are part of a political process that requires activating third parties to enter into a bargaining relationship. Managing the political resource of protest requires increasingly sophisticated protest tactics and counter-tactics. In a word, especially at critical democratic events, this means that protest itself must become more *militarized*. To be clear, this does not entail adopting violent or even substantially more disruptive repertoires of contention. Rather, it means being strategically aware of the present-day protest environment and adapting protest and contention to it.

The fact that protest is a resource means that it can be squandered. As Seattle's protesters discovered, violence tends to polarize. It frightens critical elites. And it can provide a pretext for repression. On the other hand, the disruption that has been so critical to past social movements can be very difficult to generate today. In the 1960s, protesters had the advantage in many cases of surprise. Their tactics and repertoires were unique. They could shock the public into critical awareness. Today's protester acts in a regulatory and political environment that, as noted in the previous chapter, has effectively *institutionalized* dissent. In an effort to avoid such strictly enforced conformity, protesters at recent events have sometimes turned to violent tactics.

Generally speaking, this is a strategic error. Today's protester must approach critical public events as tactically as do federal, state, and local

---

[58] Michael Lipsky, "Protest as a Political Resource," 62(4) *The American Political Science Review*, (December 1968).

officials. As difficult as coordination can be in protest environments, planning is now crucial. As they plan public displays, protesters must have effective and sophisticated technologies. They must gather intelligence, even as they know they are being watched. They must know the protest topography as well as authorities. Protesters must understand official plans for partitioning and securing militarized places. Where those plans cannot be determined well in advance of the event, they must initiate preeemptive litigation to force disclosure.[59] Protesters must cooperate to some degree across groups and ideological agendas. They must share protest space and events with those who might have different messages. Public speakers must create new symbols and frames of solidarity, ones that speak simultaneously to potential participants and a mostly complacent and disengaged public. And they must minimize, even if they cannot prevent, violence and unlawful behavior.

As the mass immigration protests in 2006 showed, disruption without violence and lawlessness is still possible. As discussed in Chapter 9 and demonstrated to some extent at the Seattle WTO protests, public speakers can use available technologies – public wireless Internet access, hand-held and worn computers, and Global Positioning Systems – to counter official tactics in real time and on the ground. They can use the contentious repertoires of past movements – sit-ins and protest marches – but must also generate new repertoires that respond to the unique features of militarized places. Old lock-step marches, for example, must be replaced with new forms of marching like "snake marches" – disjointed but coordinated movements – that resist efforts to corral and pen protesters. As always, public displays and social movements require some *movement* to be effective. Passively filing into preconfigured zones and pens produces canned messages and stale public theatre. Nonviolent resistance of spatial tactics may be used to thwart controls and, more symbolically, to highlight the irony of caged public democracy. This means that today's protester, like her predecessor, must decide when and whether it makes tactical sense to risk arrest and punishment for refusing, for example, to apply for a permit or to be confined to a "demonstration zone."

Finally, protesters must be increasingly media-savvy. Like its predecessors, the modern protest is in some sense a *production* that is intended for television and other broadcast. An effective protest must create

---

[59] Protesters have already begun to militarize protest in this fashion. They have filed lawsuits prior to both the 2008 Democratic National Convention in Denver and the 2008 Republican National Convention in St. Paul. *See* American Civil Liberties Union of Colorado v. City and County of Denver, C.A. No. 08-cv-00910-MSK-KMT (D. Colo.); Coalition to March on the RNC, et al. v. City of St. Paul, C.A. No. 08-835 JNE/JJG (D. Minn.).

both internal solidarity and external support. This requires an effective communications strategy, which in turn requires an understanding of mainstream and other media. Scholars have demonstrated that traditional media exhibit both *selection* and *description* biases in their coverage of protests.[60] They tend to focus on relatively few public events and often on the violence and conflict that occurs during those events. Studies have shown that coverage will generally be *episodic*, or focused on individual incidents within the larger course of events, rather than *thematic* in terms of the movement's agenda. Media framing of protest activity is thus often inimical to protesters' own agendas.

It is important for protesters in militarized places to influence that framing, such that militarization itself is not the only or primary story. In the case of large-scale democratic events, some coverage is generally guaranteed. Media are interested in the scale of such events and, again, their potential to produce conflict. As the "Battle in Seattle" demonstrated, violence by even a few protesters can substantially skew media coverage. There is, of course, no guarantee that a few rogue protesters will not engage in vandalism and other lawbreaking. Some peaceful and law-abiding protesters in Seattle did the right thing when they resisted vandalism by others during the WTO proceedings and later assisted in cleaning up what damage was done. Pre-event education and training should include all groups and should stress that the point is not simply to gain *publicity* but to advance a public-minded agenda through the media. Importantly, media studies have shown that more favorable coverage is produced as a result of peaceful and creative forms of disruption and civil disobedience than violent confrontations.

Even with the necessary precautions and more disciplined strategies, effective media control will be difficult for unwieldy protest movements to attain. Protest organizers and leaders should thus increasingly rely upon alternative outlets to broadcast events and frame agendas. In Seattle, for example, there were likely more cameras among the protesters themselves than among the journalists covering the events. The combination of wireless public Web access and powerful mobile personal computing devices will permit protesters to upload their own coverage of events to the Web in real time and without media filtering. Protest organizations should establish their own "citizen press" and media centers near the site of protests to facilitate coverage – both by the mainstream media and participants themselves. This does not mean that such

[60] Smith, McCarthy, McPhail, & Augustyn, *supra* note 47.

outlets are *substitutes* for traditional public forums ("adequate alternative channels"); rather, they are *supplements* to them.

In sum, in recognition of the fact that public places have been militarized, protesters must respond by militarizing public contention itself. This will require that protesters become more strategic in their planning and execution of public displays. Judges and officials cannot necessarily be relied upon to limit or prevent spatial militarization. Protesters must to some extent take it upon themselves to create the necessary breathing space for speech out of doors and collective politics at critical democratic moments.

8   PLACES OF HIGHER LEARNING

As the Supreme Court has noted, universities "began as voluntary and spontaneous assemblages or concourses for students to speak and to write and to learn."[1] Although they frequently tout their commitment to First Amendment freedoms, the policies and practices of today's American colleges and universities frequently evince ignorance with respect to basic free speech principles.[2] In particular, like many officials, college and university administrators often look with disfavor upon and seek to restrict public expression and displays of contention.

Although scholars and commentators have paid much attention to the infamous "speech codes" adopted by some universities in the 1980s and 1990s, the transformation of public spaces on university campuses has gone largely unnoticed. Places of higher learning have essentially become mirror images of the expressive topography outside campus gates. Today public colleges and universities are governed by "public order management systems" similar to those that have stifled expression in other places on the expressive topography (*see* Chapter 6). On many campuses, officials erect and enforce the same sort of buffers, bubbles, and "free speech zones" that inhibit public expression off campus. Indeed in some places of higher learning the situation is actually far worse than elsewhere on the expressive topography. In addition to often hidden but in many cases still-operative speech codes, campus administrators rely upon standardless

---

[1] Rosenberger v. Rector, University of Virginia, 515 U.S. 819, 836 (1995).
[2] Given the concern with First Amendment liberties the discussion in this Chapter will focus primarily upon *public* colleges and universities. As noted in Chapter 5, a few state legislatures and courts have required that even private universities accommodate at least some First Amendment activity. For example, California's "Leonard Law" prohibits private post-secondary educational institutions (except schools controlled by religious organizations) from making or enforcing rules subjecting students to disciplinary sanctions on the basis of what would otherwise be protected expression at a public institution. *See* Cal. Educ. Code § 94367 (a). Of course, a private college or university may always voluntarily adopt First Amendment standards for campus expression. Many indeed claim to do so.

licensing schemes, onerous fees, notice and registration requirements, restrictions on use of campus spaces by "outsiders," and even outright content and manner bans to restrict expression in public areas.

Campuses are critical places on the expressive topography. These *places of higher learning* have historically been hotbeds of social and political activism. They have served as staging grounds for a host of social movements. Today, however, in the very places where the Free Speech Movement began and where students often have their first experience with the exercise of First Amendment liberties in public places, there is less and less "breathing space" for speech out of doors on campus. In a significant sense, students in places of higher learning represent the future of public democracy in this country. We ought thus to pay special attention to the scope of expressive freedom in these places.

THE CAMPUS AS CENTER OF POLITICAL AND SOCIAL ACTIVISM

The contemporary condition of the campus as an expressive place can be traced to a substantial degree to events that occurred during the 1960s and 1970s. Campus activism had, of course, been evident on campuses long before this critical period.[3] But the defining civil rights and Vietnam antiwar movements radically reshaped campuses as expressive places. Among other things, those social movements demonstrated that places of higher learning could serve as centers of political and social activism. Free speech contests during the 1960s and 1970s brought the Constitution inside campus gates for the first time (Figure 8.1). As we shall see, this constitutional importation had both salutary and negative effects on public expression in places of higher learning.

In the 1960s, campuses across the United States literally exploded in protest. Public contention at places of higher learning initially focused on issues of student access to certain common areas of campus.[4] Indeed, the Free Speech Movement (FSM) began on the campus of the University of California at Berkeley in 1964 as a result of student's clashes with administrators over restrictions on public protests.[5] In particular, students

---

[3] For an overview of student activism from the Revolution through the 1950s, *see* Seymour Martin Lipset, *Rebellion in the University* (1976), Chs. 4–5.
[4] Don Mitchell, *A Right to the City: Social Justice and the Fight for Public Space* (2003), Ch. 3.
[5] For an account of the Berkeley Free Speech Movement, *see* Robert Cohen and Reginald E. Zelnik, eds., *The Free Speech Movement: Reflections on Berkeley in the 1960s* (2002).

Figure 8.1. Campus Gate – University of California, Berkeley.
Source: Photograph by Stuart Spivack.

objected to the University's designation of small and out-of-the-way "free speech areas" that displaced student expression.[6] They denounced and resisted efforts to remove protesters and other speakers from the area around Sproul Hall, a place that had long hosted student assemblies and other expressive activity (Figure 8.2). There, and elsewhere on campus, the university strictly banned solicitation, regulated the content of expression, and prohibited recruitment to "partisan" causes.

The FSM was ultimately successful in creating substantial public space on the Berkeley campus for political and other forms of student activism.[7] The movement ultimately spread to campuses across the country. Organized and galvanized by Students for a Democratic Society (SDS) and other activist groups, students and faculty engaged in confrontations with university and public officials. In the 1960s, protest activities occurred on anywhere from 300 to 500 of the nation's 2,000 campuses. The protests took various forms, including non-violent pickets and demonstrations, occupations of university buildings, sit-ins, riots, and strikes.[8]

Some of the student protest activities were unlawful and extremely violent. In 1969 and 1970, student radicals bombed police stations,

---

[6] *Id.* at 92–93.
[7] As Figure 8.2 shows, the plaza near Sproul Hall remains a vibrant expressive forum where students routinely engage in all manner of expressive activity.
[8] Kenneth J. Heineman, *Put Your Bodies Upon the Wheel: Student Revolt in the 1960s* (2001).

Figure 8.2. Protest on Sproul Plaza (April 2005).
Source: Photograph by Andy Ratto.

corporate offices, military facilities, and campus buildings. Twenty-
six thousand students were arrested and thousands more were injured or
expelled while engaged in protest activities. Violent and disruptive
activity that began on campuses often spilled into the public streets. In
some cases entire cities were swept up in riots and other destructive public
activity. The climax of this "climate of unrest," as the Supreme Court
would later refer to it, occurred in the spring of 1970, when four Kent
State students and two Jackson State students were killed during campus
protests.[9]

In 1972, Justice Powell reflected upon the tumult and disruption of
this period:

A climate of unrest prevailed on many college campuses in this
country. There had been widespread civil disobedience on some
campuses, accompanied by the seizure of buildings, vandalism, and
arson. Some colleges had been shut down altogether, while at others
files were looted and manuscripts destroyed . . . Although the causes
of campus disruption were many and complex, one of the prime
consequences of such activities was the denial of the lawful exercise of

---

[9] Healy v. James, 408 U.S. 169, 171 (1972).

First Amendment rights to the majority of students by the few. Indeed, many of the most cherished characteristics long associated with institutions of higher learning appeared to be endangered.[10]

But there was another, more positive, view of the campus unrest of the 1960s. The volatile mix of protest and violence on campuses arguably had several salutary effects insofar as public democracy was concerned. Public protests on campuses across the country established places of higher learning as critical places on the expressive topography. They galvanized public politics. As the late John Kenneth Galbraith argued:

> It was the universities . . . which led the opposition to the Vietnam War, which forced the retirement of President Johnson, which are forcing the pace of our present withdrawal from Vietnam, which are leading the battle against the great corporations on the issue of pollution, and a score or more of the more egregious time-servers, military sycophants and hawks.[11]

As a result of campus protests, by the 1970s courts had begun to recognize and protect students' expressive liberties. Thus, in *Healy v. James* (1972), the Supreme Court held that Central Connecticut State College's denial of recognition to the local SDS chapter on campus violated the First Amendment.[12] The president of the college had denied recognition, in part, on the ground that SDS was a "disruptive" organization. The Court observed that "the precedents of this Court leave no room for the view that, because of the acknowledged need for order, First Amendment protections should apply with less force on college campuses than in the community at large."[13] But the *Healy* Court was also careful to acknowledge school administrators' interests in preserving peace and order on campus, and in serving their primary educational mission.

In the wake of the Berkeley FSM and widespread campus disruption, officials in several states moved quickly to assert greater control over expression at places of higher learning. Many state legislatures engaged in more aggressive oversight of public colleges and universities.[14]

---

[10] *Id.*
[11] John Kenneth Galbraith, "An Adult's Guide to New York, Washington and Other Exotic Places," 4 *New York* 52 (November 15, 1971).
[12] 408 U.S. 169 (1972).
[13] *Id.* at 180.
[14] Ronald L. Rowland, Note, "An Overview of State Legislation Responding to Campus Disorders," 1 *J.L. & Educ.* 231 (1972); James L. Gibson, "The Policy Consequences of Political Intolerance: Political Repression During the Vietnam War Era," *The Journal of Politics*, 51 (1) (Feb. 1989).

Legislators and campus administrators enacted speech policies and regulations that sought to control campus contention. Some of those policies called for punishment of students who failed to comply. As a result of this new administrative regime, courts were for the first time called upon to settle a variety of First Amendment disputes between students and university administrators. As Charles Alan Wright observed at the close of the 1960s, the Constitution had officially "arrived" on campus.[15]

THE CAMPUS AS EXPRESSIVE PLACE

Over the past four decades or so, the Supreme Court has held forth on the First Amendment status of places ranging from military bases to shopping malls. Remarkably, however, the Court has never definitively addressed the relationship of college and university campuses to the rest of the expressive topography. Nor has the Court set forth clear standards that administrators must apply when regulating expressive activity in places of higher learning. In short, although campuses are among the most important places on the expressive topography, they are among the least understood in First Amendment terms.

As noted, places of higher learning have served as incubators of social and political activism. This suggests a need for substantial expressive breathing space, both inside and outside the classroom. Campuses are also, of course, connected to institutions dedicated primarily to the mission of educating students. This means that expressive liberties must sometimes yield to pedagogical and other mission-related interests. This general and universal tension substantially affects the expressive status and functioning of places of higher learning.

Physical Characteristics

Before considering the legal and constitutional status of places of higher learning, we ought first to consider the physical nature of these unique places. One thing is readily apparent: College campuses occupy a substantial amount of physical space. While figures concerning precise acreage are not available, consider that there are approximately 2,500

---

[15] Charles Alan Wright, "The Constitution on the Campus," 22 *Vand. L. Rev.* 1027 (1969).

public and private 4-year institutions of higher learning in the United States. These institutions have a combined enrollment of approximately 12 million students. In physical terms, then, college and university campuses potentially account for a significant portion of the expressive topography.

Campuses vary considerably in terms of their physical characteristics. Places of higher learning differ in terms of location, size, architecture, culture, and local geography (including proximity to local communities). Despite these variations, some commonalities can be identified. The larger institutions function essentially as self-contained towns. Campuses may have their own sanitation workers, groundskeepers, and police forces.[16] Thousands of students may live on campus, or in nearby off-campus housing. On the campus itself there are typically public streets, parking facilities, sidewalks and walkways, administrative and classroom buildings, stadiums and sports arenas, theaters, bookstores, convenience stores, restaurants, hotels, and numerous park-like plazas. In short, in terms of physical characteristics campuses frequently mirror the off-campus community.

The actual relationship of a campus to the nearby community may differ substantially, depending in particular on whether the location is rural or urban. At most public universities, nearly all of the public grounds and many campus facilities are open and accessible not only to students and faculty but also to the general public. Particularly in more urban settings, campus "insiders" like students and faculty routinely interact with campus "outsiders" like members of the community and merchants. In more isolated settings, by contrast, there may be relatively little interaction with the general public. Regardless of location, however, some itinerant speakers – such as preachers and activists – will probably visit campus owing primarily to the guaranteed presence of a substantial audience.

The geographic and architectural divide between rural and more urban campuses may be diminishing. Responding in part to student demand, some rural colleges and universities with land to spare are now seeking to "urbanize" their campuses. This entails, among other things, increasing amenities like shops and housing. One of the specific objectives of this urbanization movement is to bring an otherwise unaffiliated community into much closer contact with the university's students, faculty, and administrators. Thus, in an increasing number of instances

---

[16] *See* Pro-Life Cougars v. University of Houston, 259 F. Supp.2d 575, 582 (S.D. Tex. 2003) (describing University of Houston campus).

public universities may turn out to be less bucolic enclaves than integral parts of the larger community.

In sum, although each campus is a unique place, it also tends to consist of a diverse array of buildings, facilities, and public spaces that are in many respects the functional equivalents of off-campus structures and spaces. While some campuses remain isolated from surrounding communities, many abut and are closely integrated into proximate surroundings. Thus, we ought to consider places of higher learning both as distinct places on the expressive topography and, in many instances, as places intimately associated with other places on that topography.

"Peculiarly the Marketplace of Ideas"

As noted, the Supreme Court has said remarkably little about the expressive character and First Amendment status of places of higher learning. The Court has broadly suggested that "state colleges and universities are not enclaves immune from the sweep of the First Amendment."[17] It has also observed that the admonition in the elementary school context that neither students nor teachers "shed their constitutional rights to freedom of speech or expression at the schoolhouse gate" applies with equal, if not greater, force in places of higher learning.[18]

Justice Frankfurter once said: "It is the business of a university to provide that atmosphere which is most conducive to speculation, experiment and creation."[19] In affirming broad protection for academic freedom, the Court has observed that the university classroom *"with its surrounding environs* is peculiarly the 'marketplace of ideas.'"[20] Indeed, today most public (and many private) colleges and universities hold themselves out as marketplaces of ideas, in particular by actively publicizing their commitment to the robust exchange of ideas on campus.

With regard to the physical spaces and structures that typically comprise the nation's colleges and universities, the Court has said that "the campus of a public university, at least for its students, possesses many of the characteristics of a public forum."[21] This statement, which appears in a footnote in *Widmar v. Vincent* (1981), suggests two things. First, it

---

[17] Healy v. James, 408 U.S. 169, 180–81 (1972).
[18] Tinker v. Des Moines Indep. Cmty Sch. Dist., 393 U.S. 503, 506 (1969). *See also* Shelton v. Tucker, 364 U.S. 479, 487 (1960).
[19] Sweezy v. New Hampshire, 354 U.S. 234, 237 (1957).
[20] *Healy*, 408 U.S. at 180-81 (emphasis added); *see* Keyishian v. Board of Regents, 385 U.S. 589, 603 (1967).
[21] Widmar v. Vincent, 454 U.S. 263, 267 n.5 (1981).

indicates that campuses ought to generally be open to the basic functions of a public forum, namely "assembly, communicating thoughts between citizens, and discussing public questions."[22] Second, although one ought not to read too much into such general statements (particularly those appearing in footnotes), the phrase "at least for its students" suggests that campus "outsiders" – members of the surrounding community and visiting speakers – have somewhat lesser rights of access to the areas on campus than do students and other "insiders."

Although generally supportive of the ideal of a free and robust exchange of ideas on campus, the Supreme Court has never offered an opinion regarding either the general legal status of individual campus places or the proper approach to regulating the exercise of public liberties in places of higher learning. As a result, the First Amendment rules that apply in this particular portion of the expressive topography remain somewhat unsettled.

The First Amendment on Campus

Matters of academic freedom *inside* the classroom pose a variety of thorny First Amendment issues. These matters are generally beyond the scope of the present discussion, which is concerned instead with the manner in which the First Amendment applies to more open and "public" areas of college and university campuses. The primary First Amendment issues in these places mirror those in places beyond the campus gates: What type of place or "forum" is the campus? What standards apply to the regulation of First Amendment liberties there?

Efforts to apply the Supreme Court's "public forum" doctrine to campuses have produced conflicting approaches and decisions. Some courts and commentators have argued that as intellectual centers campuses ought to be presumptively treated as traditional expressive forums. Thus, as one court opined, a campus's "function as the site of a community of full-time residents makes it . . . more akin to a public street or park than a non-public forum."[23] As noted earlier, however, there is sometimes significant tension between the unique educational mission of the university and the robust exchange of ideas that is supposed to be

---

[22] Hague v. CIO, 307 U.S. 496 (1939).
[23] Hays County Guardian v. Supple, 969 F.2d 111, 117 (5th Cir. 1992). *See also* Rodney Smolla, "Academic Freedom, Hate Speech, and the Idea of a University," 53 *Law & Contemp. Probs.* 195, 217–19 (Summer 1990) (suggesting that although it is best to consider each campus space individually, most ought to be considered "designated" speech forums).

tolerated in traditional public forums. One federal appeals court has thus held that the entire 1,200 acres of the University of Maryland campus is a *limited* public forum – a place in which the university has broad discretion to limit expressive activity to certain subject matters and classes of speakers.[24] That court viewed the university as a "special type of enclave" devoted principally to its educational mission.[25]

As noted earlier, campuses vary widely in terms of their physical characteristics and relationships with surrounding communities. In light of these variations, many courts have taken a less categorical approach to the First Amendment status of campus spaces. Mindful of both the critical responsibility of educators to pursue educational missions and students' substantial expressive interests, these courts have generally analyzed the campus grounds on a place-by-place basis.[26] Under this approach, courts essentially treat the campus as a microcosm of the expressive topography outside its gates. As such, it contains a variety of traditional (streets), non-public (administrative offices), and limited (designated "free speech areas") public forums. In addition to allowing for a more nuanced examination of the unique characteristics of places of higher learning, this approach is consistent with the Supreme Court's statement in *Widmar v. Vincent* (1981) that the Fist Amendment does not require "that a university must grant free access to *all* of its grounds or buildings."[27]

Who is entitled to access the campus marketplace of ideas? Except for the seemingly cast-off statement in *Widmar* that a campus constitutes a marketplace of ideas "at least for its students,"the Supreme Court has not addressed this issue. As discussed below, based on a review of publicly available policies and court decisions, it seems (as one would expect) that students, faculty, and staff are generally granted the broadest rights of access to campus common spaces. The rights of "outsiders" – "Non-University Entities," as institutions often refer to them – tend to vary depending on the institution. Some colleges and universities make substantial room for "outsiders" in their access and use policies, while others substantially restrict, or in some cases even deny, the general public access to campus spaces for expressive purposes.[28]

The Supreme Court has also generally been silent with regard to the specific First Amendment standards applicable to the regulation of

---

[24] ACLU v. Mote, 423 F.3d 438, 444 (4th Cir. 2005).
[25] *Id.*
[26] *See* Alabama Student Party v. Student Gov't Ass'n of the Univ. of Ala., 867 F.2d 1344, 1354 (11th Cir. 1989) (Tjoflat, C.J., dissenting) (discussing cases).
[27] *Widmar*, 454 U.S. at 268 n.5 (emphasis added).
[28] *See* ACLU v. Mote, 423 F.3d 438 (4th Cir. 2005).

campus expression. In *Healy*, the Court rejected the general notion that the First Amendment "should apply with less force on college campuses than in the community at large."[29] In terms of time, place, and manner regulations, lower courts have essentially applied the standards applicable to the "forum" at issue. One would assume that more general rules, such as the presumption against the validity of prior restraints and the prohibition on content discrimination, would also apply on campuses. As we shall see, however, many college and university policies and regulations arguably run afoul of these and other generally accepted First Amendment doctrines.

The picture is even less clear with regard to what, if any, substantive rules may apply to regulations of public speech on campus. In the elementary and secondary school context, the Court has said that school officials may regulate and prevent disruptive behavior that "materially and substantially interferes with the requirements of appropriate discipline in the operation of the school."[30] The Court has also held that school officials, in the interest of inculcating "fundamental societal values," may prohibit "vulgar and lewd" speech directed to an immature audience.[31] Further, where the school actually provides the means for student expression or facilitates it as part of its curriculum (for example, funding a school newspaper in journalism class), the Court has said that administrators may regulate expression in any "reasonable" manner.[32] The Court has held that schools may exercise control over the *content* of expression in order to disassociate itself from certain messages or to account for the lack of maturity in the student body. Most recently, a divided Court held that a high school was permitted to discipline a high school student for displaying a message during a school-sponsored event that arguably advocated the use of illegal drugs – a message directly contrary to the school's own point of view.[33]

One would assume that college and university administrators may limit or even prohibit expressive activity that materially disrupts educational activities or materially impairs the learning environment. But the specific parameters of that discretion, as well as the general portability of the other school standards, are far from certain.[34] The Court has thus far

---

[29] *Healy*, 408 U.S. at 180.
[30] Tinker v. Des Moines Independent Community School District, 393 U.S. 503 (1969).
[31] Bethel School District v. Fraser, 478 U.S. 675 (1986).
[32] Hazelwood School District v. Kuhlmeier, 484 U.S. 260 (1988).
[33] Morse v. Frederick, 127 S.Ct. 2618 (2007).
[34] The Court has indicated that academic freedom entails substantial latitude to regulate *curricular* matters. See, e.g., Regents of Univ. of Michigan v. Ewing, 474 U.S. 214 (1985). Thus, a university is entitled to pursue what Justice Frankfurter called its "four essential

expressly declined to decide, for example, "whether the same degree of deference is appropriate with respect to school-sponsored expressive activities at the college and university level."[35] It has acknowledged on several occasions that college and university students are more mature and less impressionable than primary and secondary school students.[36] But the specific implications of that recognition for administrative discretion are not clear. In the absence of more specific Supreme Court guidance, lower courts have been forced to contend with these issues according to their own lights.[37]

The Supreme Court's declaration that its precedents "leave no room for the view that, because of the acknowledged need for order, First Amendment protections should apply with *less* force on college campuses than in the community at large" seems to suggest that college and university students are generally entitled to the same First Amendment liberties as adults in places off campus.[38] That, of course, essentially begs one of the principal questions presented in this chapter, namely whether First Amendment protections ought perhaps to apply with even *greater* force in places of higher learning.

THE "MATURE" UNIVERSITY AND THE FIRST AMENDMENT

In his reflective opinion for the Court in *Healy v. James* (1972), Justice Powell considered it fortunate that, "with the passage of time, a calmer atmosphere and greater maturity now pervade our campuses.[39] Today's college and university campuses are calmer still and, one would hope, even more "mature" than they were in the early 1970s. That does

---

freedoms" – "to determine for itself on academic grounds who may teach, what may be taught, how it shall be taught, and who may be admitted to study." Sweezy v. New Hampshire, 354 U.S. 234, 237–38 (1957) (Frankfurter, J., concurring).

[35] *Hazelwood*, 484 U.S. at 273 n.7.

[36] *See* Board of Regents of the Univ. of Wisconsin v. Southworth, 529 U.S. 217, 239 n.4 (2000) (emphasizing that "the right of teaching institutions to limit expressive freedom of students ha[s] been confined to high schools . . . , whose students and their schools' relation to them are different and at least arguably distinguishable from their counterparts in college education."); *Widmar*, 454 U.S. at 274 n. 14 ("University students are, of course, young adults. They are less impressionable than younger students."); Tilton v. Richardson, 403 U.S. 672, 688 (1971) (recognizing that "college students are less impressionable").

[37] *See, e.g.*, Nicholson v. Bd. of Educ. Torrance Unified Sch. Dist., 682 F.2d 858 (9th Cir. 1982).

[38] *Healy*, 408 U.S. at 180 (emphasis added).

[39] *Id.* at 171.

not mean, however, that the contemporary campus functions as a marketplace of ideas or the site of robust public exchanges. To the contrary, although student activism has never disappeared – and remains alive and well on some campuses today – places of higher learning have gradually come to mirror the rather anemic and diminished expressive topography outside their gates.[40] Indeed, to the extent that there are distinctions between these places, speech on today's campuses may actually be *less* free in many respects.

"Speech Codes"

In the past few decades, much of the discussion regarding free speech on the nation's campuses has focused on the debate over what is often called "political correctness." In the 1980s and 1990s, as colleges and universities opened their gates to more and more diverse student populations, officials enacted measures that they believed would ease tensions and make minority students and women comfortable on campus. Critics claimed, however, that college and university administrators were seeking to impose a liberal orthodoxy on students through restrictions on the content of their expression.[41]

On some campuses, administrators adopted extraordinarily broad prohibitions on the expression of certain beliefs and opinions. These "speech codes," as they came to be known, restricted expression across campus – in classrooms, dorm rooms, quads, and in common spaces on campus. Although the codes varied, their principal objective was to protect students from expression they might consider "offensive" or "harassing." Thus, for example, schools banned and purported to punish expression that was intended to and did cause a "loss of self esteem"; "inconsiderate" jokes; "stereotyping"; epithets; slurs; "sexually suggestive" speech that created a "hostile environment"; nonverbal gestures like ogling; and "personal abuse."[42]

The First Amendment generally forbids government from regulating or banning expression based on its offensive content. Officials are permitted to ban only certain narrow categories of "unprotected" expression.

---

[40] Tony Vellela, *New Voices: Student Political Activism in the 80s and 90s* (1988).
[41] *See* Dinesh D'Souza, *Illiberal Education: The Politics of Race and Sex on Campus* (1992); Alan Charles Kors & Harvey Silverglate, *The Shadow University: The Betrayal of Liberty on America's Campuses* (1998); Donald Alexander Downs, *Restoring Free Speech and Liberty on Campus* (2005).
[42] *See* Kors & Silverglate, *supra* note 41 at 147–83.

Among these unprotected categories are obscenity, "fighting words," and serious threats to physical safety. Campus speech codes were explicitly content-based and thus constitutionally suspect. They were not limited to unprotected categories of expression. Given their breadth, and the uncertainty speakers faced in trying to comply, the campus codes were also subject to due process challenges. It thus came as little surprise when courts quickly invalidated speech codes in effect at the University of Michigan, University of Wisconsin, Stanford University, Central Michigan University, and Shippensburg University. In 1992, the Supreme Court seemed to place the final nail in the coffin of such efforts when it invalidated a municipal ordinance proscribing "hate speech" directed toward certain ethnic and other groups.[43] The Court explicitly condemned efforts by officials to protect listeners and viewers from speech based on its potential to offend or upset an audience.

This, unfortunately, has not been the end of campus content regulation. Even after these court decisions, colleges and universities continue to purport to regulate "offensive" expression. In fact, the legal scholar Jon Gould has shown that speech codes not only did not disappear in the face of disapproving judicial precedent, but actually *increased* at both private and public institutions.[44] Gould's research shows that campus officials were essentially undeterred by the string of adverse court decisions. Many early adopters have thus retained their speech codes. More remarkably, according to Gould's research some institutions enacted new speech codes *after* the courts had uniformly condemned them.

Today content restrictions are often buried in campus "codes of conduct," disciplinary rules, and "sexual harassment policies." Although their prevalence is difficult to gauge, a recent study of publicly available policies at more than 300 institutions – primarily those highly ranked in U.S. News & World Report and other large public universities – indicated that *93 percent* still prohibit expressive content that is fully protected under the First Amendment.[45] Many of these restrictions closely mirror the speech codes of old. According to the study, for example, Furman University prohibits "offensive communication not in keeping with the community standards." The University of North Carolina-Greensboro still bans speech that demonstrates "disrespect for persons."

---

[43] R.A.V. v. City of St. Paul, 505 U.S. 377 (1992).
[44] Jon B. Gould, "The Precedent That Wasn't: College Hate Speech Codes and the Two Faces of Legal Compliance," 35 *Law & Soc'y Rev.* 345 (2001).
[45] *See* Foundation for Individual Rights in Education, "*Spotlight on Speech Codes in 2006: The State of Free Speech on Our Nation's Campuses*" (December 6, 2006).

Although these policies may be legally unenforceable, campus speakers must be aware of them all the same. Their existence raises the possibility that speakers, whether in the classroom or on the public quad, will be chilled from conveying messages some students may deem "offensive" or "disrespectful." In sum, the cloud of "speech codes" has not yet been entirely lifted from places of higher learning.

The Campus Order Management System

Conduct policies and hidden content restrictions may have some effect on student speech in common and other areas of campus. Based upon a review of publicly available campus speech policies, however, there are more serious threats to the exercise of First Amendment liberties in places of higher learning that to date have received little attention.[46]

A review of college and university speech policies generally shows that since the 1970s, administrators have gradually imported to campus various requirements and procedures similar to – and in some respects more restrictive than – the public order management system that now applies to public expression outside campus gates (*see* Chapter 6). The *campus order management system* has been implemented at many places of higher learning. An increasingly complex and heavy-handed bureaucracy, including permitting schemes, advance notice requirements, and a host of other prerequisites for expressive activity generally restricts public expression and contention on the nation's campuses.

Evidence of this extensive management system exists in the form of the variety of official policies that now govern campus expression. At a minimum, speech on the "mature" campus is typically regulated pursuant to some version of a "Public Forum Policy," an "Advertising, Distribution and Solicitation Policy," and a "Policy on Speakers and Facilities Usage." Speakers must also be familiar with the rules and regulations set forth in detailed codes like the "Office of Student Activities Articles of Registration" and the school's "Code of Conduct." Penalties for failure to comply with these and other policies range from denial of a permit, to revocation of a group's official registration, to expulsion.

In the name of public order and educational mission, college and university administrators routinely impose restrictions that chill or prevent spontaneous expression on campus. Pursuant to various speech

---

[46] The policies referred to were posted on the Web, either by the school itself or by some other entity.

policies, speakers must carefully plan any expressive activity, from simple leafleting to the staging of a mass demonstration. Most campus codes require that students obtain a permit for *any* sort of expressive activity, whether it is distributing pamphlets, displaying banners, or holding rallies or demonstrations. Some schools require advance submission of the actual materials a speaker or group will use, including flyers and brochures. Campus speech policies sometimes ban student publicity for events that have not received official approval. Leaders of student organizations are often required to meet with the Dean of Students or some other campus official prior to any planned expressive activity, to discuss the proposed event and "negotiate" its terms. Finally, administrators often insist on advance notice for expressive events ranging from 24 hours to up to 2 weeks.

Under many publicly available campus speech policies, student groups must also be officially *registered* to enjoy the full panoply of expressive rights on campus. A few of the policies direct that students may not engage in *any* type of expressive activity unless they are affiliated with a registered group. Under one such policy, an Indiana State University student was prevented from handing out fliers concerning Iraq's infamous Abu Ghraib prison on campus because he was not affiliated with any registered group. Officials informed the student that he would instead have to distribute his fliers on an off-campus sidewalk. In any other place on the expressive topography, this sort of compelled affiliation or association would likely violate the First Amendment.

Some campus permit schemes also allow for a degree of official discretion that would be patently unconstitutional if exercised elsewhere on the expressive topography. As noted, pursuant to some policies students are required to submit expressive materials prior to distribution on campus. This may lead to content-based prior restraints on expression. One policy purported to grant administrators authority to deny a request for any expressive display that does not "serve or benefit the entire University community."[47] Another purported to restrict or prohibit displays based upon their mere "potential to disrupt," a broad restriction that would, again, violate the First Amendment if enforced in other public places.[48] Administrators are sometimes granted discretion to *exempt* certain expression from permit and other requirements (although the

[47] *See* Roberts v. Haragan, 346 F. Supp.2d 853 (N.D. Tex. 2004).
[48] *See* PLC v. University of Houston, 259 F. Supp. 2d 575 (S.D. Tex. 2003). Under current First Amendment standards, the mere *possibility* of disruption or violence is not enough. The Supreme Court has required that the speaker intentionally advocate lawless action and that such action be likely to occur. *See* Brandenburg v. Ohio, 395 U.S. 444 (1969).

policies do typically note that such exemptions should not be granted based upon the content of the expression). Further, campus speech policies do not always require that permit denials be accompanied by a written statement of the grounds for denial. In many cases, no provision is made for prompt judicial or other appellate review. These and other basic protections are generally required under the First Amendment when prior restraints on expression are imposed elsewhere.[49]

In addition to the speech code provisions mentioned earlier, many campus speech policies contain explicit *content-based* regulations or bans on public expression. For example, commercial expression, which receives substantial First Amendment protection elsewhere on the expressive topography, is flatly prohibited on some campuses.[50] Some campus speech policies permit commercial advertisements to be distributed only if they are "within the bounds of good taste."[51] Others single out certain products for advertising bans. Finally, some policies even define, in rather minute detail, what administrators believe to be proper "dissent" at public events on campus. Although they do not state expressly that other forms of dissent are prohibited, the specificity of such policies rather strongly suggests an official intent to define the substantive limits of appropriate public debate. Again, this sort of restriction is flatly prohibited elsewhere on the expressive topography.

The Supreme Court has extended First Amendment protection to anonymous political leafleting in public places.[52] Yet on many campuses, anonymous leafleting and other forms of anonymous expression are banned. Campus "Literature Distribution Policies" sometimes require that *all* printed materials to be distributed on campus bear the name of the university-affiliated person or organization responsible for their dissemination. Some policies require that students speaking anywhere on campus provide identification to any official who requests it.

Some public colleges and universities have also enacted detailed rules for the erection of stationary exhibits and structures. Some of these provisions were enacted in response to antiapartheid demonstrations in the 1980s. In particular, restrictions arose in response to the erection of "shanty-town" structures on campuses across the country.[53] College and university policies sometimes expressly reserve administrators'

---

[49] *See, e.g.,* Freedman v. Maryland, 380 U.S. 51 (1965).
[50] Central Hudson Gas & Electric Corp. v. Public Service Comm'n, 447 U.S. 557 (1980).
[51] *See Haragan*, 346 F.Supp.2d at 855.
[52] McIntyre v. Ohio Elections Comm'n, 514 U.S. 334 (1995).
[53] Bradford Martin, "Unsightly Huts: Shanties and the Divestment Movement of the 1980s" *Peace and Change* 32(3), 329–60 (2007).

authority to limit expression in order to maintain campus lawns and general aesthetic values. The policies also contain detailed restrictions on the use of public bulletin boards, expressive activity near campus buildings, amplified sound, and the types of banners or signs speakers can carry. Some campus noise regulations strictly limit or even pro-scribe amplification, even in areas far removed from administrative buildings and classrooms.

The practice of charging for free speech has also reached the nation's campuses. Thus, as a condition of participating in expressive activity, some campus policies now impose fees to cover security and after-event clean-up costs. One university policy actually requires that speakers dis-tributing pamphlets provide their own trash receptacle. As do many public permitting schemes, campus speech policies sometimes require proof of insurance – for both students and "outsiders" who wish to speak in public areas. In some cases, campuses purport to make the speaker liable for the conduct of *all* members of an affiliated organization. As discussed in Chapter 6, each of the above restrictions would be constitutionally objectionable, or patently unconstitutional, elsewhere on the expressive topography.

These restrictions generally limit the rights of *students* to engage in public expression on campus. "Non-University Entities," as other speakers are often called under the policies, generally possess fewer lib-erties in campus areas. Some institutions simply bar all "outside" groups from speaking on campus. Others permit members of the general public or surrounding community to speak on sidewalks and other public spaces *bordering* campus, but not in highly trafficked spaces inside the gates. Many colleges and universities require that "Non-University Entities" be sponsored by either students or faculty in order to speak on campus.

As these examples show, the campus order management system actually allows for *less* expressive liberty than is generally available once a speaker steps outside the campus gates. Some of the restrictions, such as noise regulations that apply near classroom buildings, are of course quite sensible and necessary. But many of the provisions in campus speech policies regulate or ban expressive activity that is neither closely related to curricular concerns nor likely to disrupt pedagogical or other institutional objectives. As noted, like the "speech codes" invalidated in the 1990s, some of these rules and regulations are patently unconsti-tutional under well-established First Amendment principles and doc-trines. This has not deterred administrators from adopting and in some cases enforcing them.

Expressive Zoning on Campus

As is the case elsewhere on the expressive topography, detailed spatial rules and regulations are now rather commonplace at places of higher learning. Some of the policies, referencing precise landmarks, divide entire campuses into geographic areas subject to varying First Amendment rules. Some adopt specific "buffer zones" of anywhere from 10 feet to 25 feet around campus buildings, including student press facilities and multicultural centers. These kinds of buffers restrict access to certain contested places on campus (*see* Chapter 4). Other policies impose embodied "bubbles" designed to shield certain students – for example, those visiting campus health care facilities – from unwanted expression (*see* Chapter 3). These spatial restrictions obviously track those that have been approved and imposed outside campus gates.

The broader phenomenon of expressive zoning has also come to the nation's college and university campuses. As noted earlier, the imposition of a "free speech zone" at Berkeley actually served as the catalyst for the Free Speech Movement. Expressive zoning began to appear on campuses beginning in the 1970s, in response to activism by SDS and other student protest groups.[54] Tufts University may have initiated the contemporary use of expressive zoning in places of higher learning. In 1989, the university's president announced the establishment of "free speech" and "non-free speech" zones across campus. Tufts students promptly partitioned the campus with tape and chalk to highlight the areas in which speech was not permitted. Embarrassed by the negative media attention, Tufts eventually altered its policy.

After campus "speech codes" were invalidated in the 1990s, many college and university administrators increasingly turned to zoning policies to maintain order and control campus contention. Their attitude appears to have been succinctly summarized by the president of the University of Central Florida, who said in response to criticism of his school's zoning policy: "Free speech can occur anywhere on campus . . . But protests or other political activity must stay in the free speech zones."

The Tufts experience with expressive zoning is representative, in the sense that schools often maintain speech zones until adverse publicity (in some cases the product of litigation) forces them to alter their policies. It can thus be difficult to track precisely how many zones exist on the

---

[54] *See* Joseph D. Herrold, "Capturing the Dialogue: Free Speech Zones and the 'Caging' of First Amendment Rights,' 54 *Drake L. Rev.* 949, 955–959 (2006) (describing university speech zones); Thomas J. Davis, "Assessing Constitutional Challenges to University Free Speech Zones Under Public Forum Doctrine," 79 *Ind. L. J.* 267 (2004).

nation's campuses at any given time. Since its founding in 1999, the Foundation for Individual Rights in Education (FIRE), a nonprofit organization dedicated to expressive rights on college and university campuses, has been involved in campus speech zone controversies across the country. In large part owing to its litigation and other advocacy efforts, campus expressive zoning policies have been highlighted, altered, and in a number of cases repealed.[55]

But like speech *codes*, speech *zones* have hardly disappeared from college campuses. For example, Ohio University in Athens, Ohio has recently had approximately twenty relatively small "free speech zones" dispersed across its campus (Figure 8.3). This dispersal of expression can substantially affect certain forms of expression, such as large-scale demonstration. Moreover, although campus "free speech zones" have varied in size, like those at Ohio University they have typically been quite small relative to total campus space. In some instances, less than 1 percent of the entire campus has been approved as an open "free speech area."

A few examples will illustrate the contemporary use and effects of expressive zoning on campuses. Texas Tech University at one point limited unapproved and essentially unfettered expressive activity on a campus of 28,000 students to a single "free speech area" – a gazebo roughly twenty feet in diameter (Figure 8.4). This effectively limited *free* speech on the campus to approximately 400 square feet of expressive space on the 2,000-plus acre campus. According to the policy then in effect at Texas Tech, a speaker could engage in expressive activity on the Texas Tech campus in the designated "speech zone" without first receiving permission, but could do so elsewhere on campus only if he first notified the university and obtained permission. At one point, a law student wished to deliver a speech and pass out literature outside the gazebo expressing his religious and political beliefs that homosexuality is a sinful and immoral lifestyle. University administrators denied the student's request on the ground that his message was "the expression of a personal

---

[55] According to news accounts and other public sources, including FIRE's website, at one time or another speech zones have been in effect at the following campuses: Oklahoma State University (unknown number); University of South Florida (two zones); University of Wisconsin-Whitewater (unknown number); Western Illinois University (unknown number); University of Maryland (unknown number); Iowa State University (two zones), University of Nevada-Las Vegas (unknown number); Southwest Missouri State (one zone); Pennsylvania State University (one zone); Appalachian State University (one zone); New Mexico State University (three zones); Florida State University (two zones); Illinois State University (four zones); University of Nevada-Reno (four zones); George Mason University (two zones); Citrus College (three zones); Northern Illinois University (one zone); and the University of Mississippi (one zone). As noted, speech zoning on these and other campuses is quite fluid; thus, the circumstances reported above may have changed by the time this book is published.

Figure 8.3. Ohio University "Free Speech Zones".
Source: Map created by Kevin S. Fox.

belief and thus, is something more appropriate for the free speech area which is the Gazebo area."[56] The student challenged the designated speech zone provision and various aspects of the school's speech code. A federal district court invalidated certain provisions of the speech code, but did not ultimately reach the question whether the limitation of the student's expression to the gazebo area was unconstitutionally restrictive.

Texas Tech was not the only public university in the state of Texas to at one point designate free speech zones.[57] The University of Houston

---

[56] Roberts v. Haragan, 346 F. Supp. 2d 853 (N.D. Tex. 2004).
[57] Concerned about these and other restrictions, some Texas lawmakers eventually proposed a measure that would have limited state universities to speech restrictions no more "restrictive than necessary to protect normal academic and institutional activities." The measure was never actually voted upon.

Figure 8.4 Free Speech Gazebo at Texas Tech University.
Source: Photograph by Shelby Cearley.

limited expression to two free speech zones on its 500-acre campus. An antiabortion group sued the university after it was denied permission to display an exhibit containing pictures of dead fetuses on Butler Plaza, a centrally located and well-traveled four-acre area. The university's speech policy granted unfettered discretion to administrators to decide where on campus expression could take place based upon whether it was "potentially disruptive."[58] The Dean rejected the student group's request to display its exhibit on this ground. Indeed, the Dean testified at a hearing that he would have regarded even the silent demonstration by a single student holding a small sign proclaiming "The World is a Beautiful Place" as "potentially disruptive."[59]

A federal court ultimately invalidated the University of Houston free speech policy on the ground that it lodged "standardless discretion" in a government official to determine where and whether expression would occur.[60] Some time later, the university amended its zoning policy to expand the zones or areas on campus where expression could occur without advance permission. After the lawsuit, a university spokesman defended the use of expressive zoning and insisted that the university

---

[58] PLC v. University of Houston, 259 F.Supp.2d 575 (S.D. Tex. 2003).
[59] *Id* at 584.
[60] *Id* at 585.

"always has and always will support free speech and the free exchange of ideas."

Owing to purparted "space limitations" on its 22,000-student, 913-acre campus, West Virginia University at one point designated just *two small areas* for free speech and assembly. Each area was the size of a small classroom. Under the policy, extensive portions of the campus, including areas near the student center, the Center for Black Culture, and the building that houses the offices of the campus newspaper were located in designated speech-free zones. Thus anyone wishing to protest specific policies related to these organizations was precluded from accessing space near these *contested* places. FIRE also noted several incidents in which students seeking to exercise speech rights elsewhere on campus were prevented from doing so. For example, a student was apparently told he could not hand out flyers about corporate responsibility and human rights anywhere other than the two designated zones. In response to student complaints, media coverage, and litigation, the university initially expanded the number of approved "speech zones" from two to *six*. Sometime later the school apparently abandoned its zoning policy altogether.

These three examples are not isolated events. While some speech zones have been invalidated by courts, expanded owing to adverse publicity, or abandoned by schools that found them unworkable, many of these restrictive zones remain in place on campuses across the country. Others will likely reappear as publicity wanes, or as contention on campus increases. For example, FIRE recently asked that Valdosta State University (in Georgia) repeal its expressive zoning policy, which stated: Persons wishing to speak on campus may use the Free Expression Area (FEA) after following the appropriate reservation process. The designated site for the Free Expression Area at Valdosta State University is the stage on the Palms Quadrangle on main campus; only one person or group may utilize the area at a time. The hours of NOON to 1PM and/or 5PM to 6PM are the designated times for its use.[61] As written, this policy limits student and other expression on the 168-acre campus to a single stage area for a total of *two hours* per day.

The presence of "free speech zones" and "speech free zones" is yet another indication of just how thoroughly the broader expressive bureaucracy has now been imported into places of higher learning. Administrators have rather unthinkingly assumed that what is appropriate (and perhaps constitutional) outside campus gates is also appropriate and defensible within.

---

[61] Available at http://www.valdosta.edu/judicial/FreeExpressionAreaFEAGuidelines.shtml.

PRESERVING THE CAMPUS AS A "MARKETPLACE OF IDEAS"

Justice William O. Douglas once stated: "Without ferment of one kind or another, a college or university . . . becomes a useless appendage to a society which traditionally has reflected the spirit of rebellion."[62] Although encouraging a "spirit of rebellion" may strike some as unwise or even imprudent, Justice Douglas was surely correct that if expression is not permitted to flourish on campuses they will indeed become "useless appendages" to the expressive topography. It is imperative to First Amendment liberties and public democracy that this not occur.

Unlike so many other places on the expressive topography, places of higher learning have not yet been firmly shaped or categorized. It is not often that one writes on a relatively blank slate insofar as the First Amendment is concerned. It is thus appropriate to consider afresh what sort of "breathing space" ought to be provided for expressive liberties on campuses. We ought to ask, in particular, whether it is appropriate for administrators and courts to simply import First Amendment doctrines like public forum and time, place, and manner into places of higher learning. We ought also to more carefully consider the effects of the campus order management system on the functioning of the campus as a unique "marketplace of ideas." Finally, all of us, in particular the students who presently occupy these critical spaces, ought to think carefully and strategically about what can be done to preserve the expressive legacy of places of higher learning.

The Campus-As-Microcosm Model

So how ought we to conceive of the expressive status of college and university campuses? In certain respects, campuses look very much like *microcosms* of public places elsewhere on the expressive topography. As noted earlier, large public colleges and universities in particular have most if not all of the general physical characteristics of public areas found outside campus gates. In many if not most places of higher learning, there are thus multiple "forums" – administrative and classroom buildings, student unions, sports arenas, streets, sidewalks, parks, concourses, and plazas.

---

[62] *Healy*, 408 U.S. at 197 (Douglas, J., concurring).

Perhaps for this reason, courts have tended to import the "public forum" doctrine into considerations of First Amendment liberties on campus. As noted earlier, some courts have taken something like an "all or nothing at all" approach to places of higher learning. They have held that the campus is generally either an open public forum or something less, such as a "limited" public forum. Other courts have instead proceeded on a place-by-place basis. As between these two, the latter approach seems obviously correct – both doctrinally and in terms of the concept of expressive place. On the one hand, no one would suggest that students have a constitutional *right* to picket, demonstrate, or otherwise engage in expressive activity inside the Dean's office, inside or in close proximity to classrooms during instruction times, or on the field or floor of a sports stadium during an event. Many of these places obviously serve purposes wholly unrelated to the "free exchange of ideas." Thus not all of them can or should be treated as public forums for First Amendment purposes. On the other hand, some of the spaces on campus are indeed physically and otherwise suitable for expressive activity. To treat them all as only narrowly expressive or not expressive at all is to ignore both their tradition and their contemporary significance to public speech and democracy.

Regardless of which categorization approach a court chooses, certain campus places – quadrangles, plazas, vast park-like areas, and sidewalks – can and ought to function as open expressive forums. As noted at the beginning of this chapter, the Supreme Court has expressly acknowledged that universities "began as voluntary and spontaneous assemblages or concourses for students to speak and to write and to learn."[63] Yet the few courts that have analyzed open spaces on campuses have not generally treated them as they would similar places outside campus gates. No federal or state appeals court has yet held that campus sidewalks, parks, and streets are "traditional" or "quintessential" public forums. Indeed, some courts have held that in light of the special educational mission of the university and its need for a "quiet atmosphere," such areas are *nonpublic* forums where students and others have very few expressive rights.[64] Other courts, while finding on the facts that the university or college has designated a place like a sidewalk or open concourse as an expressive forum, have held that the designation operates for only a limited purpose – for certain speakers, for instance, or certain types of expression.[65] Other courts have ruled that open campus areas have been designated,

---

[63] Rosenberger v. Rector, University of Virginia, 515 U.S. 819, 836 (1995).
[64] *See* State v. Spingola, 136 Ohio App.3d 136, 736 N.E.2d 48 (1999).
[65] *See* ACLU v. Mote, 423 F.3d 438 (2005).

sometimes in an "unlimited" sense, for expressive activity.[66] Under the public forum doctrine, however, such "designations" (whether limited or unlimited in nature) can always be changed or eliminated by the university at its sole discretion. Thus a campus quadrangle that is an expressive forum today may cease to function in that capacity later.

As a result, in the very places it would seem courts should be applying it literally and assiduously, they have in fact departed from the campus-as-microcosm model. The open expanses of campuses in particular exist "for purposes of assembly, communicating thoughts between citizens, and discussing public questions."[67] Particularly in light of the diminished state of such places elsewhere on the expressive topography, maximum breathing space ought to be provided in these and other "quintessential" campus forums. The administrative desire for a "quiet atmosphere," while compelling in the classroom and administrative office settings, is far less so in open campus spaces. If ferment, the robust exchange of views, and perhaps the seeds of the next social movement are not to be entirely rubbed out on campus, these places at least must be considered quintessentially open to the expression of ideas.

All of this assumes, of course, that incorporation of the public forum doctrine into campus places is entirely appropriate. We have seen the damage this framework has done to public contention and First Amendment liberties elsewhere on the expressive topography. Perhaps, in light of their special historical connection to social movements and the inculcation of expressive values that occurs there, places of higher learning ought to be analyzed under a different regime altogether. To be sure, courts have grown comfortable applying the forum doctrine's cat-egorization approach to places of higher learning. But until the Supreme Court holds otherwise, they are not actually bound to apply it there.

As noted in Chapter 2, before the Supreme Court announced the public forum approach in the 1970s and 1980s, a different standard was sometimes applied. Under the "compatibility" standard, so long as the expression was considered compatible with the basic function of the place at issue it was considered appropriate there. This far more speech-facilitative standard was ultimately replaced by the deference-to-proprietors approach of the public forum doctrine. Under the compatibility standard, rather than parse the campus geography and categorize its sidewalks, streets, plazas, and quadrangles according to the public forum doctrine, courts could instead conclude that so long as the expression

---

[66] *See* Justice for All v. Faulkner, 410 F.3d 760 (5th Cir. 2005).
[67] Hague v. CIO, 307 U.S. 496 515 (1939).

is compatible with these and other campus places it ought to be permitted there. This would of course wrest some discretion from administrators wishing to impose a "quiet environment" across their campuses.[68] But it would be more consistent with the Supreme Court's observation that "the university classroom *with its surrounding environs* is peculiarly the 'marketplace of ideas' "[69] than the ossifying and speech-restrictive public forum approach.

In considering how to treat places of higher learning under the First Amendment, courts ought to at least provide the *same* level of protection to public liberties there as exists outside campus gates. There are compelling reasons, however, why the scope of expressive liberties on campuses ought to be somewhat *greater* than it is elsewhere on the expressive topography. Colleges and universities that publicly embrace robust expressive freedoms cannot simultaneously insist on a ferment-free "quiet environment." The principal functions of the public university have always included exposing students to a "marketplace of ideas" and facilitating a wide range of expression.[70] If places of higher learning are to remain "vital centers for the nation's intellectual life," there must be adequate physical breathing space within which the public exchange of ideas can occur.[71]

Rethinking the Campus Order Management System

Places of higher learning have historically facilitated "voluntary and spontaneous assemblages" and expressive displays.[72] The proliferation of detailed regulatory schemes and the rise of the campus order management system are inconsistent with the basic nature of places of higher learning. Colleges and universities must of course be allowed to pursue basic educational prerogatives and missions. Some regulation of campus

---

[68] Some First Amendment scholars argue that colleges and universities must retain substantial discretion to pursue their missions, particularly with regard to core academic matters. *See* Paul Horwitz, "Universities as First Amendment Institutions: Some Easy Answers and Hard Questions," 54 *U.C.L.A. L. Rev.* 1497 (2007). Decisions with regard to categorization of campus spaces are not closely tied to pedagogy or classroom instruction. With respect to the latter, there are sound arguments for deferring to administrators. With respect to managing campus spaces, however, arguments regarding pedagogical or mission-related discretion are far weaker.

[69] *Healy*, 408 U.S. at 180–81 (emphasis added).

[70] *See* Keyishian v. Bd. Of Regents of the Univ. of N.Y., 385 U.S. 589, 603 (1967); Bd. Of Regents of the Univ. of Wis. Sys. V. Southworth, 529 U.S. 217, 237 (2000).

[71] *Rosenberger*, 515 U.S. at 835.

[72] *Id.* at 835–36 (1995).

expression is required so that speech does not interfere with or disrupt the essential functions of these institutions. But again, this does not mean that frameworks and tactics developed elsewhere on the expressive topography ought to apply jot and tittle in places of higher learning. As noted earlier, this approach has resulted in students enjoying substantially *less* expressive freedom than speakers situated off campus.

It is important to appreciate why administrators have imported most aspects of the expressive bureaucracy onto campus and why expression has generally been constitutionalized there. To some extent, the proliferation of expressive restrictions and the incorporation of regimes like public forum and time, place, and manner are responses to the violence and disruption that occurred on campuses in the 1960s and 1970s. The bureaucratization of campus expression is also part of a broader trend toward the legalization of campus governance. Alan Kors and Harvey Silverglate have examined the explosion of "due process" regimes on campuses, pursuant to which students are prosecuted and sentenced for an increasing number of substantive "offenses."[73] Through "speech codes" and the campus order management system, expression has been similarly legalized on campuses across the country.

Unfortunately, this proliferation of legal and regulatory codes has not generally resulted in more robust constitutional liberties for students. As Kors and Silverglate note, while administrators purport to provide "due process" they often do not consider themselves bound by off-campus constitutional constraints. Kors and Silverglate argue that having internalized the disciplinary system, administrators of what they refer to as the "shadow university" generally deliver far less than the constitution requires in terms of due process. When disparities are noted, institutions quickly invoke their critical need for educational autonomy.

This is essentially what has occurred with regard to First Amendment liberties in places of higher learning. Like the due process regime, the campus order management system is now part of the "shadow university." Colleges and universities tout their openness and their special function as marketplaces of ideas. Their policies, meanwhile, often fail to allow for even the minimal expressive liberties available outside campus. When confronted by student litigants and courts, campus administrators typically invoke the need for educational and pedagogical discretion. In short, administrators often seek all of the advantages of the expressive bureaucracy while avoiding many of the strictures the First Amendment imposes on other government officials.

[73] *See* Kors & Silverglate, *supra* note 41 at 276–77.

To be fair, in some cases there may simply be a basic misunderstanding with regard to the doctrines and values of free expression. For example, the Dean of Students at the University of Mississippi defended his campus's expressive zoning policy on the ground that it would "make [ ] it easier to have areas where people know something is going on, so they can choose to listen or to avoid it."[74] The notion that public space ought to be partitioned to actually *facilitate* avoidance is fundamentally at odds with First Amendment values. At least at some educational institutions, a mandatory course for administrators on the First Amendment might be a sound idea.

Administrators ought to rethink imposing the campus order management system on their campuses. Provisions that impose restrictions on or effectively ban spontaneous assemblies and expression interfere with the basic function of campuses as "voluntary and *spontaneous* assemblages or concourses for students to speak."[75] Advance notice and meeting requirements, official recognition policies, license and permit fees, liability insurance and indemnity requirements, and other regulations that impede spontaneous gatherings and public displays ought to be substantially pruned or, better yet, eliminated. As discussed in Chapter 6, there are plausible reasons to believe that these sorts of restrictions are not necessary even in off-campus places. Similarly, there is even less reason to believe a campus would devolve into chaos without the extraordinary management system now enforced in many places of higher learning. Campus speech policies also ought to be amended, where necessary, to provide for basic things like notice of permit denials and rights of appeal and to eliminate unfettered administrative discretion. Finally, expressive zoning, particularly the sort that limits expression to a small space or spaces on often expansive campuses, ought to be discontinued altogether. Courts have already indicated that these policies are constitutionally suspect. Administrators ought not to wait for litigation and the negative publicity that typically follows to de-zone their campuses.

There are larger concerns here than a student's right to leaflet or demonstrate in a particular campus area. The restrictions described earlier interfere with social movement and other critical organizational activities on campuses. Indeed, it is doubtful that any prior social movement could have succeeded had its members complied with the array of

---

[74] Mary M. Kershaw, "Free Speech Has Its Place – or several – on USA's Campuses," *USA Today*, May 13, 2002.
[75] *Rosenberger*, 515 U.S. at 835–36 (1995) (emphasis added).

restrictions now typically imposed on college and university campuses. The campus order management system socializes students to ask permission to speak, to pay for the privilege of doing so, and to expect to be punished for unauthorized dissent and contention. This kind of inculcation reflects the antithesis of the university's traditional role as a facilitator of exchange, public politics, and even "rebellion."

In sum, administrators ought to reassess their existing public speech policies and students ought to continue to challenge the various restrictions now imposed on campus expression. This does not mean that basic things like noise restrictions and reservation systems for particularly popular areas of campus must be repealed. But in many cases, a pruning of campus speech policies could produce a thinner and more speech-friendly bureaucracy without sacrificing essential order or interfering with educational mission.

Campus Speech Standards

As noted earlier, the Supreme Court has never expressly addressed the substantive speech standards applicable in places of higher learning. Like the procedural requirements of the campus order management system, these general standards can substantially affect expression in the "public" areas of campus. Campus speech standards ought to permit the broadest range of expression consistent, as always, with the institution's pursuit of its basic mission.

Some of the First Amendment standards applicable to primary and secondary educational environments seem particularly ill-suited to postsecondary institutions. This is certainly true with regard to standards that allow school administrators to ban or limit expression owing to the supposed lack of maturity or sensitivity of the student body. As noted earlier, the Supreme Court has acknowledged that college and university students are "less impressionable" than elementary and high school students. College and university "speech codes" (overt or covert), policies that purport to define appropriate "dissent" during public displays, and bans on certain legal messages or content are all premised on the notion that there is some speech that students are not prepared to see or hear. If students are to prepare to live in a disputatious society, they must learn to encounter, tolerate, and respond to expression that is offensive or controversial. Such is the case elsewhere, including in "cyberspaces" where there are no "speech codes" or other protective policies. Thus in places of higher learning, as elsewhere on the expressive topography, regulations based upon the content of expression ought to be treated as presumptively unconstitutional.

One might object that schools, like other institutions, ought to have some discretion to limit or proscribe messages that are inconsistent with their own point of view. As noted earlier, elementary and secondary school administrators have been granted authority to disassociate themselves from certain expression. Of course, that discretion is in some sense related to the immaturity of the audience, which cannot necessarily distinguish the school's approved message from the speaker's. But in places of higher learning we must assume that more mature students are generally able to make that distinction. Outside the classroom and other administrative settings (where institutional interests generally must prevail), administrators should not be permitted to stifle debate on the ground that the speaker's or group's message is contrary to its own. If the campus marketplace is to flourish, students ought to be encouraged to engage in expressive activity even when – perhaps *especially* when – the speech challenges conventional norms or the *status quo*. This is the last opportunity most students will have to oppose governmental authority before engaging with people "off campus." The parting lesson ought not to be that students may utter only agreement with governmental policies and viewpoints.

What, finally, of the general standard of institutional "disruption"? Like elementary and secondary school officials, college and university administrators must have the authority to maintain order in the classroom and other "indoor" areas central to pedagogical affairs. But again, once one leaves these areas for the public spaces on campus, discretion to alleviate "disruption" seems far less compelling. Administrators are certainly not required to tolerate the degree of violence and disruption experienced on many campuses during the tumultuous 1960s and 1970s. But the temptation to define "disruption" in extraordinarily broad terms has clearly affected campus policies – so much so that some even seek to define proper "dissent" as that which does not cause any disruption at all. Public displays of contention are not synonymous with campus "disruption." Breathing space for public ferment must be maintained if, as Justice Douglas observed, places of higher learning are to continue to reflect a "spirit of rebellion."

The substantive standards that ought to apply to expression at places of higher learning are obviously different from those applicable at other educational levels and institutions. How different they ought to be depends to some degree on how administrators and courts perceive the function of the contemporary college or university. Of the three most commonly invoked standards in the educational context – content appropriateness, disassociation and inculcation, and disruption – only the third relates closely to the "public" areas of campus of greatest concern here. Administrators (and, where necessary, courts) ought to make certain that speech codes and other policies that rest upon this rationale do not broadly equate "dissent" with disruption. As suggested, they ought to generally apply a compatibility standard to expression in places of higher learning.

Access for "Outsiders"

As noted earlier, many campus speech policies restrict the rights of the public – "Non-University Entities" as they are often called – to engage in expression on campus. In some instances, the institution flatly prohibits outsiders to use campuses or certain areas. In most cases, however, the regulation takes the form of a "sponsorship" requirement. The Supreme Court has indicated that members of the general public do not necessarily have the *same* rights of access to campus as students (and, presumably, faculty and administrators). That does not mean, of course, that administrators cannot or should not grant them the broadest access possible. Indeed there are some very compelling reasons to do so.

Students ought not to be limited to hearing speakers with whom they, or their teachers, already agree. An evangelist who preaches at campuses nationwide was recently denied the opportunity to speak to the students on the campus of Murray State University in western Kentucky because he failed to first obtain an on-campus "sponsor" – a student organization or university department.[76] It should be obvious that sponsorship requirements like this can effectively suppress unpopular messages. Where registered student groups and faculty departments largely disagree with the "outsider's" message, these restrictions operate as heckler's vetoes. But even where there is a desire to hear the outsider's point of view, students and faculty may be reluctant to associate themselves too closely with it through official sponsorship.

Further, as noted earlier, colleges and universities are not typically isolated enclaves. They often physically border and intersect with local communities. Indeed in many cases campuses are central – geographically, socially, and culturally – to local communities. As noted earlier, some colleges and universities are seeking through building and

---

[76] A lawsuit filed by the preacher was settled after the school changed its policy. The new policy created a "free speech zone" in which all speakers, regardless of affiliation, were permitted to speak.

architecture to physically connect campuses to the community at large. This phenomenon is at least partly a response to student demands for greater connection to the community. Where architecture or geography remain something of an obstacle, exposure through interaction and expression can bring otherwise separated communities closer together.

In any event, it is inconsistent with the functioning and mission of the public university to shield or insulate students from views held by the public at large. Today, of course, substantial "outside" expression enters the campus gates through modems and wireless connections. But weblogs and ubiquitous social networking sites hardly present the full range of public ideas. Few "forums" are more appropriately considered part of the marketplace of ideas than public university concourses, parks, streets, and sidewalks. There, students may mix with the general public, in person, and exchange viewpoints on matters of concern to the university and the wider community. As elsewhere on the expressive topography, students can be exposed, sometimes unwittingly, to speakers and messages they may otherwise readily avoid. A vibrant mix of student groups, street preachers, pro-life activists, antiwar protesters, canvassers, and petition signature-gatherers must be accommodated if campuses are to serve as marketplaces of ideas.

It benefits not just the speaker but the audience as well to allow access unfettered by official "sponsorship" requirements and other restrictions on "outsiders." This does not mean that administrators cannot prefer student and faculty uses of open campus spaces over those by outside speakers, as for example by giving first preference to campus-based speakers. Nor does it mean that outside speakers need be exempt from reasonable reservation requirements that ensure availability of a requested space. But assuming the space is available, colleges and universities should not otherwise restrict the public's access to expressive places on campus.[77]

Broader considerations also counsel against limiting the speech opportunities of "outsiders" in places of higher learning. As noted throughout this book, the expressive topography is gradually eroding and shrinking. The search for alternatives to places no longer open to public expression may lead in some instances to campus gates. Why, campus officials might ask, should "our" spaces be treated as open forums? There

---

[77] Recent campus shooting incidents ought not to lead to even greater restrictions on access of outsiders to campus speech areas. For one thing, the shooters in these incidents have actually been students or former students rather than outsiders. Limiting or prohibiting activities by outside speakers will not prevent another gun-related tragedy. In any event, security experts appear to agree that restricting the general public's ability to access most campuses is simply not a realistic option.

are several reasons. In a sense, a public university *belongs* to the community as well as the students. So-called "Non-University Entities" often directly support public campuses with tax dollars. The general public also attends civic, sporting, theater, and other events on campus. Further, the institution's educational mission extends beyond the campus grounds. Faculties publish books for public consumption and conduct research with public funds. In sum, places of higher learning serve broad public functions. Barring or severely restricting public speakers from campus places is inconsistent with these important aspects of college and university missions.

Members of the public ought to be encouraged to participate in the exchange of ideas on campus. A marketplace of ideas that is limited to speakers already on campus and those who agree with them will necessarily be far less robust. Public colleges and universities should view it as part of their mission to engage not only the surrounding community but also speakers from places far beyond the campus gates.

Student Activism and the "Spirit of Rebellion"

Justice Douglas's warning about the campus functioning as a "useless appendage" speaks most directly to the students themselves. If the expressive legacy of public colleges and universities in America is to be preserved, students themselves must care enough to make it happen.

In assessing the prospects for student activism, we must realistically acknowledge that today's students face distractions, pressures, and restrictions that are very different from those of the 1960s and 1970s. New communications outlets are competing with, and in some cases replacing, more traditional and physical forms and venues of expression. Time and energy that must be devoted to classroom, extracurricular, and job market activities leave less and less time and energy for political and social activism. Today the pressures not only to attend college but also to succeed are remarkably high. The desire to succeed and pressure to conform may substantially inhibit students' willingness and ability to challenge university policies. Owing to the massive legalization of disciplinary systems at colleges and universities, many students may seek above all else to avoid academic censure and punishment.

There are other serious concerns as well. As described above, campus speech policies impose an order that presents serious obstacles for public contention. Today's students are being subtly socialized to accept the sort of anemic expressive topography they will eventually inhabit once they leave campus. There is disturbing anecdotal evidence that students are beginning to accept these limitations and even to self-censor. For example, not long ago students at Miami University engaged in protests and demonstrations against the university's treatment of sanitation and other low-wage campus workers. As they engaged in this social activism, however, students situated *themselves* in a "free speech zone" of their own making. Similarly, after successfully having their school's gazebo "free speech area" policy repealed, students at Texas Tech University continued for a time to limit expression to this location.

Nevertheless, there is some cause for optimism regarding the future of campus activism. Students, particularly those on the political right, have been quite active of late in mounting challenges to speech codes, permit requirements, and expressive zoning. Some conservative causes on campus have begun to borrow modular repertoires of contention used in the 1960s, including sit-ins, teach-ins, and boycotts. These and other student activists now have substantial assistance. Advocacy groups like FIRE are ready and willing to assist students in challenging restrictive speech policies. The Web and other media have also been critical in terms of dissemination of information regarding campus activism and student networking. Students today are better informed than their predecessors concerning the state of expressive liberties on campuses across the country.

It is far too early to declare college and university campuses "useless appendages" on the expressive topography. Evidence of a "spirit of rebellion" is actually not very difficult to find. For example, at Gallaudet University in Washington, D.C., a school attended primarily by deaf students, students recently managed to have their institution's choice of president reversed after weeks of public protest. During public protests, some students forcefully, but peacefully, shut down the campus by forming a human blockade across the front gates of the campus. Some expressed a willingness to be arrested for the cause. And in the birthplace of the Free Speech Movement, students at the University of California, Berkeley recently took not to the streets but to the *trees* – to protest a plan by the university to cut down a grove of coastal oaks in preparation for the building of a new sports arena. On some campuses, at least, Justice Douglas's "spirit of rebellion" seems to be alive and well. Whether it will flourish once students pass through the campus gates is the critical question.

9   NETWORKED PUBLIC PLACES

This final chapter examines a phenomenon that will substantially affect the expressive topography as we move into the twenty-first century. Today, many public places are being transformed into *networked* places.[1] Local communities, perhaps soon entire states, will be blanketed with public and private wireless Internet "clouds" or "meshes." In many cases these wireless networks will be linked to substantial surveillance systems. According to a recent study, there are currently more than 4,000 video cameras blanketing lower Manhattan. This is a five-fold increase from 1998. There will soon be many more. The New York City Police Department plans to implement a "Ring of Steel" around the financial district comparable to that erected by authorities in London in the 1990s. These powerful machines are able to see from a distance, and record, details as small as the lettering on a pack of cigarettes. Finally, when in public places, people are increasingly carrying or wearing sophisticated mobile technologies, including pervasive personal computing devices like multifeature cell phones and personal digital assistants. In sum, networking is a top-to-bottom technological transformation of public places.

As some scholars have noted, the networking of public places will raise serious Fourth Amendment concerns regarding searches and privacy. But it will raise less-noted First Amendment issues as well. Indeed, spatial networking ought to be added to the host of forces – privatization of public space, architectural revisions, legal restrictions on public displays of contention, public order management regimes, and "militarization" – that substantially affect the amount of breathing space available for the exercise of First Amendment liberties. In contrast to earlier chapters, this

---

[1] *See* Julie E. Cohen, "Cyberspace as/and Space," 117 *Colum. L. Rev.* 210 (2007). I have borrowed the term "networked" from Professor Cohen. But my use of the term, as will become apparent from the discussion that follows, differs in important respects from Professor Cohen's. *See* Timothy Zick, "Clouds, Cameras, and Computers: The First Amendment and Networked Public Places," 59 *Fla. L. Rev.* 1 (2007).

one primarily addresses the future prospects for public expressive liberties. Will the networking of public places revive speech out of doors in certain respects? Or will it render public expressive activity even less frequent, and more restrained, than is already the case? What specific effects will spatial networking have on public displays of contention at mass events, particularly those that occur at critical democratic moments? And what, if anything, can we do to minimize any negative First Amendment effects that might arise from the networking of public places?

THE NETWORKING OF PUBLIC PLACES

As suggested above, the networking of public places consists of three basic components. If we begin with the areas above us, the first is the adoption and construction of wireless Internet access "clouds," "meshes," or "nets." The second is the proliferation, especially during the past decade or so, of surveillance technologies that record public acts – including expressive activities. Recording devices are routinely used in public places, both in connection with official, centralized surveillance systems and as a result of increased personal recording of public events. Finally, there is the pervasive use by the public of mobile personal computing devices in public places. As we shall see, these features are not wholly independent. Together, they constitute a powerful networking *system* that will affect both the exercise and policing of public expression. Networking is still in its early stages. Its effects will likely become even more pronounced as technologies become increasingly sophisticated and embedded in public places.

Muni WiFi

Many state and local governments have taken steps to provide large-scale wireless fidelity (WiFi) connections in public places. These municipal WiFi (or Muni WiFi) projects supplement a vast existing network of private nodes and connections available in urban "hot spots" across the country. Muni WiFi systems, in particular, will alter the landscape of networked places in two significant respects. First, these systems are owned and to some degree controlled by government. This raises constitutional concerns not present where private WiFi service is concerned. Second, the physical area these public networks will cover is vastly larger than any currently existing private network. Think "hot city" rather than "hot spot."

More than 200 cities, counties, and regions are already providing some form of public wireless Internet service. While some of these programs have encountered financial and other difficulties in their start-up phases, many continue to operate and more are planned. Muni WiFi will ultimately help to drape a wireless mesh or cloud over nearly all of our public places. Suffolk County on Long Island, New York recently installed a WiFi network that will reach some 1.5 million people and cover 900 square miles. Philadelphia, one of the earliest municipal providers, has a network that covers approximately 135 square miles. Entire states, perhaps entire *countries*, may be fully wireless within the next several years.

In connection with substantial private networks, Muni WiFi networks are bringing the Web onto sidewalks and into public parks and squares. New York City has installed wireless hot spots in many of its public parks, including Central Park. Soon Web access will be available wherever a person happens to be on the expressive topography. Wireless clouds and meshes will be the backbone of a new public communications system. The new networks will allow government employees, including public safety personnel, to communicate more effectively with one another. They will allow officials to communicate more rapidly and efficiently with the general public as well.

As it has private expression, technology will transform public expression as well. Indeed, insofar as expression is concerned, "public" and "private" will merge in unique ways in fully networked places. Public WiFi will allow each of us to communicate more effectively with one another – without regard to where anyone is *physically* located. From a park bench, we will be able to communicate with audiences across the world. We will be able to report events in public, in real time. Our "private" communications networks will help transform public communication and, in some instances, public politics.

Public Surveillance Systems

The networking of public places will also involve implementation of surveillance technologies of increasing power and sophistication. Many businesses and residences have long been "secured" using closed-circuit television (CCTV) surveillance. Banks were some of the earliest adopters; they have used CCTV technology since the 1950s. Malls, department stores, and other commercial establishments have also used surveillance technologies to police and secure areas frequented by the public. More

Figure 9.1. CCTV Sign, District of Columbia.

recently, many residential complexes have installed CCTV cameras nearby and in common areas.

Indeed, in the past two decades or so, CCTV has spread across the expressive topography.[2] Most of the places where public expression is likely to occur – public streets, city centers, public parks, town squares – are now covered by an expansive surveillance network. This list covers many *inscribed* and *sacred* places that have "time out of mind" been sites of public expression and contention. (*See* Chapter 6). Cameras are popping up everywhere – on building facades, in storefronts, and on light poles (Figures 9.1 and 9.2). These camera systems have generally appeared with little public fanfare – in some cases with little public notice or opportunity for community debate. For example, without notifying members of the public – or the artist – public officials in Chicago recently affixed a CCTV camera atop an art installation. Although that particular camera was removed after a public outcry, many more remain trained on public places.

---

[2] *See, e.g.,* Jeffrey Rosen, *The Unwanted Gaze: The Destruction of Privacy in America* (2000); Marc Jonathan Blitz, "Video Surveillance and the Constitution of Public Space: Fitting the Fourth Amendment To A World That Tracks Image and Identity," 82 *Tex. L. Rev.* 1349 (2004).

Figure 9.2. CCTV Camera, District of Columbia.

Like several other transformations of the expressive topography, the proliferation of CCTV networks can be traced to the September 11, 2001 attacks. CCTV and other public surveillance technology is a major part of the plan to secure public places against future terrorist attacks. The proliferation of mounted cameras is in part a result of the massive appropriation of federal funds for homeland security. In fiscal 2006, the Department of Homeland Security requested more than $2 billion to finance grants to state and local governments for homeland security needs. A substantial portion of those funds were used to purchase and install sophisticated public surveillance systems.

As might be expected, larger cities tend to have more expansive CCTV networks. Great Britain is presently considered "the champion of CCTV surveillance."[3] But several large cities in the United States are quickly catching up. In a 2005 survey, the New York Civil Liberties Union documented more than 4,400 cameras below 14th Street in Manhattan (Figure 9.3). Another 2,000 cameras are operational in the city's subway system. As noted earlier, New York City officials plan to institute the first

[3] Christopher Slobogin, "Public Privacy: Camera Surveillance of Public Places and the Right to Anonymity," 72 *Miss. L. J.* 213, 222 (2002).

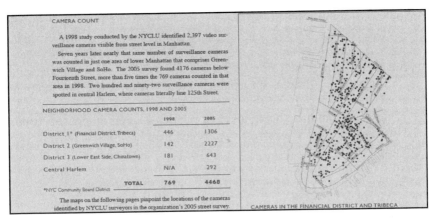

Figure 9.3. Number of CCTV Cameras in NYC Financial District, 1998–2005
Source: New York Civil Liberties Union.

London-style "Ring of Steel" in any American city.[4] The "Lower Manhattan Security Initiative" will consist of an extensive web of public and private surveillance cameras, license plate readers, and digitized movable roadblocks.[5] The system will cost $90 million. The initiative calls for 3,000 additional cameras to be installed in lower Manhattan, below Canal Street. There are also plans for a security center to be staffed by police and private security officers. The city is also considering the use of face-recognition software as part of its surveillance system.

Other large cities have also implemented extensive CCTV networks. The District of Columbia, another focus of security attention after September 11, 2001, has increased its use of CCTV surveillance. Large areas in and around the nation's capitol, including the National Mall, the Ellipse, and other places typically used by protesters and demonstrators are now under constant video surveillance by the D.C. police and the National Parks Department, which share responsibility for security in these areas. Chicago has more than 2,000 CCTV cameras in its "Homeland Security Grid," a 900-mile fiber-optic network. Its cameras are linked to a $43-million operations center that is constantly staffed by police. Baltimore, Maryland officials have used federal grants to finance a CCTV system and a $1.3 million "Watch Center." Baltimore's

[4] London's "Ring of Steel" was built in the early 1990s to deter Irish Republican Army attacks.
[5] *See* Cara Buckley, "New York Plans Surveillance Veil for Downtown,". *N.Y. Times*, July 9, 2007.

cameras are connected to a larger state highway monitoring network. New Orleans has a 1,000-camera surveillance system in which digital images are sent to a main server archive for monitoring. The Web-based archive can be accessed from any location, including from police vehicles. Philadelphia has a surveillance system with over 500 cameras trained on central parts of the city.

Questions that have been raised by academics and others concerning the efficacy of CCTV as a security mechanism have not slowed its proliferation in public places.[6] Indeed, owing to the availability of Department of Homeland Security funding, CCTV surveillance systems have been installed in a number of smaller cities like Newark, New Jersey, Tampa, Florida, Memphis, Tennessee, Virginia Beach, Virginia, and Oakland, California. Even smaller towns, including Cicero, Illinois, Newport, Rhode Island, and St. Bernard Parish, Louisiana are using CCTV technology to police public areas.

It is not just public sidewalks, streets, and parks that are covered by CCTV networks. The phenomenon is present across the expressive topography. Even places of higher learning (Chapter 8) have implemented surveillance systems. For example, with a $580,000 Department of Homeland Security grant the University of Nevada at Reno recently installed a network of 80 surveillance cameras on campus. The University of Pennsylvania has in excess of 400 CCTV cameras on its campus. Indeed, it is estimated that at least *half* of all American colleges and universities presently have some form of CCTV surveillance system in place. The number of cameras trained on campus quads is likely to increase, particularly in the wake of recent campus shooting incidents.

What makes this surveillance phenomenon potentially troublesome in terms of civil liberties is not merely the *number* of cameras focused on public areas. The latest generation of CCTV cameras has some extraordinary capabilities. Many of the cameras are automated and always-on. Most cameras now have increasingly sophisticated panning and tilting features. Some have zoom lenses that, as the legal scholar Christopher Slobogin has noted, "can read the wording on a cigarette packet at 100 yards and bring

---

[6] Although the evidence regarding the preventive efficacy of CCTV is currently inconclusive, surveillance networks have undoubtedly assisted authorities with the investigation of recent terrorist activity and other crimes. *See* Brandon C. Welsh & David P. Farrington, Home Office Research Study 252, "Crime Prevention Effects of Closed Circuit Television: A Systematic Review" (Home Office Research, Development and Statistics Directorate, August 2002), *available at* http://www.homeoffice.gov.uk/rds/pdfs2/hors252.pdf (analyzing twenty-two studies and finding that cameras reduced crime in areas under surveillance by only four percent).

nighttime images up to daylight level."[7] Next-generation cameras will likely have motion detectors, facial recognition, biometric technology, and even X-ray capabilities. Facial recognition software, which has been used at recent major sporting events and other public events, is already capable of mapping the details and ratios of individual facial geometry. Although the current technology has substantial error rates, next-generation technologies will likely be more accurate in identifying individuals in public by "reading" their faces.

Of additional concern is that the information collected as a result of all this surveillance will be digitized rather than stored on tape reels. This means that it will be possible to collect more information, to store it for longer periods of time, and to more rapidly and efficiently search what has been collected. The cameras mounted in cities, towns, boroughs, and campuses will not operate in complete isolation. They will become part of a network – in some instances spokes in a centralized surveillance grid. The CCTV cameras will link to the burgeoning public wireless network. As discussed below, the people themselves will be linked to this system too – through the technologies they carry or wear while in public places.

Mounted cameras are not the only recording devices present in public places. A running public record is being made of events on the expressive topography. Most civilians now carry camera-ready devices with them wherever they go. Police officers are also increasingly using hand-held surveillance cameras to record public policing activities. At some expressive events, police officers are stationed just a few feet away from demonstrators or protesters with cameras pointed at their faces and their signage. In New York City, public speakers recently objected when officers videotaped a small protest near the mayor's residence regarding rent laws. Officers claimed that they must sometimes tape even *lawful* public political activity in order to prevent terrorist activity and to assist in training new officers. The legal and constitutional limits of this form of public surveillance have yet to be sorted out.

In networked public places little, if anything, one does will avoid surveillance, detection, and recording. Sophisticated linked surveillance systems, supplemented by ordinary hand-held surveillance cameras, will substantially erode and ultimately may eliminate public "anonymity" and public "privacy." As discussed below, this and other aspects of public place networking may have a substantial effect not only on Fourth Amendment and other rights to privacy, but on the exercise of First Amendment liberties in public places as well.

---

[7] Slobogin, *supra* note 3 at 222.

Pervasive Personal Computing and Mobile Technologies

WiFi and public surveillance are only two components of a still-developing "digital nervous system" being grafted directly onto the existing physical topography.[8] Some of the networking that will transform public places will result not from governments and grants but from the practices and preferences of individuals and businesses. We will all contribute to the networking of public places by carrying increasingly sophisticated personal computing devices. Our physical landscape will be embedded with digital tags, sensors, and other network features. The age of what some have labeled "pervasive computing," which is "what happens when the Internet gets ubiquitous, embedded, and animated," is now upon us.[9]

Mobile and pervasive computing will alter the experiences of communicating and being in public places. With our computing devices, we will constantly give out and receive digital signals wherever we happen to be. People will essentially "announce" their presence digitally. They will enter not just a physical place, but a public digital environment. As Jerry Kang and Dana Cuff have described this environment: "Imagine not a robot, not an isolated and identifiable device, but a world saturated with networked intelligence."[10]

One of the expressive effects of this aspect of spatial networking is that anything that could be viewed or conveyed in private places can now easily be transported to public areas. The distinction between "private" expression and "public" expression will become less clear, and perhaps disappear altogether. Further, places themselves will increasingly be things we communicate with, and that communicate information back to us. Place, as location, will not exactly cease to matter. To the contrary, personal communications, advertisements, and other digital signals will be directed to us based upon our geographic position. This will occur as a result of the Global Positioning System (GPS) technologies we carry with us in cell phones and other personal computing devices. The physical environment will literally "sense" us and respond to our personal data sensors.

As discussed more fully below, the massive "digital nervous system" may give rise to new forms of communication. For example, when in public places we can let others know our whereabouts digitally. "Datasensing" will generally allow us to communicate virtually – with

---

[8] Jerry Kang & Dana Cuff, "Pervasive Computing: Embedding the Public Sphere," 62 *Wash. & Lee L. Rev.* 112 (2005).
[9] *Id.* at 94.
[10] *Id.* at 95.

places and persons – while in public.[11] This new form of communication may also facilitate public association by providing various outlets for social networking. In the not-so-distant future, dynamic digital bulletin boards may sprout up all over the public topography. Networking features will permit us to organize and communicate with social networks and groups, leave digital trails in physical places, coordinate public activities, and "virtually" signal others in our vicinity.

But pervasive personal technologies will also facilitate the policing of an increasing amount of public activity. Indeed "networked" individuals may facilitate their own surveillance. For, if others sense our presence through "datasensing," then so too will authorities. Wireless clouds will convey digital signals and locations not only to other citizens, but to authorities as well. We will not only be photographed, digitized, and videotaped while we are in public places; we may actually be tracked through GPS technologies worn on our persons or carried in computing devices. With this final networking feature in place, it may be possible for authorities to erect and enforce digital speech and assembly zones. Thus, for instance, certain public places may be accessible only to persons with the necessary digital authorization.

Networking will greatly expand communicative possibilities in public places. The manner in which we communicate, associate, and interact in public places may be fundamentally altered. As in our private environments, the things that can be said, viewed, and received in public places will expand tremendously. But in light of ubiquitous surveillance and data collection, what people are actually comfortable saying, viewing, or receiving in networked public places may be another matter.

FIRST AMENDMENT LIBERTIES AND NETWORKED PUBLIC PLACES

As noted earlier, public surveillance systems will give rise to serious Fourth Amendment questions. But the networking of public places raises substantial First Amendment issues as well. What kind of public expression and contention will be possible there? How will spatial networking affect public politics and contention at events like rallies, demonstrations, and protests? How will networking affect the primary

---

[11] *Id.*

democratic functions – identity, participation, and transparency – of public places?[12]

Public Communication and "Absent Presence"

The chapters in this book have examined a variety of obstacles to public expression. But as difficult as the exercise of expressive liberties tends already to be in physical public places, spatial networking will raise additional challenges. Networking will not sound the death knell for public First Amendment liberties. But neither will it necessarily transform our expressive topography into one that is more vibrant or robust. Ultimately, much will depend on how the people adapt to a public environment transformed by network technologies.

Let us begin with the fundamentals of public expression. In Chapter 3, we examined the many forces that already tend to inhibit *embodied* expression in traditional places. For example, physical mobility generally inhibits embodied expression in the sense that audiences rarely remain in one place for long. Public planning and architecture do not generally facilitate face-to-face interaction. And in certain circumstances, legal "bubbles" have been erected to protect particular audiences from speakers. In traditional places, however, it is generally still possible to draw attention to a display, message, or activity – even if an audience otherwise might have wished to avoid it.

One serious challenge to expression in networked public places, already apparent to anyone who has walked down a public sidewalk, is that potential speakers and audiences now tend to occupy personal "technology bubbles." In networked places, as in many non-places (Chapter 5), people increasingly address machines rather than one another. Social scientists have noted that new technologies are contributing to the phenomenon of "absent presence."[13] This means that although they are physically present in a public place, people are often mentally and psychologically elsewhere. Audiences absently ensconced within personal technology bubbles are far more difficult to interrupt or distract. Speakers who resort to more aggressive tactics to breach these bubbles – thrusting of messages or physical disruption, for example – will risk alienating intended public audiences.

---

[12] I explore some of these questions in Zick, "Clouds, Cameras and Computers," *supra* note 1.
[13] *See* Kenneth J. Gergen, "The Challenge of Absent Presence," in James E. Katz & Mark A. Aakhus, eds., *Perpetual Contact: Mobile Communication, Private Talk, Public Performance* 227 (2002).

Absent presence will substantially affect the functioning of the public marketplace of ideas. Cass Sunstein has observed that to function properly, such a marketplace requires that people sometimes hear, see, and encounter messages with which they disagree.[14] Professor Sunstein has argued that various negative information "cascades" result from one-sided communication flows. In private places like the home, new technologies are creating an increasingly insulated marketplace of ideas. As Sunstein has noted, we can program devices like personal computers such that they deliver only messages and content with which we agree, or with respect to which we are favorably disposed.

This "narrowcasting" is now fast becoming a public phenomenon. In public places, people increasingly will view only what appears on their screens. They will hear only what is presented by and through their MP3 or other personal devices. This will make it increasingly difficult for those who continue to rely upon public interaction and expression to be seen, heard, and noticed.

The look and feel of public places may also be affected by personal computing networks. Ubiquitous Web access and sophisticated personal computing devices enable people to compute and communicate outside the home and workplace. Park benches and public squares may become akin to outdoor offices and gaming venues. The multitasking public citizen may constantly communicate – but generally not with anyone in the same public place. This spatial networking effect may be felt in a variety of places on the expressive topography, from inscribed venues like public parks to "third places" like the cafes and taverns discussed in Chapter 5. People will continue to go to these places in great numbers. But they may only be *absently* present there.

As poor as the conditions for expression are in traditional public places, networked conditions may further inhibit many forms of public engagement and expression. This will allow audiences to avoid expression they do not wish to hear or see. But from the speaker's perspective, it will also make it next to impossible to gain the attention of the mobile, distracted, and narrowcasting public citizen.

"Captivity" and Virtual Harassment

As noted, there will continue to be copious amounts of expression in networked public places. As in pre-networked public areas, some of this

---

[14] *See* Cass R. Sunstein, *Why Societies Need Dissent* (2003) (discussing private programming of communications technologies to cater to personal interests).

expression will be unpleasant and offensive. Networking and crowding may make it more difficult to avoid some unwanted communications. It may also give rise to new forms of harmful and offensive expression. Thus, just as the networking of public places will place new burdens on speakers, it will also pose some new difficulties for audiences in public places.

As noted earlier, the ubiquity of the Web, brought about by the combination of WIFi and pervasive mobile computing, will begin to alter accepted notions of "private" and "public" expression. Even as "absent present" viewers and listeners, while in public places we may become "captives" to some speech we do not wish to see or hear. Technologies like mobile phones and personal computing devices will thrust the expression of networked speakers on unwilling audiences in an increasing number of public places – on the streets, in parks, and on buses and subways.

Some of this speech will be sexually explicit. Cell phone providers are already providing pornographic content in other countries; the United States market is not far behind. Thus, it will soon be possible to view sexually explicit content anywhere and at any time. The pornographic magazine or video will be digitized and transported onto the subway or bus, or into a public park, airport terminal or other public place. Unlike in traditional public places, there will be no way to zone or restrict this content in networked places. Other content may also be thrust upon the networked public citizen. New forms of targeted advertising or "public spamming" that rely upon the GPS features in personal devices may soon bombard an already advertising-saturated public.

The First Amendment will provide little, if any, protection for the "captive" listener or viewer in networked places. There is a limited First Amendment right not to receive unwanted expression.[15] That right is enforced primarily when one is in the home and cannot through rea-sonable efforts escape the expression thrust upon her.[16] One would expect or hope that social norms and decorum would prevent the most intrusive encroachments made possible as a result of spatial networking. In some circumstances perhaps self-help measures such as programming devices to reject certain messages may be relied upon. But in many

---

[15] Lehman v. City of Shaker Heights, 418 U.S. 298 (1974). *See* Franklyn S. Haiman, "Speech v. Privacy: Is There A Right Not to Be Spoken To?", 67 *Nw. U. L. Rev.* 153 (1972) (discussing doctrine of captivity).
[16] Frisby v. Schultz, 487 U.S. 474, 484–85 (1985); Consolidated Edison Co. of New York, Inc. v. Public Svc. Commn., 447 U.S. 530 (1980); Erznoznik v. City of Jacksonville, 422 U.S. 205 (1975); Cohen v. California, 403 U.S. 15 (1971).

instances, we may simply have to avert the eyes, plug the ears, or otherwise ignore public expression that we do not wish to experience. New technologies will invariably give rise to new forms of annoying, harmful, and harassing expression as well. Public voyeurism statutes have already been enacted in part to prevent the posting of invasive public photography on the Web. In networked public places, it may soon be possible to approach a recipient *virtually* and anonymously. Devices will "introduce" themselves to other nearby devices. Along with public spamming and voyeurism, we may have to address "virtual" forms of public harassment. People in networked public places may even experience a form of "public cyber-stalking" facilitated by new peer-to-peer technologies.[17] Admittedly, this is not yet a problem. But consider that a mere decade ago few had even heard of "cyber-stalking" itself. "Virtual" public stalking and similar offenses will be extraordinarily difficult to police. Thus, once again, protection from this form of networked misconduct will probably come primarily from programming computing devices rather than enacting new laws.

Public "Anonymity" and Expressive "Chill"

The First Amendment effects from "absent presence" and new forms of invasive and offensive expression may actually pale in comparison to the effects extensive surveillance could have on public expression and contention. Surveillance, digital tracking, and the attendant loss of public "anonymity" may affect both the form and frequency of public participation and public politics.

In fully networked public places, what we say and with whom we associate in public places will likely be subject to some degree of surveillance. Public and private CCTV networks and other forms of public surveillance will capture everything, including entirely lawful political activity and "private" moments in public venues. In addition, an army of "citizen-journalists," each armed with sophisticated surveillance equipment of their own, will be photographing and videotaping public places and events.

As noted, speakers do not enjoy any general First Amendment (or other) right to "privacy" or "anonymity" in public places. The Supreme Court has recognized a very limited right to anonymous public

---

[17] *See* Eugene Volokh, "Freedom of Speech from the Listener's Perspective," 1996 *Univ. of Chi. Legal Forum* 377 (describing and analyzing cyber-stalking laws).

pamphleteering.[18] As the Court has noted, political agitators from Thomas Paine to the authors of the Federalist Papers have relied upon pseudonymous and anonymous public expression. So government cannot demand that pamphleteers identify themselves, at least without very compelling reasons. Generally, however, when in public places we can indeed be discovered, observed, and made known to authorities. The limited right not to disclose one's identity on political pamphlets does not extend to all public expressive activity.

In networked public places, we will become far more knowable to others and to authorities. Public anonymity is critically important to persons other than political pamphleteers. Allan Westin has described this form of anonymity as the ability to blend into the "situational landscape."[19] Public anonymity or "blending in" can be especially critical to dissenters and others who challenge authority.[20] Like walking, wandering, and loafing in public places, the ability to blend in with others might be counted among the "unwritten amenities" of First Amendment protection.[21] As the Supreme Court has recognized:

> These unwritten amenities have been in part responsible for giving our people the feeling of independence and self-confidence, the feeling of creativity. *These amenities have dignified the right of dissent and have honored the right to be nonconformists and the right to defy submissiveness. They have encouraged lives of high spirits rather than hushed, suffocating silence.*[22]

For speakers (and others) the experience of simply *being* in public places will be different once those places are fully networked. Surveillance will reduce if not entirely eliminate the prospects of "blending in." It will expose an increasing amount of public speech activity to official view and recording. In many public places it is entirely possible that the people with whom we associate, the books and other materials we read, and our every public movement will be seen and recorded. Are these data being collected someplace? Will our public associations arouse any official suspicion? Will we even know?

---

[18] McIntyre v. Ohio Elections Commn, 514 U.S. 334 (1995).
[19] Allan F. Westin, *Privacy and Freedom* 31 (1967).
[20] *See* Marc Jonathan Blitz, "The Dangers of Fighting Terrorism With Technocommunitarianism: Constitutional Protections of Free Expression, Exploration, and Unmonitored Activity in Urban Spaces," 32 *Fordham Urb. L. J.* 677 (2005).
[21] Papachristou v. City of Jacksonville, 405 U.S. 156, 164 (1972).
[22] *Id.* (emphasis added).

Although expansive public CCTV surveillance is a relatively new phenomenon, scholars have already identified several First Amendment-specific effects on public dissent and contention from this aspect of spatial networking. Scholars in disciplines like criminology, urban geography, and sociology have observed that widespread public surveillance discourages certain groups from even being present in public places and, more generally, reduces public tolerance for "difference."[23] Public surveillance, which makes expressive and collective participation in public places more burdensome and thus less likely to occur, is another form of what political scientists call "repression." (*see* Chapter 7) If certain speakers are less inclined to even *be* in networked public places, certain messages will neither be seen nor heard there.

Privacy experts have also noted that people who believe they are being watched are subject to a phenomenon known as "anticipatory conformity."[24] Such persons tend to internalize controls and self-censor public behaviors. Anticipatory conformity can dampen or even suppress spontaneous public displays of contention.[25] As Professor Christopher Slobogin has noted:

> People who know they are under government surveillance will act less spontaneously, more deliberately, less individualistically, and more conventionally; conduct on the streets that is outside the mainstream, susceptible to suspicious interpretation, or merely conspicuous – even if perfectly harmless – will diminish and perhaps even be officially squelched.[26]

Extensive surveillance may thus affect *who* will be present, *what* they will say, *how* they will say it, and *where* contention will occur. Public speech

---

[23] *See* Hille Koskela, "Video Surveillance, Gender and the Safety of Public Urban Space: 'Peeping Tom' Goes High Tech?," 23 *Urban Geography* 257–78 (2002) (explaining gender effects of public surveillance); Katherine S. Williams and Craig Johnstone, "The Politics of the Selective Gaze: Closed Circuit Television and the Policing of Public Space," 34.2 *Crime, Law & Social Change* 183–210 (2000) (exploring how cameras are used to exclude certain groups); Jeffrey Rosen, "A Cautionary Tale for a New Age of Surveillance," 14 *Schizophonia* (August 2003), *available at* http://www.schizophonia.com/archives/cctv.htm (noting that homosexuals may be inhibited by presence of public surveillance cameras); Clive Norris, "From Personal to Digital: CCTV, the Panopticon, and the Technological Mediation of Suspicion and Social Control," in David Lyon, ed., *Surveillance as Social Sorting: Privacy, Risk and Digital Discrimination* 278 (2002).

[24] *See* Slobogin, *supra* note 3 at 243–44 (discussing research on anticipatory conformity).

[25] *See* Richard Wasserstrom, "Privacy: Some Arguments and Assumptions," in Ferdinand David Schoeman, ed., *Philosophical Dimensions of Privacy* 325–26 (1984); Daniel J. Solove, "Conceptualizing Privacy," 90 *Cal. L. Rev.* 1087, 1154 (2002).

[26] Slobogin, *supra* note 3 at 251.

may be even less robust, free, and uninhibited in overexposed networked public places than it is in the existing places on the expressive topography. The repertoires of protesters, demonstrators, and political activists consist largely of nonconforming, contentious, and sometimes disruptive acts. Even the belief that public and private surveillance systems are being used to watch and record all of this activity may deter the use of certain repertoires at rallies, demonstrations, and other public gatherings. Public assembly and association may also be affected. If public groupings are routinely watched and their activities constantly recorded, speakers may be less likely to join certain unpopular causes.

In networked public places there will be an increasingly fine line between surveillance conducted for legitimate law enforcement purposes and surveillance that simply captures all public activity. In most public areas on the expressive topography, speakers must expect to be watched and recorded. Various layers of surveillance, from mounted cameras to hand-held devices, will capture public life and various forms of public expression. As networking advances, it may cause people to avoid certain public places, increase social conformity, and decrease public dissent.

Compulsory Communication

Finally, expression in networked public places may differ in terms of its voluntariness. The First Amendment protects the right not to be compelled to express oneself, whether in private or public places.[27] But in networked public places speakers may be compelled to "speak," as they identify and authenticate themselves through digital or other signals built into the networked public infrastructure. This, too, may decrease public anonymity. Networking features may announce a person's presence and identity in situations where that person may prefer to remain unknown.

Suppose, for example, that as a condition of access to some public place the government requires some form of machine-readable compulsory identification card. In general, this would seem to be permissible under current First Amendment standards. The hypothetical compulsion does not implicate the primary concerns of the compelled speech doctrine – compulsion of some belief, creed, or thought by the speaker. It seems to be more like the sending of an administrative email, an act the Supreme Court recently found not to implicate the First Amendment's ban

---

[27] *See* West Virginia Bd. of Ed. v. Barnette, 319 U.S. 624 (1943) (invalidating compulsory flag salute for school children); Wooley v. Maynard, 430 U.S. 705 (1977) (holding that state could not compel citizens to display state motto on license plates).

on compelled speech.[28] It also appears to be closer to regulating conduct – entry – rather than speech, thought, or belief. It may be that a speaker wishing to distribute anonymous pamphlets to a crowd located in the restricted area could legitimately claim a loss of constitutionally protected anonymity under the precedent discussed above. But the general public likely would have to offer the required identification to gain entry. The foregoing hypothetical assumes that the government has made known in advance its intent to require identification. As presently interpreted, however, the First Amendment does not necessarily require that this identifying information be *knowingly* and *voluntarily* disclosed by the speaker.[29]

There is one other form of expressive compulsion that networked places may produce. The First Amendment protects not only expression of thoughts but the thoughts themselves. A person cannot be punished or regulated for merely *thinking* or entertaining bad thoughts.[30] Although this is not presently possible, next-generation facial recognition surveillance programs may well offer a window into a person's private thoughts. Facial recognition software, which as noted has already been used at major sporting and other public events, maps the details and ratios of facial geometry using algorithms. The most prevalent of these is the "eigenface," which is composed of "eigenvalues." The current technology has substantial error rates. Future models will undoubtedly be more accurate in both identifying individuals and "reading" their faces.[31]

As one commentator has stated, "Current research blurs the line between biometrics and mind reading."[32] Suppose, for example, that state-of-the-art technology permits officials to canvass a crowd, focus on a specific person identified as a potential threat of whatever nature, and

---

[28] *See* Rumsfeld v. Forum for Academic and Institutional Rights, Inc., 547 U.S. 47, 64–65 (2006) (holding that compelling campus recruiters to assist military employers with logistics of recruitment did not compel schools to speak).

[29] We shall leave aside whether this scenario violates the *Fourth Amendment's* ban on unreasonable searches.

[30] *See* Stanley v. Georgia, 394 U.S. 557, 565–66 (1969) (holding that the state "cannot constitutionally premise legislation on the desirability of controlling a person's private thoughts").

[31] U.S. Department of Defense Counterdrug Technology Development Program Office, *Facial Recognition Vendor Test 2000 Evaluation Report*, Feb. 16, 2001, available at http://www.dodcounterdrug.com/facialrecognition/DLs/FRVT_2000.pdf. Malcolm Gladwell has provided an account of the work of psychologist Paul Ekman regarding facial signaling. *See* Malcolm Gladwell, "The Naked Face: Can You Read People's Thoughts Just by Looking at Them?," *gladwell.com*, Nov. 29, 2002, available at http://www.gladwell.com/2002/2002_08_05_a_face.htm.

[32] Mitchell Gray, "Urban Surveillance and Panopticism: *Will We Recognize the Facial Recognition Society?*," 1 *Surveillance and Society* 324 (2003), available at http://www.surveillance-and-society.org.

calculate his eigenvalues. To make this more concrete, suppose a paroled child predator appears at a public park where several children are playing.[33] Assume that the predator has not approached the children or otherwise acted on whatever impulses he may then have. But his eigenvalues, captured on a public surveillance camera, reveal that he may be so inclined. Is there a lawful basis for preemptively arresting the predator, assuming these measures strongly indicate some fantasy or other invidious proclivity toward the children in the park? Under the First Amendment, the Supreme Court has said, "[t]he fantasies of a drug addict are his own and beyond the reach of government[.]"[34] But this statement was made at a time when it was not possible to "reach" fantasies. In networked public places, punishment for thought itself may one day be possible.

In sum, in addition to producing a general loss of public anonymity spatial networking may "compel" exposure of personal identity and someday even thought itself. The combination of spatial networking features may inhibit public presence, chill public expression and dissent, and even expose private thoughts in public places.

NETWORKED PLACES AND DEMOCRATIC VALUES

The effects of technology on things like expressive frequency and form are important. But they are not the most serious First Amendment concerns associated with the networking of public places. As spatial networking proceeds, we must engage larger issues concerning the future of our public places and the quality of civic life in those places. Let us return, then, to consider the democratic functions of public places first discussed in Chapter 1. How, if at all, will networked public places serve the critical identity, participation, and transparency functions that have traditionally been associated with public places on the expressive topography? And how well will they perform such functions in comparison to their non-networked predecessors?

Identity

Recall that in order to serve important identity functions, networked public places must host a critical mass of people with a diversity of backgrounds and viewpoints. They must encourage all persons and

---

[33] The hypothetical is based on the facts of Doe v. City of Lafayette, 377 F.3d 757 (7th Cir. 2004).
[34] Paris Adult Theatre v. Slaton, 413 U.S. 49, 67–68 (1973).

groups to be present and facilitate interaction among them. As we have seen in the case of traditional public places, architectures, laws, and a host of other conditions affect presence in and use of public places. Spatial networking will create some unique challenges of its own in these respects. The loss of public anonymity – the ability to "blend in" – may substantially affect the ability of networked places to support the identity claims of certain persons and groups. Surveillance and other networking features may chill more than expression. As noted earlier, networking may cause some people to feel less free to even *be* in certain public places. According to some social scientists, public surveillance in particular undermines the functioning of public places as stages for the "celebration of difference."[35]

Social science research suggests that women, the homeless, and people of color generally experience presence in public places differently than members of majority groups.[36] Some studies indicate that surveillance may disparately inhibit public presence by the homeless, teenagers, women, homosexuals, and racial minorities.[37] Further, today it is not difficult to imagine Muslim-Americans and other immigrants living somewhat chilled public lives, especially in places where every word and gesture is potentially being recorded and digitally stored. In sum, spatial networking may operate as a form of social control that inhibits the making of certain identity claims.[38]

Public surveillance systems will also make it possible for officials and private parties to control access, facilitate policing, and minimize loitering in public places. It may soon be possible to develop digital "blacklists," which can be used to automatically deny access to certain places to persons with a criminal record, a mental illness, or even a record of civil disturbance.[39] Public places might be purified of these and other "undesirable" persons by means of some combination of digital access

---

[35] Jon Bannister et al., "Closed Circuit Television and the City," in C. Norris, J. Moran, and G. Armstrong, eds., *Surveillance, Closed Circuit Television and Social Control* 24–32 (1998).
[36] *See* Laura Beth Nielsen, *License to Harass: Law, Hierarchy, and Offensive Public Speech* (2004).
[37] *See* Katherine S. Williams and Craig Johnstone, "The Politics of the Selective Gaze: Closed Circuit Television and the Policing of Public Space," 34.2 *Crime, Law & Social Change* 183–210 (2000) (exploring how cameras are used to exclude certain groups); Jeffrey Rosen, "A Cautionary Tale for a New Age of Surveillance," 14 *Schizophonia* (August 2003), available at http://www.schizophonia.com/archives/cctv.htm (noting that homosexuals may be inhibited by presence of public surveillance cameras); Blitz, *supra* note 20 at 677 (examining social implications of monitoring urban spaces for terrorist threats).
[38] *See* Clive Norris, "From Personal to Digital: CCTV, the Panopticon, and the Technological Mediation of Suspicion and Social Control," in David Lyon, ed., *Surveillance as Social Sorting: Privacy, Risk and Digital Discrimination* (2002).
[39] Kang & Cuff, *supra* note 8 at 122.

codes, mobile GPS devices, biometric technologies, and linked databases monitored by law enforcement officials. This is not a science fiction fantasy. Indeed, one company claims already to have developed "a fully automated facial recognition system based on neural network software . . . which can scan the faces of the crowd in 'real' time and compare the faces with images of known 'troublemakers' held on a digital database."[40] In the present era of "watch lists" and preemptive policing, public purification of this sort is hardly unimaginable.

Public places have traditionally supported identity claims by some very unpopular groups – Jehovah's Witnesses, Communists, Nazis, the homeless, and a host of dissenters. As noted throughout this book, physical, legal, and other barriers across the expressive topography have reduced the space in which such claims can be made. To the extent it encourages or facilitates further purification of public places, spatial networking may also drive unpopular and dissenting voices from public places.

Participation

In order to facilitate democratic participation, public places must encourage not only citizens' presence but their meaningful interaction. Although it may chill minorities and dissenting voices, networking may ultimately increase the presence of other people in places like public squares and parks. Wireless clouds and mobile computing will allow work and other things to be done in public that could once only have been accomplished in more private spaces like homes or offices. Networking features like always-on wireless Web access and personal computing devices may facilitate continued presence in and use of traditional public places. Indeed, in some cases they may even increase presence and use by re-populating abandoned or defunct public places.

The problem, as indicated earlier, lies in the *character* of the presence and use networked places will probably facilitate. As we have seen, "new urbanists" claim that things like widening sidewalks, planning communities around central places, and limiting single-use zoning may lead to more interactive and vibrant public places. All of these changes focus on making places more interactive. But urbanists and public planners have not generally accounted for spatial networking, which will in many ways *disconnect* people, thereby decreasing the amount of public interactive space.

---

[40] Clive Norris and & Gary Armstrong, *The Maximum Surveillance Society: The Rise of CCTV* 217 (1999).

As noted earlier, "absent presence" will prevent many speakers' identity claims from even being heard. It may make meaningful citizen interaction in public places much more difficult. Thus even if there is sustained, or even somewhat greater, use of public places it will not generally be of the kind or character that facilitates connections in and to public places. Transporting our home offices or gaming rooms into the public square will hardly facilitate the sort of diversified interaction that is necessary for public citizenship and democracy. Indeed, the wireless clouds above and the devices on the ground may alter our public places in a manner that renders public speech and participatory democracy far *less* likely.

Finally, whether subjective or not, the "chill" that results from being constantly watched and recorded may also reduce some traditional and critical forms of democratic participation. Even iconic and sacred public places like the National Mall will be less likely to support or facilitate robust dissent and various repertories of contentious politics once they are networked. Dissent and contention, which are critical to the participatory function of public places, may be less likely to occur in networked places across the expressive topography.

Transparency

Finally, spatial networking will affect the critical transparency functions of public places. Traditionally, public places have allowed the public to see, hear, and experience various identity claims and a diversity of expressive participation. They have also facilitated the monitoring of public policing techniques and methods by rendering these visible to the public at large. The networking of public places will undermine these transparency functions.

As a fundamental matter, much of the expression that occurs in networked public places will not be very interactive or "public." Rather, it will occur mostly with and through devices rather than persons. Tangible and physical forms of public expression help us to "know" one another, to gauge the heat, passion, and even potential danger of a particular cause or agenda. In traditional public places, the exercise of public liberties has provided visual and auditory evidence of a real, physical marketplace of ideas. Networked places will likely be less transparent in this critical respect. Although it may be possible on occasion to draw their attention to more tangible speakers and claims, the networked public citizen will generally be engaged in narrowcasting her own issues and concerns. In networked public places, the people will not even share and experience the same public *soundtrack*.[41]

Another substantial loss of transparency will occur with regard to the regulation of public expression. As noted, people may be discouraged from being present not by force, physical barriers, or public laws but rather by sensors and surveillance. The privacy scholar Jed Rubenfeld has warned of the modern state's ability, "through expanded technologies and far more systematic methods of acculturation[] . . . to watch over and shape our lives, to dispose and predispose us, and to inscribe into our lives and consciousness its particular designs."[42] Spatial networking will act as an invisible (or at least far less visible) form of social control. It will prevent the public from fully bearing witness to certain forms of repression. This particular loss of regulatory transparency affects the very legitimacy of democratic governance. The people will be left to wonder whether they are under surveillance of some sort. On occasion they may have to guess whether their behaviors are in conformity with official policies, norms, and laws. Traditional public places, which have been policed by actual persons pursuant to established public order laws, exhibited greater official transparency.

PRESERVING PUBLIC DEMOCRACY ON A NETWORKED TOPOGRAPHY

Spatial networking is going to occur; indeed in many respects it is already well under way. The manner in which people react to this transformation may substantially determine the future course of their First Amendment liberties. There are, however, steps citizens and officials can take to limit some of the more speech-restrictive effects of spatial networking in order to preserve a more vibrant and democratic expressive topography.

Legal Challenges to Public Surveillance Systems

Given its effects on anonymity and conformity, public surveillance may be the most troubling aspect of spatial networking insofar as public expression is concerned. Unfortunately, obtaining legal relief from most

---

[41] *See* Michael Bull, *Sound Moves: iPod Culture and Urban Experience* (2006).
[42] Jed Rubenfeld, "The Right of Privacy," 102 *Harv. L. Rev.* 737, 775 (1989).

of the effects of public surveillance networking will be very difficult. As with anonymity, the pressing difficulty lies in attempting to transfer "anticipatory conformity" and similar sociological effects into cognizable First Amendment harms. This requires engaging the notoriously elusive concept of expressive "chill" or deterrence.[43] It remains somewhat unclear what sort of harm a potential speaker must demonstrate in order to challenge public surveillance on the ground that it deters or "chills" the exercise of First Amendment liberties.

What is clear, however, is that a generalized claim of "chill" – that some government policy or action makes a speaker wary or nervous that speech *may* be intercepted or exposed – does not suffice. Speakers who merely surmise that they have been watched or recorded do not generally have a First Amendment "injury" cognizable by courts. The Supreme Court so held in *Laird v. Tatum* (1972).[44] In *Laird*, several civil rights protest groups challenged a United States Army covert surveillance program in which agents and officers monitored the groups' public events and meetings. The activists alleged that public surveillance of this sort "chilled" their speech and association. The Court held that the groups' allegations of expressive and associative chill were not even sufficient to raise a First Amendment claim. It held that the mere *existence* of an official surveillance program did not violate the First Amendment. In the absence of some regulatory, compulsory, or prohibitive effect stemming from the government's public surveillance, said the Court, plaintiffs were precluded from bringing their lawsuit as no "injury" had been demonstrated.

Laird poses serious difficulties for speakers seeking to mount a successful First Amendment challenge to public surveillance. As recently unsuccessful challenges to the National Security Agency's domestic surveillance program show, speakers will find it quite difficult to satisfy *Laird*'s constitutional injury requirement.[45] As in *Laird*, the essence of the public speaker's claim would be that the mere presence of cameras and other surveillance devices chills public expression. Of course, as a sociological or behavioral matter one can readily imagine that merely *knowing* officials are videotaping a public rally could chill or alter a speaker's display. And as discussed in Chapter 7, at least with regard

---

[43] *See* Frederick Schauer, "Fear, Risk, and the First Amendment: Unraveling the 'Chilling Effect,'" 58 *B.U. L. Rev.* 685 (1978); Daniel J. Solove, "The First Amendment As Criminal Procedure," 82 *N.Y. U. L. Rev.* 112, 154–59 (2007).
[44] 408 U.S. 1 (1972).
[45] *See* ACLU v. National Security Agency, 493 F.3d 644 (6th Cir. 2007), *cert. denied*, U.S. (2008) (holding that plaintiffs had failed to establish the requisite harm from national surveillance program).

to highly anticipated public protest events CCTV surveillance may be just one aspect of broader intelligence-gathering programs. As explained in Chapter 7, in advance of critical democratic events officials often engage in widespread *covert* surveillance as well. Under these circumstances, the prospects of anticipatory conformity and dampening of spontaneity may be even more acute. Yet if what is required is some evidence of a regulatory, compulsory, or prohibitory effect on public expression, even in these cases speakers will probably fail to state a First Amendment claim.

There may still be one potentially successful avenue for a First Amendment challenge to public surveillance systems. The privacy scholar Daniel Solove has argued that the First Amendment "overbreadth" doctrine might provide a basis for challenging widespread surveillance activities.[46] As Solove explains, the advantage of invoking overbreadth is that it allows a plaintiff to mount a First Amendment challenge to something like a surveillance program without demonstrating that her *own* speech activities were actually deterred in some specific way. Instead, as Solove observes, the plaintiff would argue that the surveillance program "sweeps so broadly that it captures a substantial amount of First Amendment activity."[47] The government would then at least be required to demonstrate that a 3,000-camera system was "narrowly tailored" to serve some substantial governmental interest. There is of course no guarantee that this would be a successful claim. As discussed in Chapter 7, courts are extremely deferential to government antiterrorism justifications and rarely insist on precise tailoring where public safety is arguably concerned. In light of *Laird*, however, an overbreadth-type claim may be the only avenue for a First Amendment challenge to the nation's expansive – and growing – public place surveillance systems.

Speakers may have more success enforcing limits on the *policing* of public protest pursuant to legal instruments like official guidelines and consent decrees. As noted earlier, in some cities police have videotaped public displays and demonstrations as they take place. In New York City, for example, officers have held video cameras near the faces of public protesters and then subsequently preserved the recordings. For more than three decades, the city's police department and activists have been intermittently embroiled in a dispute regarding limits on surveillance of lawful political protest activity. Back in 1971, protesters challenged surveillance and intelligence-gathering activities by police, including videotaping of

---

[46] Solove, *supra* note 43 at 159.
[47] *Id.*

lawful expressive activities, on First Amendment grounds. The parties ultimately settled the lawsuit and entered into a consent decree which set forth detailed guidelines on lawful police surveillance of public expression.[48] Similar decrees are in place in other cities, including Chicago.[49]

Although police have generally abided by these guidelines, speakers must continue to monitor compliance and seek enforcement of their terms. After the September 11, 2001 attacks, the New York City Police Department requested and received certain modifications of their public protest guidelines. Under the modified guidelines, police were authorized to videotape public protests only where an unlawful act of some kind was occurring. They were expressly prohibited from videotaping in situations where protesters were engaged in lawful political or social displays. But the police department took the position that the post-September 11 modifications allowed surveillance whenever it would be "beneficial" or "useful" to the department. They also claimed the authority to retain recordings of public events *indefinitely*.

As the district court judge overseeing the litigation noted, *Laird* plainly suggests that the mere fact of police surveillance does not violate the First Amendment – no matter how unsettling or unpleasant it may be to protesters. But the judge recently held that videotaping lawful and peaceful protests violated the terms of the consent decree. He also held that police could retain recordings of public activity for only a year in most cases, and indefinitely only if they would be useful in the context of litigation or the investigation of a crime. Although noting that these issues appeared to be settled, the court darkly prophesied that the dispute over police surveillance of public protests would probably last "as long as New York City stands."

As elsewhere on the expressive topography, resort to courts may not create a tremendous amount of additional breathing space for expression in networked public places. But the stakes with regard to surveillance are high enough to make legal challenges worth considering. At the very least, litigation with regard to widespread surveillance will raise public awareness of the extent and character of public monitoring.

Regulatory Transparency

The "digital nervous system" that is being built into the expressive topography is the product of policies that have thus far been subject to

---

[48] Handschu v. Special Services Division, 349 F. Supp. 766 (S.D.N.Y. 1972) (Handschu I); Handschu v. Special Services Division, 605 F. Supp. 1384 (S.D. N.Y. 1985) (Handschu II).
[49] *See* Alliance to End Repression v. City of Chicago, 237 F.3d 799 (7th Cir. 2001).

little public debate and discussion. Even if the speech-restrictive aspects of spatial networking cannot be prevented entirely, their effects may be lessened through greater regulatory transparency.

Muni WiFi and public surveillance systems, in particular, have often been implemented without full public consideration of their expressive effects. In the rush to digitize and otherwise network public places, officials have cast many decisions, in particular those relating to public surveillance, as matters of "public security." The expectation in some cases has been that the public ought to treat these decisions as discretionary and thus not generally open to debate.

The networking of public places is no different from other spatial modifications discussed throughout this book. Just as the people have contested the "demotion" of public places like streets and sidewalks through privatization or permitting (*see* Chapter 6), and resisted developments and "beautification" plans that will limit speech out of doors, they ought to insist on having input into how and to what extent public places will become networked. These choices ought to be treated as matters of public planning, like zoning or development issues, rather than matters within police or municipal discretion. The transformation of traditional, physical public places into networked ones ought to be the product of careful, meticulous planning with substantial and open public debate.

In this important planning process, there ought to be public notice and comment requirements for any spatial networking projects. This would include public Muni WiFi projects, which are funded with tax revenues. There ought to be clear restrictions on the nature, timing, and places of public surveillance, and strict controls on the storage, retention, and retrieval of video and other surveillance data. Following public debate, it is imperative that controls and protocols be adopted to ensure that new technologies are not subject to abuse and preserve First Amendment and other public liberties to the fullest possible extent.[50]

With regard specifically to CCTV and other surveillance technologies, the public ought to be officially notified of the location and technological capabilities of all public surveillance cameras. Further, all surveillance programs ought to be closely tailored to the publicly stated governmental purposes supporting them. The tailoring of public surveillance systems ought to include limiting the degree of surveillance

---

[50] For a comprehensive list of suggested limits on public surveillance programs, *see* The Constitution Project, *Guidelines for Public Video Surveillance: A Guide To Protecting Communities and Preserving Civil Liberties* 15 (2006), *available at* www.constitutionproject.org.

sophistication to articulated official concerns and purposes. Given their general invasiveness and their effects on public anonymity and privacy, biometrics and other such invasive technologies should not be used to monitor public places. At the very least, such technologies ought not to be used during demonstrations and other public displays.

With regard to data collection, retention, and retrieval, the people must have assurances that the public data trails they leave behind will not be collected, stored, mined, or used for improper purposes. Thus there must be clear protocols and limits regarding both Muni WiFi programs and surveillance camera networks. Officials should adopt and implement technological and administrative safeguards that will encrypt publicly transmitted data, limit access to that data, and provide clear guidelines for non-law enforcement access to surveillance records.

To this point, the recommendations have simply assumed that surveillance cameras are an inevitable feature in networked public places. Despite the lure of Homeland Security funding – and the (seemingly false) peace of mind that comes with camera surveillance – officials should consider whether there is in fact a real need for such systems. Many localities seem to be putting extensive surveillance systems in place preemptively, without any history or finding of public crime, terrorist threat, or disturbance. Critical places like the White House may indeed require some degree of external surveillance for their protection. But it is far from clear that such measures are needed to protect public places in Newark, Virginia Beach, and countless localities across the nation. Particularly in light of the uncertain First Amendment deterrent effects of CCTV, officials ought to at least consider whether security funds might not be better spent elsewhere.

It is particularly disturbing that *inscribed* and even *sacred* places like the National Mall and Central Park have been subjected to extensive surveillance. These are places in which anticipatory conformity must be minimized if not altogether prevented. Prior to September 11, 2001, police generally managed to maintain public order in such places without expansive CCTV systems. Indeed, given the extensive layers of public order management already in place (Chapter 6), disruption at even mass demonstrations on the Mall has been a rarity. There would seem to be no pressing need for constant and sophisticated surveillance of open public spaces so critical to expressive liberties.

Public involvement in the networking process may alleviate some of the transparency deficit created by CCTV surveillance and other digital infrastructure. Harmful effects like spatial purification and anticipatory conformity may be alleviated to some degree by public notice and opportunities for participation in the process by which public places become networked. These minimal steps must be taken to assure citizens that public places remain open to difference, dissent, and the exercise of First Amendment liberties. Without such assurances, an already rather anemic expressive topography may become even less vibrant.

Networked Public Contention

Earlier we focused on the negative expressive effects spatial networking may produce. Fundamental changes like absent presence are probably here to stay. But even if some traditional forms of public interaction are likely to diminish in networked public places, it is critical that public contention and dissent be preserved. In this narrow sense the networking of public places may actually have some salutary effects. Network features like personal computing devices may prove critical in terms of *counteracting* some of the most negative effects of spatial networking. To preserve traditional forms of public politics, however, the people will need to be creative in terms of adopting new repertoires of contention for networked public places and adapting traditional repertoires for networked environments.

As we learned during the 1999 World Trade Organization protests in Seattle (Chapter 7), computers can facilitate public contention in networked public places. Social networking and other "associational software" can provide some of the social capital required for successful public politics. The Web can be used to link groups of people, who can then turn virtual social capital into "swarms" and other gatherings in physical places.[51] If used creatively and effectively, the network of wireless clouds and handheld devices may facilitate things like spontaneous assemblies and real-time counter-tactics during critical moments of public politics. Protest groups and activists have already been able to use a combination of digital tags, wireless meshes, and personal computing devices to organize expressive events and conduct public displays and demonstrations. As devices and public networks become more sophisticated and more deeply embedded in the physical infrastructure, counter-protest activities may become even more effective.

There is another limited respect in which network technologies – surveillance in particular – may actually *enhance* the exercise of public liberties. Law enforcement officers and governments are not the only

---

[51] *See* Howard Rheingold, *Smart Mobs: The Next Social Revolution* (2002), Chapter 7.

ones with cameras and surveillance tools trained on public places and events. Protesters and the general public are increasingly recording public expressive activities and, more importantly, official reactions and responses to them. This citizen "press" activity is creating a counter-record of public events. This will not prevent police from engaging in unlawful, deceitful, or sometimes disproportionate acts. But it may serve as something of a defense or perhaps even a deterrent. For example, several protesters arrested at the 2004 Republican National Convention in New York City successfully defended against resisting arrest and other charges based upon video evidence of the events in question.

Citizen surveillance may be useful in other respects as well. As noted in Chapter 7, one of the most significant challenges for activists and social movements is to garner favorable media attention for their messages and causes. The media have their own agendas and coverage of public politics is often selective. Media biases have a tendency to distort messages. Technology-savvy protesters will increasingly be able to bypass the mainstream media by composing their own coverage and broadcasting it to the world – unfiltered and in real time. Protest organizations ought to strategically use new media and technologies; they should staff and operate their own media organizations at public events.

In sum, speakers can leverage the features of a new networked environment to expressive ends. To do so, they must learn to combine virtual and physical networks in ways that lead to stronger social networking and more coordinated public contention. Networked repertoires of contention, combined with sophisticated use of network features like wireless Web access and personal surveillance technologies, can help preserve and perhaps even improve upon public politics.

"Sousveillance" and Civil Disobedience

Finally, speakers can improve the transparency of networked surveillance by drawing public attention to surveillance – thereby perhaps minimizing the fear, intimidation, and chill that may accompany public monitoring. They can also rely, as speakers traditionally have, on certain mild forms of civil disobedience.

Videotaping the activities of the police is one form of "sousveillance," or surveillance *from below*.[52] This simple act creates transparency by

---

[52] *See* Steve Mann, Jason Nolan, and Barry Wellman, "Sousveillance: Inventing and Using Wearable Computing Devices for Data Collection in Surveillance Environments," 1 *Surveillance and Society* 331 (2003), available at http://www.surveillance-and-society.org. *See*

subjecting officials themselves to public surveillance. Although police have occasionally sought to have this practice enjoined, courts have generally not been receptive to claims of interference or "obstruction." For some, sousveillance of this sort resituates the technologies of surveillance in a manner that is empowering. It essentially turns the tables on authorities. It is thus one way of counteracting the "chill" and intimidation that public surveillance can produce.

Some creative activists and organizations have gone beyond mere videotaping of officials. They have more aggressively engaged CCTV cameras by charting and publishing their precise locations. This expresses not only disapproval of public surveillance and monitoring but the absence of intimidation. Activists have also created some unique repertoires of contention that focus on public surveillance cameras. For example, a group known as the "Surveillance Camera Players" has used street theater to highlight and essentially mock the operation of CCTV cameras in New York City. These activists have performed various plays and skits in front of the cameras.[53]

None of these acts will prevent extensive public surveillance. But activists have already demonstrated that adjusting to public surveillance does not have to mean living in "suffocated silence." If public politics is to survive the networking of public places, the people will simply have to learn to resist anticipatory conformity and other behavioral effects that tend to suppress spontaneous displays. To preserve breathing space for public expression and contention in networked public places, speakers will have to do what they have always done – adapt and respond to an always-changing expressive topography.

---

also David Brin, *The Transparent Society: Will Technology Force Us To Choose Between Privacy And Freedom?* (1998).
[53] Surveillance Camera Players, *We Know You Are Watching: Surveillance Camera Players, 1999–2006* (2006). The group's activities are described on their website, www.notbored.org.

EPILOGUE

As I was editing this manuscript, a group of students in South Korea initiated a series of mass protests in that country. What began as a reaction to a proposal to import beef from the United States was soon transformed into a more generalized demonstration of public dissatisfaction with government policies. Citizens from all walks of life soon joined the students in sustained public demonstrations. The images of tens of thousands of people in the streets concerned and humbled South Korea's president. In response to the mass displays, several members of the president's cabinet resigned and import policies were revised. Similarly, recent public displays in Myanmar, Pakistan, and elsewhere have profoundly affected public debate and public policy across the globe.

So much attention is focused on cyber-spaces and various forms of "virtual" expression that we tend to forget the power of such physical expression and contention. There is no question that in America, as elsewhere in the world, expressive activity has migrated in vast quantities from traditional "meatspaces" or physical forums to online forums like weblogs and social networking sites. The form and indeed the very meaning of First Amendment liberties – "speech," "press," "petition," and "assembly" – is changing in ways we are only now beginning to appreciate.

These developments have not altered the basic fact that people continue to rely upon more traditional forms of expression and expressive forums. The many examples in this book, although typically lacking the profile or effectiveness of the South Korean protests, demonstrate as much. Our long tradition of public expression, dissent, and contention, from the earliest activities in the colonies to present-day peace activists, agitators, and dissenters, has been possible owing to relatively open access to embodied, contested, inscribed, and other places on the expressive topography. We have reached a critical moment with regard to the fate of our expressive topography and the preservation of breathing space for

First Amendment liberties. As we sit in front of computer screens, an important part of our First Amendment infrastructure is being dismantled in ways that tend to receive little public attention or sustained consideration. A variety of public places that might host public expression are being altered by planners, architects, zoning officials, legislators, law enforcement officials, campus administrators, and courts in ways that restrict or suppress expressive liberties. Failure to reverse or at least limit some of these transformations places an important aspect of our expressive tradition in serious jeopardy.

As a nation that so frequently and passionately touts its commitment to personal liberty, the public search for truth, self-actualization, and self-democracy, we ought to stop and think seriously about how public places and public expressive liberties are presently valued in this country. What does it say about our solemn commitment to First Amendment liberties that a Jews for Jesus member is forced by officials in Oyster Bay, New York to obtain a permit simply to *approach* citizens in a public park? That farm workers in Bridgeton, New Jersey are charged $1,500 to march in the public streets to protest immigration laws, or demonstrators in Newark must obtain a $1 million insurance policy before receiving a permit to march? That entire downtown blocks in large cities like Houston and Minneapolis are now submerged in privately owned underground tunnels or raised into sterile elevated skyways? That large numbers of people choose to live in gated and other "secure" communities that bar "outsiders" from using the streets and sidewalks for expressive purposes? That students on vast college and university campuses are restricted to tiny "free speech zones"? And that those working on behalf of the President of the United States follow official policies on the art of "deterring potential protesters" from even attending the president's public appearances?

These and countless similar examples hardly yield the "index of freedom" Harry Kalven so proudly and optimistically wrote about in the 1960s. Today a dangerous double standard appears to be developing with regard to expression delivered physically and tangibly as opposed to virtually. A patron at the local mall is tossed out for wearing an anti-government t-shirt. A dissenter is removed from a public political event for the same reason. A "sidewalk counselor" situated in a "public forum" is nevertheless displaced owing to the discomfort and offense her expression is likely to cause. Funeral protesters are removed from public areas near cemeteries so that they can be neither seen nor heard. Students must ask permission prior to engaging in expressive displays in open campus areas. Computer codes are deemed expressive, while many deny that asking for alms in public is protected under the First Amendment. We would not tolerate such regulations or entertain such doubts in virtual places. The fact that the physical characteristics of the expressive topography *allow for* this sort of regulation, while those in cyberspace generally do not, is simply no answer. The fact is that a speaker's right to offend and attack others in the most vicious manner is vigorously defended and preserved in virtual places, while her right to approach and engage others in more traditional venues is increasingly limited or denied. This is, to say the least, a rather faint-hearted version of freedom of expression.

The problem is certainly in part attitudinal. Government officials, from the president to local police forces, seem to have calculated that the political and other costs of preventing or substantially curbing dissent and public contention are generally outweighed by the benefits of suppression and public order. This has sometimes been a very expensive calculation. Cities have been forced in the past several years alone to pay out millions of dollars in damages to persons falsely arrested or detained during public displays and demonstrations. Yet one rarely hears any significant public outcry over these substantial public expenses. The public seems to have accepted that preemptive policing and the like are necessary in an era of terrorist threats and other public dangers. We may be less free, but perhaps we are safer.

Like their leaders, many Americans seem more than ever to fear public dissent and contention. Many people simply do not *like* embodied and other forms of speech out of doors. This is, of course, not a sufficient reason to limit or ban such activity. In an age of coded security warnings and constant reported threats to public safety, however, public assemblies can indeed seem like potential mobs or opportunities for terrorist activity. Of course, Americans are by nature already less inclined than citizens in other countries to engage in public displays. This disinclination appears to be growing. As a people, we seem to be less and less comfortable with any expression that cannot be easily deleted or filtered. Simply being approached on a public sidewalk entails engaging in an increasingly foreign and uncomfortable form of personal interaction. Our daily lives are busy and frantic; when in public we seek peace, quiet, order, tranquility, and aesthetic charm. In essence, we want our public places to mirror our private ones.

As this book has demonstrated, the preservation of space for public expression and other First Amendment liberties will require a broad public and civic commitment. Courts, officials, public planners, and of course the people themselves must reevaluate the "index of freedom" in public places. Then they must set about the task of preserving, to the extent now feasible, public "breathing space" for expressive liberties.

As we have seen, courts can and do invalidate the most egregious regulations and restrictions on public expression. This is necessary, but hardly sufficient. Courts ought to take the intersection of speech and spatiality far more seriously. As noted throughout this book, the First Amendment property paradigm the Supreme Court established in the 1970s and 1980s tends to blind courts to the *expressiveness* of place. This property paradigm is firmly entrenched at this point. But as this book shows, it can be modified from within to account for the many unique ways in which place relates to expressive liberties. The disaggregated fashion in which courts examine "public forum" and "time, place, and manner" issues ought to be replaced by a more holistic consideration of the expressive topography. Generally speaking, the question is not whether a *particular* restriction on public expression is troubling, but rather whether it is so in light of the condition of the *system* of places I have called the expressive topography. Wooden categorization of places and superficial analysis of the legal "adequacy" of alternative places, which have helped create the anemic expressive topography we have today, ought to be replaced by serious engagement of the specific place at issue and its importance to the speaker. As we have seen, state courts (and legislatures) might also play a significant role in terms of carving out additional local space for speech out of doors.

Courts cannot preserve the expressive topography by themselves. Those responsible for the condition of our public physical infrastructure – public planners, zoning officials, and architects – must also be aware that their shaping and altering of public places often affects an *expressive* topography. Every sidewalk that disappears, or is folded into some private development, or recharacterized as something other than a "public forum," chips off yet another piece of the expressive topography. Every large-scale development that fails to make room for expressive activity creates yet more dead space or *non-place* on the expressive topography. Every Jersey barrier or bollard that separates the people from public buildings reduces the space for democratic contests. To some extent, the physical alterations that have been made to the expressive topography are irreversible. Entire cities cannot simply be rebuilt in Jane Jacobs's civic republican image. In many instances, however, nothing is yet finally written *in stone*. For example, new urbanist projects demonstrate how careful planning can fashion not only more vibrant public communities, but a more facilitative expressive topography as well.

In short, government officials must fully embrace the terms of the "trust" arrangement that applies to public places. As stewards of our public places, officials ought not to simply auction them off to the highest bidder. Nor should public places be treated as private conservancies or aesthetically pleasing playgrounds for the well-heeled. Public expression cannot be robust and wide-open if speakers must tiptoe (in ever smaller numbers) on manicured public lawns and avoid newly "beautified" public squares. If officials can obtain traffic impact and other alterations from developers in exchange for a variety of zoning concessions, then surely it is possible for them to demand "expressive easements" as well. More creative and civic-minded management and development of public and quasi-public places can have at least a limited salutary effect on the expressive topography.

None of this will happen unless the people themselves are committed to preserving their own expressive liberties. Although they presently have many other social and communicative options, we have seen that when properly motivated the people can overcome substantial obstacles to the exercise of these liberties. For example, permit requirements and other public order laws have been wholly ineffective in the face of an energized public assembly with a specific message or grievance to deliver. Public place activists are working hard to ensure that local communities, parks, and sacred venues like the National Mall remain open to expressive activities. And some motivated speakers continue to contest – in court and before local administrative bodies – a variety of limits placed on speech out of doors.

At this moment, however, too few citizens are so motivated. Some of their apathy is learned at home, in schools, and in social settings. But we cannot ignore the physical and legal burdens that have recently been imposed upon public expression. Who wants to stand immobile in a wire cage or protest pen? This is an act of political futility. Who wants or can afford to risk arrest, or expulsion, for merely leafleting or posting a sign? Such tactics and penalties exist because the majority tolerates and in some cases even supports them. So long as this is so, the expressive topography and public expressive liberties will continue to dissipate. Preservation of these liberties simply cannot occur unless the people can be convinced to demand access to public places, practice democracy there, and learn to tolerate public contention and dissent.

It is unlikely that the expressive topography will ever wholly disappear. As long as there are physical places and people continue to be present in them, some form of public expression will probably occur. This book has presented a rather bleak picture of our contemporary expressive topography. But imagine that topography twenty or thirty years from now. Assuming we continue down the present path, where will large public assemblies gather? Which public spaces will remain open to leafleting, petition-gathering, and proselytizing? In which suburban neighborhoods will speakers be allowed to publicly communicate with residents? What places of modernity will be open to public assemblies and expression? What kind of public expression will college and university campuses facilitate? Who will protest, and in what manner, in front of thousands of public security cameras?

Like the earth's surface, which many scientists have recently confirmed is eroding, our expressive topography is slowly but steadily shrinking. The agencies of this particular erosion are all undeniably *human*. We can ignore them, and suffer further loss of our public expressive liberties. Or as proper stewards of the expressive topography, we can begin to address these causes forthrightly and expediently. This is a choice the people must make – and soon.

INDEX